USING MICROSOFT OFFICE 2007: TUTORIALS AND PROJECTS

Craig A. Piercy
University of Georgia

Mark W. Huber
University of Georgia

Patrick G. McKeown
University of Georgia

WILEY

CREDITS

EXECUTIVE EDITOR: Beth Lang Golub
PUBLISHER: Don Fowley
ASSOCIATE EDITOR: Jen Devine
SENIOR EDITORIAL ASSISTANT: Maria Guarascio
PRODUCTION MANAGER: Micheline Frederick
PRODUCTION EDITOR: Kerry Weinstein
CREATIVE DIRECTOR: Harry Nolan
DESINGER: Michael St. Martine
EXECUTIVE MARKETING MANAGER: Amy Scholz
MEDIA EDITOR: Lauren Sapira
MEDIA PROJECT MANAGER: Andre Legaspi
ASSISTANT MARKETING MANAGER: Carly DeCandia
MARKETING ASSISTANT: Alana Filipovich

This book was set in Adobe Garamond 12/14 by Aptara, printed and bound by Bind Rite Graphics. The cover was printed by Bind Rite Graphics.

To order books or for customer service, please call 1-800-CALL WILEY (225-5945).

ISBN   978-0-470-22390-1

Printed in the United States of America

10 9 8 7 6 5 4 3 2 1

About the Authors

Craig A. Piercy has been an award-winning teacher of large numbers of students in Introduction to Information Systems, Computer Programming, and Web Development classes at the University of Georgia since 2000. Previously, Dr. Piercy taught similar courses at Towson University, and he received his MBA and Ph.D. in Management Science from the University of Georgia. As an engineer and later as an academic, Dr. Piercy has long been interested in information technology and how it can be used to solve problems and improve our lives. In addition to this book, he was the co-author of *Learning to Program with VB6*, 2nd edition, and he has co-authored *Information Systems: Creating Business Value*, published by John Wiley & Sons, Inc. in 2007. His primary area of research is in developing algorithms to support decision making. In particular, Dr. Piercy explores decision models that include multiple conflicting objectives. Dr. Piercy has been the Director for the Masters of Internet Technology program at the University of Georgia since 2006. When not teaching or writing, he enjoys spending time with his wife, Estelle, and his two sons, Nicolas and Victor.

Mark W. Huber is a Senior Lecturer in Management Information Systems in the Terry College of Business at the University of Georgia, a member of the UGA Teaching Academy, and a former Director of the Terry College's Institute of Leadership Advancement's Leadership Excellence and Development Program.

During the past eight years, he has won twelve teaching awards including recognition as Outstanding Faculty at UGA Honors Day, a Terry College Regent's Professor Award Nominee, Outstanding MIS Faculty, a Student Government Outstanding Professor Award, Alpha Kappa Psi (professional business society) Outstanding Management Information Systems teacher of the Year Award, and three UGA Career Center Student Development Awards. Dr. Huber recently completed a twenty-one-year Air Force career that included the creation and command of a Combat Communications Squadron and the management and development strategic information systems projects at the Pentagon. His research interests include collaboration and technology-supported learning, collaborative business intelligence and sustainability and sustainable IT.

His papers have been published in *Database*, the *International Journal of e-Collaboration*, *Journal of Marital and Family Therapy*, and *Communications of the Association for Information Systems*. In addition to this textbook, he has co-authored a lab manual published by John Wiley & Sons, Inc. in 2006. Away from school, he and his wife Lisa enjoy hiking, kayaking, and bicycling.

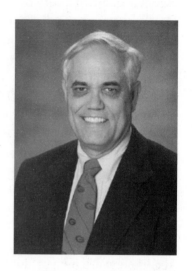

Patrick G. McKeown is Professor Emeritus of Management Information Systems in the Terry College of Business at the University of Georgia. Until his retirement in 2003, he was the founding head of that department. He was on the faculty at the University of Georgia for twenty-seven years. Before that, he taught at the State University of New York at Albany for three years and was an adjunct faculty member at New York University. He has a Ph.D. in Management Science from the University of North Carolina at Chapel Hill. He has published close to fifty articles in the areas of management science and information systems and has also written more than thirty textbooks in these areas. He is a Fellow of the Text and Academic Authors Association, only one of fifteen such honorees out of an organization of over one thousand textbook authors. In addition, in 2003, he was given the Lifetime Service Award by the UGA MIS Alumni Association and had a student scholarship created in his name by the UGA MIS Department. He is also a member of University of Georgia Teaching Academy. Dr. McKeown was a Fulbright Scholar in Portugal in 1998 at the Catholic University of Portugal and has taught internationally at universities in France, Finland, South Africa, and New Zealand. He is married to his wife of thirty-nine years, Carolyn, the father of two grown children, and the grandfather of Keegan and Katie Jane. He splits his time between Fort Myers Beach, FL, Athens, GA, and international travel.

Preface

Our computer lab modules are primarily designed to support a college level course in which there is a need to develop in the students a very basic level of computer literacy. Our primary target with the modules is to support instruction in the basic use of the most commonly used personal computing operating system (Microsoft Windows and Windows Vista) and the most popular group of business productivity software (Microsoft Office with Word, Excel, PowerPoint, and Access). In this preface, we hope to give you a clear idea of the context and goals that have motivated us to develop this set of computer lab modules.

These lab modules were first developed to support our Introduction to Information Systems course at the University of Georgia. With this course, we serve from 600 to 900 students per semester. The course is delivered with a lecture component and a lab component. The focus of the lecture component, which is usually delivered in large class sections of about 300 students, is to provide the conceptual basis of how information technology and systems are used to support business organizations. For more information about the concepts that we cover in our lecture course please see our text *Information Systems: Creating Business Value* by Mark Huber, Craig Piercy, and Patrick McKeown, ISBN 978-0471-26582-5.

The focus of the lab component is to provide the students with the basic skills of using business-oriented software. Through the lab component students learn hands-on computing skills that will be useful for their future coursework and career. Our labs are conducted in breakout sessions with 20 to 55 students per section (the class size is determined by the computer labs' capacities) and our lab sessions are taught by junior and senior level undergraduate teaching assistants.

As part of developing the course as described, we tried several of the available materials that can be used to support the lab component of our course. While there are definitely many quality choices out there, we found none that matched our particular needs. Then, we decided to develop our own supporting material. In doing so, we had the following goals in mind.

- Cover only the basics. The lab material is roughly 25% to 30% of the material that we cover in our course. This means that the amount of time and resources for both instructors and students to budget to the lab portion of the course is tight. We designed our modules to give the students what we felt is the minimum required knowledge needed to work with the software effectively.
- Provide a foundation for later skills development. Relative to the first goal, we wanted to make sure that students were capable of moving beyond the fundamental concepts when needed. So, we built into our modules instructions and motivation for using the Help features that are found with each of the software packages. This also helps the students to get in the mode of "learning to learn," which is important for continuous self-improvement in a fast changing, competitive world.
- Make our tutorials hands-on. It is well known that the best way to learn software is to use software. Each module includes an example to work through while learning the concepts. In addition, we assign additional projects that require use of the software in our course.

- Provide a low cost solution. Much of the really good material available for an instructor to choose from is very comprehensive and detailed in the coverage of the software. Our students were required to purchase a large lab text costing near or over $100 and we were only using a small portion of the material. While we feel that there are necessary costs of being a successful college student, we also felt that it was wasteful to require students to incur costs beyond those necessary for our course.
- Flexibility and agility in lab topics. To achieve this goal, we chose to write our material in loosely coupled modules. This allows us the flexibility to adjust the schedule of lab topics from semester to semester. It also allows us to pick and choose among the modules when needed for this and other courses. For example, in one semester we conducted a special research project concerning the instruction of Excel and chose not to use those modules. Even so, we easily used the modules for the other lab topics.

We have been using versions of these lab modules to support the lab component of our course since fall 2003. Our students served as the ultimate editors for our material. It can honestly be said that the material you find in our tutorials have been tested and refined by more than six thousand students at the University of Georgia. They have been well received by our students and perhaps more importantly the modules have successfully guided the students' learning. We sincerely hope that you will find them useful in instructing and supporting your students as well. Students and faculty can find additional material to support their work with this text at www.wiley.com/college/piercy.

Students and faculty can find additional material to support their work with this text at: www.wiley.com/college/piercy. For students, you can find tutorial example files and files needed for exercises and projects as required. For instructors, answer keys for all examples and exercises are available along with an instructor's manual.

Now available to educational institutions adopting this Wiley textbook is a free 3-year membership to the **MSDN Academic Alliance.** The MSDN AA is designed to provide the easiest and most inexpensive way for academic departments to make the latest Microsoft software available in labs, classrooms, and on student PCs. Microsoft Project 2007 software is available through this Wiley and Microsoft publishing partnership, free of charge with the adoptions of any qualified Wiley textbook. Each copy of Microsoft Project is the full version of the software, with no time limitations, and can be used indefinitely for educational purposes. Contact your Wiley sales representative for details. For more information about the MSDN AA program, go to http://msdn.microsoft.com/academic/.

Contents

Tutorial 1

MICROSOFT WINDOWS VISTA BASICS

After reading this tutorial and completing the associated exercises, you will be able to:

- Use the basic features of MS Windows.
- Start using software in Windows.
- Work with Windows applications.
- Use Help for Windows.

THE BASICS OF MICROSOFT WINDOWS VISTA

Microsoft Windows Vista (or just Vista for short) is a type of software known as an **operating system**. In general, operating system software is designed to handle the tasks required to manage the interaction of all of the hardware and software components that make up your computer system. So the operating system software works at a level that is closer to your computer's processor than other software you will be using. Operating system software will also contain **utility** software, which is used to handle specific tasks such as file backup, virus protection, and system security.

The combination of the operating system and the specific microprocessor used is known as the computer's **platform**. Windows Vista is designed to work with computers that run on Intel or Intel-compatible processors. Computers that use this combination are said to use the **Wintel** platform. While many other platforms exist, such as those based on the Apple **Macintosh** and **UNIX** operating systems, Wintel computers are by far the most often used for personal computing applications.

The Windows Vista Desktop

When you interact with Vista, what you see is known as a **graphical user interface (GUI)**. This means you will give most of your instructions to the computer by moving your mouse over a graphical control (often called an **icon**) and then clicking the mouse button. Some of the graphical controls that you will use with Vista will be discussed in a later section.

Using a GUI also allows Microsoft to design the display so that it follows a **desktop** analogy. With this analogy, think of your screen as the top of a desk at your office. The icons that are placed on the desktop are things that you will frequently need to use. For example, you may place a frequently used folder or a software shortcut on the desktop so that you can get to it quickly when needed. Clicking on the folder icon on the Vista desktop would be similar to picking up a manila file folder from a real desk and looking inside.

You can use the desktop for many tasks such as opening application software, working with files, and connecting to a network or the Internet, among others. What you see on your desktop depends on your computer's settings. For this reason, your desktop may look different from those on other computers or those shown in this tutorial.

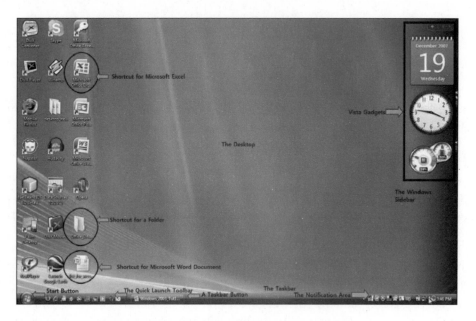

Vista Figure 1-1: The Windows Vista desktop.

The main components of the Windows Vista desktop are shown in Vista Figure 1-1. Vista Table 1-1 lists and describes the components shown in the figure.

Desktop	The main screen that you see once your computer has started and you have logged on with your username and password. It's called the desktop as a metaphor for a real, physical desktop.
Taskbar	The long horizontal bar at the bottom of your screen. The taskbar is visible almost all the time. The taskbar contains the Start button, the Quick Launch Toolbar, a middle section that can contain taskbar buttons, and the notification area.
Start button	The round button at the left end of the taskbar. The Start button provides access to the Start button dialog (further discussed in a later section).
Quick Launch Toolbar	A row of program icons that lets you start programs with one click. You may add program icons to this area.
Taskbar button	Represents a program that is currently open. A button will appear "pushed in" when it is the active program and "not pushed in" if it is open but not the active program.

Notification area	Displays icons of utility programs that are running in the background, along with the date/time control.
Vista Sidebar	A long, vertical bar that is displayed on the right side of your desktop. It contains miniprograms called gadgets, which offer information at a glance and provide easy access to frequently used tools.
Icons (shortcuts)	Small pictures that represent files, folders, and programs. They can be used to get to these items more quickly than going through the Start menu. Thus, an icon on the desktop is often referred to as a Shortcut.

Vista Table 1-1: Windows Vista desktop components.

Note: The desktop view shown in Vista Figure 1-1 is for *Windows Vista Professional.* Your own computer may look different, but the major components will work the same.

Using the Notification Area

The notification area includes icons for utility programs that typically run in the background while you are working with other applications. You can use these icons to get information about the current state of your computer as follows:

1. Some of the icons let you see information about the current state of your system when you simply place the mouse over them.

    In Vista Figure 1-2, pointing the mouse over the network-connection utility icon lets us see the current wireless networking status.

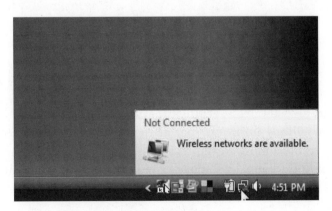

Vista Figure 1-2: Wireless access notification.

2. You can also right-click on a notification bar icon to see a context-sensitive menu.

    The options on a context-sensitive menu will be related to the context of what you are working on.

The options on the menu of Vista Figure 1-3 are related to networking.

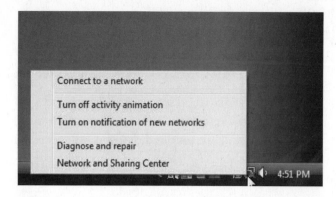

Vista Figure 1-3: Context-sensitive menu for Networking icon.

3. Clicking some icons will display a dialog for making adjustments to your system.

   In Vista Figure 1-4, pointing the mouse at the speaker icon shows the speaker volume level and the codec used for playing audio.

Vista Figure 1-4: Speaker status notification.

4. When you click on the speaker icon, a dialog appears that you can use to adjust the system volume.

   On the volume dialog shown in Vista Figure 1-5, simply adjust the slider with the mouse to adjust the volume.

   In addition to the system status icons, other icons in the notification area represent various utilities that you may have running in the background on your computer.

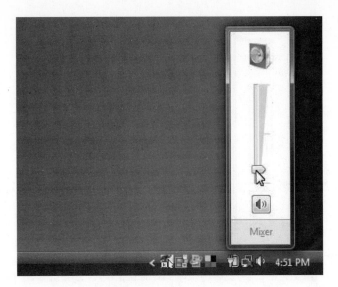

Vista Figure 1-5: The System speaker volume dialog.

Opening Applications from the Quick Launch Toolbar

On the left side of the status bar, just to the right of the Start button, you'll find the Quick Launch Toolbar. As the name implies, this toolbar allows you to start up (launch) your favorite applications quickly by clicking their shortcut icons. Let's take a look at how we can open a program from here. Later, we'll see how we can add an application icon to this toolbar.

1. Vista Figure 1-6 shows you a few icons on the Quick Launch Toolbar.

Vista Figure 1-6: Icons on the Quick Launch Toolbar.

You'll have a different mix of icons on your toolbar.

To open a program, simply click once on the icon.

2. In Vista Figure 1-6, we are ready to open the Windows Media Player from the Quick Launch Toolbar.

We see the results with the Windows Media Player open in Vista Figure 1-7.

Vista Figure 1-7: Windows Media Player opened from
the Quick Launch Toolbar.

3. It's a good idea to explore what you can do with each component of Windows
   Vista.

   One way to do that is to right-click on a component to see what is available on the
   related context-sensitive menu.

   Vista Figure 1-8 shows you the menu available by right-clicking the Quick Launch
   Toolbar.

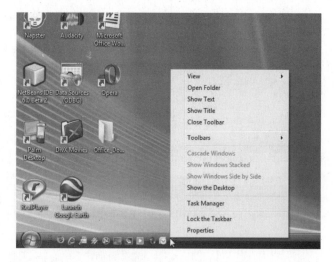

Vista Figure 1-8: Quick Launch Toolbar context-sensitive menu.

4. An especially useful command on the Quick Launch Toolbar is represented by the
   Show Desktop icon, illustrated in Vista Figure 1-9.

   When you have an application window fully open on the screen, you can get back
   to the desktop quickly by clicking this icon.

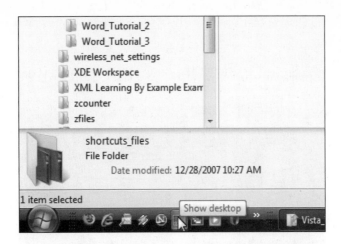

Vista Figure 1-9: The Show Desktop icon.

5. Vista Figure 1-10 illustrates what the screen may look like after you click the Show Desktop icon.

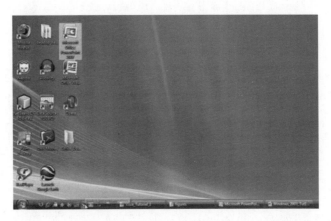

Vista Figure 1-10: After clicking Show Desktop.

6. Another useful command is represented by the Switch Between Windows icon. If you have several application windows open and click the Switch Between Windows icon, you will see a visual display like that shown in Vista Figure 1-11, called **Flip 3D**.

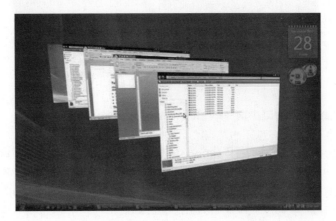

Vista Figure 1-11: After clicking the Switch Between Windows icon.

With Flip 3D, you can preview all of your open windows without having to click the taskbar.

7. Flip 3D displays your open windows in a stack as in Vista Figure 1-12.

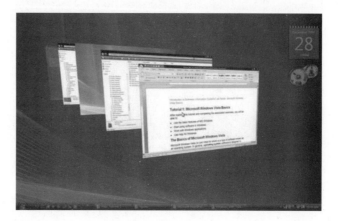

Vista Figure 1-12: Switching between windows.

At the top of the stack, you'll see an open window.

You can flip through the stack using either the wheel on your mouse (if you have one) or by holding the Windows logo key and repeatedly pressing the Tab key.

When the window that you want to display is at the top of the stack, click on it, and the window will maximize to fill the screen as shown in Vista Figure 1-13.

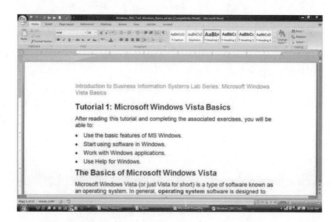

Vista Figure 1-13: The selected window.

Opening Applications, Folders, or Files Using Desktop Icons

As we discussed earlier, the desktop is the main screen area that you see after you turn on your computer and log on to Windows Vista. When you open programs or folders, they will appear on the desktop. You can also put things on the desktop, such as shortcuts to programs, files, and folders, and then arrange them however you want.

1. To open an application from the desktop, double-click on its shortcut icon.

   In Vista Figure 1-14, we are about to double-click the icon for MS PowerPoint.

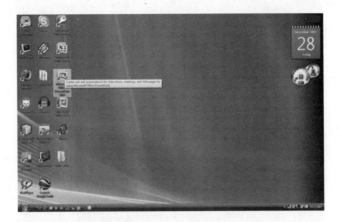

Vista Figure 1-14: Double-clicking a desktop icon.

2. After a short wait, your application will open in a window on the screen, as shown in Vista Figure 1-15.

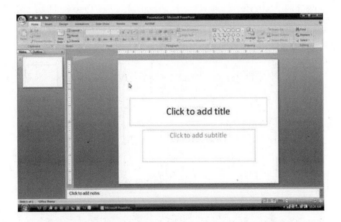

Vista Figure 1-15: The opened application.

3. As usual, if you right-click a desktop icon, you'll see a context-sensitive menu with commands that let you work with the icon and its associated application.

For example, as you see in Vista Figure 1-16, you can add a shortcut to the Quick Launch Toolbar.

Vista Figure 1-16: Desktop Icon context-sensitive menu.

4. Vista Figure 1-17 shows the results of adding a PowerPoint shortcut to the Quick Launch Toolbar.

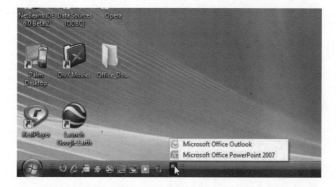

Vista Figure 1-17: A new Quick Launch Toolbar command.

THE VISTA START BUTTON

The Start button dialog is the main entry point to all of the things that you have stored on your computer. As "Start" implies, you'll often click here first to begin working with the files, folders, or applications. Through the Start button dialog you can start programs; search for and open files, folders, and programs; access the Control Panel to adjust your computer settings; access Windows Help; and log off from an account or turn off your computer. We'll take a brief look at the Start button and some of the functions available here. We'll revisit the Start button later in this tutorial and the next, when we discuss Windows Help and searching for files. Vista Figure 1-18 provides an overview of the available commands on the Start button dialog.

Vista Figure 1-18: The Vista Start button dialog.

Starting Programs from the Start Button

1. You'll find the programs that you have used recently listed in the left pane of the Start button dialog.

   You just have to click on the program in the list to open it.

   In Vista Figure 1-19 we are about to open the Windows Notepad application.

Vista Figure 1-19: Opening a recently used program.

The Notepad program is now open and waiting for use as shown in Vista Figure 1-20.

Vista Figure 1-20: The opened Notepad program.

You can access all of the programs on your system by clicking the aptly named All Programs command, shown in Vista Figure 1-21.

Vista Figure 1-21: The All Programs command.

Vista Figure 1-22: The All
Programs list.

Vista Figure 1-23: Selecting
a Program.

2. After you click All Programs, the left pane of the dialog will display a listing of the
   programs available on your system as shown in Vista Figure 1-22.

   You can navigate this list using the scrollbar to the right.

3. For some of the listings, programs will be grouped within folders.

   Click on a folder to see a listing of the programs that it contains.

   You can open a program by clicking on its name in the listing, as shown in Vista
   Figure 1-23.

Vista Figure 1-24 shows the results of clicking the Microsoft Excel program listing in the All Programs list.

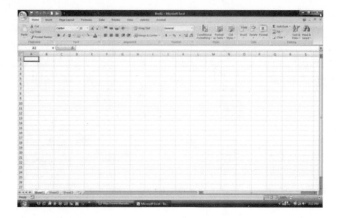

Vista Figure 1-24: The opened Excel program.

4. The Recent Items list is very convenient in opening the documents with which you have been working recently.

Click the Recent Items command to see the list of recently opened documents, as in Vista Figure 1-25.

Vista Figure 1-25: Recent items.

When you click an item in the Recent Items list, the document will be opened using its default program as shown in Vista Figure 1-26.

Vista Figure 1-26: An opened recent item.

Shutting Down Your Computer

At some point you'll want to stop working on the computer. (You've got to eat sometime!) You have several options for suspending your computer's operation or shutting it down. We'll look at a couple of those here.

1. To simply shut off your computer, click the right-facing arrow at the bottom of the Start button dialog.

    You'll see a menu with several options, one of which is Shut Down, as shown in Vista Figure 1-27.

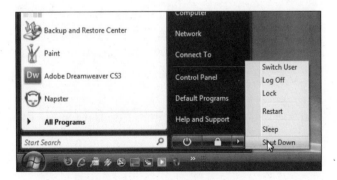

Vista Figure 1-27: The Shut Down button.

It's important to use Shut Down rather than simply turning off the power, as the operating system needs to make sure that all running software is closed correctly. Turning off the power without using Shut Down could damage files on your computer.

2. Shutting down and starting up your computer can take up precious minutes of your day.

You may prefer simply to put your computer to sleep, as demonstrated in Vista Figure 1-28.

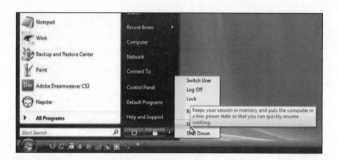

Vista Figure 1-28: The Sleep option.

Sleep mode will keep your current session in memory so that all applications and documents that you currently have open will be already opened when you return to your computer. Sleep will help conserve power when you are not actively using your computer.

If you have password protection activated, you will need to enter your username and password when starting up the computer after shutting down or putting it to sleep.

3. You can also put your computer to sleep by clicking the Sleep button, shown in Vista Figure 1-29.

Vista Figure 1-29: Sleep and Lock buttons.

The Lock button will leave your computer on but require the user to log on before using it.

WORKING WITH HELP IN WINDOWS VISTA

Windows Vista Help provides an extensive source of information about how to use Windows. In addition to the Help system that comes with Windows Vista, most application software used with Windows will also include help systems that work in a similar manner.

1. You can gain access to Windows Help from the Start button dialog as shown in Vista Figure 1-30.

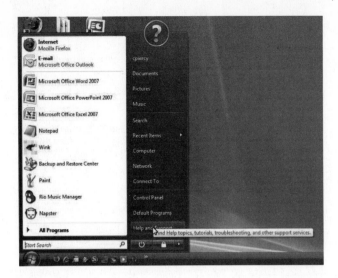

Vista Figure 1-30: Accessing Windows Vista Help.

You can also get to Windows Help by pressing the F1 key while the desktop is displayed.

Note: If you have a Windows application active and press the F1 key, you will access the application's Help system instead of Windows Help.

2. Windows Help works much like a Web browser.

You can click on hyperlinks to access other pages about topics of interest.

Navigation buttons are available on the Help window to help you move back and forth between pages and to access specific pages such as the Home page (Vista Figure 1-31).

Vista Figure 1-31: The Help Home page

You can also click a link to go to Windows Online Help for a more extensive, dynamic help system.

3. One way to find information is to browse or drill down to the topic of interest.

    Start by clicking on a hyperlink from the Home page.

    The result of clicking the Windows Basics link is shown in Vista Figure 1-32.

Vista Figure 1-32: The Windows Basics: All Topics page.

As this figure shows, some pages will include links to more specific information pages.

4. At other times, the Windows will compress to a smaller view of the list of topics.

    Vista Figure 1-33 shows the results of clicking the Table of Contents link on the Help home page.

    On all pages you can access other pages in the same way by clicking on the blue hyperlinks.

    Eventually, you will drill down to an information page as we will see in a later figure.

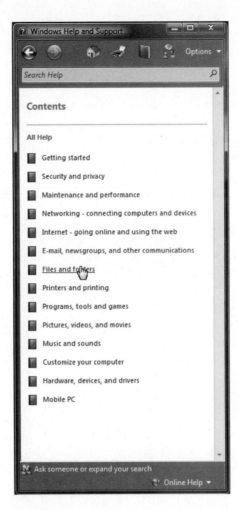

Vista Figure 1-33: Help Table of Contents.

5. Perhaps a more efficient way to use Help is to employ the Search feature.

You'll find the Search box at or near the top of every Help page as shown in Vista Figure 1-34.

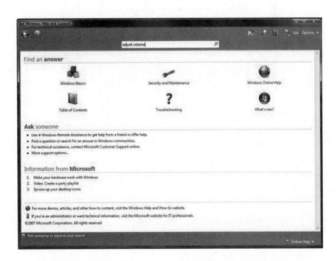

Vista Figure 1-34: Using Help Search.

This works much like an Internet search site but restricts the search to your local system or within the Windows Online Help pages.

Simply type in a keyword or phrase, such as *adjust volume,* into the search box and then click on the Search Help button (with the magnifying glass icon).

6. Most searches will result in a list of links to pages that potentially match your entered keyword.

The results for a search on the keywords *adjust volume* are shown in Vista Figure 1-35.

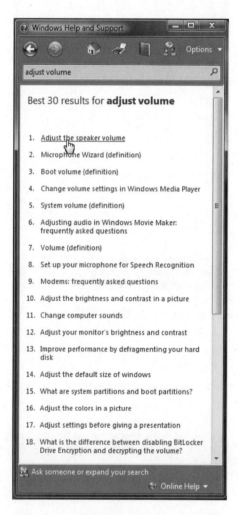

Vista Figure 1-35: Help Search results.

As in the other lists, simply select a hyperlink with a promising description and click on it to access the information that you need.

7. Whether you browse or use Help Search, eventually you will get to a Help information page such as the one shown in Vista Figure 1-36.

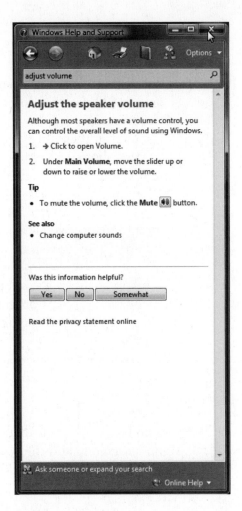

Vista Figure 1-36: Help information page.

An information page will typically provide a description of the topic, a set of steps you can follow for completing a task in Windows, and tips to help make your work easier.

You will also often find a list of links to related topics.

EXERCISES TO BUILD YOUR KNOWLEDGE OF WINDOWS VISTA

Match the term on the left with the appropriate description on the right:

_____1. Desktop

_____2. Lock

a. The analogy used for the primary Windows display.

b. Provides access to: all programs through the Start button, minimized open programs, shortcuts on the Quick Launch Toolbar, and the notification area.

_____3. Notification area

c. The main gateway that provides access to your computer's programs, folders, and settings.

_____4. Quick Launch Toolbar

d. A section of your taskbar near the Start menu where you can add shortcuts to programs.

_____5. Shortcut

e. The area on the right side of the Windows taskbar. It contains shortcuts to programs and important status information.

_____6. Sleep

f. A section of the desktop that provides a way to organize the information you want to access quickly, without cluttering your workspace.

_____7. Start button

g. A link to any item accessible on your computer or on a network, such as a program, file, folder, disk drive, printer, or another computer.

_____8. Switch Between Windows

h. A shortcut on the Quick Launch Toolbar that provides a graphical view of all the applications currently open on your computer.

_____9. Taskbar

i. A power-saving state that saves all open documents and programs, and allows the computer to resume full-power operation quickly when you want to start working again.

_____10. Vista Sidebar

j. An option that you can use so that other people cannot use your computer or see your documents while you're away but when you do not want to log off or put your computer to sleep.

11. Windows Vista is provided with a simple calculator. Describe how you can open the calculator program.

_____

_____

_____

_____

12. Open and use the Calculator program to find the answer to the following:

$$54^2 = \text{\underline{\hspace{2cm}}}.$$

13. Minimize the Calculator program and then open Paint. Describe how you can switch between the two programs.

_____

_____

_____

_____

Using Help in Windows, find and write below instructions for how you could do the following:

14. Change your desktop background image.

_____

_____

_____

_____

15. Put your system in Lock mode.

_____

_____

_____

_____

16. Check to see whether any wireless networks are available.

_____

_____

_____

_____

17. Set your default printer.

_____

_____

_____

_____

_____

18. Turn on your Windows Firewall.

_____

_____

_____

_____

_____

Tutorial 2

WORKING WITH FILES IN MICROSOFT WINDOWS VISTA

After reading this tutorial and completing the associated exercises, you will be able to:

- Recognize files and how they are organized in an information system.
- Work with files using MS Windows Explorer.
- Open and save files in common MS Windows applications.
- Work with files from the MS Windows desktop.

FILES AND HOW THEY ARE ORGANIZED IN AN INFORMATION SYSTEM

Everything in your computer storage—from the programs you run to the documents you create—is stored in files. An understanding of files and how and where they are stored is very important. If you can get a firm grasp of files, then you will be able to figure out many things about the use of computers.

A **file** is basically a group of related data stored somewhere in your computer. A file's only purpose is to hold and store data that can be read by the computer. Each file has a name, a location, a size, and other properties. Files can store data in different ways, and we often think of having different types of files. Types of files include program files, which contain sequential lists of instructions for the computer; text files, containing information that a human being can read; graphics files, containing data that will be displayed as a picture; audio and video files, containing data that may be seen and heard; web page files, containing content and instructions about how a browser should display the content; and application files, which contain data of all the foregoing types in forms that are used by various application software packages.

How you use a file depends on the type of data it stores, but there are some things that can be done with most files. You can **run** a file if it contains a program. You can **view** and **edit** a file's contents. When managing files, you can make a **copy** of a file, you can **move** a file, and you can **delete** a file. Finally, using application software you can **create** a file.

File Names

Files are labeled using two parts: the **file name** and the **file type**. The name is chosen by the user to identify the file. Most users will choose a file name that describes the contents of the file or how the file is to be used. For example, a file that contains a sales report might be called *Sales Report,* or a file that contains the program instructions for a video dance game could be called *Virtual Hokey Pokey.*

With Windows Vista, a file name can have as many as 260 characters, including spaces, and they can contain any character on the keyboard except backslash (\), forward slash (/), colon (:), asterisk (*), question mark (?), quotation marks ("), and angle brackets (< >). In reality, the file name should be shorter, since the complete **file path** (more on file path in a few moments) is included in this character count. In addition, some application programs have difficulties interpreting extremely long file names, so it is recommended to choose file names that are no longer than necessary.

The file type is used to identify the application program that is used to open a file. The file type is associated with the **file extension**, a suffix attached to the file name that in Windows is typically three or four letters long but can be longer. File extensions are used to describe the type of formatting used to store the information in the file. For example, to designate that the *Sales Report* file was created using Microsoft (MS) Word 2007 and stored using Word 2007 format, the *.docx* extension would be added after the file name to obtain *Sales Report.docx.* The file name and extension *Virtual Hokey Pokey.exe* would indicate that the file is an executable program. Notice that, when written out, the file name and extension are separated by a period. Some common file extensions are shown in Vista Table 2-1. Keep in mind that there are many more file extensions than these that you'll run across on your system.

Extension	Description	Example
.exe, .com, .bat	Program files that contain a list of instructions for the computer	EXCEL.EXE
.txt, .dat	Text files containing human-readable information (ASCII format)	Class_roll.txt
.doc, .docx	Word processing documents for MS Word (all versions up to 2003) and Word 2007, respectively	History_report.docx
.xls, xlsx	Spreadsheets for MS Excel (all versions up to 2003) and Excel 2007, respectively	Loan_Analysis.xls
.mdb, .accdb	Databases for MS Access (all versions up to 2003) and Access 2007, respectively	Moms_recipes.accdb
.ppt, pptx	Presentation for MS PowerPoint (all versions up to 2003) or 2007, respectively	MKTG_Class_Project.ppt
.jpg, .gif, .bmp, .png	Graphics files containing data that will be displayed as images	Family_vacation1.jpg
.mpg, .avi, .asf, .rm, .mp3	Audio and video files containing data that may be seen and heard	Who_Let_the_Dogs_Out. mp3

.html, .htm, .asp	Web page files containing content and instructions about how a browser should display the content	My_Home_Page.html

Vista Table 2-1: Some common file types.

File Locations

As you work with a file, the copy of the file on which you are working is located in **primary memory (RAM)**. Any files in primary memory are lost when the power is turned off. This is not as scary as it may sound, because the file that you are working with in primary memory is only a temporary copy of the file. The original is stored in **secondary storage**, which is not lost when power is turned off, such as your **hard disk**. As long as you remember to save the file that you are working with to secondary storage frequently, the changes that you make to the temporary copy will be retained.

Secondary storage provides the capability for long-term storage of your files. Several types of media and associated devices may be available for you to use as secondary storage. Each device that is available to your computer can be identified using a letter of the alphabet. A listing of common devices and their possible letter designation is shown in Vista Table 2-2. This list provides some common letter assignments, but different letters could be used on your system.

Letter designation	Medium	Device
A:, B:	Diskette (commonly used in the 1980s and 1990s but almost never found on newer computers)	Diskette drive
C:	Hard disk	Hard drive
D:	Hard disk or high-capacity removable disk (e.g., Zip disk)	Hard drive or high-capacity removable disk drive (e.g., Zip drive)
E:	CD-ROM, CD-R, CD-RW, DVD-ROM, DVD-R, DVD-RW	Compact disc or DVD drive
F: and beyond	USB flash disk, networked drive	USB memory stick; remote file server

Vista Table 2-2: Secondary storage devices and designations.

To be able to find all of the files that you will be working with, your secondary storage devices need to be well organized. Fortunately, Windows Vista provides a **hierarchical** scheme for organizing your files. A hierarchy may be thought of as a group of things arranged into ranks.

The items at each rank are arranged in subgroups, and each subgroup is under one item at the next higher rank. For secondary storage the rank is determined by storage capacity. We will see more about this in a few minutes.

The MS Windows hierarchy is based on the analogy of a typical office. We will see that this analogy carries over to many other areas of Microsoft software, such as the desktop view of the operating system and the work organization used with MS Office software. With the office analogy, you can think of your secondary storage as a file cabinet (given the amount of information that you can typically store, think of it as a colossal file cabinet). Each of the different storage devices attached to your system may be thought of as a drawer in the file cabinet. You may then organize your files by placing **folders** in each drawer of the file cabinet. Then you can obtain greater degrees of organization by placing folders within folders, or **subfolders**.

> ▶**Interesting Fact:**
> The Windows hierarchy is not really new with Windows Vista. The folder and subfolder scheme of Windows Vista is basically the same as the directory and subdirectory scheme used with MS DOS. For this reason, your professor may have a senior moment and say *directory* when he or she means *folder.* Please have patience.

With this organization scheme, you can save a file by simply placing it in the drawer of the file cabinet. This corresponds to simply saving it on the storage device in what is known as the **root folder**. While this is possible, it has some limitations. First, because of the way that the operating system works with the file hierarchy, the number of files that may be stored directly on the root directory is limited. Second, your files will quickly become unorganized and difficult to locate.

You could also create a folder on the root in which to place your files to provide more organization. Folders will typically be named to indicate the purpose of the files or to match the way in which you wish to organize your work that you are saving. For example, you may wish to create a folder on your hard drive (C:) called *MIS Class* to save all files related to your MIS class.

If you want your files to be more organized, you can create subfolders. For example, within your *MIS Class* folder you might create subfolders called *Excel Files* and *Access Files* in order to store your course work related to using Excel and Access, respectively.

Once your files have been organized, it may often be necessary to indicate *where* a file is located. One way to do this is to use the **file path**. The file path is a standard method of indicating a file's location by listing the letter of the drive on which the file is stored, followed by the names of the folders and subfolders that the file is within. For example, suppose that you have stored an Excel project file called *My Excel Project.xlsx* in the Excel file subfolder mentioned in the previous paragraph. The path for this file would be

C:\MIS Class\Excel Files\My Excel Project.xlsx

The file path always begins with the letter of the secondary storage device followed by a colon and backslash (:\). This is followed by a listing of the folders and subfolders that lead to the file. Each folder name in the list is separated using a backslash (\). Finally, the file name is listed. Reading the file path, we would say "The file *My Excel Project.xls* is on the C: drive in a folder called *MIS Class* in a subfolder called *Excel Files*." Notice that this file path scheme is one way to represent movement through a hierarchy from largest (the drive) to smallest (the last subfolder). Notice also that this scheme is much like the URL scheme that is used for locating Web pages on the Internet.

File Sizes

Another important characteristic to consider is how much storage capacity will be needed to store a file. This is based on the file size. File size is measured in bytes, or more typically in kilobytes (KB = 1024 bytes) or megabytes (MB = 1,048,576 bytes). A small file, such as a brief letter written using MS Word, may require 20 KB of storage space. A larger file, such as a 30-second video file in mpeg format, may require 3.2 MB.

You must consider file size when deciding where to store your file, because different storage devices will have various storage capacities. Vista Table 2-3 shows some typical capacities for secondary storage devices along with some other advantages and disadvantages of each.

Storage Medium	Storage Capacity	Advantages/ Disadvantages
3 1/2" diskette	1.44 MB	Very portable; lowest storage capacity; slow read-write speeds; just about obsolete (replaced by Flash drives)
Hard disk	100 GB to 500 GB	Largest storage capacity; fastest read/write speeds; not portable (unless in a laptop)
USB flash drive	64 MB to 2 GB	Very portable; high storage capacity; high read-write speeds
High-capacity removable disk	100 MB to 250 MB	Reasonably portable; medium read/write speeds; difficult to find compatible drive
Compact disc	700MB	Very portable; high capacity; high read/write speeds; most media and drives are read-only or write-once
Private network server	1 GB (portion often provided to each user)	Medium capacity; fairly high read/write speeds; may not have access away from network
Internet service provider	10 MB to 100 MB (may depend on how much you are willing to pay)	Medium to high capacity; available anywhere that you have Internet connection; read/write speeds related to connection speeds—slower for large files

Vista Table 2-3: Secondary storage capacities.

Storage capacity is constantly increasing and may have changed some since the writing of this tutorial. Also, the number of files that you are able to store on a specific device is directly related to the type of files with which you are working.

WORKING WITH FILES AND FOLDERS

Let's take a look at how we can work with these files and folders using Windows Vista. The primary means of accessing and working with your files and folders is through a folder window. We'll start there.

The Folder Window

1. There are several ways to get to a folder window.

   One way is to open the main Documents folder window by clicking the Documents option in the Vista Start menu. (See Vista Figure 2-1.)

Vista Figure 2-1: Opening the Documents folder using the Start menu.

   You can also open a folder window by clicking a folder icon on the desktop.

2. The Documents folder window is shown in Vista Figure 2-2. Notice the components that make up this window:

   - The **navigation buttons** with the right and left arrows will let you move back and forward through folders that you have viewed.
   - The **address bar** displays the path to the current folder. You can also access a list of recently visited folders by clicking the arrow on the side of the list box. You can use the address bar to navigate to a different folder without closing the current folder window.

- The **search box** will let you search through this folder and folders lower in the hierarchy based on a keyword. We will look more at search capabilities later in this tutorial.

Vista Figure 2-2: The Documents folder window.

- The **toolbar** provides icons for performing common tasks such as changing how the files and folders are displayed and copying files.
- The current folder contents are displayed in the **file list pane**. The column headings can be used to sort and group the files by type.
- The **navigation pane** shows the hierarchy of folders on your system. You can move between folders by clicking on them here.
- The **details pane** shows the properties associated with the selected file. File properties are information about a file, such as the author, the date the file was last modified, and any tags you might have added to the file.

3. After a folder is open, you can navigate to subfolders in several ways.

You can click on a subfolder in the file list pane, or you can browse for the folder in the navigation pane and click on it.

Any opened folder will be shown in a folder window with the list of its files and folders shown in the file list pane.

4. Notice how the file list appears in Vista Figure 2-3. This is the simple **List view**.

   You can change how and what you view in the file list pane.

   To do this, click the Views command on the toolbar.

Vista Figure 2-3: A subfolder.

For example, select the Tiles view, as shown in Vista Figure 2-4, from the menu to see the files displayed as in Vista Figure 2-5.

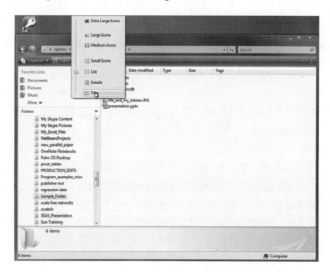

Vista Figure 2-4: The Views command.

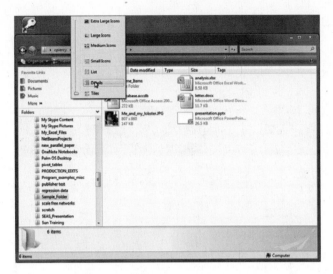

Vista Figure 2-5: The Tiles view.

5. With the Tiles view the files are listed in rows and columns.

   In most views, each file is listed using its file name and an icon.

   In some views, like the Tiles view, more information is provided, such as the file size.

   Now let's switch to the Details view.

6. The Details view, as the name implies, shows additional columns with more details about each file.

   You can click on the column heading of any of the details provided to have the files sorted in order of the selected information.

   Simply click on a heading as shown in Vista Figure 2-6 and select how you want to sort or group the files.

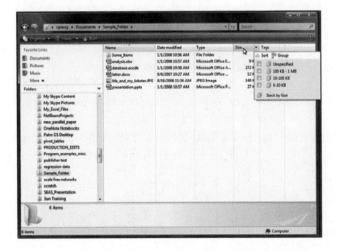

Vista Figure 2-6: Choosing to sort files by size.

7. Let's change the view one more time to Medium Icons.

We see the Medium Icon view selected in Vista Figure 2-7 and shown in Vista Figure 2-8.

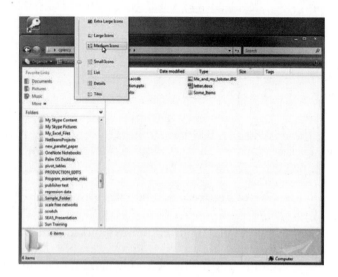

Vista Figure 2-7: Selecting Medium Icon view.

Vista Figure 2-8: Medium icons.

Here we can take a closer look at the icon styles used to display the files.

8. Notice in Vista Figures 2-7 and 2-8 that Office document icons look like sheets of paper, representing documents, with smaller icons representing the application.

Folder icons appear as open manila folders.

When the icon for a picture file is large enough, it will be a small version of the picture.

You'll see other icons for different file types, but in most cases the icon will serve to represent the file type.

Using Search to Find Your Files

Sometimes you need to find a particular file, but you may not know exactly where it's located. Also, locating the file by browsing could take a long time given that your system may have hundreds of files and subfolders. Fortunately, Vista comes with a Search feature that can make it easier to find your files, folders, and applications.

1. You can use Search to find programs, files, or folders.

   As with most things in Vista, start at the Start button menu.

   Recall that there is a search box located near the bottom of the Start button menu (Vista Figure 2-9).

Vista Figure 2-9: The Start button menu, showing search box at bottom and Search also on the menu at right.

   You might also notice the Search item in the list of options in the menu itself.

   Clicking this will open a folder window that will let you search using the folder window search box.

2. The search will begin as soon as you start typing something in the search box.

   We will demonstrate by searching for items that contain the word "Access."

Notice that as soon as we type the "A," as shown in Vista Figure 2-10, the file list disappears and the word "Searching..." appears.

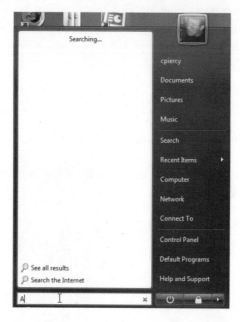

Vista Figure 2-10: Beginning a search.

3. As soon as enough characters have been entered, the list will start to be populated with potential matching items.

In Vista Figure 2-11, the search continues with some items that contain *Ac* already displayed.

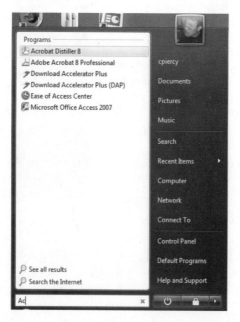

Vista Figure 2-11: Results matching *Ac*.

As soon as the item you are looking for is displayed in the list, you can click on it to open it and end the search.

4. Matching items will be divided into two sections, as shown in Vista Figure 2-12.

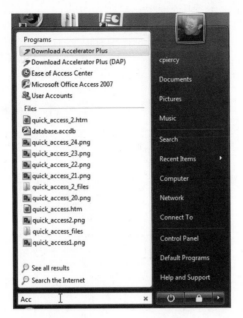

Vista Figure 2-12: Continuing the search.

Software applications will be displayed in the upper section marked Programs, while data and document files will be displayed in the Files section.

With each successive character, the search results will narrow to include only those items that match the latest keyword.

For example, notice that now that the second "c" is added, entries for "Acrobat" have disappeared from the list.

5. Vista Figure 2-13 shows the results of our search using the entire keyword "Access."

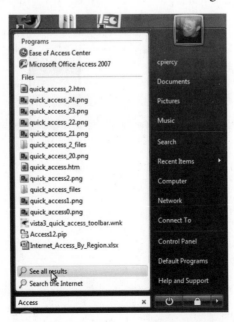

Vista Figure 2-13: Final search results.

The results in this list are only the most likely subset of the entire search results.

You can view the entire search results by clicking on the link marked "See all results."

6. After you click "See all results," a folder window will open displaying a temporary folder called "Search Results" (Vista Figure 2-14).

Vista Figure 2-14: The Search Results folder window.

The folder is temporarily loaded with the files that match your search.

Even then some keywords may have more results than are immediately displayed.

Notice the message at the top indicating that the result set is large and could be narrowed.

7. As mentioned earlier, a search box is always available on any folder window.

This search box works like the one on the Start menu, but it starts only from the current folder, as shown in Vista Figure 2-15, rather than searching the entire storage of your system.

Vista Figure 2-15: Searching from a folder window.

8. We can see similar results when using the same keyword from the Documents folder window as shown in Vista Figure 2-16.

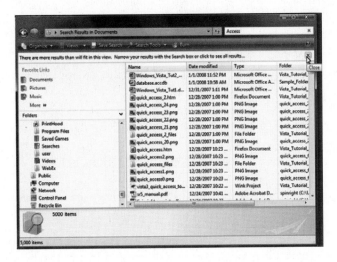

Vista Figure 2-16: Documents window search results.

EXERCISES TO BUILD YOUR KNOWLEDGE OF FILES

Match the term on the left with the appropriate description on the right:

_____1. Context-sensitive menu

_____2. File

_____3. File extension

_____4. File name

_____5. File path

_____6. Folder

_____7. Folder window

_____8. Navigation pane

a. The last part of a file name that indicates the file type.

b. An object that can contain multiple documents and is used to organize information in a GUI.

c. Listing of a file location using the drive letter and all folders that must be opened to get to the file.

d. A menu that pops up when you right-click on an object. The menu items show common things that you might do with the object.

e. The top directory in a file system of a secondary storage device.

f. An organized collection of binary data that represents a document or a program.

g. A string of characters that identifies a file and may describe the file's contents and the reason for the file.

h. A component of a folder window that shows the hierarchy of folders on your system.

____9. Root directory

i. A component of a folder window or the Start button menu that lets you find files or folders.

____10. Search box

j. A GUI dialog that lets you view and work with the contents of a folder.

11. Using folder windows, browse to a folder that contains an application file. The file name is _____ , and it uses _____ of memory.

12. The file from Question 11 was created on the following date and time: _____

Using Help in a folder window, find answers to the questions below:

13. Describe three methods you could use to copy a file from a location on the C: drive to another drive:

    1. _____

    2. _____

    3. _____

14. Give step-by-step instructions for changing display options for files or folders in a folder window.

    _____

    _____

    _____

    _____

    _____

15. How can you select more than one folder or file in a folder window?

    _____

    _____

    _____

    _____

    _____

Tutorial 1

INTRODUCTION TO MICROSOFT OFFICE 2007

After reading this tutorial and completing the associated exercises, you will be able to:

- Understand Microsoft Office and its various components.
- Start Microsoft Office applications.
- Work with the Office Interface.
- Use the Help capabilities of MS Office.

WHAT IS MICROSOFT OFFICE?

Microsoft Office is the most popular suite of productivity applications available today. By a **suite** of applications, we mean a group of applications that share a similar look and feel as well as the capability to move data easily between the applications. Microsoft Office includes MS **Word** for word processing, MS **Excel** for spreadsheet calculations, MS **PowerPoint** for creating presentations, MS **Access** for working with databases, MS **Outlook** for e-mail, and MS **Publisher** for desktop publishing documents.

In this tutorial we will be covering the common features available in the first four of those applications—Word, Excel, PowerPoint, and Access—since they are the ones most widely used in the business world by knowledge workers. MS Office has been designed to allow you to create and work with a variety of types of files. In Office Table 1-1, we show the four applications covered in this tutorial along with their file extensions.

Application	Purpose	File Extension
MS Word	Word processing	.docx
MS Excel	Spreadsheet	.xlsx
MS PowerPoint	Presentation	.pptx
MS Access	Database	.accdb

Office Table 1-1: MS Office 2007 applications and file extensions.

STARTING MS OFFICE APPLICATIONS

You can choose from several methods for starting an MS Office application. We will show you four of those methods here. Keep in mind, after we're done, that there are even a few other ways to open an Office document.

Opening an Office Application Using a Desktop Shortcut

A **shortcut** is generally represented as a small picture (icon) on your graphical user interface. You can place shortcuts in various places on your computer, but the most common is on the desktop. Opening a software application using a shortcut is very easy, as shown in the following figures.

1. In Office Figure 1-1 you can see a Windows Vista desktop with several shortcut icons displayed.

Office Figure 1-1: The Windows Vista desktop.

Four icons are for MS Office applications, namely, Excel, Word, PowerPoint, and Access.

To start an application, double-click on the corresponding icon.

2. In Office Figure 1-2, we have double-clicked on the MS Excel icon.

Office Figure 1-2: Loading an Office application.

Notice that it may take a few moments for the application to load.

While you wait, an animated graphic will appear just to let you know that something is happening while you wait.

3. After a few moments you will see the chosen software opened with a blank document ready for you to begin.

A blank Excel document is shown in Office Figure 1-3.

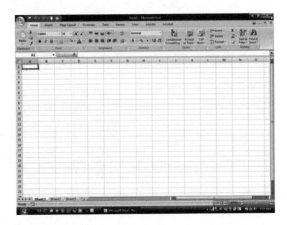

Office Figure 1-3: Microsoft Excel loaded with a blank document.

Opening an Office Application from the Start Menu

As the name implies, the primary means of getting things started in Windows is through the Windows Start button. The rest of the methods for loading an Office application will commence by clicking on the Start button.

1. The Start button is the blue button with the Windows logo that is located on the left side of the Windows taskbar, as illustrated in Office Figure 1-4.

To get started, click the Start button.

Office Figure 1-4: The Windows Start button.

2. The Start button dialog will appear, as seen in Office Figure 1-5.

Office Figure 1-5: The Start button dialog.

The left pane of the dialog contains is a listing of various programs and their icons.

The list in the top portion of this pane will remain constant while the bottom portion will show the most recently used applications.

3. As in the desktop shortcut, you can open an Office application by locating it in the list and double-clicking.

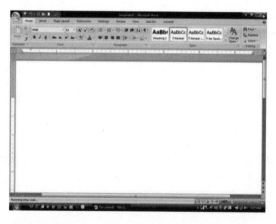

Office Figure 1-6: Microsoft Word loaded.

In Office Figure 1-6 you see the result of clicking the Microsoft Word item in the Start menu.

Note that the Start button dialog is described in more detail in our Windows Vista tutorials.

OPENING AN OFFICE APPLICATION USING A START MENU SEARCH

One of the most exciting features of the Windows Vista Start button is the search box that is located at the bottom of the dialog. Using the search box you can search for any software, file, or folder on your computer by simply typing a search term in the search box. This may be the best way to open an Office program when there are no shortcuts on the desktop or in the Start button pane.

1. To start a search, open the Start Button dialog as shown in Office Figure 1-7.

Office Figure 1-7: The Start button dialog.

Note the search box at the bottom of the dialog, which currently contains the words "Start Search."

2. Click in the search box and start typing your search term.

For our example, we want to open Microsoft Access, so we are typing the term *Access*.

Notice that the search begins as soon as you start typing.

Programs, files, and folders matching the letters you have typed will start appearing in the left pane of the dialog as you type, as shown in Office Figure 1-8.

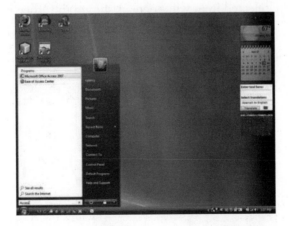

Office Figure 1-8: Typing the search term *Access*.

In most cases, your search term can be shortened to just the first few letters of the name of the item for which you are searching.

3. When the search is complete, you'll see a listing of the software, file, and folder names that match your search term (Office Figure 1-9).

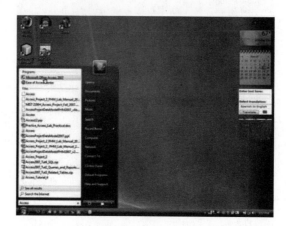

Office Figure 1-9: Search results.

The listing will include as many items as the pane can hold.

The search results will be divided into two main categories: programs and files.

For a complete listing, you can click "See all results."

You can also "Search the Internet" if needed.

4. After the search results are displayed (or sooner if the item you are looking for pops up while you are typing), click on the listing that corresponds to the item that you want.

As before, the selected item will open, as shown in Office Figure 1-10, after a short wait.

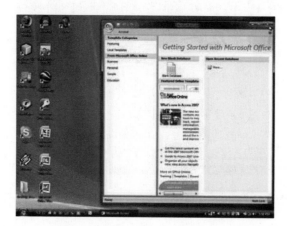

Office Figure 1-10: Microsoft Access loaded.

Opening an Office Application through the All Programs Option

The next method that we will review also begins through the Start button. You may have already noticed the option All Programs on the Start button dialog. This time we'll work through this feature to find and open an MS Office application.

1. Open the Start button dialog and click on the All Programs item in the list as shown in Office Figure 1-11.

Office Figure 1-11: The All Programs option.

2. A list of programs and program folders will appear in the left dialog pane, as they do when you perform a keyword search using the search box, but here you've asked for a listing of *any* program files and folders.

Use the scroll bar to move through the list to find the Microsoft Office folder as shown in Office Figure 1-12.

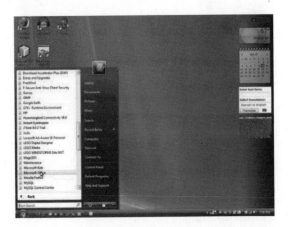

Office Figure 1-12: The Microsoft Office folder.

3. Click on the Microsoft Office folder listing.

The list will expand to see the files and folders that are located within the Microsoft Office folder, as shown in Office Figure 1-13.

Office Figure 1-13: Selecting the PowerPoint item from the list.

Find the listing for PowerPoint and click on it.

4. After a short wait, the PowerPoint application will open, ready for you to start creating a presentation, as shown in Office Figure 1-14.

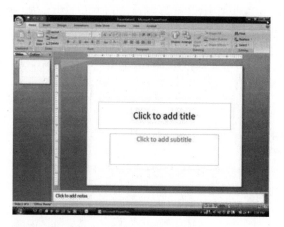

Office Figure 1-14: Microsoft PowerPoint loaded.

Opening an Existing Office Document

So far, we have seen how to open Office applications with the assumption that you are just beginning to create an Office document. Many times, however, you will already have a document file that you want to open and continue working on. There are two or three ways to do this. We will look at one method here.

1. Click the Microsoft Vista Start button.

   On the right side menu, click the Documents option as shown in Office Figure 1-15.

Office Figure 1-15: The Documents option.

2. The Documents folder window will open as shown in Office Figure 1-16.

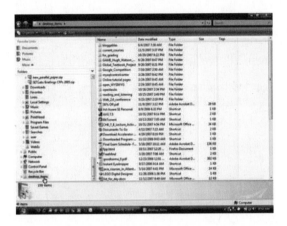

Office Figure 1-16: Documents folder window.

This window has two panes.

In the left pane, you can see a listing of folders that are available on your storage.

In the right pane, you see a listing of files and folders that are stored in the folder currently selected in the left pane.

3. You can navigate to a folder by sequentially clicking on a folder in the left pane and then click on a folder in the right pane.

Do this until you find the file that you want to open.

You can also help yourself find a file in a long list by sorting the list.

To sort the list by file type, click on the Type heading in the window as shown in Office Figure 1-17.

Office Figure 1-17: Navigating to a folder, sorting by file type.

4. Notice that after sorting by type, Microsoft Office documents are grouped together in the list.

    Choose one of the files and double-click it to open the file.

    In Office Figure 1-18, we are opening a Word file called *list_for_day.docx*.

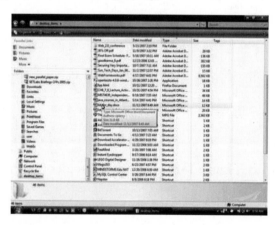

Office Figure 1-18: Selecting a Word file.

5. After a few moments, the file that you selected will open as shown in Office Figure 1-19.

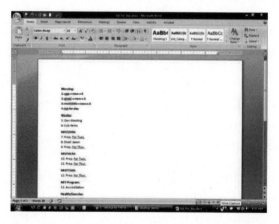

Office Figure 1-19: An open Word document.

The Office application that opens will be determined based on the file type, which is denoted by the file extension.

The file extensions for Office files are listed back in Office Table 1-1.

WORKING WITH THE MS OFFICE INTERFACE

All MS Office applications have a similar look and feel, so if you learn to use one application, you will feel comfortable learning to use the other ones as well. All applications use similar visual elements, such as ribbons, menus, and dialogs, to access the many functions that are available with each application. A **ribbon** is a strip across the top of the window that shows many of the functions the Office application can perform in a single place. A **menu** is a list of functions or submenus that are accessed via a menu bar at the top of the application window. A **dialog** is a mini-window with one or more "pages" that include commands related to a particular process or task.

Let's spend some time having a look at the various graphical elements that we will come across in any MS Office Application.

Office Ribbons

With Office 2007, Microsoft replaced the traditional menu hierarchy and toolbars with a set of ribbons. If you are used to older versions of Office, this will take some getting used to. It is our experience that, once you are past the initial shock of change, you will find that ribbons are pretty nice and can be much more efficient than the old menus and toolbars.

As described above, a ribbon is a graphical element in the shape of a strip that contains visual icons representing various application options. By clicking on an icon, you will be able to execute a command or access additional options through a menu or dialog.

Ribbons are accessed via a system of tabs known as **context tabs**. Each context tab contains a label that identifies the context that relates the various commands that are available on the tab. To switch to another ribbon, simply click on the context tab.

In the next few figures we'll take a quick look at the Home ribbon for each of the four main applications provided in Office: Access, Excel, PowerPoint, and Word. Notice that they are all very similar. This is on purpose and is the result of two major software concepts.

One is **software component reuse**. Software makers try to create reusable components that can be used in diverse applications. For example, changing regular text to bold font works the same in all four of these applications. So, once programmers figure out how to make text bold, they can write this component in such a way that it can be used over and over.

The second concept is that of a **common user interface**. Reuse allows developers to do this, but it takes a conscious effort to make it happen when creating software. The idea is to make the interface as similar as possible in multiple applications to make it easier for users to learn and switch between the different applications. Thus, not only does the command for making text bold work the same in all of these applications, but the icon looks the same and the command can be found and accessed in all the same ways. See whether you can spot other examples of these two concepts as we review the ribbons.

There are five main ribbon contexts provided in Access: Home, Create, External Data, Database Tools, and Datasheet. In addition to these main ribbons, other ribbons will become available as you work with and create various components in Access or any of the other Office applications.

The **Home ribbon** of Access is shown in Office Figure 1-20. As with all Office applications, the Home ribbon contains the most frequently used commands. Notice that the ribbon is broken up into various sections called groups. The commands in each group are related by the context label displayed at the bottom of the command group.

Office Figure 1-20: The Access Home ribbon.

Since the ribbons are organized by context, you should find it easier to remember where a command is located based on the context of what you are currently working on. For example, suppose you want to change selected text to bold. You want to change the font, and changing a font is a very common thing to do in an Office document. So, you should find the Bold command in the Font group on the Home ribbon.

Office Figure 1-21: The Excel Home ribbon.

Notice the similarities and differences between the Excel Home ribbon shown in Office Figure 1-21 and the Access Home ribbon of Office Figure 1-20. You might first have noticed that the overall appearances of the two ribbons are similar and that many of the commands are the same. Looking closer you'll start to see the differences. First of all, there are some groups on one ribbon that are not on the other. For example, the Excel Home ribbon has a Number group not found on the Access ribbon, while the Access Home ribbon includes a Records group. These differences are understandable because the two software applications are created for working with different types of documents. In Excel, you frequently do quantitative analysis, so you will more often work directly with numbers than you would when using Access.

You will also notice that the ribbon context labels are different between the two applications. In fact, the only ribbon context shared by Access and Excel is the Home ribbon. As you work through the various tutorials for the specific Office applications, you will understand why the different contexts are provided in each application and how to use the various commands provided in those contexts.

Office Figure 1-22: The PowerPoint Home ribbon.

The PowerPoint Home ribbon is shown in Office Figure 1-22. Notice the command groups on this ribbon. Again, commands that can be used in all Office applications appear in similar groups and contexts. Commands that are specific to creating PowerPoint presentation slides are also found. Fortunately, even the application-specific commands have the same look and feel as all of the other commands.

Office Figure 1-23: The Word Home ribbon.

The Word Home ribbon is displayed in Office Figure 1-23. As you look at this ribbon, you may get the feeling that understanding a ribbon display is "old hat" already. That's the power of using software that has a consistent graphical look and feel. Once you have understood how to view and access commands in one Office application, you then know how to do the same in all of the others. It then remains to learn what commands are available.

You may have noticed that near some command icons a little arrow is visible. Typically, clicking on the arrow will cause a menu or dialog to be displayed with more options related to the command icon. You may have also noticed the small box located in the lower right corner of each command group. Clicking one of these will also result in displaying a dialog with a more complete listing of commands and options related to the group context. Let's have a look at a few examples of using an Office dialog.

Office Dialogs and Menus

Other than ribbons, there are two other primary means of accessing Office commands: dialogs and menus. A **dialog** is usually presented as a smaller window or box on the screen that lets you communicate with the computer. A dialog box can be used to enter information, set options, or give commands to the computer. The dialog box gives the user options, which can be selected by clicking with the mouse. A dialog may include several pages, each of which can be accessed by clicking on tabs, much as on the ribbons.

1. In Office Figure 1-24, we see an Excel spreadsheet with a couple of cells containing text selected.

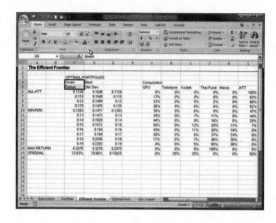

Office Figure 1-24: An Excel spreadsheet with cells selected.

We have lots of options available in the Font group of the Home ribbon that we could use to adjust the font.

However, we can get more if we use the **Format Cells dialog**.

Click on the small box located on the bottom right corner of the Font group.

2. The Format Cells dialog will appear as shown in Office Figure 1-25.

Office Figure 1-25: Format Cells dialog.

Note that this dialog has several pages of commands for adjusting cell formats.

The Font page is currently displayed, since we accessed this dialog through the Font group.

You can get to other pages of the dialog by clicking on the tabs.

On the Font page, notice that all Font options in the Home ribbon font group are available.

On some dialogs, you will find additional options as well.

3. Sometimes it's easier to find a command option on a ribbon, and sometimes it's easier to find it in a dialog.

This depends on the person and the command.

Let's look at another dialog to illustrate this.

Notice that several cells with numbers are selected in the Excel spreadsheet shown in Office Figure 1-26.

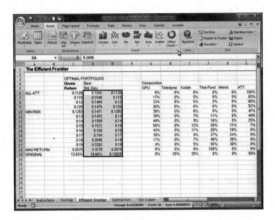

Office Figure 1-26: Cells selected in Excel.

4. Let's use a dialog to create a quick chart of these numbers.

The Charts group is located in the Insert ribbon.

By clicking in the square at the bottom right corner of the Charts group, we can access the Insert Chart dialog as shown in Office Figure 1-27.

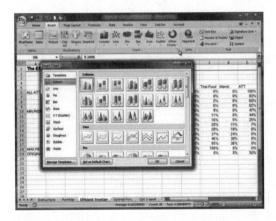

Office Figure 1-27: Insert Chart dialog.

Like many dialogs, this window contains typical Windows elements: buttons, scroll bars, lists, and icons.

5. With the Insert Chart dialog we can use either the scroll bar on the right of the dialog or the list on the right to search for an appropriate chart type.

In Office Figure 1-28, we've used the list to find the X-Y Scatter category of charts.

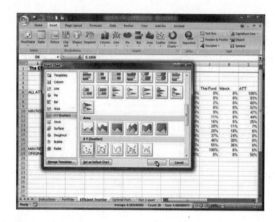

Office Figure 1-28: Selecting a chart type from a dialog.

We then selected the one we like by clicking on its icon and then clicking on the OK button.

6. The inserted chart will then be displayed on our spreadsheet as shown in Office Figure 1-29.

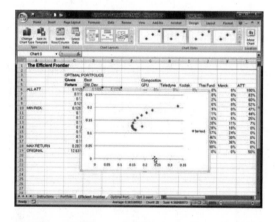

Office Figure 1-29: The inserted chart.

Complete instructions for creating Excel charts are included in our Excel tutorials.

A menu is a common and important visual element that you will run across while using Office software. A menu is basically a listing of command options from which you can click on to select. A menu may also have one or more submenus that are displayed, depending on the menu option selected.

One of the most important menus available in Office software is known as a **context-sensitive menu**. This menu is always accessible by right-clicking on a document element. The name of this menu is derived from the fact that the provided menu items will depend on the context of the element that you clicked on. For example, if you select and right-click on a phrase that you typed in Word, you'll see context-sensitive menu items such as Font, Paragraph, and Styles. These are all command options that would be useful in the context of working with text in Word. Let's look at a quick example in the context of the Excel chart.

7. If you select and right-click on the chart, you'll see a menu like that shown in Office Figure 1-30.

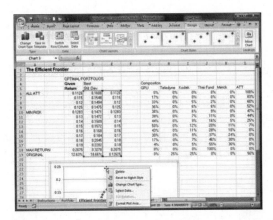

Office Figure 1-30: Context-sensitive menu for Excel chart.

Notice that the options on this menu are related to an Excel chart.

8. To select a menu item as in Office Figure 1-31, simply click on it, and the command will be executed.

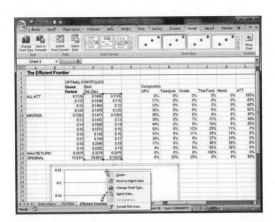

Office Figure 1-31: Selecting a context-sensitive menu option.

Some items will be listed with a small, right-facing arrow, which signifies that a submenu will be displayed when clicked.

Other menu options may be followed by ellipsis (...), which means that a dialog will be displayed when selected.

The Office Button

An important and sometimes hard to discover component of the Office user interface is the **Office button**. The Office button is the big circle marked with the Office logo on the top left of any Office application window (and you thought this was just for decoration!) The Office button provides a dialog with the commands that are common to all of the Office applications, such as Save and Print.

1. As we mentioned, the Office button is located on the top right side of the application window.

   Click this button to see the dialog as shown in Office Figure 1-32.

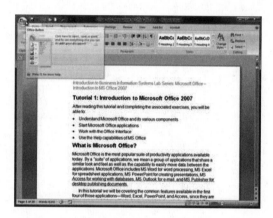

Office Figure 1-32: The Office button.

2. The Office button dialog will be displayed as shown in Office Figure 1-33.

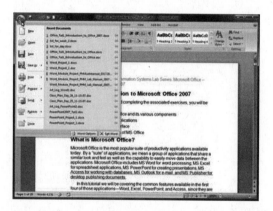

Office Figure 1-33: The Office button dialog.

Note that the primary commands are located in the pane on the left.

When the dialog is first opened, a listing of the most recent documents that you have opened will appear in the left pane.

3. If you hover the cursor over one of the primary commands in the left pane, a list of secondary commands will appear in the right pane.

In Office Figure 1-34, we have the mouse hovering over the Save As command.

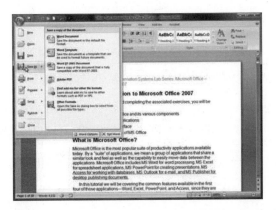

Office Figure 1-34: The Save As command.

Note the different file formats to which we can save a Word document.

4. You can click on a primary command in the left pane or select and click on a secondary command in the right pane.

In Office Figure 1-35, we see that the Save As dialog will appear when we click directly on the Save As command.

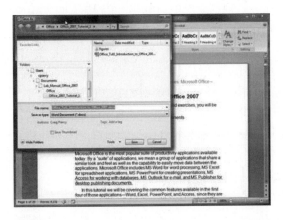

Office Figure 1-35: The Save As dialog.

5. Take a few moments to check out the commands available on the Office button dialog in each of the Office applications.

In Office Figure 1-36, we show you the Word Print options from the Office button dialog.

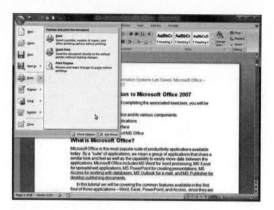

Office Figure 1-36: The Office button Print options.

6. Another button that you should note is the Word Options button located at the bottom of the Office button dialog, as shown in Office Figure 1-37.

Office Figure 1-37: The Word Options button.

This button provides access to commands that let you configure Word to work as you would like.

Each of the Office applications has an Options area that you can access in this manner.

7. Clicking the Options button will bring up the Word Options dialog, shown in Office Figure 1-38.

Office Figure 1-38: The Word Options dialog.

Take a few moments to navigate this dialog in one of the Office applications to see what options you can set.

We'll use one of the pages here to change some application settings in the next section.

The Quick Access Toolbar

While the Office Button contains the most frequently used commands that are common to most all office applications, you will want to get to some of these commands more quickly. That's where the Quick Access Toolbar comes in, as shown in the following examples.

1. The Quick Access Toolbar is located in the title bar at the top of the application window next to the Office button.

   The Quick Access button, shown in Office Figure 1-39, includes three buttons: Save, Undo, and Redo.

Office Figure 1-39: The Quick Access Toolbar.

   In addition, the arrow icon provides a menu for customizing the Quick Access Toolbar.

2. You use a command on the Quick Access Toolbar just as you would any other command on a ribbon or dialog.

   For example, click the Save icon as shown in Office Figure 1-40 on the Quick Access Toolbar to get the dialog shown in Office Figure 1-41.

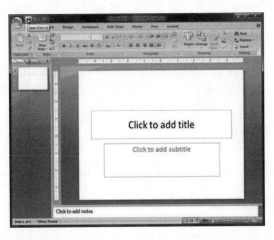

Office Figure 1-40: The Quick Access Save command.

3. For example, by clicking on the diskette-shaped icon, the Save As dialog will be displayed as shown in Office Figure 1-41.

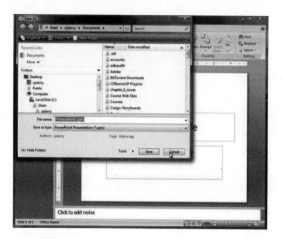

Office Figure 1-41: The Save As dialog
from Quick Access Toolbar.

4. In Office 2007 applications you can customize the Quick Access Toolbar so that it includes the commands that you frequently use.

To begin, open the Microsoft Office button dialog and click on the Options button at the bottom of the dialog.

In Office Figure 1-42, we are starting to customize the Quick Access Toolbar for PowerPoint.

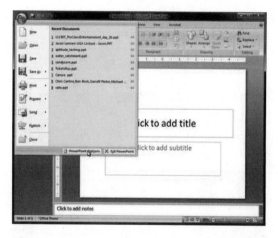

Office Figure 1-42: The PowerPoint Microsoft Office button.

5. Click on the Customize option in the list in the left pane of the dialog.

In the right pane of the PowerPoint Options dialog, you'll see the Customize the Quick Access Toolbar page.

This page is composed of two main areas as shown in Office Figure 1-43.

Office Figure 1-43: Customize the Quick Access Toolbar.

In the area on the left you can view a listing of all of the available commands that you can put on the toolbar.

6. You can change the listing by selecting a category in the list box above this area.

In the right area you'll see the list of commands that are currently on the toolbar.

To add a command, select it in the left area, then click the Add button as shown in Office Figure 1-44.

Office Figure 1-44: Adding a Quick Access command.

You can choose to add it for all documents or only for the current document.

7. After clicking the Add button, you'll see the new command appear in the right area.

In Office Figure 1-45 you can see that we added the file Open command to the Quick Access Toolbar.

Office Figure 1-45: The added Open command.

8. With the new button added to the right pane, you can also change the position in which it will appear on the Quick Access Toolbar.

   Simply click the up or down arrow on the right of the dialog with the command selected.

   In Office Figure 1-46 we have moved the Open command to second place. The topmost item in the list will appear as the leftmost command on the toolbar.

Office Figure 1-46: Adjusting the position of the added command on the Quick Access Toolbar.

9. In Office Figure 1-47, we have added additional commands to the toolbar. Namely, we added the New and New Slide commands.

   When you have added all of the commands to the Quick Access Toolbar that you want, click the OK button.

Office Figure 1-47: Adding more commands to the Toolbar.

10. Our final Quick Access Toolbar configuration is shown in Office Figure 1-48.

Office Figure 1-48: The final Quick Access Toolbar.

MS OFFICE HELP

Our last topic in this introduction to the use of MS Office is a brief discussion of the Help system that is common to all MS Office applications. This help system is quite extensive and can be accessed in a number of ways—for example, by pressing the F1 function key or by clicking the Help button on the far right end of the menu bar at the top of the application window. In the following examples, we'll explore the Help feature available in MS Access.

1. With Access, you actually get some help as soon as you open the application.

The opening window, shown in Office Figure 1-49, includes links to starter database structures and to Office Online.

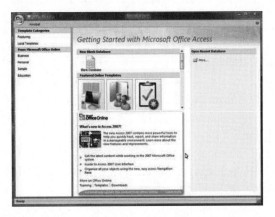

Office Figure 1-49: Opening page of MS Access.

2. After you have begun to work in a database, there are two main ways to access Help.

   You can press the F1 key on the keyboard, or you can click the Help button found in the upper right corner of the application window, as shown in Office Figure 1-50.

   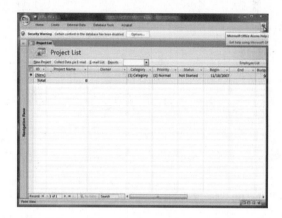

   Office Figure 1-50: The Microsoft Access Help button.

   The Access Help dialog will appear.

3. Think of the Help dialog as a searchable reference book where you can find answers to all of your questions about using Access (Office Figure 1-51).

   Office Figure 1-51: The opening page of Access Help.

   In the left pane, there is a table of contents with links to topics.

   Near the top of the window, there is a search box.

   Any item in blue is a hyperlink to more information.

4. When you load Access on your computer, an Access Help knowledge base is loaded along with software.

   The Help dialog makes the knowledge base accessible.

If you are connected to the Internet, you can get access to a larger and more up-to-date knowledge base.

Look at the button in the lower right corner of the Help window. If it reads "Offline," click it to get a pop-up menu that allows you to "Show content from Office Online," as shown in Office Figure 1-52.

Office Figure 1-52: Changing connection status.

5. After connection to Office Online, the only immediately visible change is the connection status button in the lower right corner, which should now read "Connected to Office Online," as shown in Office Figure 1-53.

Office Figure 1-53: Connected to Office Online.

The main difference is in the amount of information available to you.

In most cases, you probably don't need to be connected, but at times it can be very helpful.

Let's click on the "Getting Help" link in the right pane of the dialog.

6. Now the page in the right pane has changed to provide a listing of help topics.

Browse the list and click on any topic of interest.

In Office Figure 1-54, we are clicking on the link that reads "Using Microsoft Office Online."

Office Figure 1-54: Clicking a Help topic.

7. Eventually, for any topic you will get to a page where you can read about the topic, as shown in Office Figure 1-55.

Office Figure 1-55: Entry for getting Help online.

These pages will include text and images about the Help topic of interest as well as links to related topics.

8. You can also browse for topics using the Table of Contents pane.

If an entry in the Table of Contents is preceded by a book icon, then it contains a more detailed list.

You can click on the book icon to expand this list as shown in Office Figure 1-56.

Office Figure 1-56: Navigating the Table of Contents.

9. Entries that are preceded by the Help icon will lead to the Help entry for the topic.

In Office Figure 1-57, we have clicked on the topic "Access Glossary."

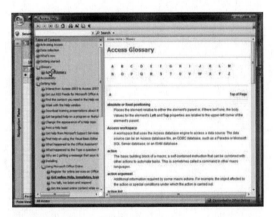

Office Figure 1-57: The Access Glossary.

This is a nifty page to know about if you want to look up an Access term.

10. No doubt you have already noticed the other icons and controls available on the Help dialog.

For example, scrollbars are available for each of the window panes when a list or Help entry is too big to view in the pane.

In addition, there is a toolbar at the top of the dialog with several commands (Office Figure 1-58).

Office Figure 1-58: The Help dialog toolbar.

11. The Help dialog toolbar contains commands that work much as they would in a Web browser: buttons for paging back, paging forward, printing, and others.

    In Office Figure 1-59, we have clicked the Home button on the toolbar to get back to the entry page for Access Help.

Office Figure 1-59: Back to the Access Help Home page.

EXERCISES TO BUILD YOUR KNOWLEDGE OF MICROSOFT OFFICE

Match each of the Office terms with its description.

_____1. Access

a. The Microsoft Office application that lets you create text documents such as letters and term papers.

_____2. Dialog

b. The Microsoft Office application that lets you create quantitative models and analyze numeric data.

_____3. Excel

c. The Microsoft Office application that lets you create slide shows to use in a presentation.

_____4. Help

d. The Microsoft Office application that lets you create and manage a database.

_____5. Office button

e. A knowledge base full of information about how to use Office software.

_____6. Office Online

f. A button that provides access to commands, such as Print and Save, that is common to all Office applications.

_____7. PowerPoint

g. A long, thin graphical element located at the top of an Office application window that contains commands for working with your document.

_____8. Start button

h. The Windows Vista button that you can use to find and start your Office programs.

_____9. Ribbon

i. A mini-window with one or more "pages" that include commands related to a particular process or task.

_____10. Word

j. A collection of Office Help information, templates and other helpful Office tools that is available on the Microsoft Office Web site.

Answer the following questions page to reinforce your knowledge of Microsoft Office basics.

11. List the main software components that are available in Microsoft Office. Describe the primary purpose of each component.

_____

_____

_____

_____

_____

12. Open MS Word on your computer. List the names of the first five icons found on the Home ribbon. Describe what happens when each of these icons is clicked.

_____

_____

_____

_____

_____

13. Using Word Help, find out how you can make newsletter-style columns in your document. List the main steps here.

_____

_____

_____

_____

14. Using Word Help, search Microsoft Office Online to find Office templates. List the names of four templates that you find.

_____

_____

_____

15. Customize your Word Quick Access Toolbar to include the following command icons: Save, Undo, Redo, Open, New, and Quick Styles.

Tutorial 1

INTRODUCTION TO MICROSOFT WORD 2007

After reading this tutorial and completing the associated exercises, you will be able to:

- Open and start using Microsoft Word.
- Work with the Word Interface.
- Perform basic tasks with text using Microsoft Word.
- Prepare to print your document.

MICROSOFT WORD: YOUR DOCUMENT CREATION SOLUTION

Do you write letters to your grandmother, a pen pal, or your local newspaper editor? Are you an aspiring author? Or are you interested in creating formal business documents? You may be thinking: "Who writes letters? I'm a techno road warrior who communicates through e-mail, instant messaging, and social networks." While this may increasingly be the case, there will come a time when an electronic document won't do, and you'll need to create a document suitable for printing. In these cases, knowledge of Microsoft Word will benefit you.

Microsoft Word is the part of the Microsoft Office suite of programs that provides you with tools for creating, editing, formatting, adding tables and pictures, color coding, linking or embedding your Excel spreadsheets or other software-created objects, correcting grammar and spelling, writing equations, and distributing and sharing documents. (Whew!) While Word was primarily designed with the printed document in mind, recent versions have included tools for creating electronic documents, such as the ability to include hyperlinks in your document or save the document that you create as a Web page. These tools, along with Word's powerful formatting features, provide you with capabilities for using Word as your e-mail, blog, and Web page editor.

In the next few pages, you will learn the basics of working with MS Word. In this tutorial, you will cover the basic skills of setting up Word for your needs and will start creating useful and vibrant documents.

WORKING WITH THE WORD INTERFACE

As with other software you may have learned, before getting maximum mileage out of Word you need to become familiar with the Word interface. Fortunately, because of Microsoft's use of objects and a common user interface, many of the same interface elements that you find in other Windows-based software—menus, toolbars, status bar, and so on—are available and have the same look and feel in Word.

In this section, you will be introduced to the standard interface. The interface for MS Office software in general was described in the Office tutorial chapters, so the focus will be on interface features that are unique to Word. You can open MS Word by double-clicking the MS Word icon on your desktop or by selecting it from the Start menu system.

Word Interface Overview

Open Word and try to identify the items indicated in Word Figure 1-1 and listed in Word Table 1-1. In general, when you start the Word software, the assumption is that you want to start a new document, and a blank page will be ready for you to use. We'll see later how we can start a new document while Word is already open.

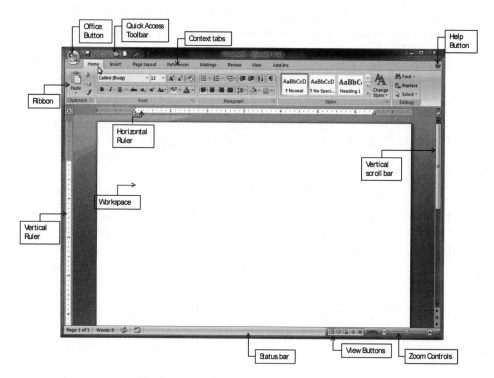

Word Figure 1-1: The Word interface.

Component	Description
Ribbon	A visual component that shows the most commonly used Word commands for a given context, such as Insert, as described in the Office tutorials.
Context tab	One of a row of tabs displayed above the ribbon, on which you can click to switch to a particular ribbon.
Status bar	A component that provides information on the status of Word, such as the current page and document page count; the word count of the document; whether Caps Lock is activated; whether changes are being tracked; and whether typing inserts characters before the character at the cursor or overtypes the characters to the right of the cursor.
Horizontal scrollbar	The horizontal scrollbar lets you move the workspace horizontally to view more of the workspace. This may be needed if you zoom in to view your page and it becomes wider than the screen.
Vertical scrollbar	Often your document will be taller than the screen. The vertical scrollbar lets you move between your pages.
Zoom control	Allows you to adjust the display size of the workspace quickly.
Office button	By clicking this button, you'll have access to commands that are common to all the various software in Microsoft Office, such as Open, Save, and Print.
Quick Access Toolbar	Using the Office button, you can add icons here for commonly used commands.
Help button	A button that, when you need to do something that you don't know or have forgotten how to do, you can click to access the Word Help facility, which is full of good content that describes anything that you might want to do in Word.
Horizontal/ vertical ruler	A ruler is a tool that allows you to see and adjust how components of your document are aligned on the page. The horizontal ruler is used for working with the horizontal alignment of components while the vertical ruler deals with vertical alignment.
Workspace	This is the area in which you can add, view, and work with the items in your document.
View buttons	These buttons allow you to view your document in different ways: Print, Full Screen, Web Layout, Outline, and Draft views.

Word Table 1-1: Components of the Word user interface.

Tour of the Word Ribbons

As you can see in Word Figure 1-1, Word typically has seven different ribbon contexts that make it easy to find the commands that you need. Additional ribbons may also appear when you add components such as tables or images to your document. You can actually customize Word and add one or two more if needed. The next several figures will provide a quick overview of the primary Word ribbons. You will get very familiar with these as you work through these tutorials, so there's no need to memorize them now. Just take a quick look now and then refer back to these pages as needed.

Notice that each ribbon has some things in common. As described in the Office tutorials, commands are arranged in a series of groups. Each group includes a set of controls that lets you do related tasks. Some controls are accompanied by downward-pointing arrows. When these are clicked, a menu or palette with more related options is displayed. You should also notice that each group has a small arrow in a box in the lower right corner. By clicking this arrow you can open a dialog box for the group that provides even more options that you can use to complete your work.

Word Figure 1-2: The Home ribbon.

The Home ribbon (Word Figure 1-2) contains the most commonly used Word commands. Commands such as Copy, Cut, and Paste are located here in the Clipboard group. Text-formatting commands are provided in the Font, Paragraph, and Styles groups. Finally, the Editing group provides some more commonly used commands.

Word Figure 1-3: The Insert ribbon.

You'll find many different objects that you can add to your worksheet on the Insert ribbon, shown in Word Figure 1-3. The types of objects that you can use are included in the groups Pages, Tables, Illustrations, Links, Header & Footer, Text, and Symbols.

Word Figure 1-4: The Page Layout ribbon.

The Page Layout ribbon (Word Figure 1-4) provides commands that you can use when you want to control how the overall document will be printed or appear on the screen. The commands on this ribbon are organized into the groups Themes, Page Setup, Page Background, Paragraph, and Arrange.

Word Figure 1-5: The References ribbon.

The References ribbon (Word Figure 1-5) includes commands that let you quickly and easily reference the sources for your document and create elements useful for large documents such as books. Commands of the Table of Contents group can be used to automatically make and format a table of contents based on the headings in your document. Footnotes ribbon commands allow you to add footnotes (or end notes) to the pages in your document. Other groups on this ribbon include commands that let you add or create Citations & Bibliography, Captions, an Index and a Table of Authorities.

Word Figure 1-6: The Mailings ribbon.

The Mailings ribbon (Word Figure 1-6) provides commands to help you work with documents that are meant to be sent through the postal system. You'll find commands that help you create envelopes and boilerplate letter templates. "Boilerplates" are letters like those you get from sweepstakes or other advertisers that are basically all the same except for the recipient's name, which has been inserted in the right places. You can make them look much better using Word. The commands on this ribbon are divided into groups called Create, Start Mail Merge, Write & Insert Fields, Preview Results, and Finish. You can find out how to use some of these commands in our Office Integration Tutorials.

Word Figure 1-7: The Review ribbon.

Options available on the Review ribbon (Word Figure 1-7) are typically used when you are working with other people on the document. These commands allow you to check the spelling and grammar of the text (Proofing group), add comments to selected text for you or others to read (Comments group) and track the changes made to the document by you or others over time (Tracking and Changes groups). You can also compare one document with another (Compare group) or allow only authorized users to view or change the document (Protect Document group).

Word Figure 1-8: The View ribbon.

The View ribbon (Word Figure 1-8) provides commands that you can use when you want to control how the overall document will be displayed on the screen. The commands on this ribbon are organized into the groups Document Views, Show/Hide, Zoom, Window, and Macros. A macro is a saved set of Word or programming commands that you can create to automate repetitive tasks as you work on the document.

WORKING WITH TEXT IN A WORD DOCUMENT

The primary component of any Word document is text. So let's take a look at some basic ways to work with text. When a new Word document is first opened, all you have to do is start typing text in, as shown in Word Figure 1-9.

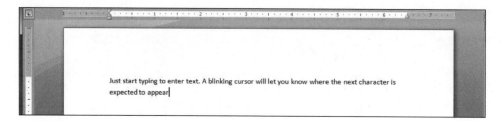

Word Figure 1-9: Typing Text.

A blinking cursor will be displayed at the location where the next character will appear when typed. Notice that, as you come to the end of a line, the next text will automatically appear on the next line. This feature is known as text wrapping.

You can move the cursor to any location that you wish within the current document by simply pointing your mouse to the location and clicking. To insert text, simply click on the page (workspace) at the location where you wish to insert the new text. Let's start to change the text by selecting part of it, deleting that part, and then inserting something new to replace it. When you wish to move, copy, delete, or modify existing text, you will first need to select the text.

Selecting and Deleting Text

1. To select some text, first click in the workspace just before or just after the text that you want to select.

   For, now click just after the word *will* as shown in Word Figure 1-10.

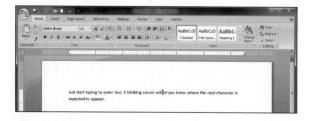

Word Figure 1-10: Positioning the cursor.

2. Hold the mouse button and drag the cursor over the text that you want to select.

   The selected text will be highlighted.

Select the words *let you know* as shown in Word Figure 1-11.

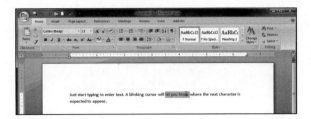

Word Figure 1-11: Selecting some text.

3. Once text has been selected, you can do various things with it.

   For now, we'll simply remove it.

   While the text is highlighted, press the Delete key. The text will be removed and the space closed up as shown in Word Figure 1-12.

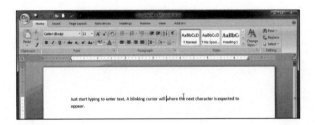

Word Figure 1-12: Deleting text.

Word provides some shortcuts for selecting text. For instance, you can select a whole word by double-clicking on it. To select a whole paragraph, just triple-click within the paragraph. You can choose an entire document using the Select All command in the Editing group on the Home ribbon or by using the keyboard shortcut Ctrl-A.

You also have other methods available for deleting text. As you've seen, you can delete text by first selecting it and then pressing the Delete key on your keyboard. Alternatively, you could place the cursor just after the text to be deleted and then use the Backspace key until the text has been deleted. Or, you could place the cursor just before the text to be deleted and then press the Delete key to delete one character at a time until the text has been deleted.

Undoing an Action

If you're anything like the authors of these tutorials, it's not uncommon to make an editing mistake. Fortunately, if you find that you have made a mistake while working with Word, you can often undo what you have done.

1. The Undo command is on the Quick Access Toolbar as the counterclockwise arrow (Word Figure 1-13).

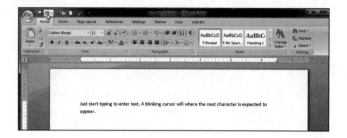

Word Figure 1-13: Clicking the Undo icon.

When you click it, the last action that you completed will be undone.

2. For instance, if you click the Undo icon just after you delete the selected text, the text will reappear as if you hadn't deleted it, as shown in Word Figure 1-14.

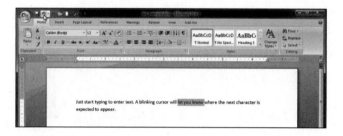

Word Figure 1-14: Undoing text deletion.

The action was undone.

3. After an action has been undone, a clockwise arrow icon appears on the Quick Access Toolbar as shown in Word Figure 1-15. This is the Redo command.

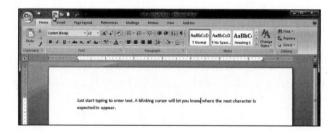

Word Figure 1-15: The Redo icon.

You can click this to redo an undone command, which is useful when you want to repeat an action. If you have not undone an action, the arrow is counterclockwise and downward and enables you to repeat the previous action.

4. The Undo feature will store a list of the last several actions that you did during the current session.

Click the small arrow and select the action to undo from the list as shown in Word Figure 1-16.

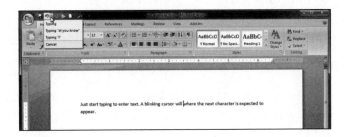

Word Figure 1-16: Undoing a previous action.

Inserting Text

Inserting text in the middle of something we've written is just as easy as deleting text. You simply click where you want to insert the text to position the cursor and then start typing. Let's try it from the point where we deleted the text snippet "let you know."

1. Click on the document between the words *will* and *where* in the sentence.

    The blinking cursor will now be positioned there as shown in Word Figure 1-17.

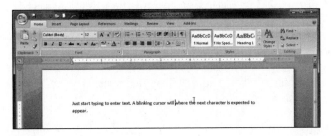

Word Figure 1-17: Positioning cursor for text insertion.

2. Type the text snippet *appear at the location* now.

    The snippet will be inserted within the existing sentence as shown in Word Figure 1-18.

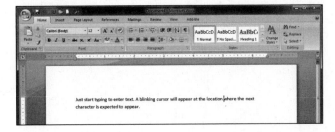

Word Figure 1-18: After inserting some text.

SAVING, CLOSING, AND STARTING WORD DOCUMENTS

Once you've started working on a document, even before you've completed it, you're going to want to save it. You'll also want to be able to close a document you are working on and start a new one. Let's take a quick look at how we can do these things in Word.

Saving Your Document

Commands for saving you document are available on the menu accessible through the Office button and on the Quick Access Toolbar.

1. Click the icon that looks like a diskette on the Quick Access Toolbar as shown in Word Figure 1-19.

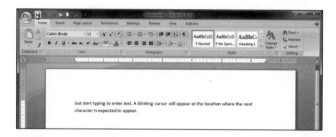

Word Figure 1-19: The Save icon on the Quick Access Toolbar.

If you're not sure which icon, hover the cursor over an icon. The name and the shortcut of the command will be displayed.

2. If you have already saved the document before, you will see a brief notice on the status bar that your file is being saved.

If it is the first time that you are saving the document, you will see the Save As dialog.

You can use the dialog to set the location where you want to save the document, give the document a file name, and even choose the type of file.

When you are done setting these options, click the Save button as shown in Word Figure 1-20.

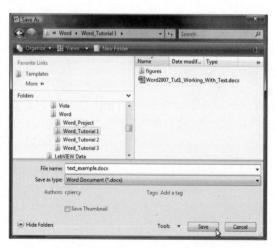

Word Figure 1-20: The Save As dialog.

Closing a Document

Documents can be closed without actually closing the Word software. This is convenient when you want to stop working on one document and then immediately begin another.

1. Click the Office button, found on the top left corner of the Word window.

   Note the various options available on the menu that appears.

   For now, click on the Close option, as shown in Word Figure 1-21.

Word Figure 1-21: Closing a document.

2. If you have not changed your recent changes, a message will be displayed asking you whether to save the document (Word Figure 1-22).

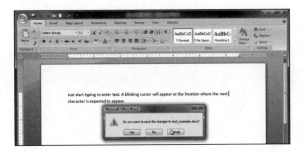

Word Figure 1-22: Save File message.

Starting a New Document

You may have noticed the New option that is available on the Office button menu. It's almost too obvious to be worth noting that this is used when you want to begin a new document.

1. Click the Office button.

Now, select the New command as shown in Word Figure 1-23.

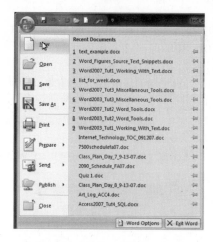

Word Figure 1-23: The New option.

The New Document dialog shown in Word Figure 1-24 will be displayed.

Note that you have several options for what kind of new document to start. These options are provided as a list of templates on the left of the dialog. You should take some time to look through the list to see what is available.

When you select a template category, one or more options for that category will be listed in the center pane of the dialog window.

2. Make sure that the Blank and recent template category is selected.

Select Blank document in the center pane as shown in Word Figure 1-24.

Word Figure 1-24: The New Document dialog.

On the right of the dialog is a preview pane.

Once you are satisfied with your selection, click the Create button.

3. A new, blank document will appear that is ready for you to begin writing, as shown in Word Figure 1-25.

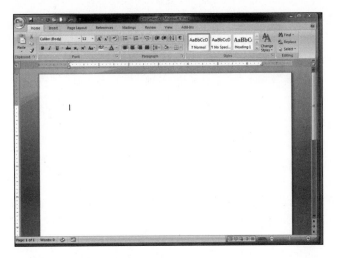

Word Figure 1-25: A new document.

FORMATTING TEXT

Selected text may also be formatted. Formatting of text can involve changing the look or style of the text, adjusting the alignment, or adjusting the spacing between the text. Formatting commands may be found on the Home ribbon, on the Page Layout ribbon, and on pop-up toolbars and menus. Let's have a look these various methods of formatting text.

Formatting the Text Font

1. We'll start with the text shown in Word Figure 1-26.

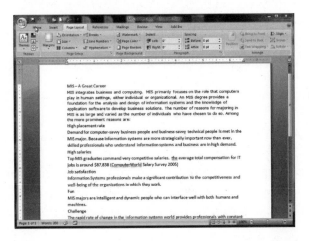

Word Figure 1-26: Unformatted document *MIS_Careers.docx.*

You can download this starter file from the tutorials Web site. The file is called *MIS_Careers.docx.*

We'll start by formatting the heading for the document that says *MIS – A Great Career* to make it stand out using a bold font style.

2. First, select the text that we want to format, as in Word Figure 1-27.

Word Figure 1-27: Selecting text to apply formatting.

One way to make this text bold is to click the Bold command, found in the Font group on the Home ribbon.

3. Now, select the line in the text with the words *High placement rate.*

Immediately after selecting the text, move the mouse pointer to the right and upward.

You should see a Quick Format toolbar appear (Word Figure 1-28).

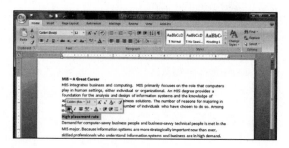

Word Figure 1-28: Formatting with the Quick Format toolbar.

Click the Bold icon here to format the selected text.

4. Let's change the font face of all of the text.

Press Ctrl-A on the keyboard to select all the text in the document.

In the Font group on the Home ribbon, you'll find a list of fonts, each one displayed in its own face as shown in Word Figure 1-29.

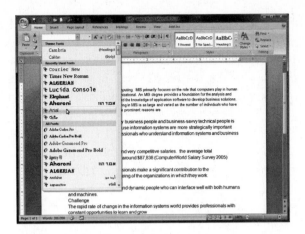

Word Figure 1-29: Setting the font face.

Click the arrow on the list box to see the list.

Select the Arial font to convert the entire text.

5. While the entire document is still selected, we'll adjust the font size as well.

   Next to the font face list in the Font group you'll find the font size list.

   Click the arrow to see a list of sizes in points.

   We'll set our font size to 12 points as shown in Word Figure 1-30.

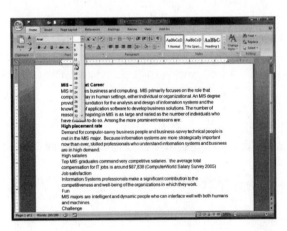

Word Figure 1-30: Adjusting font size.

The **point** (pt) is a traditional printing measure equal to $1/72$ of an inch. A 12-point printed character occupies a vertical space up to $12/72$, or $1/6$, of an inch. Fonts displayed on the screen will be approximately this scale.

Note that there are a few other ways to adjust the font size. You can make the font smaller or large by using the Grow Font and Shrink Font buttons in the Font group. You could also use the keyboard shortcuts Ctrl+>. and Ctrl+<, to grow and shrink the font, respectively.

Working with Spacing

In addition to determining the formatting of the text that you place in a document, you should also think about how you can format the blank areas of your document. The blank areas are known as **white space.** Proper formatting of white space can dramatically affect how easy your document is to read.

The white space can be managed using several tools. Among these are the vertical and horizontal rulers and the paragraph commands on the Page Layout ribbon.

1. Let's use spacing to set the document title apart from the first paragraph.

   Find the Spacing commands in the Paragraph group on the Page Layout ribbon as shown in Word Figure 1-31.

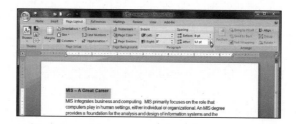

Word Figure 1-31: Paragraph spacing commands.

   Here you can adjust the amount of white space before or after a paragraph.

   Set the Before setting to 0 pt and the After setting to 12 pt. Notice how the spacing between the text has adjusted.

2. Let's use a different method to adjust the spacing of the first paragraph.

   First, select the text of the first paragraph.

   Then, right-click to see the context-sensitive menu and toolbar (Word Figure 1-32).

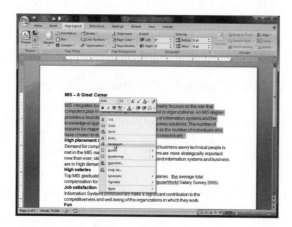

Word Figure 1-32: Paragraph option on the context-sensitive menu.

Select the Paragraph option on this menu.

3. The Paragraph dialog will appear as shown in Word Figure 1-33.

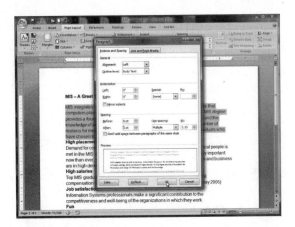

Word Figure 1-33: The Paragraph dialog.

This dialog includes two pages with commands that can be used to adjust how a paragraph is laid out.

You'll notice that the Spacing options look like those you used on the Page Layout ribbon.

Set the Before and After spacing to 6 pt and then click OK.

Using the Format Painter Tool

After you have decided on and set some formatting in your document, you may have other text elements that you want to have the same formatting. You can save some time by using the Format Painter tool to effectively copy a format from one area to another.

1. Use the methods discussed earlier to set the paragraph heading *High Placement Rate* to Bold font style.

Also set the Before and After paragraph setting to 6 pt.

Once the format is set, select the heading text and click the Format Painter tool command, shown in Word Figure 1-34.

This is the icon that looks like a paintbrush found in the Clipboard group on the Home ribbon.

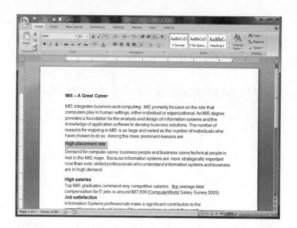

Word Figure 1-34: The Format Painter tool.

2. Now move the cursor next to the text to which you want to copy the format.

   In this case, move it next to the heading that reads *High Salaries* as shown in Word Figure 1-35.

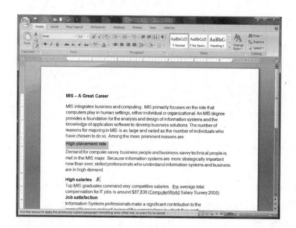

Word Figure 1-35: The active Format Painter tool.

You should see that the cursor currently appears as a paintbrush. This is your signal that the Format Painter is currently active.

3. Click and drag the cursor over the text *High Salaries*.

   You should immediately see that the format of this text has changed.

   In effect, it has been painted with the format of the previous heading (Word Figure 1-36).

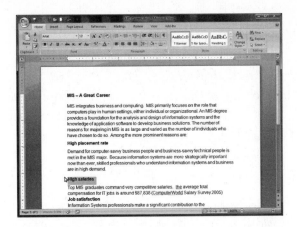

Word Figure 1-36: The Format Painter results.

4. Use the Format Painter tool to format the remaining headings with the same format.

   Also, use the Format Painter to copy the format of the first paragraph to the other paragraphs in the document.

   Your results should look like those shown in Word Figure 1-37.

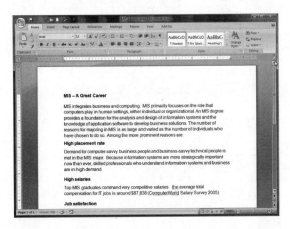

Word Figure 1-37: Results for the rest of the document.

Using the Ruler

The rulers, both horizontal and vertical, may be used to adjust margins, set tabs, and set how the text is indented. The horizontal ruler is shown in Word Figure 1-38.

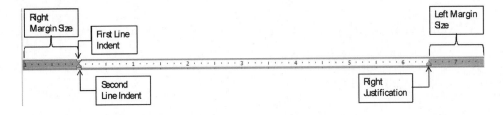

Word Figure 1-38: Horizontal ruler.

You can work with the ruler by dragging the mouse. For example, you can drag the edge of the shaded regions to adjust the right or left margin size. The triangles on the ruler can be dragged to adjust the right and left indentation of selected text. You may also use the ruler to set tab stops (click on the location on the ruler where you want a tab stop). The ruler will change appearance if you have divided the page into columns. You can use the ruler to adjust column sizes by dragging the appropriate edges on the ruler. We'll take a brief look at using the ruler on our *MIS Careers* document.

1. Select the first paragraph in the document.

   Click on the downward-pointing triangle, labeled First Line Indent in Word Figure 1-38, and drag it to the half-inch mark on the ruler as shown in Word Figure 1-39.

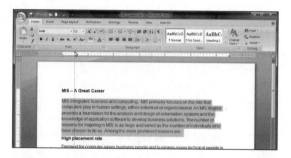

Word Figure 1-39: Setting first line indent.

A line will appear on the document as a visual guide.

2. The results should appear as shown in Word Figure 1-40.

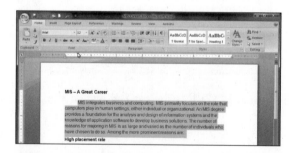

Word Figure 1-40: Results of changing first line indent.

Notice that only the first line has been indented.

The remaining lines in the paragraph are justified to the left of the page as before.

3. Now select the list of reasons for selecting a career in MIS (everything below the first paragraph).

   Click on the small rectangle below the second line indent triangle.

Drag it to the quarter-inch mark on the ruler as shown in Word Figure 1-41.

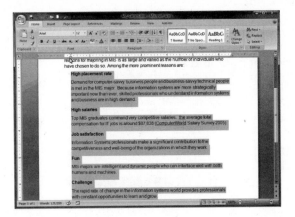

Word Figure 1-41: Indenting all lines in a paragraph.

Notice that by moving the rectangle, both the first line indent and the indent for the rest of the paragraph have been moved together.

4. We can also adjust how far the text is allowed to extend on the right of the page.

Click on the right indent triangle (the downward-pointing triangle at the right side of the paragraph) and drag it to ¼ inch from the right margin of the page.

Your document should now appear like that in Word Figure 1-42.

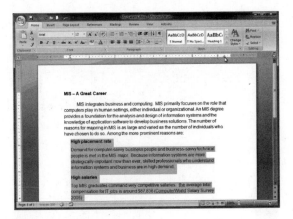

Word Figure 1-42: Right indenting the paragraph.

PREPARING TO PRINT YOUR DOCUMENT

Of course, you will want to print many of your documents on paper. Word has features that allow you to preview what your document will look like before actually printing it. In addition, when you are ready to print, you can choose which printer to use, the number of copies you want, and other, more advanced options. Let's have a look at how you can use some of these features.

1. The Print commands are found on the menu associated with the Office button (Word Figue 1-43).

   Here you can choose to:

   - Print: Select options and then print.
   - Quick Print: Print right away using the default options.
   - Print Preview: Have a look at the document on the screen as it will appear on paper so that you can make some changes if necessary before printing.

   For now, select Print Preview.

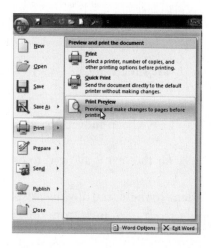

Word Figure 1-43: Print options.

2. The Print Preview view will appear as shown in Word Figure 1-44.

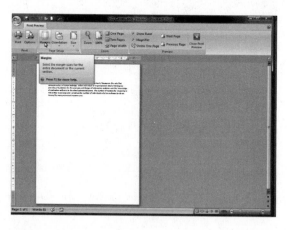

Word Figure 1-44: The Print Preview view.

This view includes the Print Preview ribbon.

There is also a view of your document that will show how it should look when printed based on your current selection.

Click the Margins command in the Page Setup group to see how to make some adjustments.

3. With the Margins command we can get a list of preset margins to choose from.

   Note that we could also click an option at the bottom that will allow us to set some custom margins.

   Let's select the preset margins that are all set to 1 inch as shown in Word Figure 1-45.

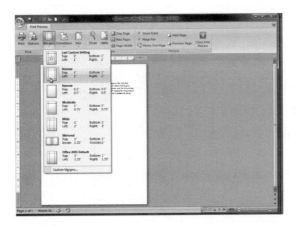

Word Figure 1-45: Setting print margins.

4. You can also choose to print your document either vertically (**portrait**) or horizontally (**landscape**) on the page.

   These options are found under the Orientation command in the Page Setup group.

   Select Landscape as shown in Word Figure 1-46 to get a peek at how the document would look with this setting.

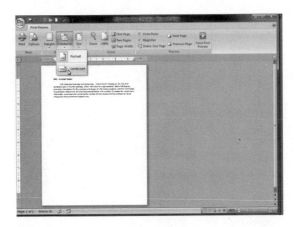

Word Figure 1-46: Choosing page orientation.

5. The document in Landscape orientation will look as shown in Word Figure 1-47.

   Change back to Portrait orientation before continuing.

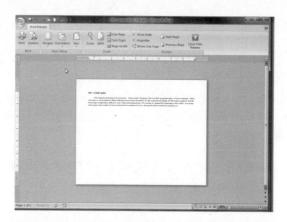

Word Figure 1-47: Document in Landscape orientation.

6. When you are satisfied with how your document looks, you can print by clicking the Print command on the ribbon, shown in Word Figure 1-48.

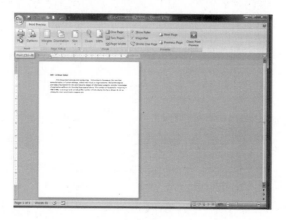

Word Figure 1-48: The Print command.

Note that you could also find this command on the Office button menu or by pressing the keyboard shortcut Ctrl-P.

7. The Print dialog will appear as shown in Word Figure 1-49.

Word Figure 1-49: Print dialog for printing the document.

The Print dialog offers you options for setting the number of copies to print, the name of the printer to use, and the actual pages that you want to print in the document, among other options.

Have a look at the options available and then either click OK to print the document or click Cancel to leave the dialog without printing.

8. When you are done with the Print Preview view, you can return to the normal document view by clicking the Close Print Preview command as shown in Word Figure 1-50.

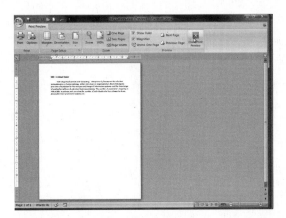

Word Figure 1-50: The Close Print Preview command.

EXERCISES TO BUILD YOUR KNOWLEDGE OF MS WORD

Match the term on the left with the appropriate description on the right:

_____1. First line indent a. Area of document devoid of text and other items.

_____2. Format Painter b. The location where the first line will begin relative to the left margin.

_____3. Landscape c. One of two special tools, one of which is located below the ribbon and the other on the left side of the screen. They are used to place and show tabs, margins, indents, and cell dimensions.

_____4. Portrait d. A Word command that allows you to copy the formatting of one paragraph and apply it to another paragraph.

_____5. Print Preview e. A preformatted document that serves as a model for starting new documents.

_____6. Quick Print f. A section located at the bottom of the window that contains information about many formatting options such as current font, insert and overtype mode, and page number.

_____7. Ruler

g. A feature in Word that allows you to see how your document will look on the page before it is printed.

_____8. Status bar

h. A Word command that allows you to print your document using the default printing options.

_____9. Template

i. When your document is oriented horizontally (the page is wider than it is tall).

_____10. White Space

j. When your document is oriented vertically (the page is taller than it is wide).

Fill in the blank with the Word ribbon and group that is home to each of the following commands. You'll have to look for them because we have not discussed some of them yet.

Command	Ribbon	Group
11. Align	_____	_____
12. Change Styles	_____	_____
13. Find	_____	_____
14. Insert Caption	_____	_____
15. New Comment	_____	_____
16. Page Color	_____	_____
17. Split	_____	_____
18. Start Mail Merge	_____	_____
19. Symbol	_____	_____
20. Zoom	_____	_____

21. Write two brief paragraphs about something that you enjoy (ideas: an event, a hobby, a sport). Use options on the Format menu, Formatting Toolbar, and Ruler to do the following:

- Set some words to make bold, italic, and underlined.

- Indent the first line by $\frac{1}{2}$ inches using the ruler.

- Set spacing above and below each paragraph to 6 pt.

- Set the spacing to double spaced.

Use Word Help to find the answers to the following questions:

22. How could you add a special symbol such as the Greek letter β or the copyright symbol, ©, to your document?

_____

_____

_____

23. What are Quick Styles? Where can you find them if you want to use them?

_____

_____

_____

24. What is a font theme? Why would you use one?

_____

_____

_____

25. Suppose that you often want to format text using a strikethrough style (~~like this~~.) It would be nice to have a shortcut button always visible to do this. Use Word Help to figure out how you can add such a shortcut button. Write the main steps here:

_____

_____

_____

WORD TUTORIAL 1: MINI-CASE 1

Scenario: Daniel Waterhouse couldn't believe what he was reading on his credit card statement. The Credit Express statement listed: $575 for a plane ticket to Mexico City, $200 for tourist sombreros, $98 at a restaurant called Gringo Paradiso, and $150 for a tour of Tenochtitlan. The thing is, Daniel has never been to Mexico in his life. His first thought is that Credit Express has made a mistake. His second thought scared him a little— "What if I'm a victim of identity theft?" He had heard about people who had lost a lot of money and even more time trying to recover from identity theft. Given this possibility, Daniel sat down to consider his options. After that, he immediately got started with the items on his list. First, he checked his other accounts and requested his credit reports online. Second, he made sure that he put a hold on all activity on his Credit Express card. Third, he sat down to write a letter to Credit Express to refute the bogus charges.

Your Task: Pretend that you are Daniel and write a brief business letter to the (fictitious) credit card company Credit Express. You are writing in relation to the unauthorized charges that Daniel has noticed on his account statement. Use the following guidelines:

- Begin your letter with the address of the person to whom you are writing and a respectful salutation.
- The body of your letter should consist of three parts. Part 1 should contain a sentence or two of greeting and how you have been happy with the company's service in the past. In part 2, describe the problem in detail. In part 3, close the body of the letter by politely but firmly stating what action you would like for the company to take.
- End your letter with a closing line ("Sincerely," "Respectfully yours," or the like), a space for your signature, and your (Daniel's) printed name. Include appropriate formatting and use of white space.

WORD TUTORIAL 1: MINI-CASE 2

Scenario: Karen Murphy is attending the fall semester of her senior year at Midwest University. It's the recruiting season, so, in addition to keeping up with her coursework, Karen is on the hunt for a job to begin her career after graduation. She has great grades and has a very active extracurricular record. With her outstanding qualifications, Karen has lots of options. But she can't just rest on her laurels; she needs to get to work on her job applications. One item that she will need is a recommendation from one of her professors. She has worked closely with Dr. Clumseau and decides that she should ask her for a letter of recommendation. Knowing how busy the life of a university professor can get, Karen has decided to write a brief letter politely asking Dr. Clumseau for some recommendation letters.

Your Task: One of these days you may find yourself in Karen's shoes. Why not get some practice now by writing a request for recommendation letter to Dr. Clumseau for Karen? Make sure that your letter includes the following:

- Begin your letter with your name and address justified on the left of the page.
- Follow this with the address of the person to whom you are writing and a respectful salutation.
- The body of your letter should consist of three parts. Part 1 should contain a sentence or two of greeting and a description of the job position or graduate work for which you have applied. In part 2, remind the professor of which class you took or how they might otherwise remember. Discuss any items you have enclosed with the letter to help them in preparing your recommendation. In part 3, close the body of the letter by politely asking for the recommendation letter. Be sure to provide any information such as a due date or recipient e-mail that the professor will need to complete the letter for you.
- End your letter with a closing line ("Sincerely," "Respectfully yours," or the like), a space for your signature, and your (Karen's) printed name. Include appropriate formatting and use of white space.

Tutorial 2

FORMATTING YOUR MICROSOFT WORD 2007 DOCUMENT

After reading this tutorial and completing the associated exercises, you will be able to:

- Work with headers, footers, and page numbers.
- Organize text with lists and columns.
- Work with tables.

WORD DOCUMENT FORMATTING TOOLS

Now that you have learned how to enter text content into a Word document, this tutorial will show you how to use Word tools to make your document more elegant. Specifically, you will learn how to organize and format various elements of your page in a manner that is both easy to read and easy on the eyes. Since you are no doubt on the edge of your seat, chomping at the bit and having a hard time holding your horses, we'll get to it without further ado. (By the way, one way to improve your writing is to try not to overuse clichés or mix metaphors. Get the picture?)

WORKING WITH HEADERS, FOOTERS, AND PAGE NUMBERS

You may not realize it, but each page of your Word document is made up of at least three parts. Of course, there is the body of the page, where you are used to typing information. Another part of each page, known as the **header**, consists of text that is added to the top margin of every page, such as the date the document was created or the title of the document. Like the header, the **footer** is added to each page in the document, at the bottom in this case.

Adding a Header

As just mentioned, the header is an area in the margin at the top of the page. With its simplest use, whatever you place in the header will appear at the top of all of the pages in your document. Let's use the header to show the title of the document at the top of our *MIS_Careers.docx* example file.

1. Open the *MIS_Careers.docx* file in Word. It should be formatted as we finished up with in the previous tutorial.

   To add elements to the header, click on the Header command, which is located in the Header & Footer group on the Insert ribbon as shown in Word Figure 2-1.

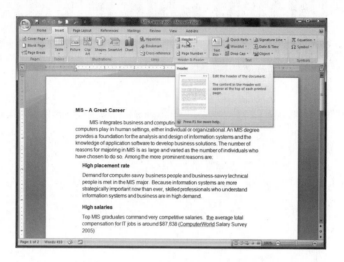

Word Figure 2-1: Inserting a header.

2. When you first click the Header command, you'll see a list of built-in header templates from which you can choose.

   You can choose to create your own by clicking the Edit Header command at the bottom of the list.

   For our example, select the Header template labeled "Alphabet," as shown in Word Figure 2-2.

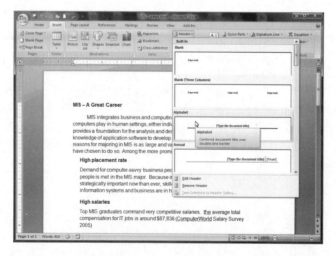

Word Figure 2-2: Selecting a header template.

3. The inserted Header template will appear as shown in Word Figure 2-3.

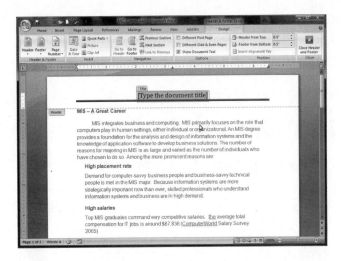

Word Figure 2-3: Appearance of the inserted header template.

When any header is inserted or active for editing, you'll see a dashed line separating the header work area from the body of the document. The body of the document will appear faded.

This template has a title field for your to fill in.

4. Click on the title field and type *MIS – A Great Career* in the box.

Your header should now appear as shown in Word Figure 2-4.

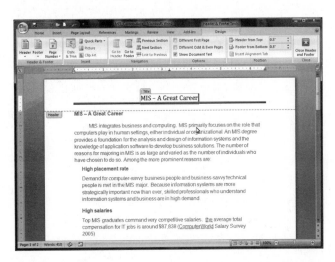

Word Figure 2-4: The completed header.

Adding a Footer

The footer works just like the header, but it appears at the bottom of the page. It's a good place to display such things as page numbers, document dates, and copyright notices. We could insert a footer in the same manner as we started creating the header. But since we already have the Header & Footer Design ribbon available, we might as well start from there.

1. You probably noticed that while you are working on the header, a Header & Footer Tools Design ribbon is available. (If you have already exited the header double-click in the header area to get back in.)

   Click the Go To Footer button.

   You'll find this button in the Navigation group as shown in Word Figure 2-5.

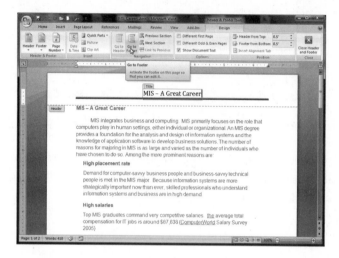

Word Figure 2-5: The Go To Footer button.

2. The view will switch to the bottom of the page (Word Figure 2-6).

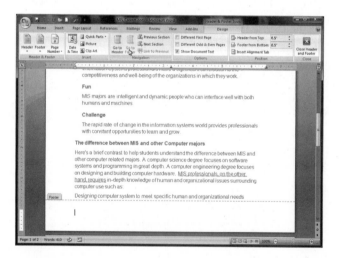

Word Figure 2-6: The view of the footer.

As with the header, the body of the document is faded, while the area at the bottom of the page is now available for you to add document components.

A footer component could be an automatic field such as a page number or the date, or it could be custom text that you want to type.

Adding Page Numbers

1. Let's add page numbers to our footer.

    Click the Page Number command located in the Header & Footer group, as shown in Word Figure 2-7.

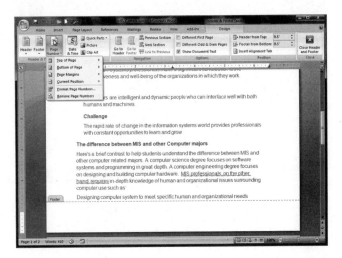

Word Figure 2-7: Adding a page number.

Notice that you can choose to place the page number just about anywhere in the document.

The popular choice is usually in the header or the footer.

We'll put it in the footer, so select Bottom of Page.

2. You should now see a list of prebuilt page number formats and locations.

    Place the page number in the bottom right corner of the page by selecting Plain Number 3 as shown in Word Figure 2-8.

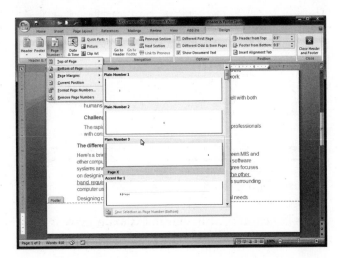

Word Figure 2-8: Selecting page number format and location.

3. You should now see the page number appear right-aligned in the footer as shown in Word Figure 2-9.

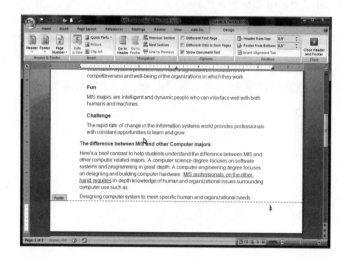

Word Figure 2-9: The inserted page number.

If you were to scroll to later pages, you would see sequential page numbers in the same location on each page.

Adding the Date

1. While still working on the footer, click the Date & Time command.

This command is found in the Insert group of the Design ribbon, as shown in Word Figure 2-10.

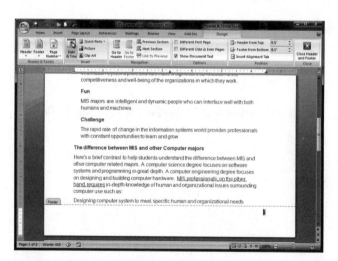

Word Figure 2-10: Adding a date to the footer.

2. The Date and Time dialog will appear as shown in Word Figure 2-11.

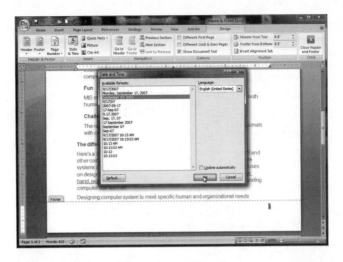

Word Figure 2-11: The Date and Time dialog.

This dialog provides a list of data and time formats all shown with the current date.

Select one that you like and click OK.

In Word Figure 2-11, we have chosen the format *September 17, 2007*.

3. After clicking OK, you'll see the date inserted in the footer at the cursor location.

In our case, this is right up against the page number as shown in Word Figure 2-12.

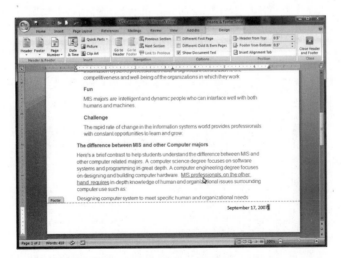

Word Figure 2-12: The inserted date.

In general, it is a good idea to place the cursor where you want a component before inserting it.

But we can fix that easily enough.

4. With the cursor still flashing between the date field and the page number, press the Tab key on the keyboard a couple of times.

This should move your data field to be left-aligned in the footer.

One thing you should notice is that tabs and spacing can work a little differently in the header and footer than in the body of the document. This can take some practice before you get accustomed to how this works (Word Figure 2-13).

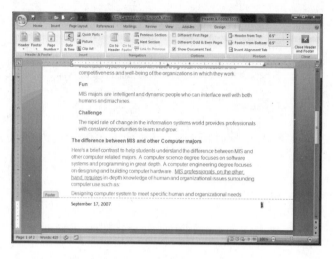

Word Figure 2-13: The final footer.

Footnotes

The upper and lower margins of the page can also be used for other important document components. For example, an important reference can be added to a page as a footnote. The footnote will typically be added near the bottom of the page just above the footer.

1. Word has a command called Insert Footnote, located on the References ribbon (Word Figure 2-14).

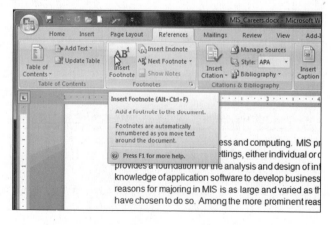

Word Figure 2-14: Inserting a footnote.

Before clicking this command, place the cursor on the page next to the text that you want to cross-reference with the footnote.

For our example, place the cursor just after the first heading, *MIS – A Great Career*, and click the Insert Footnote command.

2. The view will switch to the bottom of the page with your cursor flashing just after an inserted footnote number.

   You'll also notice that the font size has decreased (Word Figure 2-15).

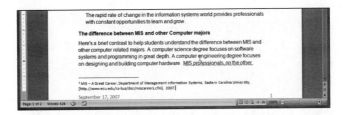

Word Figure 2-15: Typing the footnote.

Enter the following text, which is the reference for the text in our example:

MIS – A Great Career, Department of Management Information Systems, Eastern Carolina University, [http://www.ecu.edu/cs-bus/dsci/miscareers.cfm], 2007.

3. One way to finish is to simply double-click on the body of the document.

   Scroll up to the main title, and you'll find a number that corresponds to the footnote number at the location where your cursor was before starting your insertion (Word Figure 2-16).

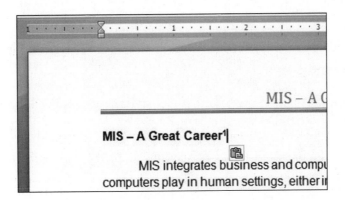

Word Figure 2-16: The footnote reference.

ADJUSTING THE TEXT LAYOUT WITH LISTS AND COLUMNS

There are several ways in which you can change how text is laid out on your page. A couple of the most commonly used methods are to use a bulleted or a numbered list and to place your text in two or more columns (most of the time just two). The following will show you how to use these features.

Bulleted Lists

The author of this tutorial is a big believer in lists (so much that he even includes things like breakfast and lunch on his list of things to do for the day). Lists are good for providing brief descriptions of things and to highlight important items.

1. To begin, select the group of text that begins with the line *Designing computer systems...* as shown in Word Figure 2-17.

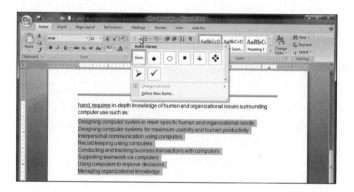

Word Figure 2-17: The Bullet Library.

On the Home ribbon, click the arrow next to the bulleted list icon found in the Paragraph group.

This will open the **Bullet Library**, which displays a list of bullet styles you can use for the list.

2. Place the cursor over any of the bullet styles in the Bullet Library, and you'll see a preview of the bullet style on your list.

In Word Figure 2-18, you can see how the list looks with the usual solid black round bullets.

Go ahead and click on this bullet style to select it.

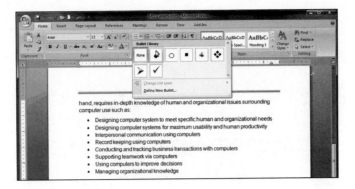

Word Figure 2-18: Solid black round bullets.

3. After selecting the solid black round bullets, check out the Bullet Library again.

   Notice that there are two new sections (Word Figure 2-19).

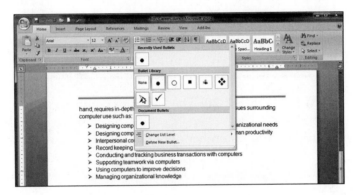

Word Figure 2-19: Previewing other bullets.

One section shows recently used bullets, while the other shows bullets already used in the document.

Keep in mind that you can also choose to use numbered lists. These lists work similarly to bulleted lists. When making a numbered list, you will have a choice of the numbering style to use. Arabic numbers, uppercase or lowercase letters, and Roman numerals (1, 2, 3,...; a, b, c,...; I, II, III, IV,...) are some of the options available for numbered lists.

Placing Text in Columns

Another way to adjust the text layout is to place the text into columns. You may want to use this to make your document look professional (like a newspaper or magazine) or to save space (for lists with short entries, you can use columns to get the entire list on one page).

1. First, select the text that you want to display in multiple columns.

In this case, select the list of MIS Careers on page 2.

Now, navigate to the Page Layout ribbon.

In the Page Setup group, click on the command icon labeled Columns as shown in Word Figure 2-20.

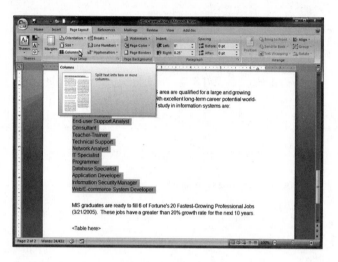

Word Figure 2-20: The Columns command.

2. A list of available column number options is displayed for you to select from.

   For our list, select the two-column option from the menu as shown in Word Figure 2-21.

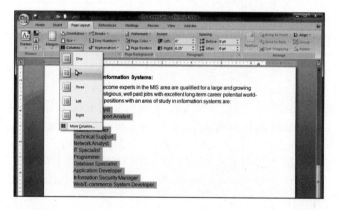

Word Figure 2-21: Creating two columns.

3. The results should look like those displayed in Word Figure 2-22.

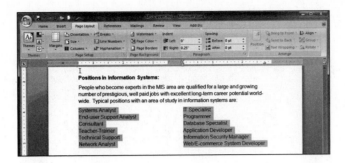

Word Figure 2-22: Text in two columns.

WORKING WITH TABLES

A **table** is an important tool for displaying information. A table can also be a useful tool for controlling the layout of your text on the page.

Tables consist of **rows** and **columns**. They can be formatted with borders or without borders. The row heights and column widths may be sized as a group or individually. Rows can be set up that contain varying numbers of cells. The table and the text within the cells of the tables can be aligned horizontally and vertically. These are just a few of the table attributes that you can set to control the format of your tables.

You may be getting the idea that tables in Word are very versatile. You'll see just how versatile in the next several pages.

Creating Tables

1. To insert a table, place the cursor in the document at the location where you want the table to be.

   In our document, highlight the text placeholder that reads *<table here>*. Find and click the Table command, which is in the Tables group on the Insert menu, as shown in Word Figure 2-23.

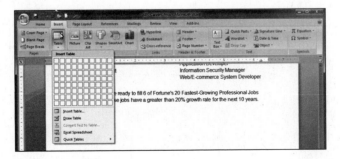

Word Figure 2-23: Inserting a table.

2. You'll see the Table dialog shown in Word Figure 2-24.

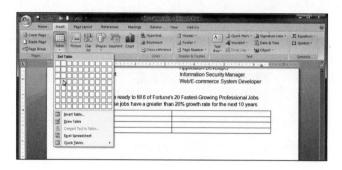

Word Figure 2-24: Setting table size.

The grid here is used to specify the size of the table you want.

Simply drag the mouse over the grid to highlight the squares representing the number of rows and columns in the table.

For this example, we'll initially insert a table with four rows and two columns, as shown in Word Figure 2-24.

3. Your new, blank table will appear in your document, and some special Table Tools ribbons will be displayed, as shown in Word Figure 2-25.

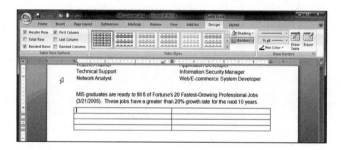

Word Figure 2-25: A new, blank table and Table Tools Design ribbon.

The Table Tools ribbons will be displayed any time the cursor is located in the table.

Note that the default format for a table is rather plain with black borders and no colors. We'll fix that shortly.

Adding Text to a Table

Now we need to add text or other components to our table. For our example, we will be displaying a list of MIS careers and their corresponding percentage growth rates. The table should be easy for the reader to understand, so we will start by adding some column headings. We'll then add the main content into the table.

1. Obviously, tables are composed of columns and rows.

   We can refer to the intersection of a row and column as a table **cell**.

   To add text to a table, you simply click in the cell to make it active and type.

   Click in each cell in the top row of the table and type the headings shown in Word Figure 2-26.

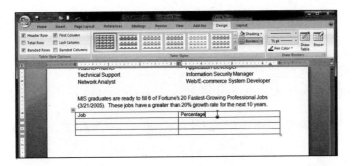

Word Figure 2-26: Adding table heading text.

2. You can select one or more table cells in the same way that you select text: by clicking on a document location and then dragging the mouse to select.

   Do this to select the top two cells.

   Now click the Bold command on the Home ribbon or press the keyboard shortcut Ctrl-B to make the headings bold as shown in Word Figure 2-27.

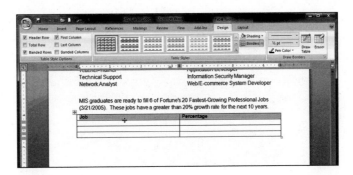

Word Figure 2-27: Selecting and formatting table text.

3. If you want to change data in a table cell, you can select it or place the cursor where you want to insert or delete text, as shown in Word Figure 2-28.

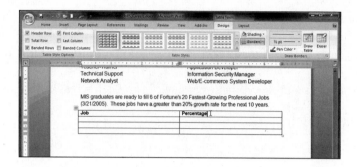

Word Figure 2-28: Editing table text.

Let's change the heading in the second column to *Percentage Growth Rate*.

4. The final table headings should appear as shown in Word Figure 2-29.

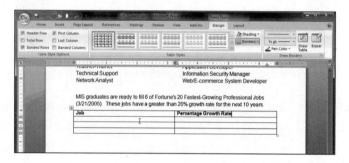

Word Figure 2-29: Final table headings.

5. Now let's enter the text in the body of our table.

Click in each cell and type the text shown in Word Figure 2-30.

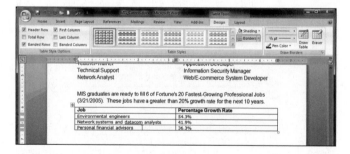

Word Figure 2-30: Entering table text.

6. It turns out that three rows won't be enough for our job listing.

We'll need to insert some more rows.

Make sure that the cursor is in one of the cells of the last table row and then right-click.

The context-sensitive menu will be displayed as shown in Word Figure 2-31.

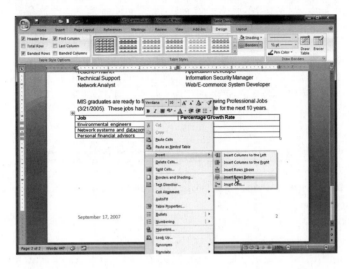

Word Figure 2-31: Context-sensitive menu for table cell.

Select Insert from the menu.

You have several options to choose from here. Be sure to have a look at the available options before making a final selection.

We'll take the option Insert Rows Below.

7. You should now see a new, blank row added to your table as shown in Word Figure 2-32.

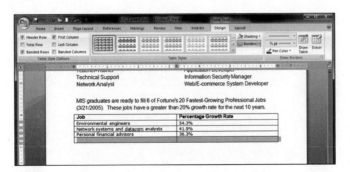

Word Figure 2-32: An inserted table row.

8. Add rows and text to complete the table as shown in Word Figure 2-33.

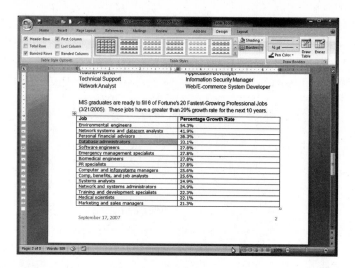

Word Figure 2-33: The table with additional rows and text.

Formatting a Table

Our current table is kind of plain. That's okay for many purposes because there is something to be said for keeping things simple. However, it might be nice to jazz it up a little with some nice formatting. Let's see what we can do.

1. Commands for giving your table a pretty format are located on the Table Tools Design ribbon.

   One of the best places to start is with the set of prebuilt templates in the Table Styles group.

   Click the lower arrow next to this group on the ribbon as shown in Word Figure 2-34.

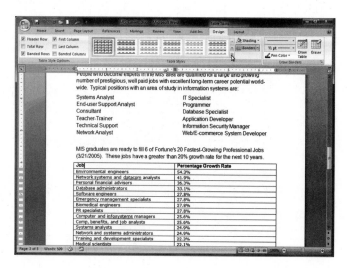

Word Figure 2-34: The Table Design ribbon.

2. A dialog with a large list of prebuilt styles will appear as shown in Word Figure 2-35.

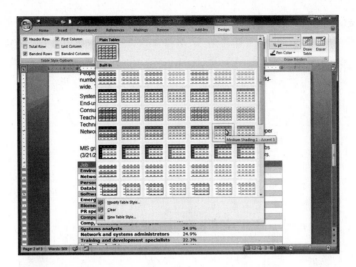

Word Figure 2-35: Selecting a prebuilt table style.

You can see more by scrolling with the toolbar on the right of the dialog.

When you hover the cursor over a style, the table on the document will adjust to give you a preview of your table in that style.

3. If you choose the prebuilt style labeled Medium Shading 1 – Accent 5, your table will look like the one shown in Word Figure 2-36.

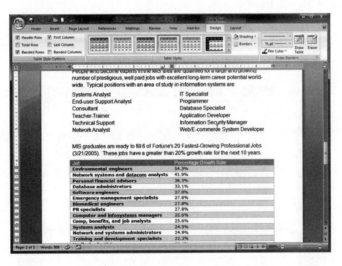

Word Figure 2-36: A styled table.

4. You should pick a style with an eye toward making it easy for the reader to understand your main point.

In this table, we'd like to highlight those jobs related to MIS. The current style doesn't do that.

Changing the style of the table is easy. While the cursor is located somewhere in the table, we simply select a different prebuilt style as shown in Word Figure 2-37.

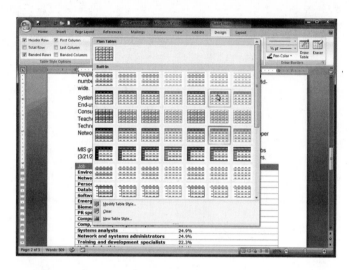

Word Figure 2-37: Changing the table style.

5. This time, we picked a style that has only the heading row filled with a background color.

Let's adjust the table so that MIS careers are filled with a light color and all others are filled with a darker color.

To start, highlight all table rows except the header row, and right-click to display the context-sensitive menu as shown in Word Figure 2-38.

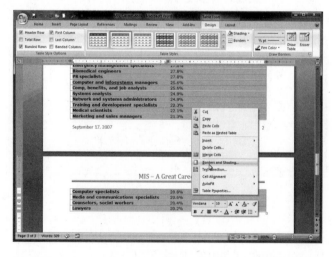

Word Figure 2-38: The table context-sensitive menu.

6. Select the menu option Borders and Shading.

The Borders and Shading dialog will appear with various commands you can use to adjust the table borders or put a color shade in the cells.

For now, have a look at the items available on the Borders page, shown in Word Figure 2-39.

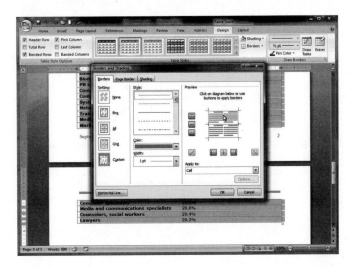

Word Figure 2-39: The Borders page of the Borders and Shading dialog.

7. Click the Shading tab near the top of the Borders and Shading dialog window.

The Fill list currently shows No Color, as shown in Word Figure 2-40.

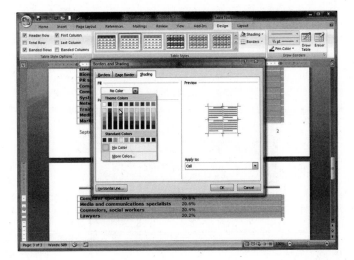

Word Figure 2-40: The Shading page of the Borders and Shading dialog.

Click the arrow on the Fill list to get a palette of color choices in the left pane of the dialog.

In the right pane, you can see a preview of the options that you select.

8. When you've selected a color, the table sample in the Preview pane will show your change.

We selected a light blue color for our example in Word Figure 2-41.

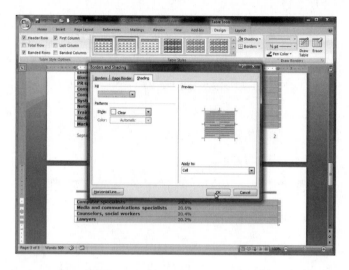

Word Figure 2-41: Selecting a fill color.

When you have made a selection, click the OK button to return to the document.

9. Our current table is shown in Word Figure 2-42.

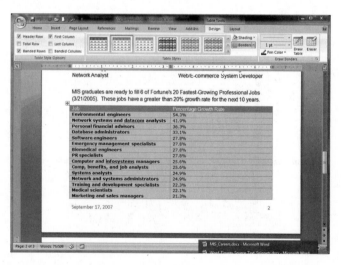

Word Figure 2-42: Table after selecting fill color.

We still need to do something to highlight the MIS careers in this table.

We'll do that by changing the fill color for only those cells.

10. Select the Job and Percentage Growth Rate cells for the Network Analysts position as shown in Word Figure 2-43.

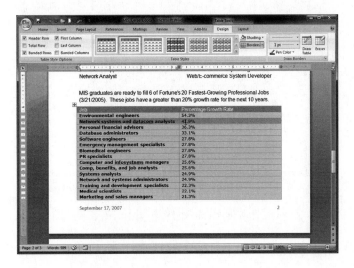

Word Figure 2-43: Selecting two cells.

11. Right-click and navigate the menu and dialog to adjust the shading.

Select a different color for these cells.

In Word Figure 2-44, a light green fill color has been chosen for the MIS career cells.

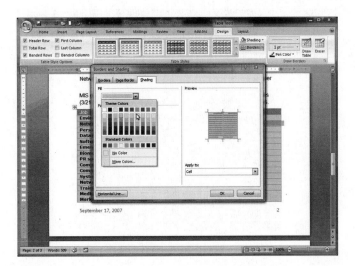

Word Figure 2-44: Selecting a fill color for selected cells.

12. Our table will now look like that shown in Word Figure 2-45.

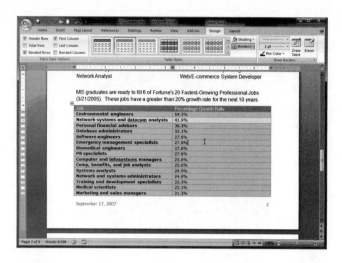

Word Figure 2-45: Table cells highlighted by fill color.

With this format, you can see how this portion stands out well from the rest of the table.

13. Have a look at the table in Word Figure 2-46.

This table includes a few more entries and several more highlighted careers.

Use what you've learned to complete your table to look like the one in Word Figure 2-46.

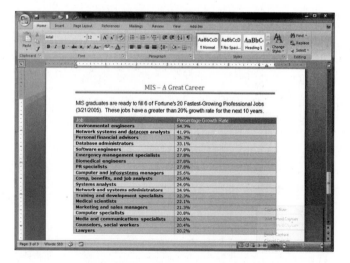

Word Figure 2-46: The final table.

EXERCISES TO BUILD YOUR KNOWLEDGE OF MS WORD

Match the term on the left with the appropriate description on the right:

_____1. Borders

_____2. Bullet Library

_____3. Design

_____4. Fill

_____5. Footer

_____6. Footnote

_____7. Header

_____8. Layout

_____9. Reference

____10. Shading

a. The contents of an area located within the top margin of a page.

b. The contents of an area located within the bottom margin of a page.

c. An explanatory note inserted at the foot of the page referring to a point within the text; in Word it is usually in a smaller text font than the body of the text.

d. A list of prebuilt symbols used to mark items in a list.

e. A dialog window used to adjust the colors of a table.

f. A dialog window used to adjust the color, style, and thickness of the lines surrounding table elements.

g. The background color of a cell in a Word table.

h. The Table Tools ribbon that includes commands that affect how table elements are styled.

i. The Table Tools ribbon that includes commands that affect how the table elements are arranged on the page.

j. A Word ribbon that includes commands that allows you to insert footnotes.

Write a document describing how to do something that you enjoy. Use the elements discussed in this tutorial in your document.

11. Include your topic and your name in the header.

12. Include page numbers in the footer.

13. Use a bulleted or numbered list.

14. Use columns in your document.

15. Add a table to your document.

Use Word Help to find the answers to the following questions:

16. In what ways can you use the keyboard instead of a mouse to navigate around a table?

_____

_____

_____

_____

17. The Bullet Library comes with a set of prebuilt bullet styles. Can you add new styles to this list? If so, how would you do it?

_____

_____

_____

_____

18. Can you sort the contents of a table? How?

_____

_____

_____

_____

19. How would you use the Word ruler to adjust how columns are laid out in your document?

_____

_____

_____

20. What is a multilevel list? How would you make one?

_____

_____

_____

WORD TUTORIAL 2: MINI-CASE 1

Scenario: Holly Short is feeling a bit stressed. She has so many things to do and can't seem to find the time to do it all. There's the term paper for English. There are the team project for her biology class and the software project for her MIS course. On top of that, she is the president of the Delta Epsilon Iota honor society chapter for her school and there are just so many tasks she needs to do for the upcoming new member induction banquet. The list goes on. "List!" thinks Holly. "That's what I need." Holly knows that one of the best tools for keeping organized is simply to keep a list of items that need to be taken care of. She could even keep track of the status of the items of her various tasks. She's so busy right now, though, that it would be very helpful if you could work up that list for her.

Your Task: You've agreed to help Holly by making a template for her daily list. The idea is that you will create a document that Holly can open and then enter her "to-do" items. Make this document by using the following guidelines:

- In the header, add Holly's name and a field that will automatically display the current date. (Use Word Help to find out how to insert a field.)
- Use a table to lay out the items on the page. Your table should have three columns and five or six rows. The borders should not be displayed when the document is printed.
- The first column of the table is to be used to indicate the category (such as MIS class, DEI, Home) within which each task fits. Also, include a clip art figure related to the category as a visual reference.
- The second column is where Holly will write her list. In each cell in this column, make a bulleted list of five or six blank lines for writing using the underscore (_) character.
- In the third column, place five or six small boxes, using the Shapes command on the Insert ribbon. These should be placed vertically and lined up with the lines that you added to the second column. Holly can use these to check off the items that she has completed.

WORD TUTORIAL 2: MINI-CASE 2

Scenario: You're excited! For your summer internship you found a position as an assistant to the event planner for the local convention center. Your boss, Ms. Lea Sidhe, is in charge of organizing and planning the logistics for up to 50 major conventions a year. Responsibilities include facilities setup, organizing food and amenities, and sometimes the planning of the conference schedule. It's this last task that Ms. Sidhe has decided to trust you with. She has decided that what is needed is a nice schedule template that can be saved and then modified as new conferences and conventions are being planned. She wants you to make such a template using Word 2007. It's a big responsibility for your first job, but with your knowledge of Word, you're up to the task.

Your Task: Your task is to create a conference agenda template with sample data. Your template can then be used when planning future conferences at the center. Make this document by using the following guidelines:

- In the header, add the conference title (left aligned) location (centered) and dates (right aligned).
- Add the document title *Conference Agenda* centered at the top of the page in a large, bold font.
- Create a table with two primary columns: one column for times of day and the second to list the conference activity for that time. To begin, include at least 10 rows. Complete the table as follows:

  - The conference lasts from Monday through Thursday. You need to have a separation row within the table for each day. In the first row, merge the two cells into one large row. Set centered text alignment and type *Monday* into the cell. Change the font style and format and the cell fill color to set this apart as a heading.
  - Create similar heading rows for the remaining days of the conference.
  - For each day of the conference, enter appropriate session times in the left column. For example, the first session on Monday might take place from 8:30 am to 9:30 am.
  - For each session, enter a list of activities that are taking place during that time. Use bulleted, numbered, or multilevel lists as appropriate. For example, the first session on Monday might include a welcome speech by the conference organizer and a keynote speech by a prominent speaker.
  - Use table styles and borders and shading commands to make your table look nice.

Tutorial 3

ILLUSTRATING AND REVIEWING A MICROSOFT WORD 2007 DOCUMENT

After reading this tutorial and completing the associated exercises, you will be able to:

- Add images to a Word document.
- Check grammar and spelling.
- Create a simple Web page using Word.

ILLUSTRATING AND COMPLETING YOUR DOCUMENT

"What's this," you're thinking. "You mean that I'm not finished with my document after I type and insert all of the content?"

The answer is: It depends!

If all you want to do is create a document and then simply store it to your hard disk, then you might be finished. Or, if you only need to create a document and submit it to your professor in electronic format, then you could be ready to go. Of course, this assumes that you have checked and proofread your document and corrected any errors that may be found. Fortunately, Word provides tools that allow you to take care of most of the proofreading chores while you create the document.

What about the increasingly common times when you want to post your document as a Web page? Word also has features that can help you convert your document to a Web format.

In addition, you may want to jazz up your document with some images, following the old saw, "A picture is worth a thousand words." A good figure or photo can make your document more interesting and may communicate to your reader better than any words you can type. Of course, MS Word allows you to add and work with images in your document.

Completing this tutorial will provide you with the knowledge necessary to use these features.

ADDING GRAPHICS TO A DOCUMENT

You can use graphics to illustrate and highlight important concepts and to add "pizzazz" to your documents. The primary way to insert a graphic into your document is through the Insert ribbon. On this ribbon you will find several types of graphics that you can use in the Illustrations group. These options include Picture, Clip Art, Shapes, SmartArt, and Chart. Let's start by adding a Clip Art graphic to our *MIS Careers* example document.

Adding Clip Art to a Document

The Clip Art option provides a collection of cartoon-style graphics that are categorized by theme. Using the Clip Art collection you can find a graphic to illustrate just about any topic. Word comes with a nice size library of Clip Art installed, but you can access a lot more by going online to the Microsoft Web site.

1. Start by opening up the *MIS Careers* example document that you created in the first two Word tutorials.

   Place the cursor just before the first paragraph as shown in Word Figure 3-1.

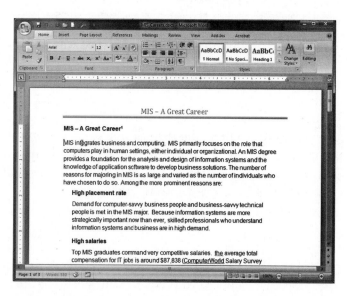

Word Figure 3-1: *The MIS Careers* example document.

2. Click the Insert ribbon tab.

   Notice that there are several types of graphics objects that you can insert through the commands in the Illustrations group. One of these is Clip Art. Click that icon.

   The Clip Art dialog window will appear docked on the right side of the Word window as shown in Word Figure 3-2.

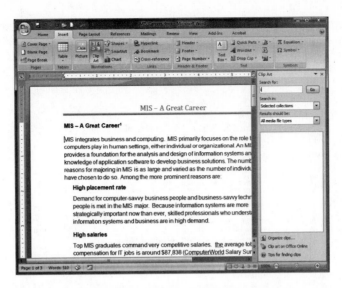

Word Figure 3-2: The Clip Art dialog.

3. The Clip Art dialog provides several options.

Possibly, the most useful option is the Search for: text box.

Here, you can type in a keyword and then search for images that are somehow related.

Type the word *business* in the Search for: text box and click Go as shown in Word Figure 3-3.

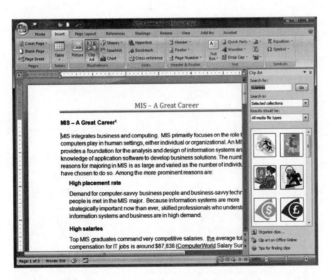

Word Figure 3-3: Searching for a clip art image.

4. After a moment, images from the collection will be displayed in the preview window as shown in Word Figure 3-4.

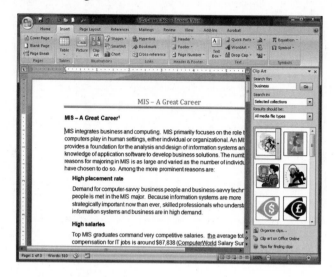

Word Figure 3-4: Selecting a clip art image.

Notice that you could also choose to search through collections on your hard disk, if you have any, or on Office Online.

When you find an image that you like, simply double-click the image to insert it into your page.

5. The clip art image will be inserted into the document at the current cursor location.

The image that we chose is shown in Word Figure 3-5.

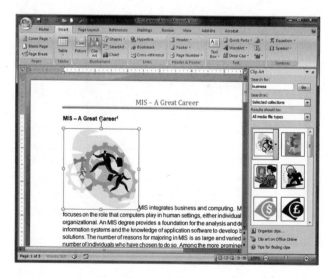

Word Figure 3-5: The inserted clip art image.

Note the line and small boxes around the edge of the picture.

This shows you that image is currently selected.

6. The small boxes at the corners of the outline of the clip art are called **sizing handles**.

    You can adjust the size of the image by placing the cursor over a sizing handle and then dragging until the image is the right size as shown in Word Figure 3-6.

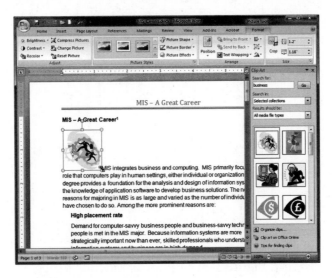

Word Figure 3-6: Adjusting the clip art size.

Notice that when the image is selected, a new ribbon, titled Format, is available.

Commands on this ribbon can be used to adjust the image in various ways.

7. You can access other commands by right-clicking the selected image and viewing the context-sensitive menu.

    Right-click now, and you'll notice options such as Edit Picture, Change Picture, Insert Caption, Text Wrapping, Size, and Format Picture, as shown in Word Figure 3-7.

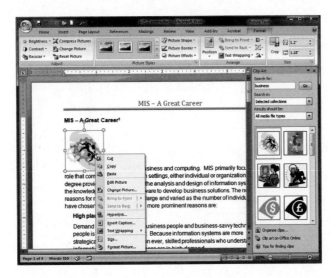

Word Figure 3-7: The picture context-sensitive menu.

8. Selecting an option on the context-sensitive menu will typically result in a dialog box with related commands.

In Word Figure 3-8, you can see the dialog box related to the Format Picture option.

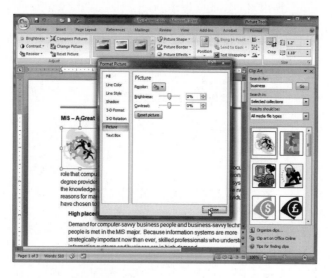

Word Figure 3-8: The Format Picture dialog.

9. You can also adjust how the image is displayed on the page in relation to the text.

To do this, select the Text Wrapping option on the context-sensitive menu.

A menu of text wrapping options is provided.

We'll select Square for our example, as shown in Word Figure 3-9.

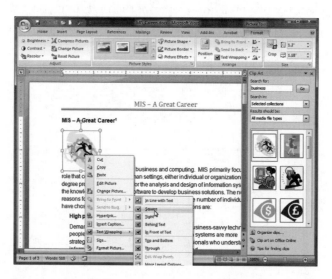

Word Figure 3-9: Setting text wrapping to Square.

10. You should now see that instead of the text following the image, it flows neatly around it as shown in Word Figure 3-10.

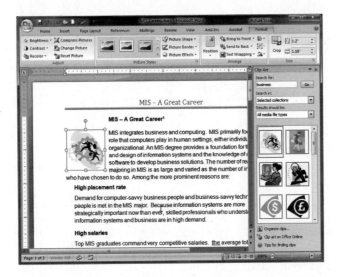

Word Figure 3-10: The results of text wrapping.

Try some of the other text wrapping options to see the differences.

Once the image is completed, you can close the Clip Art dialog by clicking on the close box (✕) at its upper right, as with any other window.

Inserting an Image from a File

When you want to insert an image from a file, you will be able to browse for the file using a dialog box similar to that used when you open a Word document file. Word will allow you to insert most graphic file formats. Working with an image from a file works just like working with a clip art image.

1. Start by placing the cursor at the end of one of the lines in another paragraph in the document as shown in Word Figure 3-11.

We'll insert an image from a file here.

Note that you will need to have a picture file stored on your computer's storage.

Click the Picture command found in the Illustrations group of the Insert ribbon.

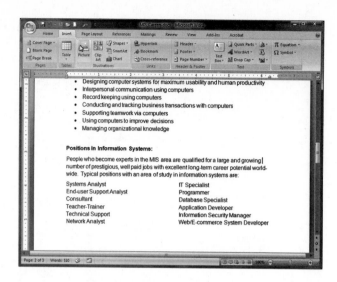

Word Figure 3-11: Selecting a spot to insert a picture.

2. The Insert Picture dialog will appear.

   This dialog looks just like the File Open dialog and works the same.

   Navigate to the folder where your picture file is stored and select the picture file.

   When the file is selected, click the Insert button as shown in Word Figure 3-12.

Word Figure 3-12: The Insert Picture dialog.

3. Word will read the file and insert the picture at the cursor location, as shown in Word Figure 3-13.

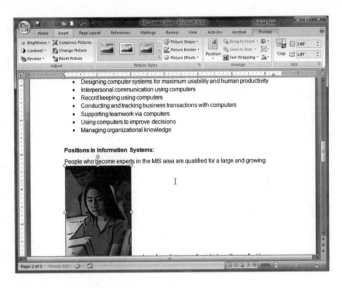

Word Figure 3-13: The inserted picture file.

Note how the text is split around the photo because of where the cursor was located.

4. Let's adjust the text wrapping to Square as we did with the clip art image.

Right-click the image and choose Text Wrapping and then Square from the menus.

The text should then flow around the image as shown in Word Figure 3-14.

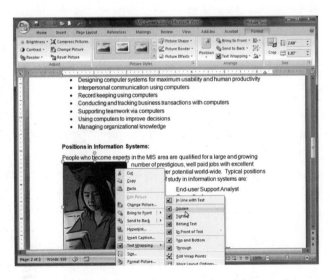

Word Figure 3-14: Setting text wrapping.

5. Recall from Word Figure 3-12 that originally we placed the cursor on the right side of the document in order to insert the image there.

The picture is not currently there, but we can move it easily enough.

Select the image and place the cursor over it.

The cursor should appear in the shape of a cross.

Click and drag the image where you want it to be as shown in Word Figure 3-15.

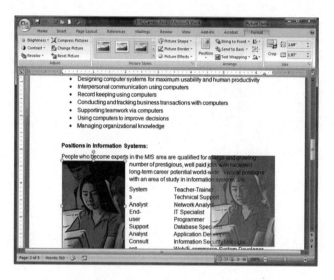

Word Figure 3-15: Moving the image.

6. The final image for our example appears as shown in Word Figure 3-16.

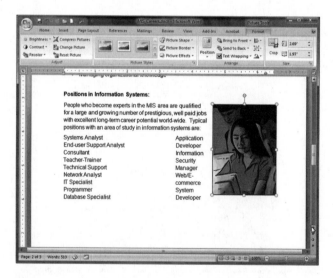

Word Figure 3-16: The picture file inserted in its final position.

Keep in mind that you can do a lot more with images if needed by using commands on the ribbons and the context-sensitive menus.

USING SPELLING AND GRAMMAR TOOLS

Word provides several tools that can help you ensure that your document follows accepted standards of grammar and spelling. We will discuss the tools listed here:

- An AutoCorrect feature that can automatically correct misspelled words

- Color-coded indicators of questionable grammar and spelling

- A thesaurus that can help you to find synonyms for the words in your document

The Word AutoCorrect Feature

Word can be set to correct many commonly misspelled words and punctuation marks automatically using its **AutoCorrect** feature. Try it! Open Word and type a sentence. Try to spell the word *another* without the *r* on the end. What happens? Did the *r* appear at the end of the word anyway? If so, then you have witnessed AutoCorrect in action.

At its simplest, AutoCorrect is a stored list of commonly misspelled words that matches the common misspelling with the correct spelling. As you type, Word in a sense watches what you enter. When it sees a word that it doesn't recognize (i.e., a word not in the Word dictionary), it will check the AutoCorrect listing. If the misspelling is in the list, the misspelling will be automatically replaced with the correct spelling. It turns out that you can access the AutoCorrect list and add items to or delete items from the list.

> ▶ **Cool tip:**
> You can add your own AutoCorrect words to the list. Sometimes you can use this to save yourself some typing. In the next few steps you'll see this in action as you add ASAP to the AutoCorrect list. Watch what happens the next time that you type *ASAP* into a document.

1. To get to the AutoCorrect dialog, you need to go through some of the menus of the Office button.

   Recall that this is the button in the top left corner of an Office window.

It's where you go for saving and printing as well as other options displayed in Word Figure 3-17.

Word Figure 3-17: The Office button and its dialog window.

2. At the bottom of the Office Button menu you'll find a button labeled Word Options.

   Click the Word Options button, as shown in Word Figure 3-18, to access the Word Options dialog.

Word Figure 3-18: The Word Options button.

3. The Word Options dialog is where you will find most options for customizing Word to the way that you work.

   You should take a few minutes to explore the various pages of this dialog.

   You'll find a button for AutoCorrect on the Proofing page, shown in Word Figure 3-19.

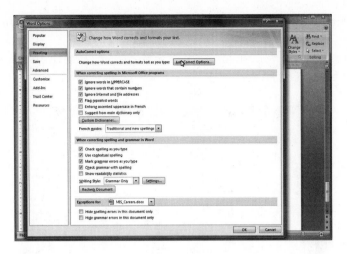

Word Figure 3-19: The Proofing page of the Word Options dialog.

4. The AutoCorrect dialog has several pages with various themes.

   For instance, you can adjust settings for how Word automatically formats various items in your document using AutoFormat.

   The settings you will need to adjust are on the AutoCorrect page as shown in Word Figure 3-20.

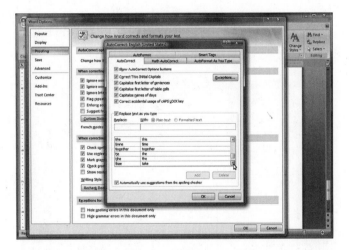

Word Figure 3-20: The AutoCorrect dialog.

5. Note that there are several areas on the AutoCorrect dialog.

   First, you can set various grammatical corrections by checking the corresponding checkboxes.

   In the bottom half of the dialog there is a list of corrections.

   Browse through this list to see what corrections will be detected.

You'll find common misspellings represented, such as *teh* for *the* or *cxan* for *can*.

You can even add your own as noted in the *Cool Tip* at the beginning of this section (Word Figure 3-21).

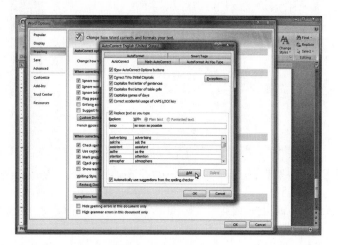

Word Figure 3-21: Adding an AutoCorrection entry.

6. Let's return to the document (by clicking OK on the AutoCorrect and Word Options dialogs) to see AutoCorrect in action.

   Find a blank line in your document. Type the letter combination *tje* (a common mistyping for *the* since the *j* is next to the *h* on the keyboard), as shown in Word Figure 3-22.

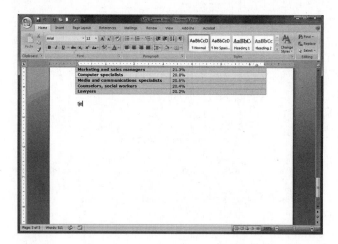

Word Figure 3-22: A common mistyping of *the*.

   Hit the space bar after typing those letters.

7. What happened?

You should now see the word *The* in place of what you typed, as shown in Word Figure 3-23.

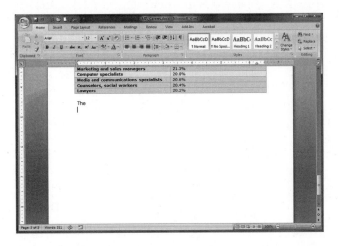

Word Figure 3-23: *The* AutoCorrected.

The mistyping, and the lowercase letter at the beginning of a sentence, have been autocorrected.

8. Now let's try the AutoCorrection entry that we added.

Type the letters *asap* (as shown in Word Figure 3-24) and then a space.

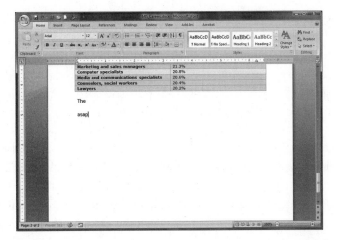

Word Figure 3-24: Trying an added AutoCorrection in action.

9. You should now see that *asap* has now been automatically changed to *As soon as possible* (with automatic capitalization as well), as shown in Word Figure 3-25.

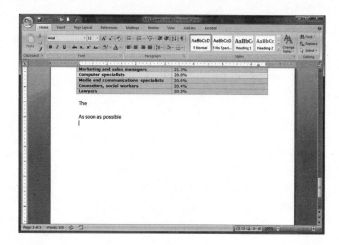

Word Figure 3-25: *asap* changed to *As soon as possible.*

Checking Spelling and Grammar "As You Type"

As you type, Word continuously compares your text to the words that it contains in its dictionary. It also compares the way that you phrase your words to a **knowledge base** of grammar rules. When an error is found, the offending language will be underlined with a colored squiggly line. The color indicates the type of error that has been found.

Handling Spelling Errors

Any word that is not recognized by Word as being in its dictionary is considered to be a spelling error. The dictionary contains most English words. You can even choose to use more dictionaries for most other natural languages. When the software determines that a word is misspelled, it will indicate the offending word by underscoring it with a red squiggly line.

Keep in mind that not all words indicated with the red line will actually be misspellings. It works well for regular English words, but Word often indicates things like proper names as misspellings since they are usually not found in the dictionary. Fortunately, if you have a word or name that you use often, you can add it to the dictionary. Let's see how we can work with misspellings in Word.

1. Notice in Word Figure 3-26 that the word *business* has been misspelled as *busness.*

   Place the cursor within the indicated misspelled word and then right-click. A context-sensitive menu will appear.

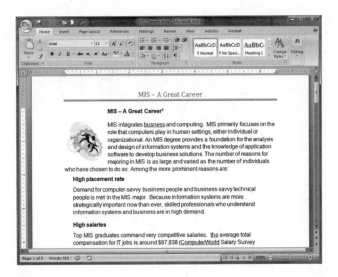

Word Figure 3-26: Misspelling indicated by red underscore.

2. Suggested words are listed at the top of the menu. Click on the correct word if it appears, as shown in Word Figure 3-27.

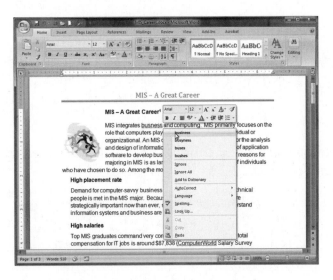

Word Figure 3-27: Spelling suggestions.

You can choose to ignore this word while in this document or add it to the dictionary for all documents.

This is a good thing to do for specialized words or proper names that you often use.

3. Select the correct spelling of *business* from the list.

The context-sensitive menu will disappear, and the correct word will replace the misspelled word in the documents, as shown in Word Figure 3-28.

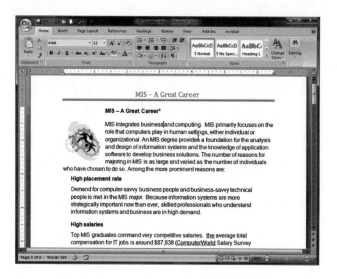

Word Figure 3-28: Corrected word.

Handling Grammar Errors

Word also has grammatical rules for the language, stored in a **rules base**. While you type, Word will automatically check your grammar against these rules. Like misspelled words, a grammatical error will be indicated by a squiggly underscore, but the line will be green instead of red.

1. Notice that a grammatical error has been indicated for a phrase in the document shown in Word Figure 3-29.

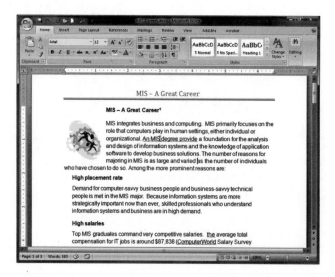

Word Figure 3-29: Grammar error indicated by underscore.

Place the cursor within the indicated grammar error, and then right-click.

2. A context-sensitive menu will appear.

   A suggested correction will appear at the top of the list. Simply click on it to use or revise as suggested as shown in Word Figure 3-30.

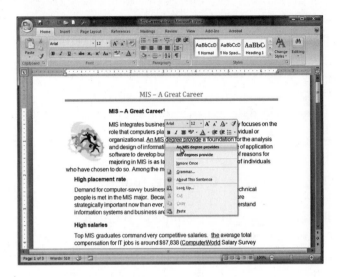

Word Figure 3-30: Grammatical suggestions.

Choose Ignore Once if you prefer your grammar to the suggested correction.

3. After you select a suggestion from the list, the text will be altered to reflect your selection as shown in Word Figure 3-31.

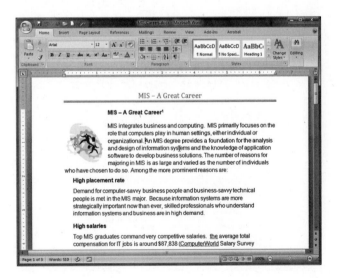

Word Figure 3-31: The corrected grammar.

> **▶ Caution:**
> Remember that Word compares your text with what it has stored in its dictionary, thesaurus, and grammar knowledge base. While these lists are extensive, they have their limitations. There might be items missing. Also, sometimes a word may be a correctly spelled word, but not the one you intended that fits the context of your sentence. For example, if you type manger—a feed trough for farm animals—when you mean manager, Word will not catch this error since manger is spelled correctly. A spelling checker may not catch such words. There is no guarantee that these tools have corrected every problem in your document. This means that you should always visually proofread your documents.

Running the Spelling & Grammar Checking Tool

There are also several tools available in the Proofing group on the Review ribbon that you can use to check your document. One of the most important of these is the Spelling & Grammar checker. With this tool you can review the entire document, checking and adjusting spelling and grammar errors one by one. You should make a habit of using this tool before completing any Word document.

1. Navigate to the Review ribbon.

   You'll find the Grammar & Spelling command in the Proofing group on the ribbon as shown in Word Figure 3-32.

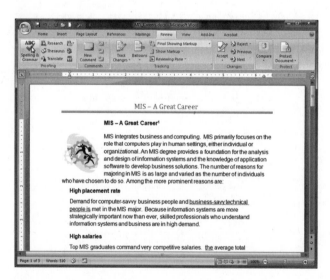

Word Figure 3-32: The Grammar & Spelling command.

Click the Grammar & Spelling command.

2. Word will start reviewing your document starting from the current location of the cursor.

   When a potential error is found, either spelling or grammar, a dialog box will appear as shown in Word Figure 3-33.

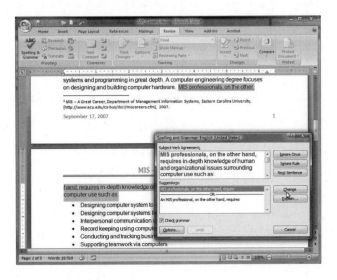

Word Figure 3-33: A grammar error.

   The dialog contains two panes. In the upper pane, the suspected error is displayed. Again, green is for grammar and red is for spelling.

   The bottom pane will contain suggested corrections.

   If desired, you can click on one of the suggested solutions to select it.

   For a grammatical error, several buttons are also provided that allow you to ignore the error; ignore the rule (thus, no further suspected errors of this nature will be displayed); go on to the next sentence; change the error to the selected correction; or explain (causing Word Help to display a page explaining the grammatical rule).

3. A similar dialog will appear for a suspected misspelled word as shown in Word Figure 3-34.

   In the lower pane will be displayed potential correct spellings for the word in question.

   For a spelling error, buttons are provided that allow you to ignore the error; ignore all (thus, no further occurrences of this suspected misspelling will be displayed); add the word to the dictionary so that it will not appear as an error in any other document; change the error to the selected correction; change all; or use the AutoCorrect feature.

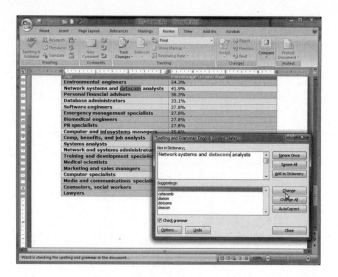

Word Figure 3-34: A spelling error.

4. At times, words will appear as misspellings when they are not (as with proper names, as shown in Word Figure 3-35).

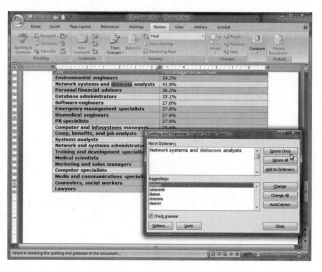

Word Figure 3-35: A proper name presented as a spelling error.

For these, you can ignore the error.

You should be careful to ignore only when really needed.

5. When a word indicated as a misspelling is indeed misspelled, as shown in Word Figure 3-36, select the appropriate spelling and click the Change button.

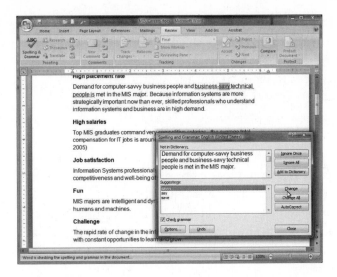

Word Figure 3-36: A correctly identified misspelling.

The next error if any will be displayed.

6. After all of the suspected errors have been inspected, a message will be displayed indicating that the check is completed (Word Figure 3-37).

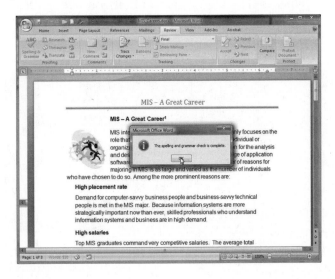

Word Figure 3-37: Check is Complete message.

CREATING WEB PAGES WITH WORD

Web pages are made up of content, text, and graphics, along with Hypertext Markup Language (HTML) and other programming code. To become a professional Web developer and create e-commerce sites with all of the bells and whistles expected today, you would need to learn several languages and technologies. However, to create a simple Web page for your own use, all you need is Word. The Save As option lets you do this. In general, follow these steps to create your Web page:

- Create the content for your page using Word.
- Save the page as a Web Page.
- Copy the file to your server.

Creating page content is easy with Word. You simply need to insert your content—text, tables, pictures, and all—just as you would into a normal Word document. Format the content just as you would in your regular Word pages. Just think about how things should look in a Web page and format your content to match. The HTML that is required by the browser to display your page correctly will be automatically generated when you save the file as a Web page.

Inserting Hyperlinks

An important component of a Web page is the hyperlink. A hyperlink is a pointer to another page that is stored on the network (usually, the Internet and World Wide Web). A hyperlink is made up of two parts: the text that the user can see and the Uniform Resource Locator (URL). You may know the URL better as a "Web address."

1. To create a hyperlink, highlight the text that you want to make into a hyperlink.

   Then right-click it (Word Figure 3-38).

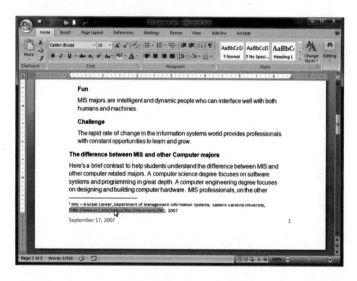

Word Figure 3-38: Highlighting text for a hyperlink.

2. You'll see that one of the options on the context-sensitive menu that is presented says "Hyperlink..." as shown in Word Figure 3-39.

   Select this option.

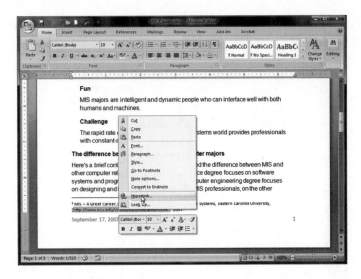

Word Figure 3-39: The Hyperlink option.

3. The Insert Hyperlink dialog will be displayed as shown in Word Figure 3-40.

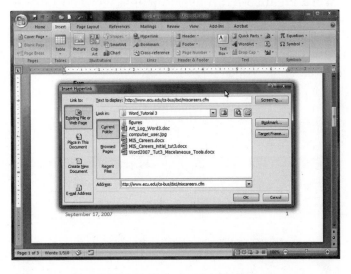

Word Figure 3-40: The Insert Hyperlink dialog.

Note that you can link to other items such as those within the current document or folder.

For a link to a Web page, make sure that the URL you want is entered into the Address text box.

You should also note the text in the Text to Display box. This is what the user will see in the document. It can be different from the address (and usually is).

4. When you have finished filling the dialog, click the OK button.

The dialog will disappear, and you will see that the text you selected looks like the typical hyperlink on a Web page, as shown in Word Figure 3-41.

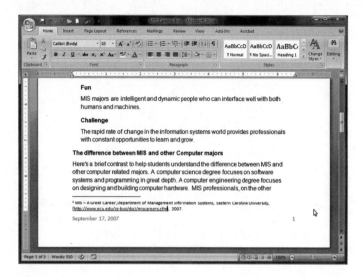

Word Figure 3-41: A hyperlink in a Word document.

To test the link, press and hold the Ctrl keyboard button and click on it.

The Web page should open in your browser.

5. You can also access the Insert Hyperlink dialog from the Insert ribbon, as shown in Word Figure 3-42.

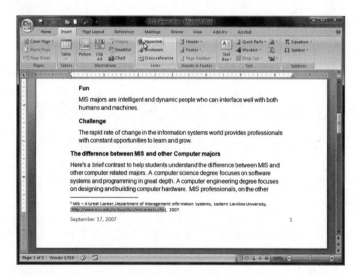

Word Figure 3-42: The Hyperlink command on the Insert ribbon.

After that, it works the same as previously shown.

Saving Your Document as a Web Page

1. You start saving your document as a Web page by accessing the Office button menu.

   Click on the Save As option as shown in Word Figure 3-43.

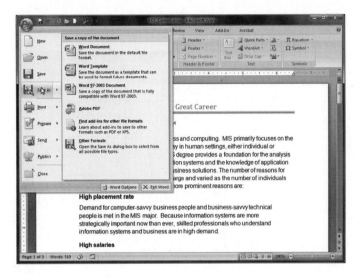

Word Figure 3-43: The Office button menu.

2. The Save As dialog will be displayed.

   As with saving a file, first navigate the folders until you find the location where you want to save the Web page file.

   Now, click the arrow on the Save As Type list.

   You'll see a list of many file types from which to choose, as shown in Word Figure 3-44.

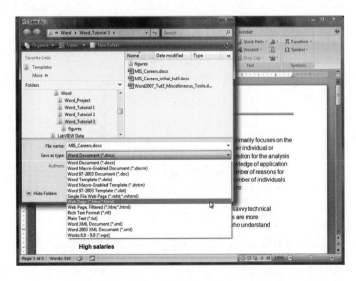

Word Figure 3-44: The Save As dialog.

3. Typically, the file type labeled "Web Page (*.htm,*.html)" is the best file type for a general Web page.

After selecting the file type, you should see that the File Name entry has changed with an extension that reflects the new file type.

Click Save to save the file with the new format, as shown in Word Figure 3-45.

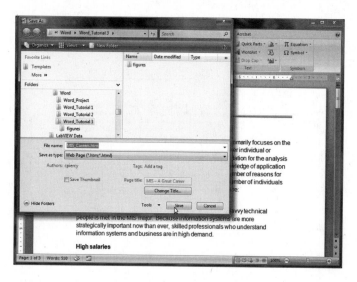

Word Figure 3-45: Saving after choosing Web Page file type and entering new file name.

4. Sometimes components of a document will work within some file types but not in others.

The Word Compatibility Checker will scan and notify you when an incompatible document component is found, as shown in Word Figure 3-46.

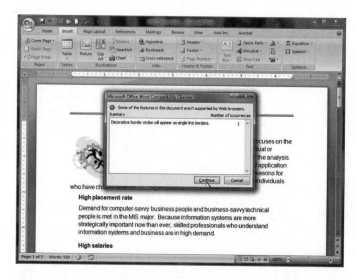

Word Figure 3-46: The Word Compatibility Checker.

Click Continue to accept these known items and continue scanning.

You can Cancel if you do not like a change.

5. After you save the document as a Web page, the document view will change so that you can preview how your document will appear in an actual browser, as in Word Figure 3-47.

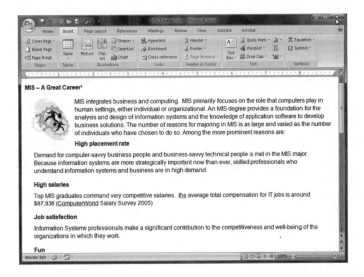

Word Figure 3-47: The Web Page document.

You can also open the document in an actual Web browser to view it.

Any edits that you make can now be saved directly to your new Web page document.

▶ Caution:

Since only text may be stored in an HTML file, some elements of your Web page will not be saved in the actual HTML file. Most graphics are usually stored as binary files. You need to be aware of how Word handles this when posting your file to the Web page in order to have your graphics appear on your page. Here is what Word does when creating your page. Assume that you are naming your page *Home.html*.

1. Word will create a folder called *Home_files* (the name of the folder is based on the name that you enter for the Web page).

2. Graphics will be stored as separate, binary files in this new folder.

3. In the Web page, an HTML tag that will make sure the picture appears in the appropriate location on the page will replace the graphic.

What all this means for you is that when you copy the file to your server, you will also need to post the associated folder with the images.

---

6. Word Figure 3-48 displays a view of Windows Explorer where the Web page document (*MIS_Careers.html*) file has been saved.

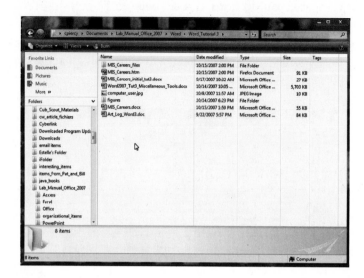

Word Figure 3-48: The folder location of *MIS_Careers.html*.

Notice that there is also a folder called *MIS_Careers_files*.

7. Take a look inside the *MIS_Careers_files* folder.

Several files related to the Web page document are stored here.

Image files (with extensions such as jpg, gif, png, or bmp) associated with the Web document are stored here, as shown in Word Figure 3-49.

Word Figure 3-49: The *MIS_Careers_files* folder.

Where Web Pages Live

The Internet works like a very huge **client/server** network. When you browse to a Web site, your computer becomes a client that is requesting a file from a server. All of the Web pages that are available for viewing on the Internet are stored on computers that have been set up as servers. This means that in order to make your pages available for others to view over the Internet, you will need to have a server available to which you can copy your files. You may also need to learn software such as WS-FTP so that you can transfer (post) your files to a Web server.

EXERCISES TO BUILD YOUR KNOWLEDGE OF MS WORD

Match the term on the left with the appropriate description on the right:

_____1. Compatibility Checker   a. An image from a library of line type drawings.

_____2. AutoCorrect

     b. A Word feature that checks to see whether the objects in your document are compatible with the file type.

_____3. Clip Art   c. The common file extension for a Web document.

_____4. html

     d. A feature that you can adjust that affects how the text flows around an inserted picture.

_____5. Text wrapping

     e. A collection of commands for adjusting Word to support how you want to work.

_____6. Word Options

     f. A tool that helps you to proofread your document by checking for errors.

_____7. Spelling & Grammar   g. An address to a resource on the World Wide Web.

_____8. URL

     h. A Word feature that allows you to choose a word and then look up synonyms.

_____9. Thesaurus

     i. A Word feature that will sense when you have made a common spelling mistake and then automatically replace your error.

_____10. Hyperlink

     j. Setting up text in your document as a pointer to another content source (i.e., document portion, another document, Web page). When you click on this text, the other content will open.

11. A friend has asked you about some of your favorite Web sites. In a Word file, make a bulleted list of Web sites for your friend. Use the name of the site in your list. Then, make each item into a hyperlink to the actual Web site.

Add the following corrections to your AutoCorrect list in Word:

Replace:	With:
12. MIS	Management Information Systems
13. CS	Computer Science
14. lol	Laughing out loud!
15. Your University abbreviation	Your University complete name

Use Word Help to find the answers to the following questions:

16. What is Compatibility Mode? When and why would you want to work in this mode?

_____

_____

_____

17. The Word Options button on the Office button menu provides many features for customizing your copy of the Word software, but it's not the only place to look for customization. For instance, you may want to change the default font formatting for your Word documents. You can do this without accessing the Word Options. How would you set default font properties?

_____

_____

_____

18. In the United States and much of the rest of the world, Word uses a built-in English dictionary by default. But what if you wanted to use Word to compose a paper for your French class? How could you change the dictionary used by Word to the French dictionary instead of the usual English dictionary?

_____

_____

_____

19. In addition to creating Web pages, you can also use Word to write entries for your blog. What steps would you take in Word to allow you to write and post entries to a blog?

_____

_____

_____

20. People often work in teams on an important document. When a document is shared among team members, it can be difficult to keep up with different versions of the document. What Word feature is available for keeping up with modifications made to a Word document by team members? What would you do to get started using this feature?

_____

_____

_____

WORD TUTORIAL 3: MINI-CASE 1

Scenario: Amy Shaftoe wants a job. She's created a nice résumé but wants to make it readily available for recruiters to find and read. Not only that, but she doesn't really feel that her one-page résumé tells her whole story. In addition to her soon-to-be-completed business degree, Amy has been active in several student organizations. For the last two semesters, she has been the president of Delta Epsilon Iota, a very selective honor society. In addition, she had worked summers since she was 16 as a salvage diver on her boat. She feels that she has many successes and learned many lessons from each of these activities. Amy wonders how to get all of this across in the limited space available on a one-page resume. Finally, it comes to her: "A Web site!" But she doesn't know the first thing about HTML or making Web pages. Fortunately, a friend reminds Amy that she can make a simple but adequate Web page using Word.

Your Task: Write a document that could become Amy's home page on the Web. Use the following guidelines when creating your home page:

- Include information about Amy's activities and hobbies.
- Add a list of links to some of her favorite Web sites.
- Use a table without borders to align things in the document as you want them to appear in the browser.
- Use at least one picture on your page.
- Check the document for spelling and grammar.
- Preview how your document would look when printed and make a printout of your pages.
- Save your file as a Web page. How many actual files were created when you saved it this way? Where are the images stored?

- View your page in a Web browser (such as Internet Explorer or Firefox). Does your page look as it did when you were viewing it in Word? How is it different? How would you change your page to make it look better?
- If you have a Web server available, post your pages to your account. What difficulties, if any, did you encounter? What steps did you take to overcome these difficulties?

WORD TUTORIAL 3: MINI-CASE 2

Scenario: It's Marco Carson's dream job. He has just taken a marketing position with the International Society for Ecotourism. Marco is so excited because the job will combine his two great loves: travel and ecological conservation. As the name implies, the society provides resources to support ecotourism. Ecotourism involves nature-based tourism, which involves education and interpretation of the natural environment and is managed to be ecologically sustainable. For his first project, Marco has been tasked with developing promotional materials for a society-sponsored trip to the rain forests of Borneo. The trip will involve learning about and helping to catalog the flora and fauna of these endangered forests. The trip will include a week-long stay at a society-owned "jungle treehouse" lodge. Participants will help a group of scientists explore the area and record information about the plants and animals that they find there. In addition to the work, participants will have the opportunity to take part in evening seminars presented by the resident naturalist. For an additional cost, a beach weekend option is available for unwinding after the hard but rewarding work in the jungle.

Your Task: Use Word to write a brochure to describe the eco-travel opportunity. Use the following guidelines when creating your brochure:

- Include information about the trip, such as activities, schedule, benefits to potential travelers, prerequisites, pricing and options, trip planning, and contact information.
- Use a three- or four-column format and spread your brochure over two pages that can later be printed on the front and back of a single page.
- Add a links to the organization's Web site and e-mail address.
- Use tables without borders as necessary to align things in the document as you want them to appear in the browser.
- Use images to illustrate the brochure.
- Check the document for spelling and grammar.
- Preview how your document would look when printed and make a printout of your brochure. Be sure to print on two sides of the sheet. How can you do this?
- Save your brochure file as a Web page. How many actual files were created when you saved it this way? Where are the images stored?
- View your page in a Web browser (such as Internet Explorer or Firefox). Does your page look as it did when you were viewing it in Word? How is it different? How would you change your page to make it look better?
- If you have a Web server available, post your pages to your account. What difficulties, if any, did you encounter? What steps did you take to overcome these difficulties?

MICROSOFT WORD PROJECT 1: WRITING A RÉSUMÉ AND COVER LETTER

By reading the business case section and completing this project you will:

- Extend your knowledge of MS Word.
- Learn how to apply MS Word to solve business problems.
- Understand résumé creation using tables.
- Understand how to create a Merge Document and an associated Data Source.
- Discover resources for creating effective résumés and cover letters.

PROJECT INTRODUCTION

Two essential tools used by students to obtain internships or jobs or to apply to graduate school are résumés and cover letters. This project will help you create these essential career-oriented tools. Given that most students apply for more than one position with more than one company, a MS Word feature known as Mail Merge may save you some labor.

THE COVER LETTER AND RÉSUMÉ PROJECT

Parts A and B Business Case

Sometime during your college career you are likely to apply for an internship, a job, or graduate school. Employers and graduate schools will expect you to send them a well-written cover letter accompanied by a professional résumé. For tips on creating professional cover letters and résumés, you should check with your school's career center. You also may want to visit http://www.career.uga.edu/students/writingeffectivecoverletters.html and http://www.career. uga.edu/STUDENTS/resumes.html. Lastly, you can search the World Wide Web to find even more information on cover letters and résumés.

Part A, Résumé: Problem Definition

Your task is to create a one-page, professional résumé. A résumé is a brief summary of your education and your work experience. Another way to view a résumé is as a one-page snapshot of you. Often, you submit a résumé (and cover letter) as part of an application for an internship or a job. Potential employers often make an initial assessment of your suitability for a position based on the content and appearance of your résumé. Although your résumé will be attached to your cover letter, it is generally a good idea to create your résumé and then create a cover letter. After you have decided what to include on your résumé, it will be easier to choose what to highlight in your cover letter.

Creating a meaningful and professional résumé that captures your educational and professional achievements can be a difficult task. The question of what to include and how to describe what you've done (content), the order in which headings and topics should appear (style), and how to lay out your one-page résumé (format) are all significant questions that need to be answered. To help you get started, here are some ideas regarding content, style, and format.

When deciding which of your accomplishments to include on your résumé, try to highlight the most important achievements *relative to the position* for which you are applying. If you are applying for an internship, look for relevant job experience in which you might have displayed leadership, technical knowledge, and so forth. On the other hand, if you are applying for a scholarship, leadership may be important, but including more of your educational achievements rather than job-related ones might be more appropriate.

Content Tip: Regardless of your purpose, you are creating a résumé for a target audience (e.g., a corporate recruiter). For each item on your résumé, you should be sure to answer the following questions: What did I do? What was the impact? Who cared? So, if you were the president of a student organization, you might present it on your résumé as follows:

President, The _____ (fill in) National Honor Society, 2006.

- Responsible for leading 600+ members involved in career seminars and over 100 hours of community service per semester.
- National and Recording Secretary, 2004–2005.

Similarly, if you had an internship and were now applying for an IS position, you might list the internship like this:

Intern, E-National Restaurant Business, Inc (ENRB) Corporate Headquarters, Atlanta, GA Summer 2005.

- Member of Restaurant Information Systems team. Interacted with ENRB operators across the country.
- Established connectivity between in-store POS servers and ENRB servers in over 30 stores throughout US.
- Successfully modified and implemented software written in Java and used by over 100 stores.
- Named "ENRB Corporate Intern of the Year" for positive impact on store operations nationwide.

Notice how, in both examples, the important questions—What did I do? What was the impact? Who cared?—were answered directly. For the student organization presidency, the "who cared" question is left for consideration as an interpretive question.

Style Tip: What's the best style for your résumé? The answer to this may depend on your major, the company to which you are applying, and many other requirements. For example, business school majors often list their educational accomplishments first, followed by internships or work experience, while journalism students may list internships with media companies first and then highlight their scholastic achievements. You should consult your advisor, career center, corporate recruiters, and successful alumni for the latest guidance on style.

Formatting Tip: Are you a person who has too much to list on one page? Are you still using your word processor like people used to use a typewriter? The many formatting features found in MS Word can help you manage the type (written items) and the white space (e.g., spacing between lines) to create a professional appearance that enhances readability and content yet allows you to squeeze more items on a page. Let's look at controlling line spacing as an example of how to manipulate white space to put more lines on a page.

First, open a new document in MS Word. Next, locate the Show/Hide Paragraph icon (the ¶ button) on MS Word's Home ribbon. Make sure this button is clicked on. You'll know whether you've done this, because if you have, there will be paragraph marks (¶) at the end of every paragraph and you will see spaces (dots) between words. Once you've done these two things, type the résumé items listed above.

Notice there appears to be a line between the last line of the "President" item and the first line of the "Intern" item. Try to put your cursor in this white space—you can't. This is because this 12-pt space was created as part of the paragraph formatting feature in MS Word, accessible from the Paragraph group on the Home ribbon. If you needed less space, how could you do this? See what happens if you change the spacing after and before. Sometimes you can use as little as 3-pt after-line spacing and still have enough white space between items to allow them to be easily read. There are many more formatting features available in MS Word to help you manage content and white space. The commands on MS Word's Home and Page Layout ribbons, along with Help, can help you craft a concise and professional one-page résumé.

Part A, Résumé: Problem Requirements

You should create a professional one-page résumé that is suitable to send to an employer or a graduate school. If you are not yet applying for internships, jobs, or graduate school, you should imagine that you are applying and should create a one-page résumé that you can use in the future. If your résumé is to be posted to the Web, you may want to consider the amount of personal contact information that you include and the layout of your Web version. An e-mail may be sufficient contact information, and you may not want to post home addresses and phone numbers. Ask your instructor about what he/she would like you to include and whether or not you should create a "Web-publishable" version.

Part B, Cover Letter: Problem Definition

A cover letter is a letter that is usually sent with an application for an internship or job. Cover letters state the purpose of your application (e.g., applying for an IS-related summer internship) and highlight those qualifications that, you feel, make you a strong candidate for the position.

Your task is to create a cover letter that will serve as the starting document for your Mail Merge and that, once merged with the data, will be the cover letter you send to employers or graduate schools.

Before you begin creating your cover letter, here is some general background information on Mail Merge. Mail Merge is an MS Word feature that enables you to:

1. Create your own form letters and, using the same starting document, merge data into the document for different recipients and purposes (e.g., internship with Companies X, Y, and Z and part-time position with Company A).

2. Create a data source that can be customized by adding fields as needed and that can be used as the data source for more than one starting document.

If you are unsure of what to do, you can use MS Word Help to guide you (try using "mail merge" or "form letter" in the field below the "What would you like to do?" question).

Part B, Cover Letter: Problem Requirements

You should create a professional cover letter that is suitable to send to an employer or a graduate school. If you are not yet applying for internships, jobs, or graduate school, you should imagine that you are applying and should create a letter that you can use in the future. When you build the Data Source that will be merged into the Starting Document, you should create data on at least five companies that you would like to intern with or work for. You may make up contact information for the company employees/recipients of the letters. Each recipient should have a different title (Dr., Mr., Ms., etc.) a different Job Title (Director of Recruiting, Recruiting Manager, etc.), and so on.

Interpretive Questions

Based on your experience with this project, answer the following questions.

1. Why is MS Word considered word-processing software and not electronic typing software?

2. What are some sources that might answer the "Who cared?" question regarding some of your achievements?

3. What is the relationship between your résumé and your cover letter? Having created both documents, do you agree or disagree with the authors' suggestion that it is better to create the résumé before the cover letter?

4. What resources exist at your school to help you create résumés and cover letters?

MICROSOFT WORD PROJECT 2: CREATING AN ORGANIZATION NEWSLETTER

By reading the business case section and completing this project you will:

- Extend your knowledge of MS Word.
- Learn how to apply MS Word to solve business problems.
- Understand how to create a newsletter.
- Understand how to create a merge document and an associated data source.
- Discover resources for designing effective newsletters.

PROJECT INTRODUCTION

The Global River Conservancy (GRC) is a nonprofit environmental group whose primary purpose is the protection of free-flowing rivers. Lisa Rios, a business school graduate, has recently become a Corporate Communications specialist for a major corporation. In her spare time she works as a volunteer for the GRC.

The GRC is interested in improving its communications with various constituencies, such as volunteers and donors. One way to do this is through a newsletter. Many organizations keep in touch with their members and supporters through newsletters. Although Web sites and downloadable documents are replacing traditional paper newsletters delivered by a postal service, newsletters remain an important form of communication regardless of delivery method. MS Word makes it easy to create professional-looking newsletters. By completing this project, you'll be able to create newsletters for the organizations to which you belong. Additionally, since most organizations have many members and other stakeholders, you'll also learn about a laborsaving MS Word feature known as Mail Merge that can help you prepare a newsletter for a traditional mass mailing.

In Part A you will help Lisa create GRC's newsletter, and in Part B you will help her complete the Mail Merge that GRC will use to send out the newsletter.

THE NEWSLETTER PROJECT

Parts A and B Business Case

Organizations need to communicate with various individuals and with other organizations. For example, local chapters of many national organizations publish periodic newsletters to keep their members up to date. Here are two sites that can help you get started: Microsoft Office Online: Help and How To, Microsoft Corporation, 2008, http://office.microsoft.com/en-us/help/HA010818671033.aspx and Create the perfect business or organization newsletter, Roger C. Parker's NewEntrepreneur.com, 2000, http://www.newentrepreneur.com/Resources/Articles/12_Step_Newsletter/12_step_newsletter.html. You can also search the Web on your own to find even more information on creating effective newsletters and similar types of business communication.

Part A, Newsletter: Problem Requirements

Your task is to create an effective and appealing newsletter for an organization. You should create a professional newsletter that is suitable for use by an organization of which you are a member. If you don't belong to any organizations, create a newsletter that could be used by the academic department for your major or intended major. Your newsletter should be visually appealing and contain accurate, interesting, relevant, and timely content (information represented by text, clip art, photos, and so forth). Content is very important, but creating an easy-to-read newsletter also requires careful thought about layout and design issues.

One specific design concern is the appropriate use of white space. As discussed in the Word tutorials, white space includes the background, border areas, and space between paragraphs, lines, and characters. Managing this space allows you to control the attention of your readers and can make your document easier to read. White space is often paired with formatting changes for increased emphasis.

Here's an example of the use of white space and formatting

The extra space before and after the line of text drew your eyes to that line, and they stop at the end of it. This served to focus your attention. Enlarging the font size and boldfacing the text increased your focus on the line.

The specific requirements for your newsletter project are as follows:

1. The newsletter you create for GRC should be at least two pages long.

2. The header for the newsletter should contain the organization's name and a graphical display of its organizational logo or symbol.

3. The footer for the newsletter should contain the contact information for the organization and the page number.

4. The first page should be formatted into two columns with a picture or graphic inserted in the middle of one of the columns.

5. The second-page formatting is up to you, but it should be visually appealing and facilitate the display and understanding of the information presented.

6. Your instructor may add further requirements.

Part B, Mail Merge: Problem Requirements

Newsletters are mailed to various GRC supporters and other interested parties. Your newsletter will serve as the starting document for your mail merge; once merged with the data, it will be mailed out by GRC. When you build the data source that will be merged into the starting document, you should create data for at least five individuals who will receive the newsletter. You may use your friends or family as members or you may make up contact information for the recipients of the newsletters. Each recipient should have a different title (Dr., Mr., Ms., etc.), a different address, and so on. However, before you begin creating your newsletter, here is some general background information on mail merge.

Mail Merge is a Word feature that enables you to:

1. Create different versions of documents (e.g., "form letters") by using the same starting document and merging specific data into the document for different recipients and purposes

2. Create a data source that can be customized by adding fields as needed and that can be used as the data source for more than one starting document.

You can access Mail Merge from the Mailings ribbon. If you want to, you can use Word's Step by Step Mail Merge Wizard. This tool is found on the Mailings ribbon on the Start Mail Merge drop-down menu. In addition, Microsoft Word Help provides the Mail Merge process as follows:

1. Set up the main document.

2. Connect the document to a data source.

3. Refine the list of recipients or items.

4. Add placeholders, called mail merge fields, to the document.

5. Preview and complete the merge.

You can find more instructions on completing a mail merge by accessing Word help and performing a search using the keywords "mail merge."

Interpretive Questions

Based on your experience with this project, answer the following questions.

1. Why is MS Word considered word-processing software and not electronic typing software?

2. Given your use of columns and graphical media in the newsletter, what is the impact of white space on the appearance of your newsletter?

3. What are the possible ways that the GRC can get their newsletter into the hands of their members?

4. GRC could decide not to mail your newsletter physically to its constituents or as an attachment to an e-mail. When printing, the fields in a mail merge are generally "filled in" when the document is printed. If the organization decided to publish your newsletter as an attachment to an e-mail, would it be possible to create electronic versions of the "filled-in" mail merge documents? What would you need to do differently?

Tutorial 1

INTRODUCTION TO MICROSOFT POWERPOINT 2007

After reading this tutorial and completing the associated exercises, you will be able to:

- Open and start using Microsoft PowerPoint.
- Work with the PowerPoint interface.
- Create a basic MS PowerPoint presentation.

WHAT IS MICROSOFT POWERPOINT?

Uh oh! You've been chosen by your team to make the class presentation on your project. Or, as president of a school club, you need to present your plans for resolving the financial problems you inherited from your predecessor. Even better, you've been asked by a recruiter to make a short presentation on why she should hire you for a great job that you would love to have. If any of these or a wide variety of other situations involving presentations apply to you, then knowledge of Microsoft PowerPoint may benefit you.

PowerPoint is the part of the Microsoft Office suite of programs that provides you with tools for creating, editing, and formatting presentations that can be shown to small or large groups of interested parties. You can also add tables, pictures, graphics, video, and audio files to your presentation. You can link or embed your Excel spreadsheets or other software-created objects. You can also create hyperlinks to files or locations on the World Wide Web. That sounds like a lot, and these are only just a few of the things you can do, but, fortunately, PowerPoint is probably the easiest of the Office programs to learn and use.

In this tutorial you will cover the basic skills of setting up PowerPoint for your needs and will start creating useful and vibrant presentations.

WORKING WITH THE POWERPOINT INTERFACE

As with other software you may have learned, before getting maximum mileage out of PowerPoint you need to become familiar with its interface. Fortunately, because of Microsoft's use of objects and a common user interface, many of the same interface elements that you find in other software—menus, ribbons, status bar, and so forth—are available and have the same look and feel in PowerPoint as in other Office applications. In addition, the user interface is flexible and changeable, meaning that you can adjust some elements of the interface to match how you want to work with PowerPoint for maximum productivity.

You can open MS PowerPoint by double-clicking the PowerPoint icon on your desktop, single-clicking the icon on the Taskbar if it appears there, or by selecting it from the Start menu system.

PowerPoint Interface Overview

Open PowerPoint and try to identify the items indicated in PPT Figure 1-1 and listed in PPT Table 1-1. In general, when you start the PowerPoint software, the assumption is that you want to start a new presentation document, and a blank slide will be ready for you to use.

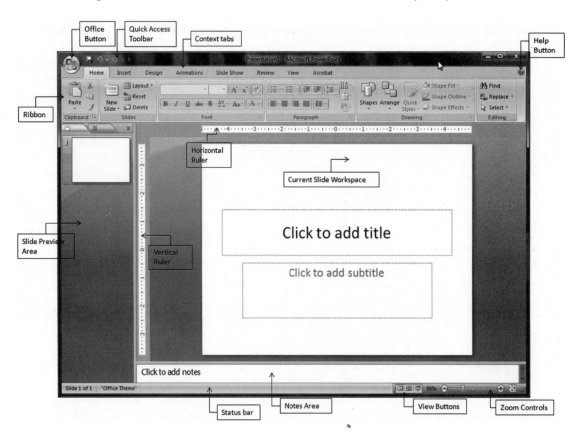

PPT Figure 1-1: The PowerPoint interface.

Component	Description
Ribbon	A visual component that displays the most commonly used PowerPoint commands for a given context, such as Design.
Context tab	One of a row of tabs displayed above the ribbon, on which you can click to switch to a particular ribbon.
Status bar	A visual component at the bottom of the PowerPoint window that provides information on the status of PowerPoint, such as the number of slides in the presentation and the design themes used.
Zoom control	A component that allows you to adjust the display size of the workspace quickly.
Office button	The round button at top left of the PowerPoint window. By clicking this button, you'll have access to commands that are common to all the various software that are provided with Microsoft Office. Commands such as Save and Print are found here.
Quick Access Toolbar	A place on the window where you can add icons for commonly used commands.
Help button	A button that, when you need to do something that you don't know or have forgotten how to do, you can click to access the PowerPoint help facility, which is full of good content that describes anything that you might want to do in PowerPoint.
Horizontal/vertical ruler	A tool that allows you to see and adjust how components of your document are aligned. The horizontal ruler is used for working with the horizontal alignment of components, while the vertical ruler deals with vertical alignment.
Current slide workspace	This is the area in which you can add, view, and work with the items in the current slide of your presentation document.
View buttons	These buttons allow you to view your document in different ways, such as Normal, Slide Sorter, and Slide Show views.
Slide preview area	An area where you can preview the current and other slides in the presentation. You can view these in either Slides or Outline formats.
Notes area	An area where you can enter speaker notes for the current slide.

PPT Table 1-1: Components of the PowerPoint user interface.

In looking at PPT Figure 1-1, you can see that the Normal view of the PowerPoint interface is very much like the Microsoft Office interfaces you've dealt with earlier. The main difference is that the PowerPoint interface is slide oriented instead of document oriented as in Word or table oriented as in Excel or Access. This means that, while in Normal view, the interface is set up to enable you to create multiple slides, with the current slide being shown in the Current slide workspace. The Slides page of the slide preview area provides you with a graphical list of the slides that you have created so far. The Outline page of the slide preview area will display and outline of the textual information provided on the slides of your presentation. On the bottom of the normal view you will find the Notes area. Here, you can enter speaker notes that you can refer to when you deliver your presentation.

The View buttons enable you to select a particular view of the slides, either Normal view (the one you use for editing the current slide); Slide Sorter view, in which all of the existing slides are shown together at thumbnail size, allowing you to reorder them by dragging them to new positions; Slide Show view, in which the slides are shown taking up the full screen in the form you would use to make a presentation; and the Notes Pages view, which allows you to view slides and related notes. You can print these pages to refer to while giving your presentation.

Tour of the PowerPoint Ribbons

As you can see in PPT Figure 1-1, PowerPoint typically has seven (or more) different ribbon contexts that make it easy to find the commands you need. You can actually customize PowerPoint and add one or two more if needed. The next several figures will provide a quick overview of the primary PowerPoint ribbons. You will get very familiar with these as you work through these tutorials, so there's no need to memorize them now. Just take a quick look now and then refer back to these pages as needed.

Notice that each ribbon has some things in common. Commands are arranged in a series of groups. Each group includes a set of commands that let you do related tasks. Some controls are accompanied by downward-pointing arrows. When one of these is clicked, a menu or palette with more related options is displayed. You should also notice that each group has a small arrow in the lower right corner. By clicking this arrow, you can open a dialog box for the group that provides even more options that you can use to complete your work.

PPT Figure 1-2: The Home ribbon.

The Home ribbon (PPT Figure 1-2) contains the most commonly used PowerPoint commands. Commands such as Copy, Cut, and Paste are located here in the Clipboard group. The Slides group includes commands for adding and deleting slides as well as choosing a slide layout. Text formatting commands are provided in the Font and Paragraph groups. The Drawing group has commands that will let you add drawing components to your slides. Finally, the Editing group provides some more commonly used commands.

PPT Figure 1-3: The Insert ribbon.

You'll find many different objects that you can add to your worksheet on the Insert ribbon (PPT Figure 1-3). The types of objects that you can use are included in the groups Tables, Illustrations, Links, Text, and Media Clips.

PPT Figure 1-4: The Design ribbon.

The Design ribbon (PPT Figure 1-4) provides commands that you can use when you want to control how the overall presentation document will be printed or appear when displayed on the screen. The commands on this ribbon are organized into the groups Page Setup, Themes, and Background.

PPT Figure 1-5: The Animation ribbon.

The Animation ribbon (PPT Figure 1-5) includes commands that let you control how animated elements behave when your presentation is displayed as a slide show. The Preview command lets you preview the animations associated with the current slide. The Animations group includes commands that you can use to add and manage animation behavior for the individual components on your slide. The Transitions group includes features that let you control how the presentation transitions from one slide to another.

PPT Figure 1-6: The Slide Show ribbon.

The Slide Show ribbon (PPT Figure 1-6) allows you to view your presentation as a slide show and control how it will behave when viewed as a slide show. Command groups located on this ribbon include Start Slide Show, Set Up, and Monitors.

PPT Figure 1-7: The Review ribbon.

Options available on the Review ribbon (PPT Figure 1-7) are used to make sure that you have completed a quality presentation. They are also useful when you are collaborating with others to create the presentation. These commands allow you to check the spelling and grammar of the worksheet (Proofing group) and add comments to cells for you or others to read (Comments group). You can also allow only authorized users to view or change the document (Protect Document group).

PPT Figure 1-8: The View ribbon.

The View ribbon, shown in PPT Figure 1-8, provides commands that you can use when you want to control how the overall document will be displayed on the screen. The commands on this ribbon are organized into the groups Presentation Views, Show/Hide, Zoom, Color/Grayscale, Window, and Macros. A macro is a saved set of programming commands that you can create to automate your work in PowerPoint.

CREATING A BASIC POWERPOINT PRESENTATION

You can create a basic PowerPoint presentation document by following some typical steps:

1. Choose a design for your presentation.

2. Add text content.

3. Add more complex content such as graphics, sound, and video.

4. Set up slide show elements such as animations and transitions.

5. Review and proof the presentation.

6. Present the presentation.

In this tutorial we will concentrate on the first two items in the list. In later tutorials we will discuss the use of more complex content, preparing your presentation for final display, and presenting it as a slide show. The primary content components of any PowerPoint presentation are text and graphics. So our discussion in this tutorial will look at some basic ways to work with them.

Choosing a Presentation Design

It's very easy to format an entire document with a professional design by applying a document design theme. A theme provides a set of unified design elements that provides a consistent look for your document by using color, fonts, and graphics. A presentation theme is a set of formatting choices that include colors, fonts, and effects. PowerPoint comes with a collection of built-in design themes (accessible on the Design ribbon).

As the theme will affect how the content on your page will appear, it is usually better to select the design theme before adding content. By doing this, you can add your content within the theme constraints as you go rather than having to adjust it afterward. This being said, you should have some idea of your topic so that you can select an appropriate theme. Let's see how to apply a theme.

1. As you saw in PPT Figure 1-1, when you start PowerPoint, it automatically brings up a slide that has text boxes for a title and a subtitle or author with different-sized fonts for each as shown in PPT Figure 1-9.

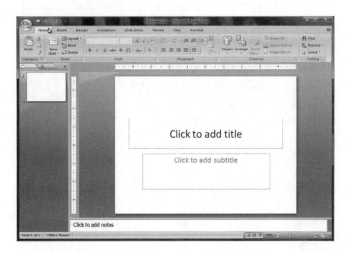

PPT Figure 1-9: A new PowerPoint presentation.

The slide is blank with no design theme applied.

2. Select the Design ribbon.

In the center of the ribbon, you'll find a command group labeled Themes.

With the commands in this group, you can choose a color theme, a font theme, an effects theme, or an overall theme that includes all three.

A few of the overall themes are displayed, but you can click the *More* arrow next to the overall themes, as shown in PPT Figure 1-10, to see the complete list.

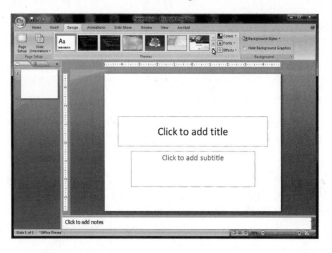

PPT Figure 1-10: The PowerPoint Design ribbon.

3. The All Themes dialog is divided into three main panes as shown in PPT Figure 1-11.

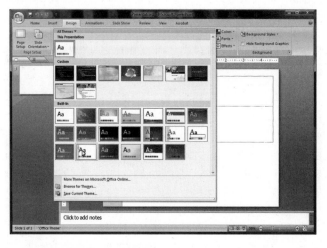

PPT Figure 1-11: The All Themes dialog.

The top pane will display the current theme.

The middle pane includes custom design themes. These are themes that you have created or downloaded.

The final pane includes built-in themes.

4. You can preview the theme on your slide by hovering over the small image of it on the ribbon or the All Themes dialog.

Select one of the themes by clicking on it.

The design theme chosen will be applied to your current slide and any slide that you add to the presentation.

For the design in PPT Figure 1-12, we chose the built-in theme called "Solstice."

Adding Text to the Title Slide

Adding text content to a slide is pretty easy. You can type your content directly on the slide, or, as we will see later, we can add text through the Outline view. Let's add some text to our title slide.

1. As you can see in PPT Figure 1-12, there are two areas on the current slide where you can add text.

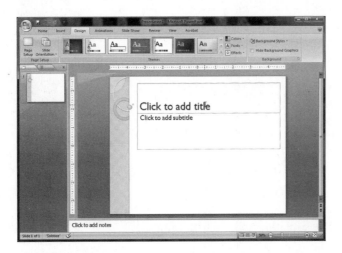

PPT Figure 1-12: A slide with a design theme.

Click in the field labeled "Click to add title."

Your slide will now appear as in PPT Figure 1-13.

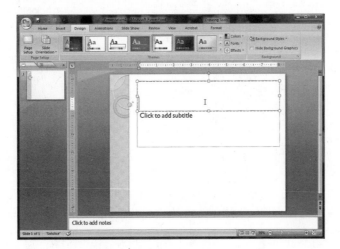

PPT Figure 1-13: A slide text field.

The cursor will be flashing in the area and waiting for you to type text.

2. As you type, your text will appear on the slide.

   Notice that you will also see it on the Slide Preview area on the left side of your PowerPoint window.

   Add the title: *Choosing a Business Major* (PPT Figure 1-14).

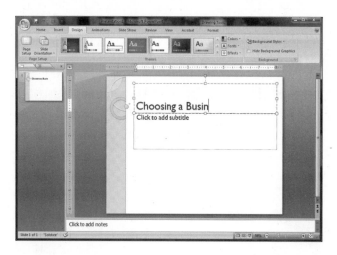

PPT Figure 1-14: Entering text on a slide.

3. Adding the subtitle works just the same.

   Click in the subtitle area and type: *Which one is right for you?* as shown in PPT Figure 1-15.

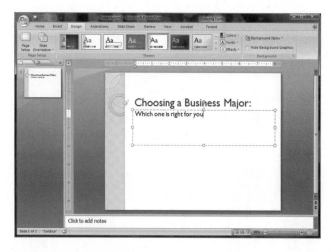

PPT Figure 1-15: Adding a subtitle.

4. The title slide will appear as shown in PPT Figure 1-16.

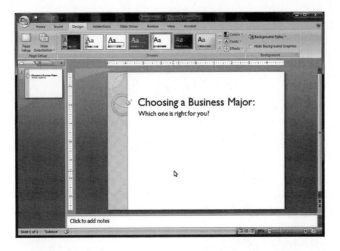

PPT Figure 1-16: The completed title slide.

Adding a New Slide

Of course, a PowerPoint presentation is usually made up of more than just a title slide. We'll need more, so let's see how to insert a slide.

1. The New Slide command is located in the Slides group on the Home ribbon.

   By clicking directly on the New Slide command, you'll insert a new slide with the same layout as the current slide, as shown in PPT Figure 1-17.

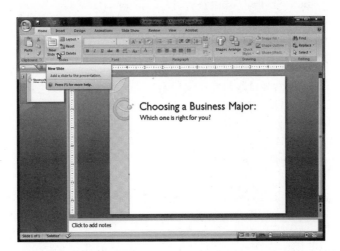

PPT Figure 1-17: The Insert Slide command.

   You can also do this by using the keyboard shortcut Ctrl-M.

2. Instead of clicking the command directly, click the small arrow at the bottom of the command icon.

A dialog with a list of slide layouts will be displayed as in PPT Figure 1-18.

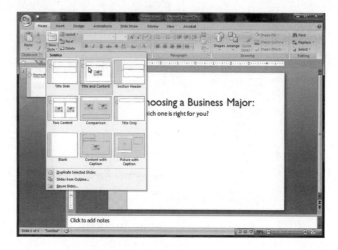

PPT Figure 1-18: New slide layouts.

The layouts provided may look different depending on the theme that you have chosen for your presentation.

3. Select the layout labeled Slide and Content.

A new slide with this layout will be inserted as shown in PPT Figure 1-19.

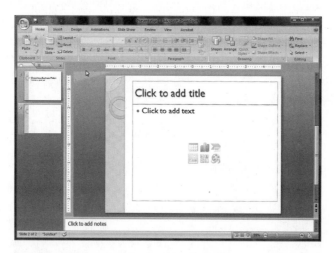

PPT Figure 1-19: A new slide with Slide and Content layout.

The new slide will be displayed in the current slide workspace.

You'll also see the new slide added in the preview area.

4. You can now enter text on the new slide in the same way that you added text to the title slide.

Enter the word *Introduction* as the title.

Add the text shown in PPT Figure 1-20 as the main content of the slide.

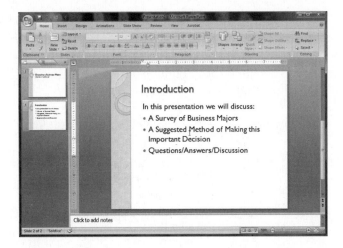

PPT Figure 1-20: Text on the new slide.

Formatting the Text on a Slide

Once text content is on a slide, it can be formatted in much the same way that text is formatted in any of the Microsoft Office software. Most of the text formatting commands are found in the Font and Paragraph commands on the Home ribbon. Usually, you can also access these commands by highlighting the text that you want to change and moving the mouse slightly up to the right to show a context-sensitive toolbar and menu. In the following examples, we will use the commands on the ribbon to demonstrate text formatting options.

1. To begin formatting text, you need to either select the specific text or select the text box within which the text resides.

   Go ahead and select the title text *Introduction* on the second slide of our example presentation, as shown in PPT Figure 1-21.

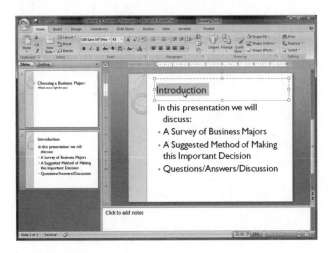

PPT Figure 1-21: Selecting text for formatting.

2. Sometimes we will be interested in adjusting the font of text.

   You can change the font by selecting a font name from the list available on the Home ribbon.

   Access the list, as shown in PPT Figure 1-22, by clicking on the arrow next to the name of the current font.

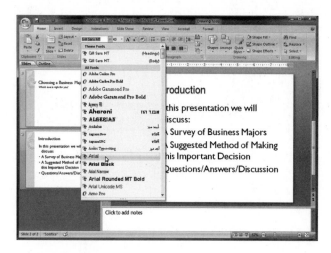

PPT Figure 1-22: Changing the text font.

   Experiment by changing the current title to *Arial* font.

3. You can adjust the font size by selecting an exact size from the font size list or by using the increase/decrease arrows as shown in PPT Figure 1-23.

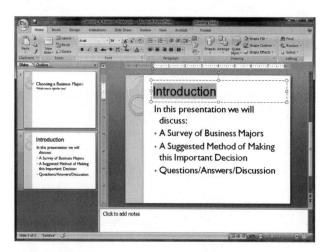

PPT Figure 1-23: Adjusting font size.

   Any adjustments made will immediately display on the current slide.

4. Keep in mind that the original font name and size were part of the overall theme of the presentation.

You should take great care in choosing whether to actually change the font, and if you do so, choose one that complements your chosen design theme.

In this case, we are going to use the Undo command, as shown in PPT Figure 1-24, to return to our original font name and size.

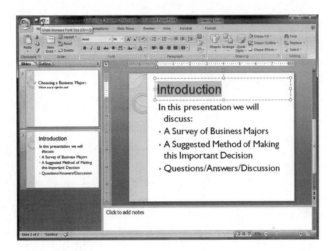

PPT Figure 1-24: The Undo command.

5. We can also adjust the text style using commands in the Font group.

   While the title is selected, click the Bold button in the Font group of the Home ribbon as shown in PPT Figure 1-25.

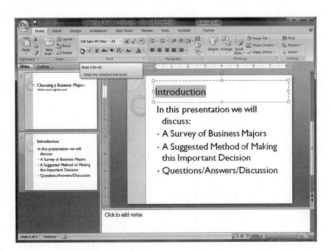

PPT Figure 1-25: Setting text to bold.

Note that you could also use the Ctrl-B keyboard shortcut.

Other font styles available here include underline, italic, and strike-through.

6. You can also use commands on the Home ribbon to adjust how items in a list are presented.

Add the line *List may change slightly by University* under the first line in the bulleted list, as shown in PPT Figure 1-26.

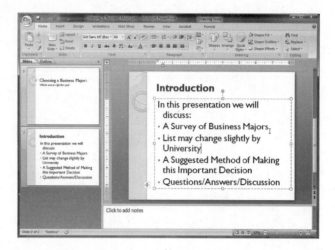

PPT Figure 1-26: Formatting a text list.

We'll use this as part of our example on list manipulation.

7. Highlight the new line.

Our goal is to "demote" this line from the current list level.

In effect, we will make it a list within a list.

You'll find the Increase List Level button in the Paragraph group. This is the button with the right-facing arrow.

Click this arrow as shown in PPT Figure 1-27 to change the list level of the selected text.

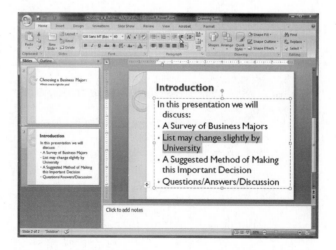

PPT Figure 1-27: Increasing the list level.

8. You should now see (PPT Figure 1-28) that the selected line has been shifted over underneath the previous line.

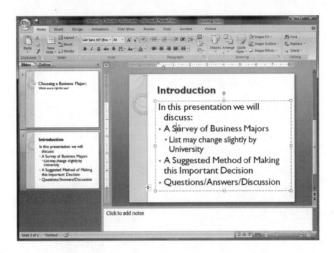

PPT Figure 1-28: The new list level.

Also, notice that the font size has been decreased so that the items at this list level appear as a sublist related to the list item just above.

9. With the new list level selected, click the Decrease Font arrow until the selection fits on one line as shown in PPT Figure 1-29.

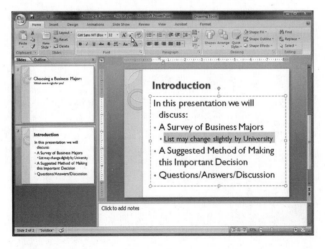

PPT Figure 1-29: New list level with decreased font.

10. You can also adjust the style of buttons used with the list.

   Click the arrow next to the Bullets button.

   You'll see a list of bullet styles.

For the example in PPT Figure 1-30, we've selected the arrow bullets.

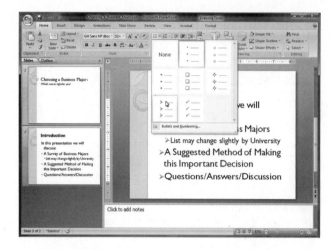

PPT Figure 1-30: Changing bullet style.

11. You can choose a different style for list items at different levels.

Select the sublist item.

Now, select the original filled round bullets for the sublist as shown in PPT Figure 1-31.

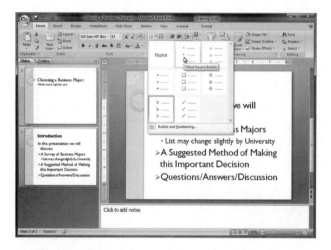

PPT Figure 1-31: Selecting sublist bullet style.

12. The slide after you have completed your formatting is shown in PPT Figure 1-32.

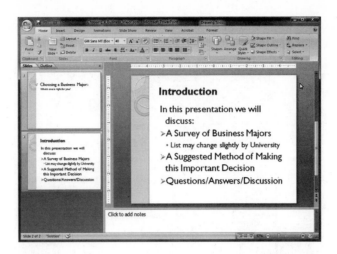

PPT Figure 1-32: The completely formatted slide.

Placing Text in Columns

1. It's also possible to adjust the way that text is arranged on the slide.

    For instance, we can take a list of items and arrange them into two or more columns.

    To begin, create a new slide like that shown in PPT Figure 1-33.

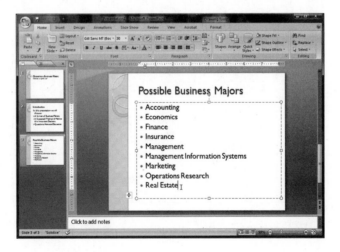

PPT Figure 1-33: A single-column list.

2. Highlight the items in the list.

The Columns command of the Paragraph group on the Home ribbon is shown in
PPT Figure 1-34.

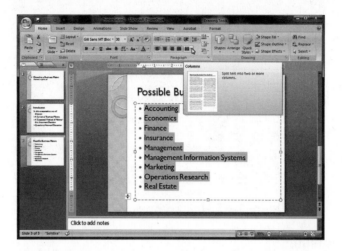

PPT Figure 1-34: The Columns command.

3. Click the arrow on the right side of the Columns command.

Several Columns options will be displayed as shown in PPT Figure 1-35.

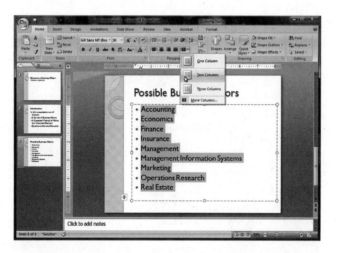

PPT Figure 1-35: Columns command options.

4. Select the Two Columns option.

The list of majors will now appear in two columns as shown in PPT Figure 1-36.

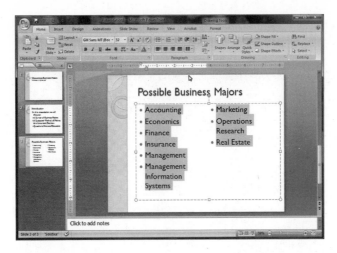

PPT Figure 1-36: Text in two columns.

Jazzing Up Text with SmartArt

PowerPoint is also equipped with several other features that allow you to present your content in a pleasing and professional manner. One of these features is called **SmartArt**. A SmartArt graphic is a visual representation of your information. You'll get the idea as we work with SmartArt to improve the format of the majors listed in the slide.

1. The SmartArt command is located on both the Insert ribbon and the Home ribbon.

    For this example, we will use the SmartArt command in the Paragraph group of the Home ribbon.

    With the text highlighted, click the arrow next to the Convert to SmartArt command (PPT Figure 1-37).

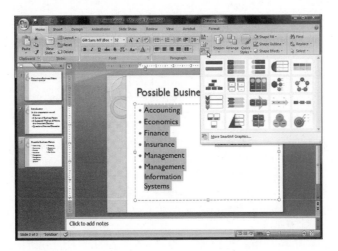

PPT Figure 1-37: The Convert to SmartArt command.

2. You can also access SmartArt options using a context-sensitive menu.

With the text selected, right-click and then select the Convert to SmartArt option (PPT Figure 1-38).

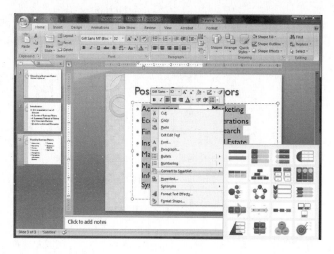

PPT Figure 1-38: SmartArt command on context-sensitive menu.

3. The Choose a SmartArt Graphic provides a collection of visual options.

   You can browse through all of them or narrow them down by selecting a category.

   We've selected the Basic Block List from the List category as shown in PPT Figure 1-39.

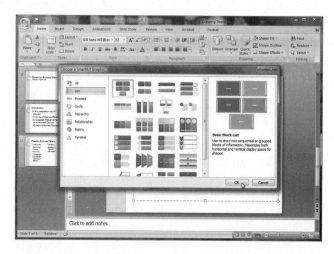

PPT Figure 1-39: Selecting a SmartArt graphic.

You should take some time to browse the available options.

4. Your text will now be displayed within the selected SmartArt as shown in PPT Figure 1-40.

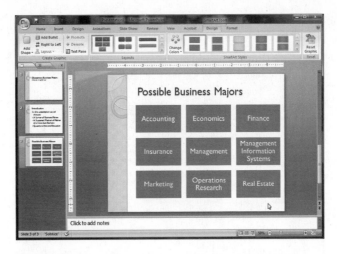

PPT Figure 1-40: Text displayed with SmartArt.

Working in Outline View

So far, we have been entering text directly on a slide, but there's another way that we can add text content. Text content can be added to your presentation by using the Outline page in the left-hand (slide preview) pane of the PowerPoint window. In fact, this may be the best way to enter your text, since it gives you a good place to organize your thoughts while creating the presentation.

1. In the preview pane, click on the tab labeled "Outline."

   You should now see the text that is currently in your presentation in outline form, as shown in PPT Figure 1-41.

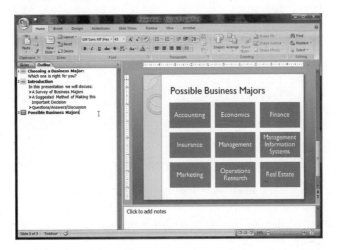

PPT Figure 1-41: The Outline view.

Notice that each slide is indicated by a number and a slide icon.

You can click on one of the slide icons to select a slide and its contents.

2. Click and place the cursor in the Outline view just after the title of the last slide.

Press the Enter key.

You should see that a new slide has been created both in the Outline view and in the current slide workspace as shown in PPT Figure 1-42.

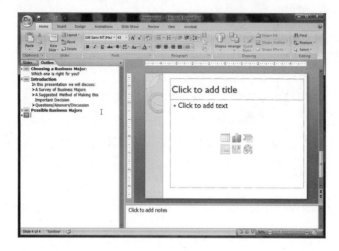

PPT Figure 1-42: Adding a slide using Outline view.

3. With the cursor still in the Outline view, type the title *Accounting* for the slide (PPT Figure 1-43).

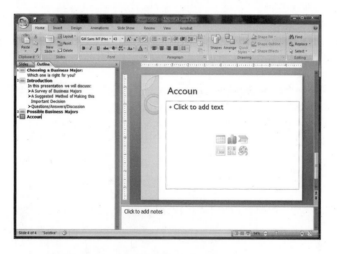

PPT Figure 1-43: Typing the slide title.

Notice that, while you type in the Outline view, what you are typing is entered into the title area on the slide.

4. Let's use the Outline view to add text content in the body of the slide.

After typing the slide title, press the Enter key.

Whoa! What happened! A new slide was created, as shown in PPT Figure 1-44, but we wanted to work with the same slide.

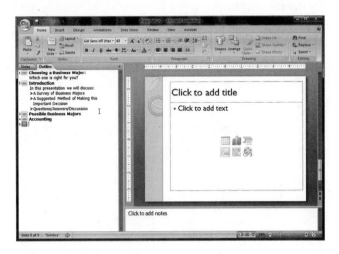

PPT Figure 1-44: A new slide in Outline view.

What's needed is to demote this new slide a level.

5. With the cursor placed just after the new slide icon, press the Tab key.

You should see the cursor move over slightly and the slide returned to the Accounting slide.

You could have also used the Increase Level command to achieve this.

The Shift-Tab key combination will move the level in the other direction.

Now you can type text in outline view that will be entered into the body of the slide.

In PPT Figure 1-45, we have added text describing an Accounting major and slide titles for other business majors.

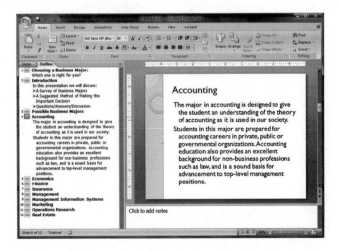

PPT Figure 1-45: Adding text to the body of the slide.

Saving Your Presentation

The process of saving your file works the same in most all of the Office software packages. In case you haven't seen this in action, we'll review it here.

1. Click on the Microsoft Office button in the upper left of the PowerPoint window.

    You'll see the menu displayed in PPT Figure 1-46.

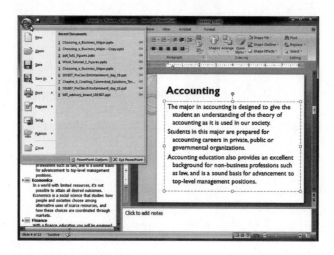

PPT Figure 1-46: The Microsoft Office button menu.

This menu includes commands that are more or less common to all Office software.

2. Click the Save As menu option.

    A list of available saving options will be presented to you.

    Note that you might save your file to be compatible with older versions of PowerPoint or as an Adobe PDF file.

    We'll simply choose PowerPoint Presentation as shown in PPT Figure 1-47.

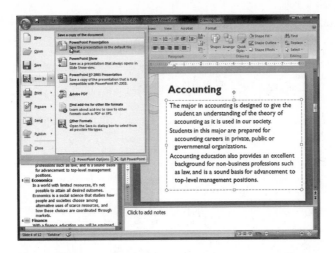

PPT Figure 1-47: Saving as a PowerPoint presentation.

3. The Save As dialog will appear as shown in PPT Figure 1-48.

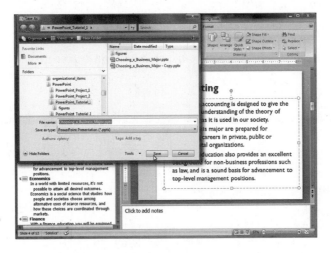

PPT Figure 1-48: The Save As dialog.

With the dialog you can choose the location where you want to save the file and one of many file formats using the Save as Type options.

You can also name your file.

For now, navigate to a folder where you want to save the file and give it a name.

Click the Save button.

4. If it is the first time a file of that name has been saved at that location, the file will be saved, and you will be returned to PowerPoint.

If a file already exists of that name, then you will be prompted as shown in PPT Figure 1-49.

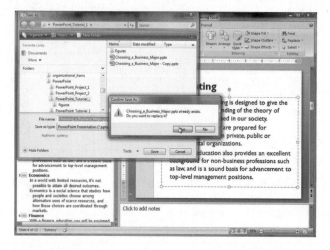

PPT Figure 1-49: Confirm Save As dialog.

Choose wisely whether you want to replace the current file.

You can always choose a different name for the current file if you aren't sure.

USING POWERPOINT HELP

An important feature of the Microsoft Office software suite is the extension collection of definitions, how-to's, and explanations that make up Office Help. When you get stuck or you're having a problem remembering how to do something, your first thought should be: "Maybe I can find something about this in Office Help!" Although Help looks and works the same in all of the Office products, the content is generally specific to the software that you are currently using. Let's see how we can use Office Help in PowerPoint.

1. You can access the Help feature by clicking the Help icon in the upper-right corner of the PowerPoint window (PPT Figure 1-50).

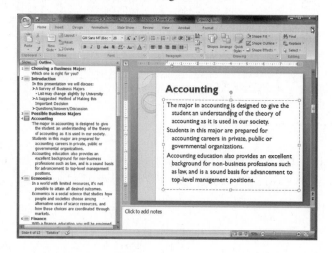

PPT Figure 1-50: The Office Help button.

2. The first page that you will see in PowerPoint Help is a table of contents listing the main categories of Help information.

    You can browse to a topic by selecting the most likely category and then clicking the link to drill down to find the topic of interest.

    In PPT Figure 1-51, we are selecting the category Creating a Presentation.

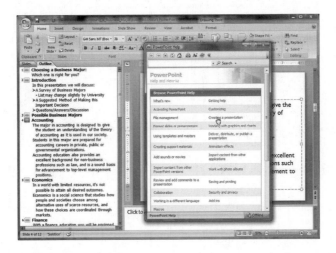

PPT Figure 1-51: The PowerPoint Help table of contents.

3. Within each category, you'll find a list of subtopics.

    Scroll through the list and click on the most likely link to your topic of interest.

    In PPT Figure 1-52, we are selecting the topic Delete a Slide.

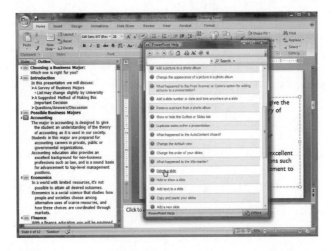

PPT Figure 1-52: Browsing through PowerPoint Help.

4. Eventually (after two or three clicks) you will reach a page with information about your topic of interest.

Most entries will also include links to pages of related information (PPT Figure 1-53).

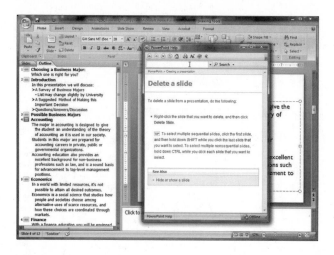

PPT Figure 1-53: The Help entry for how to delete a slide.

5. If browsing the Help pages is not your style, you can also enter keywords into the search box and search for your topic of interest.

   Try searching for how to *insert a table* as shown in PPT Figure 1-54.

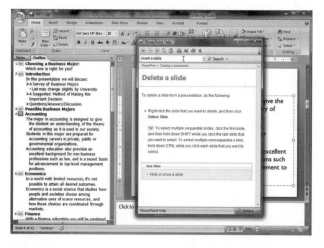

PPT Figure 1-54: Entering a Help search term.

6. A list of links that are related to your search terms will be displayed (PPT Figure 1-55).

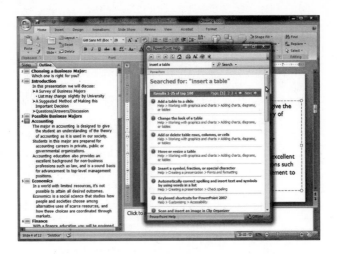

PPT Figure 1-55: Help search results.

From this point, you're back to browsing and clicking the links until you find what you are looking for.

While there is a large amount of information built into PowerPoint, if you are connected to the Internet, you will also have access to Help online, which is even more extensive and often more up to date.

EXERCISES TO BUILD YOUR KNOWLEDGE OF MS POWERPOINT

Match the term on the left with the appropriate description on the right:

_____1. Notes area

    a. The left pane of the PowerPoint window, where you can see a listing of the slides in your presentation.

_____2. PowerPoint Help

    b. Used to demote content from a high list level such as a slide title to a lower list level such as slide content.

_____3. Shift-Tab

    c. The primary window where you design your slides.

_____4. Current slide workspace

    d. A set of built-in templates that are used to define positioning and formatting for content that will later appear on a slide.

_____5. Slide layout

    e. A collection of templates that provide a visual representation of your information.

_____6. Slide preview area

    f. A set of formatting choices that include a set of colors, a set of fonts, and a set of effects.

_____7. SmartArt

g. Provides information on the status of the PowerPoint such as the number of slides in the presentation and the design themes used.

_____8. Status bar

h. Allows you to adjust the display size of the workspace quickly.

_____9. Themes

i. A large knowledge base available to you with PowerPoint that can assist you in finding out how to do anything that you want in PowerPoint.

_____10. Zoom control

j. An area where you can enter speaker notes for the current slide.

Fill in the blank with the PowerPoint ribbon and group that is home to each of the following commands. You'll have to look for them because we have not discussed some of them yet.

Command	Ribbon	Group
11. Arrange		
12. Effects		
13. Layout		
14. Movie		
15. New Comment		
16. Record Narration		
17. Shapes		
18. Slide Sorter		
19. Transition Sound		
20. WordArt		

Practice by using PowerPoint to expand your knowledge:

21. Create a presentation with at least two slides. Be sure that there are both text and pictures. What else you put on them is your choice. Practice using keyboard shortcuts (see Help) to speed up your work. For example, highlighting text and pressing the Ctrl key while holding down the B key will boldface text. Perhaps the most important keyboard shortcut is Ctrl plus S. What does this do? Create a third slide that lists at least six more keyboard shortcuts that you discovered. Save your file.

22. After completing the preceding item, add a blank slide to your presentation. On this slide you will experiment with the Illustrations group on the Insert ribbon and discover that a PowerPoint slide can have more layers than a cake!

On the Insert ribbon, click the Shapes command in the Illustrations group. Select a rectangle from the Rectangles group on the drop-down menu or an oval from the Basic Shapes group. Add some shapes to your slide. Also add a text box by selecting Text Box from the Basic Shapes group. Now use some the options on the Format ribbon, which appears whenever a shape is selected. You can change the stacking order of shapes using the commands in the Arrange group. You can fill the shapes in with different colors using commands in the Shape Styles group.

What happens to your shapes when you select an object and then use "Send to Back" or "Bring to Front"? Can you use layering and colors to create different shapes and effects? Try it!

POWERPOINT TUTORIAL 1: MINI-CASE 1

Scenario: Oscar Tabb and several of his friends are taking a careers seminar from his university's career center. After investigating the various business majors available, Oscar has decided to major in Information Systems (IS). He is excited about all of the possible jobs he can have after he graduates, but he is unsure which one might be right for him. He knows that internships are a great way to learn about working in IS, and several companies are offering internships for next summer. Oscar plans to apply for several internships to jump-start his IS career planning. As a part of his careers seminar, Oscar needs to create a presentation that highlights five companies for which he might like to intern. Oscar decided to use PowerPoint to create his presentation.

Your Task: Create a PowerPoint presentation to present to your class that highlights five companies who hire entry-level IS professionals and who offer internships (*there is no file to download for this mini-case*). You should choose companies that you might like to intern with/work for regardless of your personal choice of major. Almost every company hires IS professionals to help it create business value, so it's likely that a company that you want to work for will be one that you can use to complete the tasks listed below.

- Think about the purpose, content, and audience of your presentation. Select a slide design that supports the effective communication of your message to your target audience.
- You should create a title slide that includes the title of your presentation, your name, and the date. Center all of your information. The title of your presentation should be in a larger font than your name and the date.
- For each of the five companies you've chosen, create a bulleted-text slide that contains the name of the company, one fact about the company, and why you are interested in the company. Also include a URL to the part of each company's Web site where internships are listed or described.
- On the next to last slide, add bullets that will give the class an idea of what criteria you will use to decide which internships to apply for.
- The last slide should be a summary of what you've presented.

- Don't forget to save the file when you complete your work.
- If you are not sure how to do some of the above tasks, be sure to use PowerPoint Help to find out how.

POWERPOINT TUTORIAL 1: MINI-CASE 2

Scenario: You have just started your job with Acme Products, Inc. Your boss, Ms. Bertille Canis-Latrans, has asked you to familiarize yourself with the new products in the catalog. In fact, she not only wants you to know about the products, but also wants you to create a presentation about them for an upcoming Acme marketing meeting to be held in Phoenix, Arizona. If you do a good job on the presentation, Ms. Canis-Latrans promises to take you with her to the meeting.

Your Task: Create a PowerPoint presentation to describe one of your company's products. You can base your presentation on any product that you are familiar with and use. Your presentation should briefly describe the product, the user problems it solves, and the audience for which it is intended. You should also outline different models or options available. Be sure to incorporate the following content in your presentation:

- You should create a title slide that includes the title of your presentation, your name, and the date. Center all of your information. The title of your presentation should be in a larger font than your name and the date.
- Include an overview slide that lists the topics that you will discuss.
- Use two or more slides to outline the features of your product. Be sure to group features into logical categories and to state the user benefit of each feature.
- Try to use a real user example to discuss how the product or service can be used by different groups.
- Provide relevant technical specifications, using as many slides as necessary.
- Provide pricing and availability information.
- The last slide should be a summary of what you've presented.
- Don't forget to save the file when you complete your work.
- If you are not sure how to do some of the above tasks, be sure to use PowerPoint Help to find out how.

Tutorial 2

USING GRAPHICS, ANIMATION, AND MULTIMEDIA IN MICROSOFT POWERPOINT 2007

After reading this tutorial and completing the associated exercises, you will be able to:

- Increase interest in your slides by adding graphic elements.
- Create a figure using the Drawing toolbar.
- Add motion using animation and transitions in slide shows.
- Apply "Best Practices" rules to your PowerPoint presentations.

INCREASING INTEREST WITH MULTIMEDIA ELEMENTS

You can increase interest in your presentation by adding multimedia elements to slides. By **multimedia**, we mean all types of nontextual elements, including graphics like those you used in the first PowerPoint tutorial, photos, animations, charts, tables, diagrams, objects, and hyperlinks, as well as video and sound. You can also create your own graphics using components from the Drawing group on the Home ribbon. In this section, we will discuss how to add these various elements to our example presentation.

Adding Clip Art to Slides

PowerPoint comes with a large collection of clip art: graphic images or symbols that can be inserted into your document. In terms of visual complexity, clip art is usually much simpler than a photograph or a complex graphic design. The collection of clip art that is provided with PowerPoint is quite extensive and is divided into thematic categories. You can browse within a particular category, or you can use a search capability to find images that match your keyword. Although the installed clip art library is extensive, you can find even more online at the Microsoft Office Web site. Let's add clip art to our presentation.

1. The Accounting slide from our business majors presentation is displayed in PPT Figure 2-1.

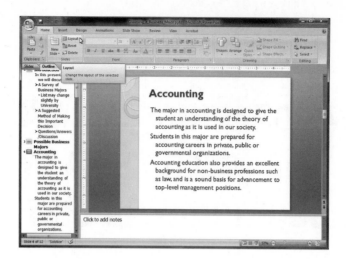

PPT Figure 2-1: A slide to edit.

We'd like to add a piece of clip art to this slide, but there doesn't seem to be enough space.

One solution would be to adjust the slide layout for additional content.

The Layout command is located in the Slides group of the Home ribbon.

2. Click the small arrow next to the Layout command to access the layout options for the current theme (in this case, Solstice) as shown in PPT Figure 2-2.

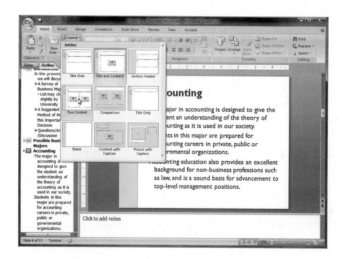

PPT Figure 2-2: Selecting a new layout.

Select the Two Content option, since we would like a second content component.

3. The current content will be included in one of the content areas, as shown in PPT Figure 2-3. Note that we will want to adjust it to fit.

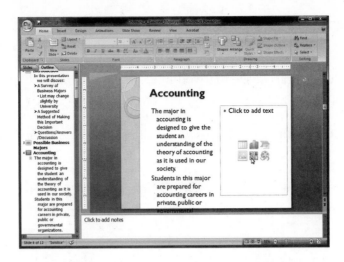

PPT Figure 2-3: The Two Content layout.

A second content area is now available for us. Let's add clip art to this second area.

Click on the clip art icon in the center of the bottom row in the content area.

4. The Clip Art dialog window will appear docked on the right side of the PowerPoint window.

The Clip Art dialog provides several options.

Possibly, the most useful option is the Search for: text box.

You can type in a keyword and then search for images that are somehow related.

Type the word *business* in the Search for: text box, as shown in PPT Figure 2-4, and click Go.

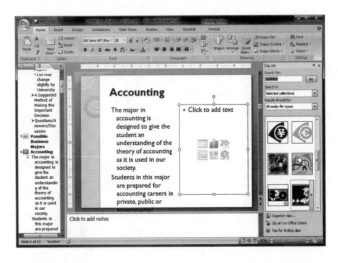

PPT Figure 2-4: The Clip Art dialog docked.

5. After a moment, images from the collection will be displayed in the preview window.

When you find an image that you like, simply double-click the image to insert it into your page.

Your selected clip art will appear on the slide, centered in the content area, as shown in PPT Figure 2-5.

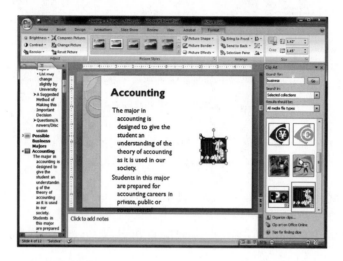

PPT Figure 2-5: Inserting a clip art graphic.

6. You may prefer a larger image.

Notice that a new Format ribbon is provided that will let you format the clip art.

You could adjust the size there, or you could simply grab one of the sizing handles (small boxes around the edge of the image) and drag it to the preferred size, as shown in PPT Figure 2-6.

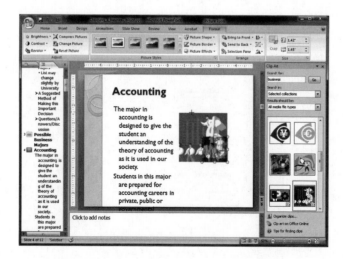

PPT Figure 2-6: Resizing the clip art.

7. We'd also like to adjust the text on the slide.

   Click the text content area to select it.

   You can tell that the entire area is selected when the line around the boundary is a solid line as shown in PPT Figure 2-7.

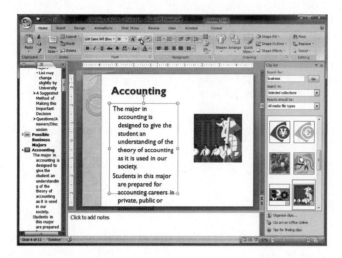

PPT Figure 2-7: Adjusting the text size.

Now use the font decrease command in the Font group to adjust the text to fit.

8. The completed slide with clip art is shown in PPT Figure 2-8.

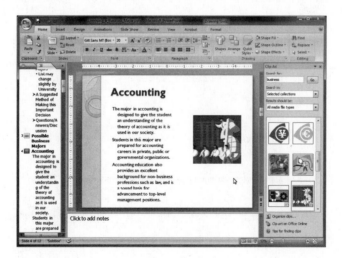

PPT Figure 2-8: The completed slide with clip art.

Drawing in PowerPoint

PowerPoint includes some powerful features for creating your own drawings. Most of these commands are available on the Home ribbon in the Drawing group, but they can also be found on a special Drawing Tools Format ribbon, once you've started a drawing, and on the context-sensitive menu for some objects.

For our example, assume these are the steps to be followed to select a business major:[1]

1. Start process by thinking about your interests in business.

2. Review information on the various majors.

3. Select a major to which to apply.

4. Go through application process.

5. If accepted into desired major, go to Step 6; otherwise go back to Step 2.

6. Take classes in major required for graduation.

7. Graduate!

We'll use this decision process as the basis for drawing a flowchart on a slide in our example presentation. Fasten your seatbelt. This is going to be a longer ride than usual.

1. Start by inserting a slide at the end of your current presentation as shown in PPT Figure 2-9.

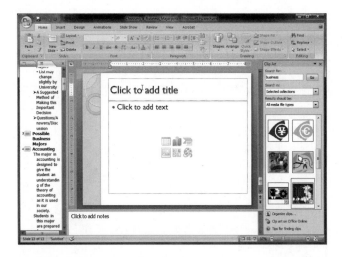

PPT Figure 2-9: A new slide for our drawing.

Change the layout to Title Only, because the content for this slide will be a drawing that we will create.

---

[1]This is *not* meant to be a representation of the major selection process at any specific college or university; just a general process for this decision.

Add the title *Choosing a Major.*

2. Most of the commands that we will be using are found in the Drawing group of the Home ribbon.

   Click the arrow under the Shapes command.

   You may see this as a collection of shapes. If so, then click the More arrow (the lowest of the three arrows at the right of the collection).

   You'll now see the complete list of predrawn shapes available in PowerPoint, as shown in PPT Figure 2-10.

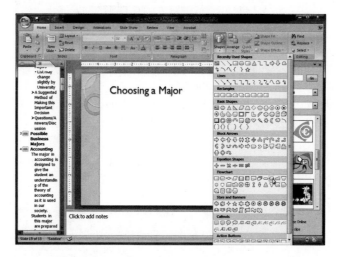

PPT Figure 2-10: The Shapes collection.

3. Notice that one of the Shapes categories is labeled Flowchart.

   Browse the shapes in the Flowchart category until you find and click on the shape labeled Preparation.

   Now, use the mouse to draw a rectangle on the slide at the location where you want the new shape.

Try to locate the shape like that shown in PPT Figure 2-11.

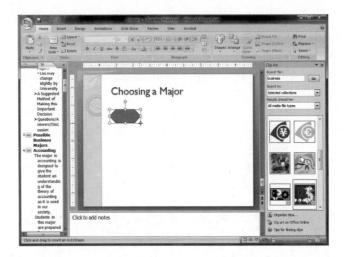

PPT Figure 2-11: Adding the Preparation flowchart shape.

4. With the shape selected (click on it to select it again if needed), start typing the label *Start Process.*

You should see that the words you are typing start to appear within the shape as shown in PPT Figure 2-12.

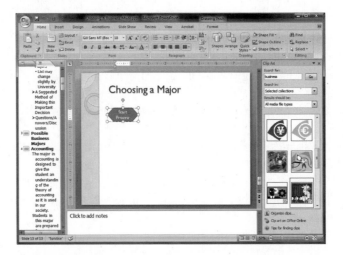

PPT Figure 2-12: Typing a label within a shape.

The shape was created initially using a default style that fits with the presentation theme.

Using Quick Styles, you can quickly adjust the shape's style as discussed in the next step.

5. With the shape selected, click the Quick Styles command from the Drawing group.

You'll see a palette of shape styles to choose from.

For the shape in PPT Figure 2-13, we used the style labeled Light 1 Outline, Colored Fill–Accent 1.

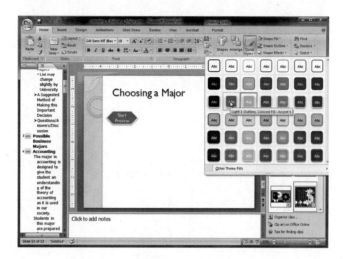

PPT Figure 2-13: Selecting a Quick Style.

6. Flowcharts are good for showing the steps for getting something done.

   Once we begin, we need to include steps that actually do something.

   To that end, let's add the shape for a Flowchart: Alternate Process, as shown in PPT Figure 2-14.

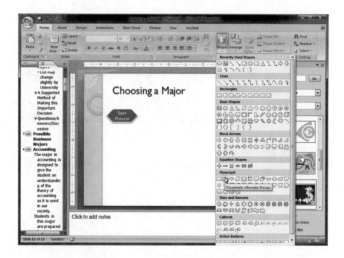

PPT Figure 2-14: Adding another shape.

7. Place the Alternate Process shape just to the right of the Preparation shape, as shown in PPT Figure 2-15.

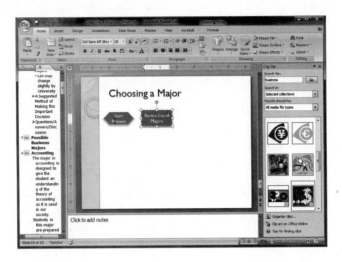

PPT Figure 2-15: The Alternate Process shape.

Type the label *Review List of Majors* into the new shape.

Use the Quick Styles command to make the shape style match the previous shape.

8. We need a few more processes in the flowchart (three, to be exact).

We could take the time to create them as before, but we could also save a little time by copying the process we already have.

Right-click on the process shape and choose Copy on the context-sensitive menu, as shown in PPT Figure 2-16.

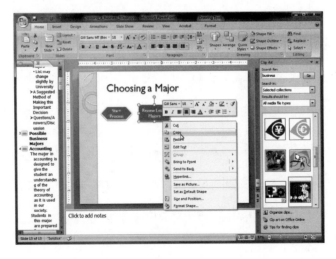

PPT Figure 2-16: Copying a shape.

9. Now right-click somewhere on the slide.

This time, choose Paste from the context-sensitive menu that appears, as shown in PPT Figure 2-17.

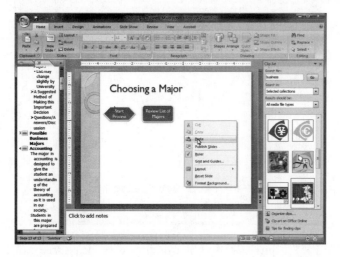

PPT Figure 2-17: Pasting a copied shape from the Clipboard.

10. Notice that the pasted shape will appear almost right on top of the original copy, as shown in PPT Figure 2-18.

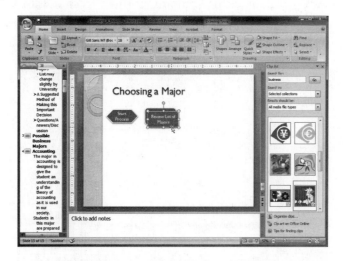

PPT Figure 2-18: The pasted shape.

Click on the shape and drag it to where you want to place it.

11. Move it over to the right in line with the other two shapes.

Highlight the existing text and then type *Select Major.*

Your drawing so far should appear as shown in PPT Figure 2-19.

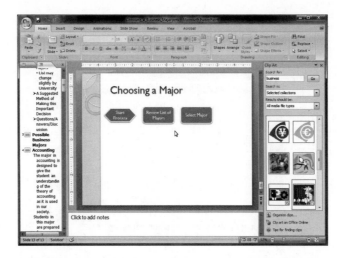

PPT Figure 2-19: The drawing with three shapes.

12. Let's select the three drawing objects to adjust their alignment.

To select all of the objects, click just above and to the side of one of the objects and drag to create a rectangle that contains all three, as shown in PPT Figure 2-20.

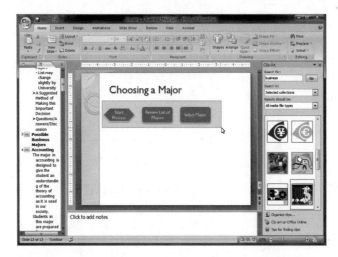

PPT Figure 2-20: Selecting more than one drawing object.

When you let the mouse button go, all of the objects that were enclosed in the rectangle will be selected.

13. It may be that your shapes are not quite aligned correctly.

Not to worry—there are some easy ways to correct this.

With all three shapes selected click the Arrange command.

Notice that you can adjust the order, grouping, and positioning of objects using the options here.

Select Align, and then select Align Middle from the submenu, as shown in PPT Figure 2-21.

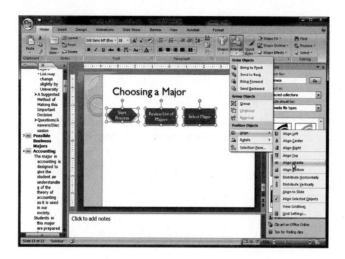

PPT Figure 2-21: Aligning objects.

14. The Align submenu also includes commands for distributing your components equally either horizontally or vertically.

    With the three shapes still selected, select the Distribute Horizontally command from the Align submenu, as shown in PPT Figure 2-22.

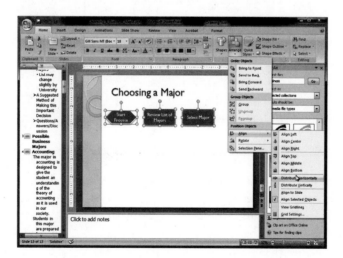

PPT Figure 2-22: Distributing objects.

15. Your shapes should now appear as shown in PPT Figure 2-23.

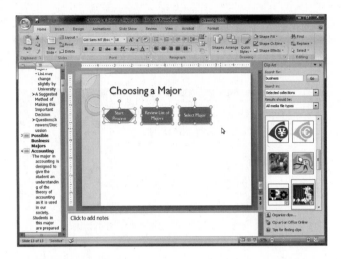

PPT Figure 2-23: Aligned and distributed shapes.

The shapes are aligned vertically and distributed equally across a horizontal middle line.

16. Go ahead and add the shapes shown in PPT Figure 2-24.

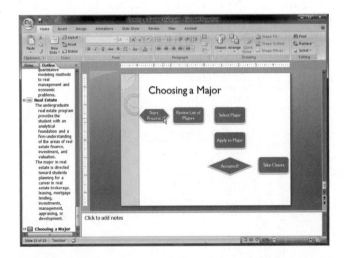

PPT Figure 2-24: Final shapes for the flowchart.

Be sure to make sure that their style is compatible with the existing shapes.

Also, make sure that the shapes are well aligned.

Select one of the shapes in our drawing.

17. Notice that when one or more shapes are selected, there is a special ribbon, Format (under Drawing Tools), with commands for working with a drawing.

We need some arrows connecting our drawing, so let's click on the arrow in the Insert Shapes group of this ribbon, as shown in PPT Figure 2-25.

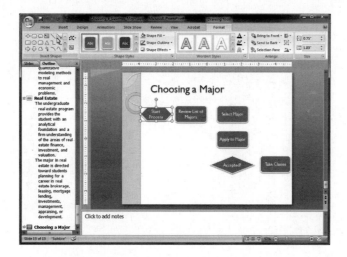

PPT Figure 2-25: The Format ribbon.

We want to use arrows both to connect the shapes in our drawing and to illustrate the order in which one would move through the decision process.

18. An arrow is a drawing object that can act as a connector between other shapes.

   While a connector is being inserted, red indicators appear on the currently selected shape as shown in PPT Figure 2-26.

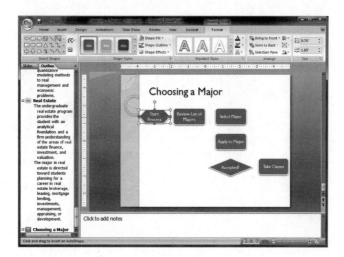

PPT Figure 2-26: Connection point indicators.

The red squares indicate connection points that are available on the selected shape.

19. Click the rightmost connection point of the Preparation shape.

Then drag to make an arrow connector to the leftmost connector of the first process, as shown in PPT Figure 2-27.

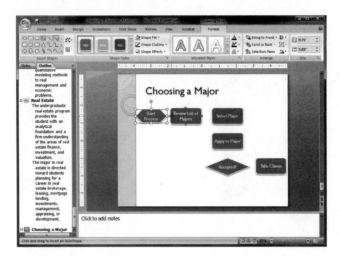

PPT Figure 2-27: Adding a connection arrow.

Notice that, as you approach the next shape, the red connection indicators will appear on that shape.

20. The inserted arrow is shown in PPT Figure 2-28.

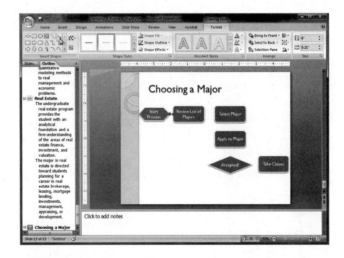

PPT Figure 2-28: The inserted connection arrow.

21. Use the arrow connector to add the arrows shown in PPT Figure 2-29.

Be sure to note that one of the arrows uses a slightly different type of arrow connection than the others.

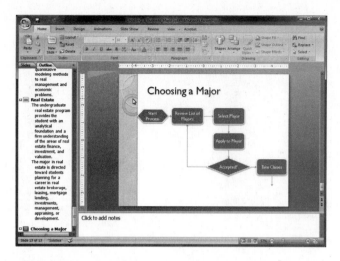

PPT Figure 2-29: Arrows connecting the flowchart components.

22. We'd like to add some more components to the chart later, but it's getting kind of crowded.

    Use the mouse to trace a rectangle around the entire drawing to select everything as shown in PPT Figure 2-30.

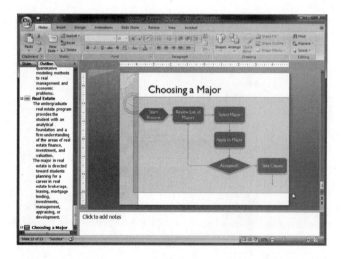

PPT Figure 2-30: Selecting the entire flowchart.

    You can tell that everything is selected by the presence of sizing and moving handles (little boxes) on the edge of each component.

23. With the entire set of drawing components selected, use the mouse to drag the flowchart up and over to the left, as shown in PPT Figure 2-31.

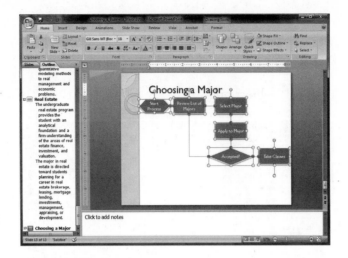

PPT Figure 2-31: Moving the flowchart components as a group.

If you see that you've left some components behind, first undo the move and then reselect everything, making sure that your rectangle includes all components this time.

24. You may also want to move the title of the slide up a little higher.

At this point, your slide should look like that shown in PPT Figure 2-32.

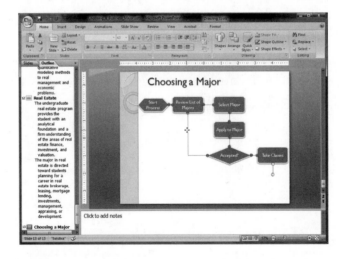

PPT Figure 2-32: The repositioned slide components.

Let's select the arrows to make them a little thicker.

First, select one arrow.

Then, hold down the Ctrl key and click on another to select it.

Notice that both arrows are now selected.

25. Using the mouse and Ctrl key in combination, select all of the arrows.

    Now, right-click on a selected arrow to get the context-sensitive menu.

    Select the Format Object option as shown in PPT Figure 2-33.

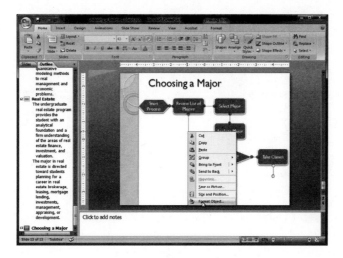

PPT Figure 2-33: Context-sensitive menu for the arrows.

26. You should now see the Format Shape dialog.

    The commands found here may also be found on the Drawing Tools Format ribbon.

    Use whichever you find most convenient.

    Adjust the Line Style Width, as shown in PPT Figure 2-34, until it is set to 3 pt.

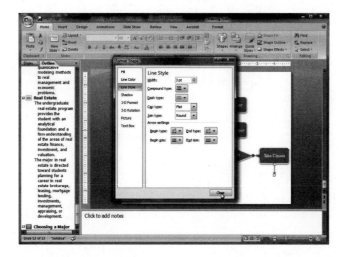

PPT Figure 2-34: Adjusting line style of arrows.

27. Your drawing should now look as shown in PPT Figure 2-35 with the thicker arrows.

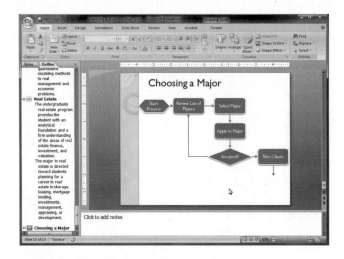

PPT Figure 2-35: The drawing with thicker arrows.

28. We can also apply Quick Styles to the arrows.

Select all of the arrows again and then click the Quick Styles command on the Format ribbon.

Notice in PPT Figure 2-36 that the shapes shown on the Quick Styles options have changed to reflect the type of object selected.

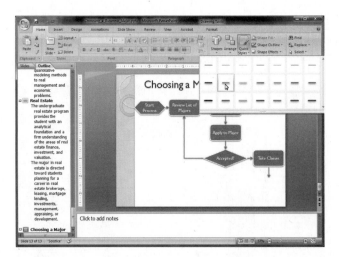

PPT Figure 2-36: Using Quick Styles with arrow objects.

Select a compatible style for the drawing.

29. The latest version of the drawing with thicker, more stylish arrows is shown in PPT Figure 2-37.

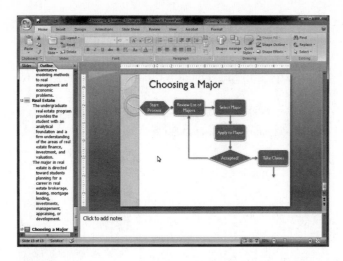

PPT Figure 2-37: The latest version of the drawing.

Adding a Picture from a File

In addition to drawings and clip art, we will often want to add graphics stored in files. These might be drawings created with another graphics program or photographs. We can add images stored in just about any of the common graphics file formats in use today to a PowerPoint slide. Let's see how to do that by adding an image from a file to our Flowchart drawing.

1. Make sure that the Flowchart slide is the current slide.

   Now, find the Picture command in the Illustrations section of the Insert ribbon, as shown in PPT Figure 2-38, and click it.

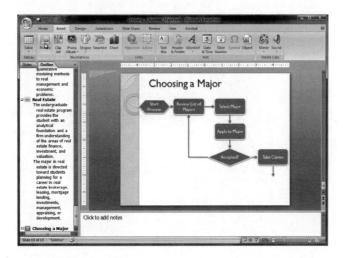

PPT Figure 2-38: The Insert Picture command.

2. The Insert Picture dialog will appear.

   This dialog works just like the Open File dialog.

Navigate to the location on your computer's storage where the picture file is located.

Select the picture file and then click on the Insert button, as shown in PPT Figure 2-39.

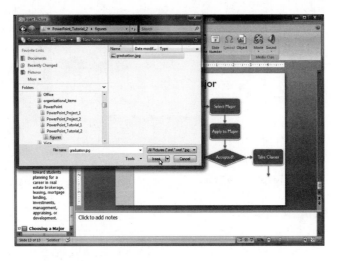

PPT Figure 2-39: Locating the picture file.

3. PowerPoint will read the image file and insert the image onto the slide.

Typically, the image will be inserted in the center of the slide, as shown in PPT Figure 2-40.

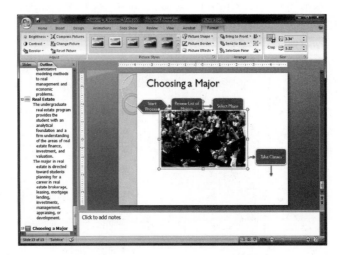

PPT Figure 2-40: The inserted image.

Its size will depend on the stored size of the image.

We want to shrink the image and then place it in the lower right corner below that "arrow to nowhere" in the drawing.

4. With the picture selected, move the cursor over the image.

The cursor should change shape to appear as a cross with arrows on its endpoints.

This is a signal that if you click and hold, then you can drag the object around on the slide.

Go ahead and move it to the lower right corner, as shown in PPT Figure 2-41.

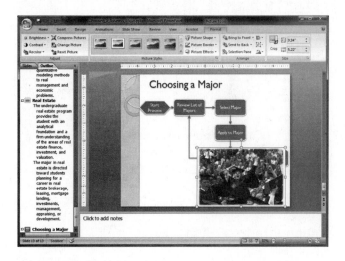

PPT Figure 2-41: Moving the picture object.

5. The shape of the cursor can be a signal that PowerPoint is ready to perform other functions as well.

With the picture still selected, place the cursor over the sizing handle in the upper left corner.

The cursor is now a double-sided arrow pointing in the directions in which you can adjust the image size, as shown in PPT Figure 2-42.

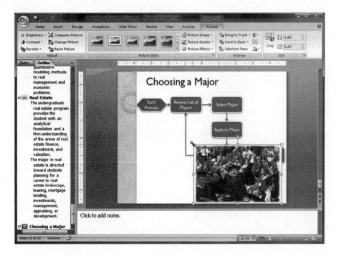

PPT Figure 2-42: Adjusting picture size.

6. Click on the sizing handle and drag the cursor until the image is about the size shown in PPT Figure 2-43.

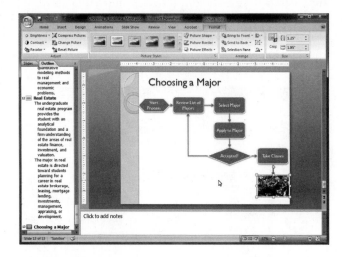

PPT Figure 2-43: Decreasing the picture size.

Inserting Other Components to a Slide

As with a picture from a file, there are several things that we can insert on a slide available on the Insert ribbon. Have a look at this ribbon to see what is available. Our drawing is almost complete, but we need a few text labels. Let's see how we can add text to our drawing by adding a text box.

1. The current drawing with the inserted picture is shown in PPT Figure 2-44.

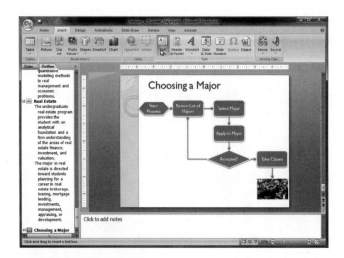

PPT Figure 2-44: Drawing with inserted picture.

Let's add a label just below the graduation picture.

A text box is a convenient way to add text in the default theme format.

With the slide with our drawing current, click the Text Box command on the Insert ribbon.

2. Now click somewhere on the slide near where you want the inserted text to appear.

   A small box with a flashing cursor will appear, waiting for you to enter some text, as shown in PPT Figure 2-45.

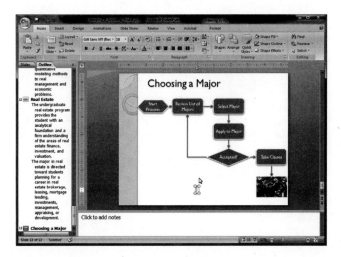

PPT Figure 2-45: The inserted, waiting text box.

The line around the box and the sizing handles are convenient while working with the text box, but they will typically disappear when the text box is not selected.

You can, however, adjust the format of the text box to display the boundary line if desired.

3. Type the phrase *Graduate!*

As you type, the characters will appear within the text box, as shown in PPT Figure 2-46.

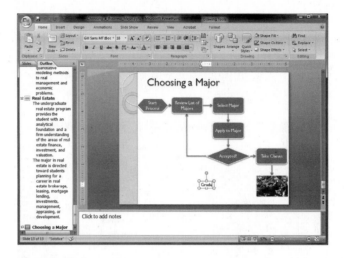

PPT Figure 2-46: Adding text to the text box.

4. With the text box selected, move it just below the graduation picture, as shown in PPT Figure 2-47.

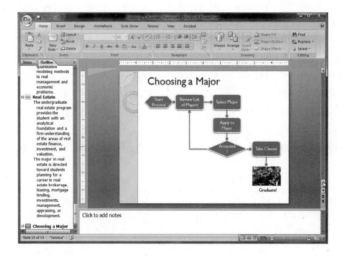

PPT Figure 2-47: The almost completed drawing.

Are there any other labels needed for this drawing?

If so, go ahead and add them where needed.

Inserting a Table

Another useful visual display of information is a table. With PowerPoint, you can create a table from scratch, or you can insert one from another source, such as Word, Excel, or Access. In the following example, we'll see how to create a table from scratch to add a slide showing the top job positions in terms of expected growth rate.

1. To start, insert a new Title and Content slide somewhere in the presentation.

    Add the title *Career Growth Rate* to the slide.

    In the content area, click on the icon that represents a table, as shown in PPT Figure 2-48.

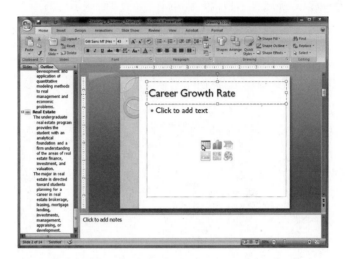

PPT Figure 2-48: A new slide for the table.

Alternatively, you could insert a table through the command on the Insert ribbon.

2. The Insert Table dialog will appear, prompting you to enter the number of rows and columns to create in the table.

    We need a table with 2 columns and about 20 rows, as shown in PPT Figure 2-49.

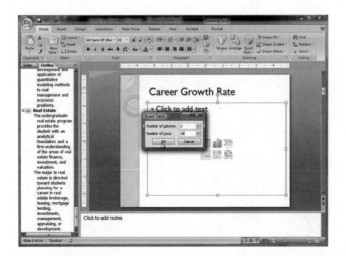

PPT Figure 2-49: The Insert Table dialog.

3. A table will now be inserted.

The style of the table is chosen automatically to complement the theme of your presentation.

Note from PPT Figure 2-50 that two additional ribbons are now available: Design and Layout, both under Table Tools.

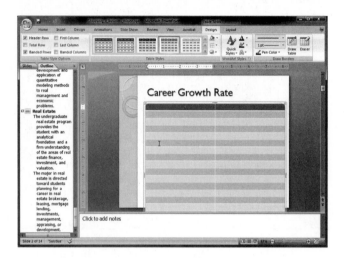

PPT Figure 2-50: The inserted table.

You can use commands on these ribbons to alter how the table looks.

4. Assuming that we like the table design, we now just need to add data to the table.

Simply click in a cell and type.

In PPT Figure 2-51, we are in the midst of entering the column headings *Job* and *Percentage Growth Rate*.

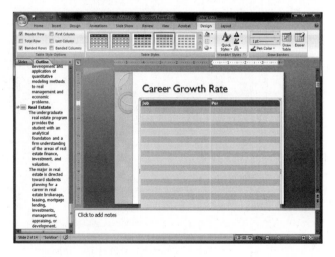

PPT Figure 2-51: Adding column headings.

5. Go ahead and add the data shown in PPT Figure 2-52.

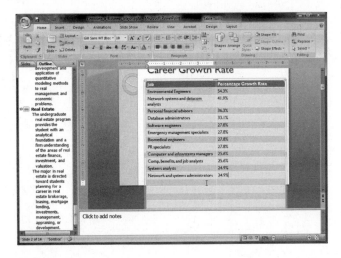

PPT Figure 2-52: Adding data to the table.

For adding data to the table, you can select each table cell by clicking in it.

Alternatively, you can press Tab and Shift-Tab or the arrow keys on the keyboard to move between table cells.

6. It turns out that we have more rows than we need.

Let's delete a few of these.

One way to do this is to highlight the rows for deletion first, then right-click.

You can now choose the Delete Rows option on the context-sensitive menu as shown in PPT Figure 2-53.

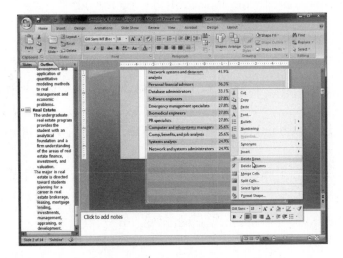

PPT Figure 2-53: Deleting table rows.

Where else do you think you might find this command?

Be sure to note the other options available here for future use.

7. The final table is shown in PPT Figure 2-54.

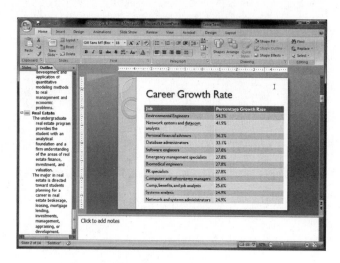

PPT Figure 2-54: The final table.

Try experimenting with the design and layout commands on the Table Tools ribbons until you have a table that you can be proud of.

Adding Audio to Your Presentation

Text and images are not the only way to present information. You may want to incorporate richer forms of media such as audio or video. In general, audio and video clips will be stored in separate files and will need to be inserted into your presentation. Both types of media can be inserted in much the same way. Here, we'll show you how to add an audio file to your presentation. We'll leave experimentation with video up to you.

1. Make the presentation title slide the current slide.

    We'll add an audio file that will be set to play automatically when this slide is displayed in slide show view.

    You'll find the Sound command in the Media Clips group of the Insert ribbon.

    Click the small arrow at the bottom of the command to see the options that you have for adding audio to a presentation.

    Select Sound From File... (PPT Figure 2-55).

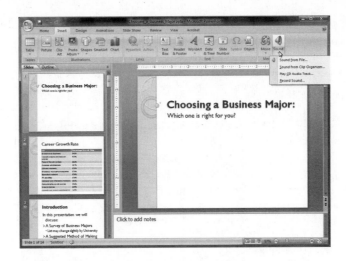

PPT Figure 2-55: The Sound command.

2. The Insert Sound dialog will appear.

    Look familiar? This is the standard file navigation dialog that you have used to open a PowerPoint file or to search for a picture file to insert.

    If you have a sound file, navigate to it, select it (as shown in PPT Figure 2-56), and then click OK.

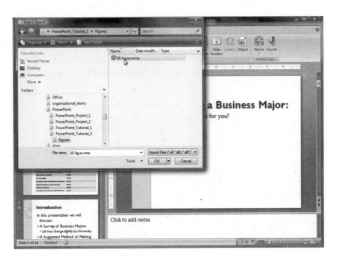

PPT Figure 2-56: The Insert Sound dialog.

3. A question box will appear asking how you want the audio file to start.

    You can choose to have it start automatically or wait of the presenter to click it.

For our presentation, we will select to have the audio file start playing automatically, as shown in PPT Figure 2-57.

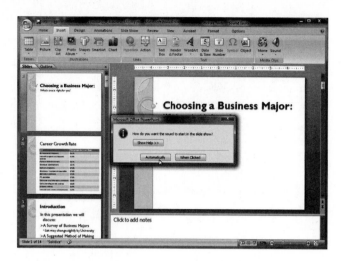

PPT Figure 2-57: Insert Sound question box.

4. A small icon in the shape of an audio speaker will appear on the slide.

This icon represents the audio object that you have just inserted (PPT Figure 2-58).

PPT Figure 2-58: The PowerPoint sound object icon.

By default, this will appear only while you are editing the presentation and will not appear during the slide show.

5. When the audio object is selected, you'll see an Options ribbon under Sound Tools.

This ribbon, shown in PPT Figure 2-59, includes commands that allow you to adjust how the audio file will appear on the slide and how it will play.

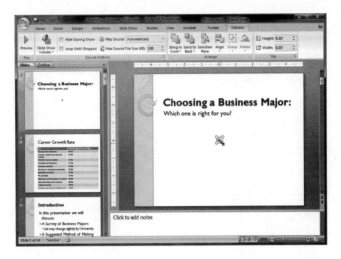

PPT Figure 2-59: The Sound Tools Options ribbon.

Take a moment to familiarize yourself with the commands available on this ribbon.

MAKING YOUR SLIDES MOVE

Another way to make your presentations more interesting and dynamic is through the use of transitions and animations. A **transition** refers to the manner in which the contents of slides will appear as you move from one slide to the next. Transitions can include a variety of effects with which the text and images are displayed when a new slide is displayed. With a transition, all of the elements of a slide are displayed in the same manner.

Animation, on the other hand, refers to the use of action or motion within a slide and can affect some or all of the elements of a slide. Transitions are generally set to occur automatically when a new slide is displayed, while animations must be activated by some action, usually a mouse click. Both transitions and animations can be applied to single slide or to all slides, and they can be combined.

Working with Transitions

1. Make the slide for which you want to add a transition the current slide.

You'll find the Transition to This Slide group on the Animations ribbon, shown in PPT Figure 2-60.

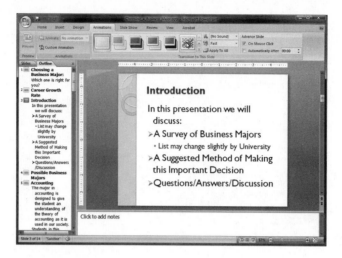

PPT Figure 2-60: The Animations ribbon.

As the name of the group implies, you can adjust how a transition is made as the slide show progresses from the previous slide to this one.

Try selecting a transition, such as Dissolve, shown in the figure.

2. When you place the cursor over one of the transition styles you'll see a preview of it with the slide.

We caught the slide in the middle of the Dissolve transition in PPT Figure 2-61.

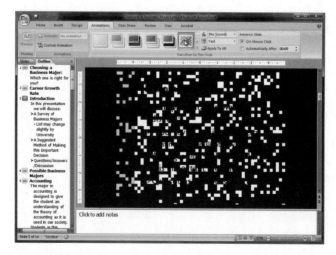

PPT Figure 2-61: The Dissolve transition.

3. After the transition preview, the slide will return to edit mode.

Note the other options available in the Transition to This Slide group, such as the transition speed, whether the transition is accompanied by a sound, and when the transition will occur.

Click the More arrow beside the transitions listed to see the full transition library, as shown in PPT Figure 2-62.

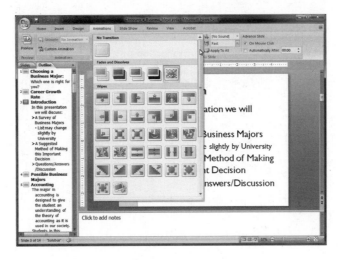

PPT Figure 2-62: The transition library.

4. The transition library is broken down into categories named for a general transition behavior.

Again, a preview of the slide transition will be shown as you select from the group.

Try a few and select one that you like for the slide.

In PPT Figure 2-63, we've chosen Cover Left from the Push and Cover category.

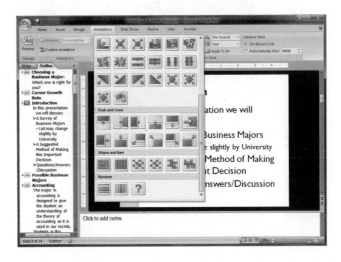

PPT Figure 2-63: Selecting a transition.

5. After selecting the transition, let's set the transition speed to medium.

   You can choose from three speeds (slow, fast, and medium), using the list box on the right side of the Transition to This Slide group as shown in PPT Figure 2-64.

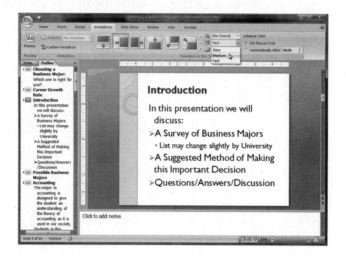

PPT Figure 2-64: Setting transition speed.

6. Just like when you selected a transition style, after changing the transition speed you'll see a preview of the transition.

   A preview of the Cover Left transition is shown in PPT Figure 2-65.

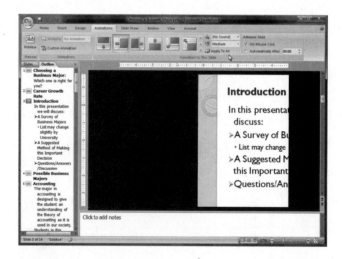

PPT Figure 2-65: Preview of transition speed.

Animating Slide Content

1. We can also add movement to components within a slide.

   We'll get you started with a simple one here, but keep in mind that you can make quite complex animations using the PowerPoint Custom Animations dialog.

To start, select the slide with the SmartArt list of business majors, as shown in PPT Figure 2-66.

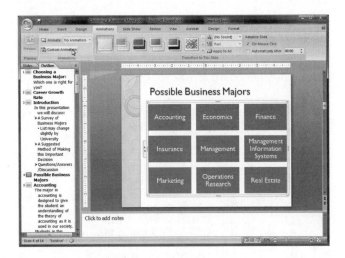

PPT Figure 2-66: The SmartArt list object.

2. We are going to add some custom animation to the SmartArt object itself.

   Select the SmartArt list object and then click the Custom Animation command found on the Animations ribbon.

   The Custom Animation dialog will appear docked on the right of the PowerPoint window.

   Once a component on a slide is selected, we can add movement by clicking on the Add Effect command, as shown in PPT Figure 2-67.

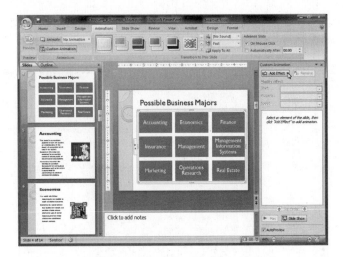

PPT Figure 2-67: The Custom Animation dialog.

3. Animation Effect options include Entrance, Emphasis, Exit, and Movement Paths.

Entrance effects are used when you want the component to enter the slide in a dynamic manner.

If you select one of these options, you will see a submenu with the various effect styles.

Let's select the Checkerboard Entrance effect as in PPT Figure 2-68.

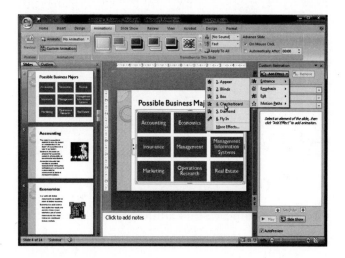

PPT Figure 2-68: Selecting an Entrance effect.

4. After you select the effect, it will be entered into a list of effects that have been added to our slide.

   Since the Entrance effect is currently the only effect on the slide, it is first in the list.

   In addition, you can adjust several properties of the effect such as: how it starts (On Click); the direction of the effect (Across); and the speed (Very Fast), as shown in PPT Figure 2-69.

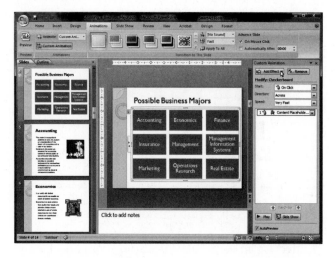

PPT Figure 2-69: The added Entrance effect.

5. Just the opposite of an Entrance effect is the Exit effect.

   When active, an Exit effect will allow an object to leave the slide in a dynamic manner.

   As with the Entrance effect, there is a library of effects to choose from.

   The initial list includes the most popular effects, but you can get to more by selecting the More Effects option as shown in PPT Figure 2-70.

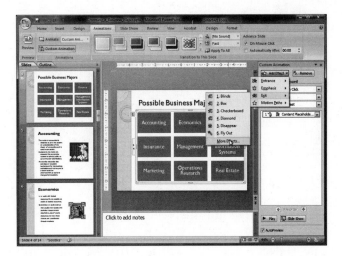

PPT Figure 2-70: Adding an Exit effect.

6. You'll see a dialog with a complete, categorized list of effects that you can choose from.

   Each time you click on an effect option, you will see a brief preview of it on the slide, as shown in PPT Figure 2-71.

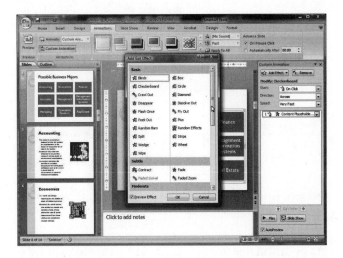

PPT Figure 2-71: Selecting an Exit effect.

Try a few, and then select one that you like.

7. For our slide, we will select the Boomerang style for our Exit effect as shown in PPT Figure 2-72.

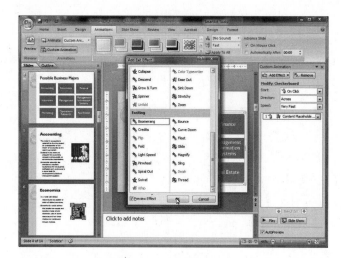

PPT Figure 2-72: Selecting the Boomerang effect.

Select your preferred style and then click OK.

8. When the new effect is added, it will appear in the list of animations for the slide, as shown in PPT Figure 2-73.

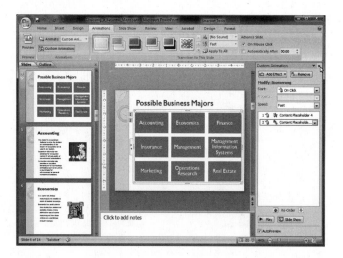

PPT Figure 2-73: The added Exit effect.

You can preview your complete list of animation effects at any time by clicking the Play button.

Experiment by adding animation effects to this and other slides.

MAKING GOOD PRESENTATIONS

Now that you know how to create a presentation, let's take a look at some common rules for making good presentations. Think of these rules as the *Seven Rules of Highly Effective Presentations.*

Rule 1: Don't try to cram too much information on a single slide. Have only one topic per slide, and use the **6 x 6 principle**—no more than six lines of text, with no more than six words per line.

Rule 2: Wherever possible, use bullets rather than numbers, because bullets do not imply a significance or order, and numbers do.

Rule 3: Use a readable font type and size. A sans serif font is good for titles (such as Arial, Verdana, Helvetica, etc.), and a serif font can be used for bullets or body text (e.g., Times New Roman, Garamond, Goudy, Palatino, etc.). This matches what most people are used to looking at in print formats. Font sizes should be at least 36 point for titles and 24 point for text.

Rule 4: Be careful about your choice of colors. Colors should be easy to read; light text against a dark background is considered better than vice versa. Avoid placing saturated primary colors (red, green, blue) next to each other, as they can create a third color where they meet.

Rule 5: Use simple tables and charts to present your numbers. In charts, use colors instead of fill patterns to convey a clear, bold message.

Rule 6: Be careful with graphics, photos, and so on to ensure they are readable by your audience and are a meaningful part of your presentation rather than a distraction.

Rule 7: Do *not* read your presentation to your audience! Use it to augment your verbal presentation rather than being the same.

EXERCISES TO BUILD YOUR KNOWLEDGE OF MS POWERPOINT

Match the term or icon on the left with the appropriate description on the right:

_____1. 6 x 6 principle   a. A collection of icons, buttons, and other useful image files that can be inserted into slides.

_____2. Arrange   b. A library of prebuilt shapes that can be inserted onto a slide to make a drawing.

_____3. Clip art   c. Combinations of different formatting options that are displayed for your selection at thumbnail size in various galleries.

_____4. Custom Animation   d. A set of commands on the Home ribbon and Drawing Tools Format ribbon that allow you to position the items quickly on a slide.

_____5. Distribute   e. An Arrange command that helps you to position several items evenly either horizontally or vertically.

_____6. Illustration   f. A set of commands that lets you add movement behavior to items on a slide.

_____7. Multimedia   g. A set of graphic objects that is available on the Insert ribbon.

_____8. Quick Styles   h. No more than six lines of text with no more than six words per line.

_____9. Shapes collection   i. Provides a variety of effects for moving dynamically between slides.

_____10. Transition   j. Graphics, photos, audio, video, animations, and other nontext elements.

Practice by using PowerPoint to create a presentation with the following:

11. Create an informative presentation about five outdoor-oriented locations in your area. You may highlight state parks in your area or discuss your favorite places to sit and relax, hike, bike, kayak, and so forth.

12. Add pictures of your favorite outdoor places.

13. Use layers to add text to the photographs you insert.

14. As you create the slides, include text or bulleted items explaining why these places are special to you.

15. Be sure to include any special information such as hours of operation or entrance fees.

16. Use transitions that enhance the flow of your slide show.

17. Add a sound clip that conveys the tranquility (mountain overlook) or excitement (Class IV rapids) of the location. Be sure it runs when the slide opens.

Use PowerPoint Help to answer the following:

18. Is it possible to play a movie full screen instead of as part of a slide? If so, how would you do it?

_____

_____

_____

19. What options are available for animating a SmartArt object?

_____

_____

_____

20. When your presentation is ready, how do you go about displaying it as a slide show?

_____

_____

_____

POWERPOINT TUTORIAL 2: MINI-CASE 1

Scenario: Your favorite high school guidance counselor, Ms. Empa Thee, contacted you and asked you to create a presentation like that shown in PowerPoint Tutorial 1. She wants your presentation to provide information on the business majors available at your college or university. The presentation should be fun and interesting so that high school students will watch it. Also, your presentation should be capable of running in a continuous loop so that it can be displayed on a computer screen in Ms. Thee's office.

Your Task: There is no file to download. Your presentation should include at least the following slides:

- A title slide with an appropriate title, your name, and some clip art graphic other than that shown in the tutorial.
- A new slide after the title slide that explains the purpose of the presentation that is in the two-column Text and Content design and uses a picture or logo from your business college Web page for added interest.
- Transform the picture or logo into a hyperlink that students can use to access the business school's Web site.
- A slide that lists the various business majors at your school. If there are specialties included within a major, use subheadings to list those as well.
- A slide immediately after the list of business majors at your school or college; use actual or fictitious data for the percent of students in each major to create a pie chart on the new slide with an appropriate title.

Remember the following items:

- Choose a design that complements your presentation, with an appropriate background color and texture for all the slides in your presentation.

- Insert information in a footer that includes the date, which will change automatically based on the date the presentation is shown, the slide number, and the title of the presentation.
- Add transitions, animations, and timings that will allow students to view your presentation, read the content on each slide, and see the next slide without having to click a mouse or press the space bar or any key.
- Save your presentation. Finally, print your presentation using the Handouts option in pure black and white, with six slides per page.

POWERPOINT TUTORIAL 2: MINI-CASE 2

Scenario: You have created a PowerPoint presentation to describe one of your company's products for your boss, Ms. Bertille Canis-Latrans, for your job with Acme Products, Inc. (See Mini-Case 2 of PowerPoint Tutorial 2.) Ms. Canis-Latrans is happy with the content of your presentation, but in her words, "It lacks a certain *je ne sais quoi.*" She wants you to jazz it up some by adding graphics, transitions, sounds, and animation.

Your Task: Create a PowerPoint presentation to describe one of your company's products. Either create it from scratch or use the one that you created for PowerPoint Tutorial 1. Be sure to incorporate or add the following in your presentation:

- A graphic (photo or drawing) of the product.
- Charts for any slide with data.
- A corporate logo for Acme Products in the lower corner of all slides. (See whether you can figure out how to add this to the Master Slide.)
- A slide that lists the various products sold by Acme. If there are subcategories of products, use subheadings to list those as well.

Remember the following requirements:

- Choose a design that complements your presentation with a suitable background color and texture for all the slides.
- Add transitions, animations, and timings that will allow viewers to see your presentation, read the content on each slide, and see the next slide without having to click a mouse or press the space bar or any key.

MICROSOFT POWERPOINT PROJECT 1: CREATING A PROMOTIONAL PRESENTATION

By reading the business case sections and completing this project you will:

- Extend your knowledge of MS PowerPoint.
- Learn how to apply MS PowerPoint to solve business problems.
- Understand the basic questions underlying the creation of effective presentations.
- Understand how to create a PowerPoint template.
- Learn how to use the slide master view.

PROJECT INTRODUCTION

Assume that after applying for an internship, you've been selected as a summer intern by your hometown Chamber of Commerce. During your interview for the internship, you mentioned that you knew how to use MS PowerPoint. The Chamber wants you to create a PowerPoint presentation that it can use to promote your hometown and the surrounding area. At the end of your internship, you will make a presentation to the Chamber of Commerce using the PowerPoint presentation that you developed.

Project Presentation Instructions

There are no files to download for this project. You will create the files that you need.

THE POWERPOINT AUTO CONTENT WIZARD AND CREATING A TEMPLATE

Business Case

You are excited about the opportunity to demonstrate your technical and communication skills. You know that references earned through a successful internship carry great weight with potential employers. You should use your knowledge of your home city, town, county, state, and country to provide the initial knowledge for your presentation. To this content you will add information gained through research. The World Wide Web is a great place to look for information about places, historical and recreational opportunities, and pictures. Be sure to give proper credit to any source you use and to avoid using copyrighted pictures without the copyright holder's permission. If you have the chance, you could even take your own pictures and use then in your presentation.

Problem Definition

You need to create an effective presentation for your local Chamber of Commerce. Presentations are one way to communicate a message to an audience. Here are a few hints on how to create an effective presentation regardless of delivery method. To communicate your message effectively through a presentation, you should ask yourself some basic questions.

First you should ask yourself, "What is my message?" or "What do I want to get across to my audience?" Answering either of these questions focuses your thinking about the reason for your presentation. You must focus, because any topic of importance is likely to be too broad to cover completely in a brief presentation. Hopefully when you complete your presentation, you can complete a sentence similar to the following: "When my audience reads/hears my presentation, they will know/believe that _____ is a great place to visit/live."

In order to answer either of the first two questions effectively, you should also be thinking of your answer to this question: "Who is my target audience?" For this project, if you come from a small town, you may target people of all ages from your region. If you grew up in New York City, London, or Cairo, you may need several presentations targeted to reach international audiences in any age and socioeconomic group likely to travel long distances.

After considering your message and your audience, you will have created knowledge that will guide you and help you to select the content or information that you will include in your presentation. Rather than start from scratch, you've decided to use PowerPoint's Auto Content Wizard to create a basic outline for your project. One way to do this is to open a new PowerPoint file and select New from the Office Button menu. Here you will find many different slide show templates that will contain preselected themes and styles. You can select from templates currently on your computer, or you may download a template from Microsoft Office Online. Several templates in the Presentations Business category may be helpful. After selecting a template, you will have to customize it to fit your purposes. Using the Slide Sorter view, you can open one or more templates and then copy and paste slides into a new presentation to create your own template. You can save this file as a template by using the Save As command from the Office button menu and choosing Design Template as the file type.

Before moving on to the requirements for this project, here are some final tips regarding PowerPoint presentations (you can find additional materials at many sites on the Web):

1. Create an outline of your presentation in Outline view or using a word processor. You can import a word processor outline into your template and then edit for content and presentation considerations.

2. As you revise your template, consider what information will be common to all slides (e.g., slide number). PowerPoint provides a place for such information known as the **slide master**. Any items placed on the slide master, such as a date, page number, or your hometown's official seal, will appear in the same place on every slide. You can find out more about the Slide Master view by using PowerPoint's Help function.

3. Use complementary colors, graphics, and images but use them sparingly to enhance your content and not to distract from it.

4. As with graphics, transitions and special effects (e.g., animations) should be used with content to make a point and generally not just because of the "gee-whiz" factor.

5. Try to use 28-point font or larger and limit the amount of text on each slide. Three to five bullets per slide is considered an effective norm.

6. Use charts instead of tables of numbers to present data. You can add additional details by including remarks in the notes section of the slide and creating handouts for the audience. You can also put the tabular data at the end of your presentation, after a blank slide, and refer to the data during audience questions.

7. Having said that, as you create your presentation, try to anticipate the questions your audience might ask.

8. Practice, practice, practice before giving your final presentation. Ask a friend to be the imaginary audience and have her/him ask questions and critique your presentation. Brainstorm potential physical locations where you might make your presentation and evaluate how your choice of slide design, background color, and text attributes (size, color, etc.) will appear to the audience.

Problem Requirements

This project requires you to create an effective presentation for your local Chamber of Commerce. The requirements listed below are minimum requirements to get you started. Your instructor may add requirements.

Slide 1, Project Title Slide: This slide should include your class title, your instructor's name, your name, the date, and the project name as found on your syllabus.

Slide 2, Title Slide for Your Presentation: This slide will serve as the first slide of your Chamber of Commerce presentation. You should have an appropriate title, your name, and the date that you are presenting to the Chamber of Commerce (you can make up a date).

Presentation Body: The slides from the third slide on are the body of your presentation. There should be an appropriate number of slides to get your message across and to comply with your instructor's requirements. Within these slides, you should craft a presentation that uses images, data, and other elements to present your hometown to your audience and to highlight the wealth of activities in your local area. You should include hyperlinks to local resources and points of interest and visit these links as part of your presentation. If you haven't covered the use of hyperlinks in presentations, you can use PowerPoint Help to guide you (try entering *insert a hyperlink* into the text box below the "What would you like to do?" question). Add transitions, sound, and animations as necessary to make your point and keep the presentation *interesting*. Remember to provide citations for others materials just as you would for any other class project. Be careful not to use copyrighted materials without the copyright holder's permission.

Next-to-Last Slide, Summary: Summarize your main points and reinforce your main message.

Last Slide, Questions? Create a slide that prompts the audience for questions.

<u>**Interpretive Questions**</u>

Based on your experience with this project, answer the following questions.

1. What are some other attributes of audiences in addition to age and socioeconomic level that you may want to consider when determining your target audience for the Chamber of Commerce project?

2. Is using a ready-made template the easiest way to complete the project in this case? How could you have created your own template outside of PowerPoint and then implemented it using PowerPoint? *Hint:* Think of the relationship between an architect and a house.

3. If the Chamber of Commerce asks you to create a Web-publishable version of your presentation, how might you do this using PowerPoint? In addition to the issue of how to publish your presentation to the Web, what other issues might you need to consider?

MICROSOFT POWERPOINT PROJECT 2: MANAGEMENT INFORMATION SYSTEMS PRESENTATION

By reading the business case sections and completing this project you will:

- Extend your knowledge of MS PowerPoint.
- Learn how to apply MS PowerPoint to solve business problems.
- Understand the basic questions underlying the creation of effective presentations.
- Understand how to create a PowerPoint template.
- Learn how to use the Slide Master view.

PROJECT INTRODUCTION

Management Information Systems (MIS) departments at schools around the country are experiencing a similar problem: there are more job openings for MIS graduates than there are students graduating with a MIS degree. For this project, assume that you are an MIS major. Your professor is the MIS Department Head and has asked you to develop a presentation highlighting the MIS major. Specifically, she wants you to answer two frequently asked questions: "What is MIS?" and "What can I do with a MIS major?" If your school does not have a MIS major, choose a major that closely matches MIS. Some possible choices are Information Science/Information Technology (IS/IT), Computer and Information Science (CIS), and Decision Sciences and IT. Your goal is to create a presentation that will inform and attract students to the MIS major. Your professor plans to use your presentation as part of the MIS Department's recruiting efforts. When completed, you will present your presentation to a select group of alumni, some of whom might want to offer you a job!

Project Presentation Instructions

There are no files to download for this project. You will create the files that you need.

THE POWERPOINT AUTO CONTENT WIZARD AND CREATING A TEMPLATE

Business Case

You are excited about the opportunity to demonstrate your technical and communication skills. You know that the connections you make with the alumni may help you get an internship or a job after graduation. Additionally, your work will be presented to other students at your school and beyond. You'll need to research the MIS major as well as follow on careers. An especially useful link is to the Career Center at the University of Georgia and its Major Decisions page: http://www.majordecisions.uga.edu/major/major/major.asp. Your school may have a similar page, and it would make a great starting point. Be sure to give proper credit to any source you use and to avoid using copyrighted pictures without the copyright holder's permission. If you have the chance, you could even take your own pictures and use them in your presentation.

Problem Definition

You need to create an effective presentation for your school's MIS Department. Presentations are one way to communicate a message to an audience. Here are a few hints on how to create an effective presentation regardless of delivery method. To communicate your message effectively through a presentation, you should ask yourself the answer to some basic questions.

First you should ask yourself, "What is my message?" or "What do I want to get across to my audience?" Answering either of these questions focuses your thinking about the reason for your presentation. You must focus, because any topic of importance is likely to be too broad to cover completely in a brief presentation. Hopefully when you complete your presentation, you can complete a sentence similar to the following: "When my audience reads/hears my presentation, they will know/believe that MIS is a great choice for a major and that it provides several paths to interesting, high-paying, fun, and successful careers."

In order to answer either of the first two questions effectively, you should also be thinking of your answer to this question: "Who is my target audience?" For this project, you may need to consider multiple audiences such as other students, faculty, alumni, and high school students.

After considering your message and your audience, you will have created knowledge that will guide you and help you to select the content or information that you will include in your presentation. Rather than start from scratch, you've decided to take advantage of the pre-built templates available with PowerPoint. One way to do this is to open PowerPoint, click on the Office button, and select New and then select Presentations from the list under Microsoft Office Online. Once you are at the Microsoft Office website, choose a presentation template that will help you "sell" the MIS major to other students. Regardless of which template that you choose, you will have to customize it to fit your purposes. You may even choose to use more than one template. You can open multiple templates in PowerPoint and view them arranged side by side. Next, you could switch to the Slide Sorter view and copy and paste slides into a new presentation to create your own template. You can save this file as a template by using Save As command on the Office button menu and choosing Design Template as the file type.

Before moving on to the project requirements page, here are some final tips regarding PowerPoint presentations (you can find additional materials at many sites on the Web):

1. Create an outline of your presentation in outline view or using a word processor. You can import a word processor outline into your template and then edit for content and presentation considerations.

2. As you revise your template, consider what information will be common to all slides, such as the slide number. PowerPoint provides a place for such information known as the slide master. Any items placed on the slide master, such as a date, page number, or your school's official seal, will appear in the same place on every slide. You can find out more about the Slide Master view by using PowerPoint's Help.

3. Use complementary colors, graphics, and images, but use them sparingly to enhance your content and not to distract from it.

4. As with graphics, transitions and special effects (e.g., animations) should be used with content to make a point and not just because of the "gee whiz" factor.

5. Try to use 28-point font or larger and limit the amount of text on each slide. Three to five bullets per slide is considered an effective norm.

6. Use charts instead of tables of numbers to present data. You can add additional details by including remarks in the notes section of the slide and creating handouts for the audience. You can also put the tabular data at the end of your presentation, after a blank slide, and refer to the data during audience questions.

7. Having said that, as you create your presentation, try to anticipate the questions your audience might ask.

8. Practice, practice, practice before giving your final presentation. Ask a friend to act as the audience and ask questions and critique your presentation. Brainstorm potential physical locations where you might make your presentation and evaluate how your choice of slide design, background color, and text attributes (size, color, etc.) will appear to the audience.

Problem Requirements

This project requires you to create an effective presentation for your school's MIS department. The requirements listed below are minimum requirements to get you started. Your instructor may add requirements.

Slide 1, Project Title Slide: This slide should include your class title, your instructor's name, your name, the date, and the project name as found on your syllabus.

Slide 2, Title Slide for Your Presentation: This slide will serve as the first slide of your MIS Major presentation. You should have an appropriate title, your name, and the date that you are presenting to the group of alumni (you can make up a date).

Presentation Body: The slides from the third slide on are the body of your presentation. There should be an appropriate number of slides to get your message across and to comply with your instructor's requirements. Within these slides, you should craft a presentation that uses data (such as starting salaries) and images to present the MIS major to your audience. Your images could include corporate logos of companies that hire MIS grads, pictures of student/ faculty social events, alumni, or alumni working in offices. You should include hyperlinks to the e-mails or Web pages of alumni who are willing to speak with students about the MIS major (your instructor may allow you to make up names and URLs). If you haven't covered the use of hyperlinks in presentations, you can use PowerPoint Help Answer Wizard to guide you (try entering *insert a hyperlink* into the field below the "What would you like to do?" question). Add transitions, sound, and animations as necessary to make your point and keep the presentation *interesting*. Remember to provide citations from other materials just as you would for any other class project. Be careful not to use copyrighted materials without the copyright holder's permission.

Next-to-Last Slide, Summary: Summarize your main points and reinforce your main message.

Last Slide, Questions? Create a slide that prompts the audience for questions.

Interpretative Questions

Based on your experience with this project, answer the following questions.

1. What are some other attributes of audiences, in addition to age and educational level, that you may want to consider when determining your target audience for the MIS Major presentation project?

2. Is using a ready-made template the easiest way to complete the project in this case? How could you have created your own template outside of PowerPoint and then implemented it using PowerPoint? *Hint:* Think of the relationship between an architect and a house.

3. If the MIS Department asks you to create a Web-publishable version of your presentation, how might you do this using PowerPoint? In addition to the issue of how to publish your presentation to the Web, what other issues might you need to consider?

Tutorial 1

INTRODUCTION TO MICROSOFT ACCESS 2007

After reading this tutorial and completing the associated exercises, you will be able to:

- Open MS Access.
- Create tables using MS Access.
- Create forms and use them to enter data into tables.

Note: Be sure to work through the examples in this tutorial as you read. This is the way you will learn by doing.

MICROSOFT ACCESS: A RELATIONAL DATABASE APPLICATION

Microsoft Access is a **relational database** application that is part of the Microsoft Office suite of applications. A database is an organized way to store data, and database software usually provides features that allow a user to add, delete, update, and manipulate (transform) data. A relational database, such as MS Access, stores data in **tables**. A table consists of rows (**records**) and columns (**fields**). Although the appearance of the records and the fields resembles the rows and columns you may have seen or may study later in a Microsoft Excel worksheet, Access is a much more powerful tool than Excel for organizing, storing, and retrieving data. Much of this additional power comes from the relational model that is implemented by MS Access.

With Excel, you can create data tables that list all data for a particular entity (customer, product, etc.) in a row of the worksheet. So, if a customer makes 100 purchases and a business tracks the customer's address in a database, that address would be listed 100 times. The relational model used by MS Access allows us to store data in separate tables and then link tables via common fields—the **primary key/foreign key** relationship.

A primary key in a table is a field that contains a unique value for each and every record in the table. In other words, if a field is a primary key, you can't use a specific value more than once in that column. A foreign key is a field in one table that contains values that are stored in a primary key in another table. If we look at the foreign key for a specific record, we can use the value to look up more data in the table where that field is used as a primary key. We are then guaranteed to find only one record that matches that value. Basically, a foreign key field provides a **reference** to a record in another table.

For example, suppose we have a *Customer* table, in which there is a field *CustomerID* that is a primary key in that table. If a copy of the *CustomerID* is stored as a foreign key in a *CustomerLoan* table, then information such as the customer's address is stored only once, in the *Customer* table, but can be accessed from any customer loan record. This reduces data redundancy and improves updating and other database functions.

Most of this module will be spent *learning by building.* First you will create a database consisting of one table, and then you will create a form to enter data. In later modules, you will learn how to query this table for information and to create reports based on this information. You will also learn how to add tables to this database; then you will create the remaining tables; and finally you will link the tables by creating relationships and to query a multi-table database.

STARTING A NEW ACCESS DATABASE

Let's start by opening a new Access database and taking a quick look at the MS Access interface.

1. Open MS Access by clicking its icon on the desktop or selecting it from a Windows menu.

    You should now see the "Getting Started with Microsoft Office Access" screen shown in Access Figure 1-1.

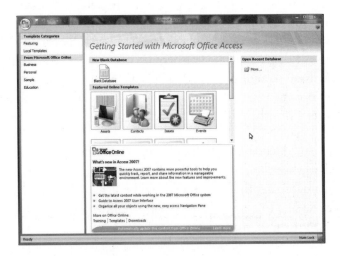

Access Figure 1-1: Opening MS Access.

With this screen you have several options. You can work on a database that you created earlier by selecting it from a list of Recent Databases on the right side of the screen, or you can start a new database. If you choose to start a new database, it can be a blank one for which you will build all components from scratch, or you can choose from a library of prebuilt templates. Microsoft has supplied a large library of templates of commonly used database applications. For our purposes, we'll start a new blank database.

2. Click on the Blank Database icon.

   A window will appear on the right side of the screen that will prompt you to enter a file name for your database.

   We'll enter *Example_Database* for now.

   Note that Access 2007 uses.*accdb* as the file extension for Access database files, as shown in Access Figure 1-2.

Access Figure 1-2: Starting a new blank database.

After entering the file name, click on the Create button.

Note that in Access Figure 1-2 you can see the location where the new database will be stored just below the text box where you enter the new database name. To change this, click on the folder to the right of the text box, then navigate to the location where you want to store the file.

THE MS ACCESS INTERFACE

You should now see the main Access interface that you will be working with as you create or modify an Access database. The basic structure of the Access user interface is shown in Access Figure 1-3, and its components are listed in Access Table 1-1.

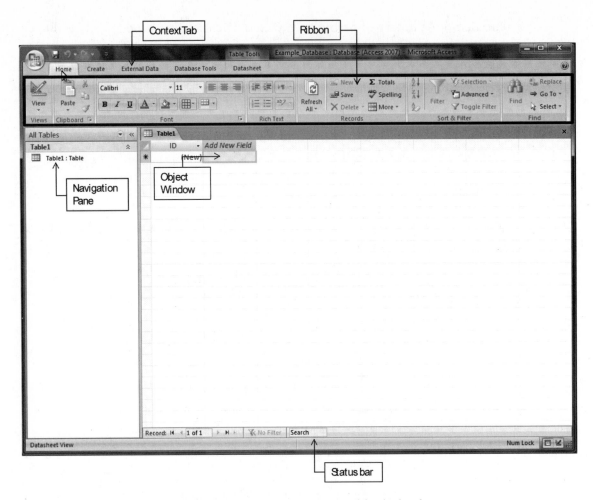

Access Figure 1-3: Starting a new blank database.

Component	Description
Context tab	Tabs above the ribbon that allow you display different commands based on the category that you choose.
Status bar	Part of the window that provides information about the progress of any ongoing process.
Navigation pane	The area that displays the objects included in your current database. You can use this to navigate to the object that you want to work on.
Ribbon	A strip across the upper part of the window that contains commands that reflect the active context tab and the object that you are currently working on.
Object window	The area of the window that displays any open database objects.

Access Table 1-1: Components of the Access user interface.

In order to understand the names of some of these components, you need to understand that an Access database is generally a collection of **objects**. These objects could be tables, forms, queries, reports, and macros. In this tutorial, we will work with two of these types of Access objects: tables and forms. You'll see other object types in later tutorials. As indicated in Access Figure 1-3 and Access Table 1-1, the object window will display the object you are currently working on. The look of this window will change depending on what the object is. To select an object to work with, we usually find it in the navigation pane.

Access Ribbons

In Access Figure 1-3, there are four main Access ribbon context tabs displayed, which make it easy to find the commands that you need. (You can actually customize Access and add one or two more if needed.) In addition, other ribbons will become available as you work with various objects. For example, the context tab for the Datasheet ribbon is shown in Access Figure 1-3 because we started a new Access database and the software assumes that we are currently working with a new table.

The next several figures will provide a quick overview of the primary Access ribbons. You will get very familiar with these as you work through these tutorials, so there is no need to memorize them now. Just take a quick look now and then refer back to these pages as needed.

Notice that each ribbon has some things in common with all the others. Commands are arranged in a series of groups. Each group includes a set of commands that let you do related tasks. Some controls are accompanied by downward-pointing arrows. When these are clicked, a menu or palette with more related options is displayed. You should also notice that each group has a small arrow in the lower right corner. By clicking this arrow you can open a dialog box for the group that provides even more options that you can use to complete your work.

Access Figure 1-4: The Home ribbon.

The Home ribbon, shown in Access Figure 1-4, contains the most commonly used Access commands. The Views group provides commands that let you change how a particular object is displayed. Commands such as Copy, Cut, and Paste are located here in the Clipboard group. Formatting commands are provided in the Font and Rich Text groups. The Records group provides commands for working with the records (rows) of an Access data table. The Sort & Filter group commands can be used to display only items that fit a given criteria. Finally, the Find group provides tools for searching for items in your database.

Access Figure 1-5: The Create ribbon.

The Create ribbon, shown in Access Figure 1-5, includes commands that are used to create various Access objects. The Tables group provides commands for creating tables, the Forms group provides commands for creating forms, and the Reports group provides commands for creating Reports. The Other group provides commands for other types of objects such as queries and macros.

Access Figure 1-6: The External Data ribbon.

The primary purpose of Access is to work with data. The External Data ribbon, shown in Access Figure 1-6, provides commands that let you do more with your data. The Import group provides commands for bringing data in to your database from external sources. The Export group provides commands that allow you to use the data in your current database in other applications. The Collect Data group provides commands that let you collaborate to communicate or collect data. The SharePoint Lists group provides commands that allow you to collaborate using Microsoft Windows SharePoint services.

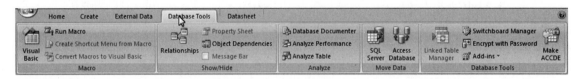

Access Figure 1-7: The Database Tools ribbon.

The Database Tools ribbon, shown in Access Figure 1-7, provides commands that let you work with your database is various ways. The Macro group has commands that let you work with **macros**, which are saved sets of instructions for automating a task in Access. The Show/ Hide group has commands for working with relationships between objects in your database. The Analyze group has tools for checking your database and improving its performance. The Move Data group commands let you make connections to a server to send or retrieve data. The Database Tools group provides miscellaneous commands that do not fit well in the other groups.

BUILDING AN ACCESS TABLE

For this unit on MS Access, we will use a database example involving an Internet-based bank. We will start with a table that has information on the types of loans that the bank makes: home, auto, student, and so on. This information will include an ID number for each type of loan, the name of the loan type, the interest rate on this type of loan, and the minimum amount on this type of loan that the bank will extend. Later on we will add tables on the bank's customers and the loans made to customers.

1. Start by opening Access and creating a new database.

    Give the name: *Bank_Database_Example.accdb* to the database.

    You should be looking at a screen like that shown in Access Figure 1-8.

Access Figure 1-8: The new Bank Database Example database.

A new database table is shown in the Access Object window.

Notice that the navigator pane shows only one object: the current table.

A new Access database table is now shown in its Datasheet view. We'll see it using another view, the Design view, a little later. Notice that the current context ribbon matches what you are seeing, namely, the datasheet ribbon.

Although the datasheet view of a table resembles the grid that you may have seen if you have used Excel, it does not work the in the same way. When the table has been completely created, you will be able to enter data in rows and columns, but the cells (intersection of rows and columns) usually do not refer to each other as they might in Excel.

Let's continue and see how we can create a table that fits our requirements. To create the table, we need to define the fields. Remember that a table represents some "things" that we want to keep data about. In this case, the things are types of loans that a bank wants to offer. The fields are the categories of data that we want to remember for each thing.

Usually, field names are created by combining the name of the entity that corresponds to the table and a logical name for the attribute that will be stored in the field. Since this table will store data about loans, all of our field names will start with the word *Loan*. We then come up with a name for the particular field. Note that it is often acceptable to abbreviate the first part of the name. For example, *CustID* might be an acceptable name for the primary key in a *Customer* table. Also, it is customary to capitalize the first letter of each word in the field name. You will do this later in this module when you create the fields *LoanType*, *LoanRate*, and *LoanMin*. The goal is to keep the names easily identifiable, understood, and not susceptible to being mixed up.

For this example, we would like to store a loan ID, a loan type, a loan rate, and a minimum loan amount for each type of loan. These will be our fields. There are several ways to add fields to our table. We'll show you how to add fields in several of these ways.

    2. Our first method for entering a new field will be right on the datasheet.

        Double-click on the tab that reads Add New Field.

        Type the field name *LoanType* as shown in Access Figure 1-9.

Access Figure 1-9: Adding the *LoanType* field.

        That's almost it! You've actually added a new field.

        Fields have several settings that we may want to change. The settings for this field are the defaults.

When you create a field for your database table, you need to set several field properties. It turns out that there are a lot of field properties you could set, but only a few are essential. Access Table 1-2 lists the most commonly set field properties. Some of these we can set using commands on the Datasheet ribbon.

Data Type	Used to define the type of data that is to be stored in the field. Some Access data types include Text, Number, Date/Time, Currency, and AutoNumber. This is probably the most important field property that you need to set. If not changed, the field is Text data type by default.
Format	Determines how the data is displayed. Examples are percent and currency formats. The format does not affect the actual data that is stored in the field, only how it looks.
Unique	Sets whether a value in a field must be unique. When this property is set, Access will not allow you to add a new record if the entered value has been used in another record.

Is Required	Sets whether a value is required in this field. When this property is set, Access will not allow you to add a new record unless a value is entered for this field.
Field size	Technically, this determines the amount of memory needed to store a data value in the field. With Text fields it can be set by specifying the number of characters that can be used in the field (maximum 255). With numeric data types, the size is determined by specifying the type of number to be stored in the field (Long Integer, Double, etc.).
Input mask	With this property you can specify a pattern for all data values that you want to enter into the field. It's a good way to help make sure that all data will be entered with correct values.
Default value	A value that will be included in the field unless changed by the user entering the data.

Access Table 1-2: Commonly set field properties.

3. Some of the field properties can be set using the commands in the Data Type & Formatting group on the Datasheet ribbon.

    While the *LoanType* field is selected, click the arrow for the Data Type list to see the possible data types you can select.

    Select the *Text* data type for this field as shown in Access Figure 1-10.

Access Figure 1-10: Setting the *LoanType* data type.

    Note the other field properties that you can set using the commands on this group.

4. Let's try another way to add a new field.

Click on the New Field command in the Fields & Columns group on the Datasheet ribbon, as shown in Access Figure 1-11.

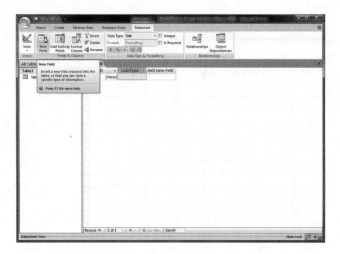

Access Figure 1-11: Using the New Field command.

5. You should now see the Field Template list appear on the right side of the Access workspace.

This is a list of predefined fields that you can choose from. Most of the commonly used field types are there.

You can choose one that should be close to what you want and then adjust field properties to tailor the field to your needs.

Select a Number field from the list as shown in Access Figure 1-12.

Access Figure 1-12: Selecting the Number field template.

6. A new field (column) with the Number data type has now been added to the table.

   Notice that the field name has also been filled in with the rather unimaginative name *Number* as shown in Access Figure 1-13.

Access Figure 1-13: The new Number field.

Let's change that quickly.

7. To rename the field, double-click on the field name in the table.

   Then type the field name *LoanRate* as shown in Access Figure 1-14.

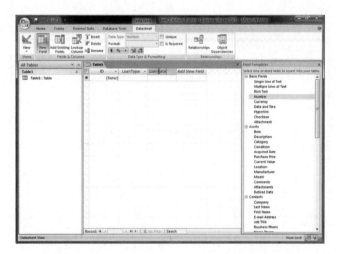

Access Figure 1-14: Naming the *LoanRate* field.

8. Interest rates on loans are generally expressed as percentages.

   Notice the quick formatting icons available in the Data Type and Formatting group.

   Click the % icon to format this field to percent.

You should see that the Format box now displays the word Percent as in Access Figure 1-15.

Access Figure 1-15: Formatting the field to Percent.

We've been working in the Datasheet view. We'll find that we have far more options if we work in Design view.

9. To get to there, select Design View from the View options on the Datasheet ribbon as shown in Access Figure 1-16.

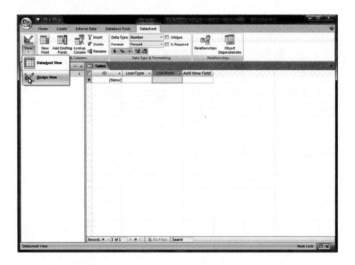

Access Figure 1-16: Changing to Design view.

Before switching to Design view, Access will prompt you to save your new table.

10. Type the name *loans* into the text box and click OK as shown in Access Figure 1-17.

Access Figure 1-17: Saving the table.

Important: Saving in Access is unlike saving in other Office software such as Word or Excel. Access saves the components that you create and the data that you enter as you work. You have to click the Save icon only on special, rare occasions.

11. The object window should now change to display a listing of the fields in your table as shown in Access Figure 1-18.

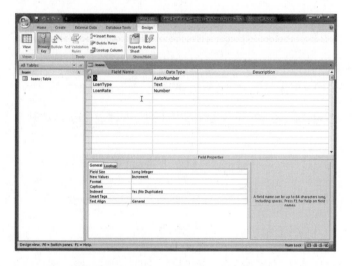

Access Figure 1-18: *loans* Table in Design view.

Notice that the names and data types of the fields that that we have entered are already listed in the upper table.

We'll use the Design view to add another field and change some current field properties.

12. To add a new field in the Design View, simply type a new field name in the Field Name list in the upper part of the Object window.

Add the field name *LoanMin* to the list as shown in Access Figure 1-19.

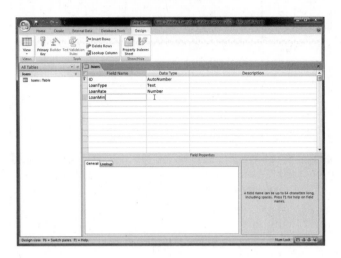

Access Figure 1-19: Adding *LoanMin* field in Design view.

When you do, the Data Type will automatically show up as Text. The lower part of the window will display a list of field settings and values.

13. A minimum loan amount is a number that represents currency.

Click the arrow on the data type box for this field and select the Currency data type from the list as shown in Access Figure 1-20.

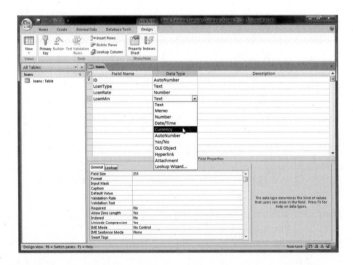

Access Figure 1-20: Setting *LoanMin* data type in Design view.

You should notice that the field setting list will change to present options available for fields of this data type.

Let's take a look at the fields in our table and make any adjustments needed to complete the table. First, have a look at the first field name, *ID*. Recall that this field was automatically included when we created a new table. This is the primary key for the table. Remember, a primary key is a field in a table that will contain a unique value for each and every record in the table. It's important that all tables in your databases include a field that can serve as the primary key. So, Access simply assumes that you want a field that can do this and includes the *ID* field by default. You can tell that this is the primary key field because there is a key icon displayed to the right of the field name in the list.

Access also assumes that you want this field to use the AutoNumber data type. AutoNumber is a special data type provided by the Access software to use with primary keys. Access will automatically fill a field using the AutoNumber data type with the next unique value. Access makes sure that an AutoNumber field is unique by never assigning a value to the field again, even after a record is deleted. The default field size for an AutoNumber field is Long Integer. The **field size** determines how much memory will be used to store numeric data in each field. For numbers, the amount of memory and format is set when you choose a numeric data type for the field type. You need to be aware of this. When a primary key is used as a foreign key in another table, you need to make sure that the foreign key uses a data type that is compatible with the data type of the primary key (Long Integer for AutoNumber).

►Thinking Critically:
Would you use the AutoNumber data type if the bank has its own loan identification system? Why or why not?

For our needs, the AutoNumber data type will work well, but it would be nice to have a more descriptive field name.

14. Click the field name for *ID* and change the name to *LoanID* as shown in Access Figure 1-21.

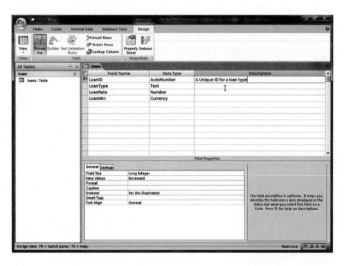

Access Figure 1-21: Adjusting *LoanID* field name.

Have a look at the field properties available for this field and their current settings. We'll leave the rest of these settings as is.

15. Let's also add a description for this field.

Type *A unique ID for a Loan Type* in the Description column for the *LoanID* field as shown in Access Figure 1-22.

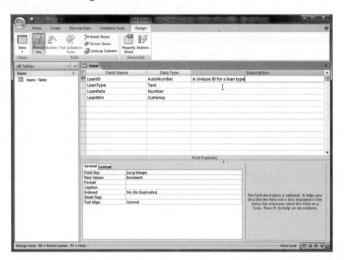

Access Figure 1-22: Adding a field description for *LoanID*.

Descriptions can be a very important part of documenting your database. They can help others working with your database recognize the purpose of a field.

16. After entering the description, you'll probably see an icon that looks like a lightning bolt with an arrow next to it.

This provides a list of Property Update Options.

Whenever you see this icon, you should click the arrow (don't ignore it!) to see available options, as shown in Access Figure 1-23, and select the one most appropriate for your use.

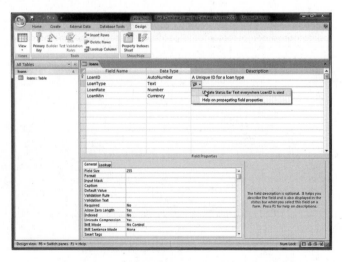

Access Figure 1-23: Property update options.

For now, select the option that starts: "Update Status Bar…"

17. You'll probably get the same message that we got, as shown in Access Figure 1-24: "No objects needed to update."

Access Figure 1-24: Message from Property Update.

This is because we have no other objects in our database besides this table.

If there were other objects, it would be a good idea to update the property as we did in Step 16. So, it's good to start getting into the habit now.

18. Now go ahead and add field descriptions for the rest of the fields as shown in Access Figure 1-25.

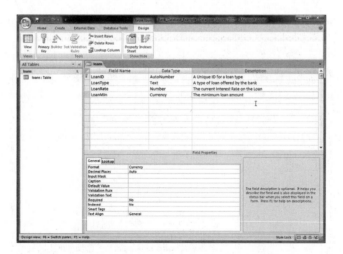

Access Figure 1-25: Field descriptions.

19. The default field width for a text field is 255 characters. This is longer than we will need for our *LoanType* field.

Select the *LoanType* field.

Now, adjust the Field Size in the field property list to 100 (Access Figure 1-26).

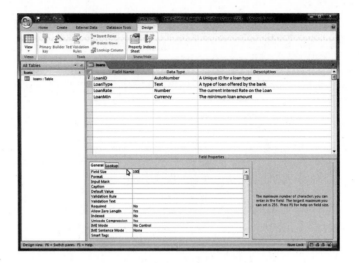

Access Figure 1-26: Setting field size for *LoanType*.

This means we can enter any text into this field that is 100 characters or less.

20. Now have a look at the *LoanRate* data type.

The default field size for a Number data type is Long Integer. This means that we can store only integer values (values with no fractional part) in the field.

Of course, percents are all about fractions.

Click the arrow for the field size box and select Double, as shown in Access Figure 1-27.

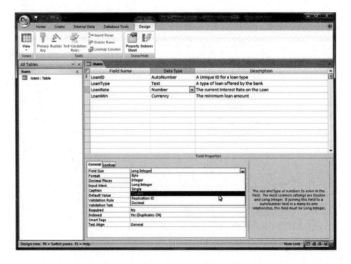

Access Figure 1-27: Setting Field Size for *LoanRate*.

Double will allow us to store values with decimal portions. The difference between Double and Single is that the values stored in a Double field can be more precise.

▶Thinking Critically:

Are there any other field properties that you think should be changed? If so, what? Go ahead and make those changes before moving on.

At this point, we are finished with designing the structure for our table. Next, we will take a look at how we can enter data into the table. In general, we could enter data using the Datasheet view, or, even better, we can create a form object to use for data entry. If you are creating a database with more than one table, *you should wait* and enter data only after all tables and their relationships are created. We'll add more tables to this example database in a later tutorial.

USING AN ACCESS DATASHEET FOR DATA ENTRY

With the table in the Datasheet view, we can simply type a data value into its appropriate field (column). To do this, we need to return to the Datasheet view.

1. Click the View command on the Design ribbon.

    You'll notice that you have a few more options this time to choose from, including PivotTable and PivotChart Views, as shown in Access Figure 1-28.

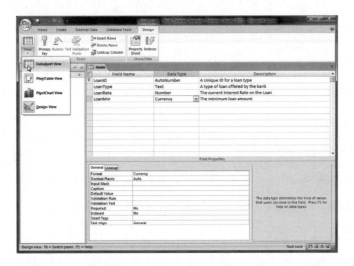

Access Figure 1-28: Selecting DataSheet view.

We'll select Datasheet view. Go ahead and select that now.

2. Access requires that you save significant changes to the database as you go along.

    So, before moving to the Datasheet view, you will be prompted to save the table as shown in Access Figure 1-29.

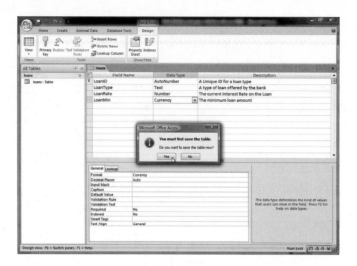

Access Figure 1-29: Saving table changes.

Click Yes to save the table and move to the DataSheet view.

3. Now you'll see the table in the Datasheet view once again. This time, however, all of the fields that you've added to the table are displayed as columns as shown in Access Figure 1-30.

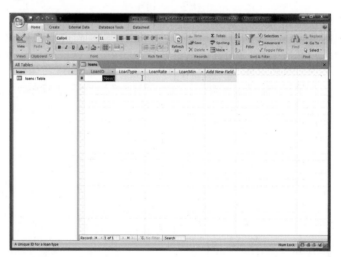

Access Figure 1-30: The Datasheet view with all table fields.

Notice the bar at the bottom of the Datasheet that shows which record you are currently highlighting (1 of 1). Later, you can use these controls here to browse through the table if desired.

4. To enter data using the Datasheet view, you simply click in the field where you want to type data and type it.

Click the *LoanType* field.

Now type the loan type: *15 Year Mortgage* as shown in Access Figure 1-31.

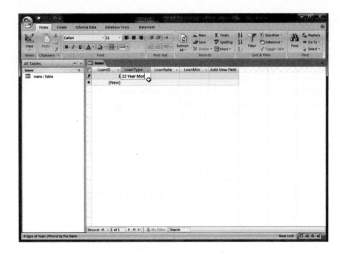

Access Figure 1-31: Entering *LoanType* data.

Notice that the number 1 appeared automatically in the *LoanID* field. Why?

5. As you enter data into a field, the *(New)* record moves to the line below the one in which you are typing.

Go ahead and enter the two records shown in Access Figure 1-32.

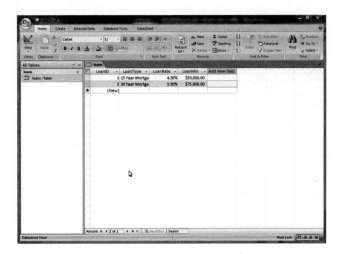

Access Figure 1-32: Entering database records.

In the next section, we'll see another way to enter data into a database table.

USING AN ACCESS FORM FOR DATA ENTRY

You will now learn how to create an Access form to use in data entry. Forms are used to provide a more formal and sometimes easier method of data entry than simply using the Datasheet view of a table. They are also important when you want users to enter data but you don't want them to have access to the actual table. To enter more data into the *loans* table, you will create the *loans* form. Let's begin.

1. While viewing the table, click on the Form command.

   You'll find it in the Forms group of the Create ribbon as shown in Access Figure 1-33.

Access Figure 1-33: Creating a form

2. You should now see a form for the *loans* table as shown in Access Figure 1-34.

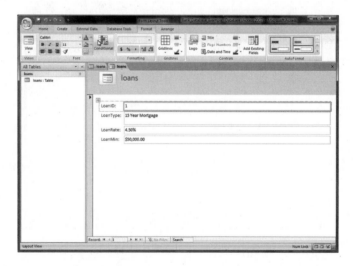

Access Figure 1-34: The *loans* form.

Notice that this form contains a label and text box for each of the fields in our database.

These text boxes are provided for data entry.

This form is bound to our table. When a value is entered into a text box, the value will be entered into the corresponding field of the table.

As you can see in Access Figure 1-34, the binding between the form and the table works both ways. The data in the currently selected record, record 1, is displayed in the form. You can move through the records using the browsing buttons (▯Record ◄ ◄ ▯   ► ►► ▯) at the bottom of the form. The ◄ and ► arrows will move one record at a time, and the ►◄ and ►► arrows will move to the first record in the table and the last, respectively. The number indicates the number of the record that is currently displayed.

The form is functional as is, but it's not very pretty. Let's first make the form look a little better. Then we'll use it to add a new record or two. The new form is currently in Layout view. While in Layout view, you'll notice that two form-related ribbons are available: the Format and Arrange ribbons under Form Layout Tools. These ribbons include commands that let us change how the format looks and how its elements are arranged.

3. On the Format menu you'll find the AutoFormat group. Click the More arrow to get a menu of format choices.

   Pick one that you like and see how the look of the form changes.

   We chose one called "Trek" as shown in Access Figure 1-35.

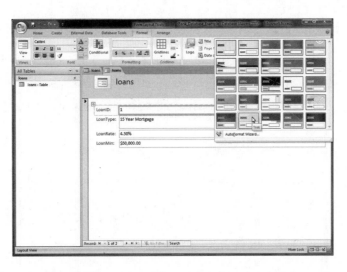

Access Figure 1-35: Selecting a form AutoFormat.

4. We can also easily adjust the labels on the form.

   Notice that the labels used are derived from the table name and the field names.

   Because it will be users (not you the designer) who are likely to enter data, we want to make these labels clearer for them.

Click on the Form title. Replace *loans* with the form title *Loan Type Entry Form* as shown in Access Figure 1-36.

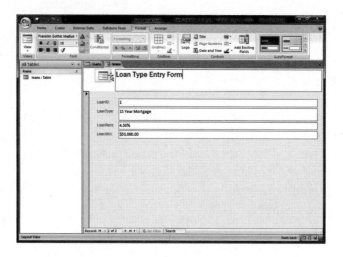

Access Figure 1-36: Editing the form title.

5. You can edit the field labels in the same way.

   Click the label *LoanID*.

   Edit it by adding a space to make *Loan ID* as shown in Access Figure 1-37.

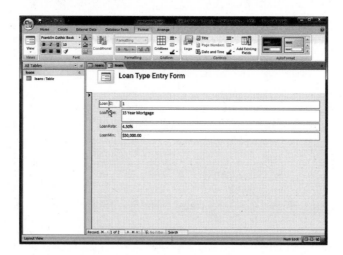

Access Figure 1-37: Editing the field label *LoanID*.

6. Edit the rest of the field labels to be more user-friendly as shown in Access Figure 1-38.

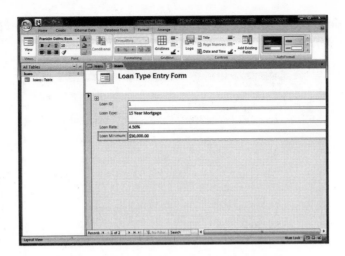

Access Figure 1-38: Editing field labels.

7. Let's make sure that our changes have actually been made to the form.

   Click the Save icon on the Quick Access Toolbar at the top left of the Access window.

   Save the form with the name *loans* (Access Figure 1-39).

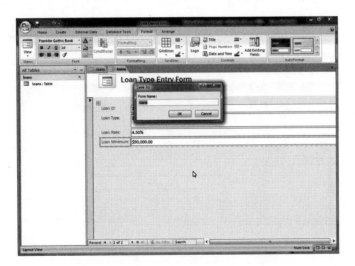

Access Figure 1-39: Saving the *loans* form.

You'll notice that this is the same name as the table. Won't it cause a problem to name two components with the same name?

8. After saving, you'll notice a change in the navigation pane.

   You should see that the components in your database, the *loans* table and the *loans* form, are listed in separate areas by object type.

If you don't see this, click the arrow at the top of the navigation pane and select All Access Objects as shown in Access Figure 1-40.

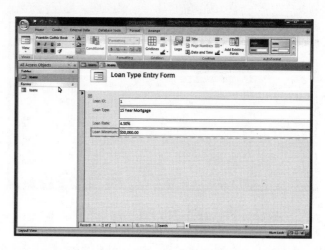

Access Figure 1-40: Database components in navigation pane.

Now that our form looks the way we want and we have it saved, let's use it to add some new data records.

9. Make sure that the form is in Form view so that you can add data.

Do this by selecting Form View from the View menu from the Format ribbon as shown in Access Figure 1-41.

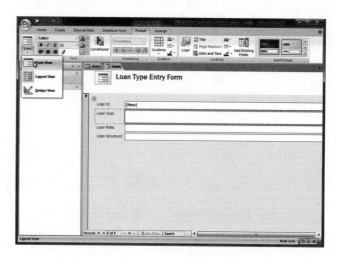

Access Figure 1-41: Changing to Form view.

10. Now click on the New Record button, 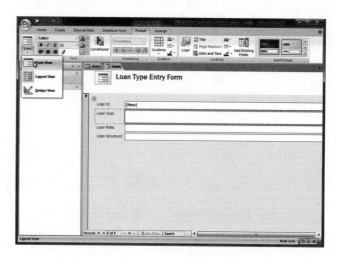, which is part of the form navigation button at the bottom of the Object window, as shown in Access Figure 1-42.

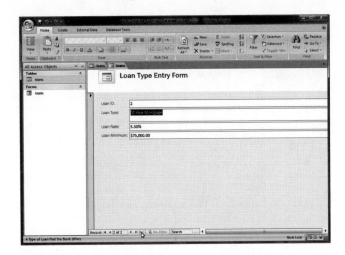

Access Figure 1-42: The New Record navigation button.

11. You'll see a new, blank record on the form as shown in Access Figure 1-43.

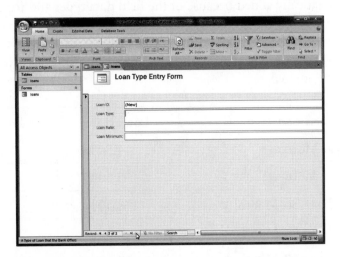

Access Figure 1-43: A new blank record in the form.

Notice that the *LoanID* field gives you a big clue that this is a new record.

12. To enter data, simply type data into the appropriate text box.

For this example, enter *Auto Loan 36-Month* for the loan type, *8.5* for the loan rate, and *5000* for the loan minimum as shown in Access Figure 1-44.

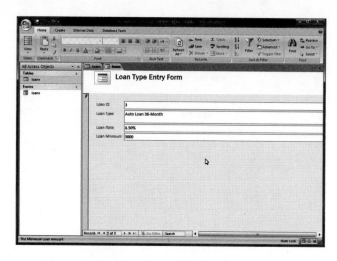

Access Figure 1-44: Adding a new record.

There is no need to type the % or $ symbols for the loan rate and minimum. They are automatically added because of the field data types and formats.

Using your form, add data until you have all six of the records shown in Access Table 1-3. If you have been following along, then the first three records should already be entered.

Loan ID	Loan Type	Loan Rate	Loan Minimum
1	15 Year Mortgage	4.50%	$50,000.00
2	30 Year Mortgage	5.50%	$75,000.00
3	Auto Loan 36-Month	8.50%	$5,000.00
4	Auto Loan 48-Month	9.50%	$7,500.00
5	Auto Loan 60-Month	10.50%	$10,000.00
6	Student	5.00%	$2,000.00

Access Table 1-3: *loans* data.

13. When completed, you should see the last record in the form as shown in Access Figure 1-45.

You can use the navigation buttons to browse the records and make any necessary corrections.

Let's check to see what the new records look like in the Datasheet view of the table.

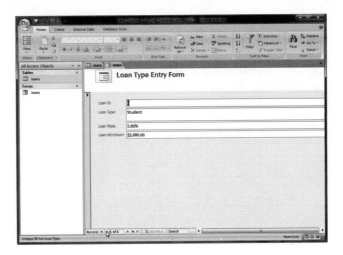

Access Figure 1-45: Last data record for *loans*.

14. Click on the *loans* table in the Navigation pane.

    Select the Datasheet view from the View options.

    What's this? Only the first two records that we entered directly into the Datasheet are listed as shown in Access Figure 1-46. What the heck is going on?

Access Figure 1-46: The *loans* table Datasheet view.

15. It turns out that there's nothing wrong. The view just needs to be refreshed.

    To do this, go to the Home ribbon and click Refresh All as shown in Access Figure 1-47.

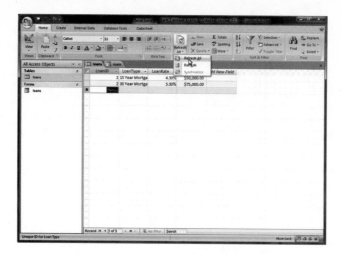

Access Figure 1-47: Refreshing the Datasheet view.

16. After refreshing the Datasheet view, you should now see all six of the records that you added as in Access Figure 1-48.

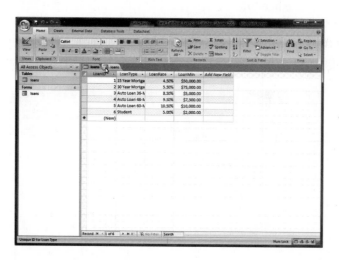

Access Figure 1-48: The refreshed DataSheet view.

Whew! Nothing lost!

Now, you've got a good start at building an Access database. You can build a table for storing data, and you can build a related form to use for entering the data. In later tutorials we'll add to your skills so that you can include multiple tables, ask questions about the data using queries, and make reports based on the data in the database.

EXERCISES TO BUILD YOUR KNOWLEDGE OF ACCESS

Match each of the Access terms with its description.

____ 1. Datasheet view

a. A way to store data by organizing it into tables made up of columns and rows.

____ 2. Design view

b. A collection of data about an entity or object in a relational database.

____ 3. Field

c. A data value about an entity, represented by a column in a relational database table.

____ 4. Foreign key

d. A collection of data about an instance of an entity, represented by a row in a relational database table.

____ 5. Form

e. A field in a relational database that is required to contain a unique value for each record in the table.

____ 6. Object window

f. A field in a relational database table that is used to refer to records in another table.

____ 7. Primary key

g. A type of object that you can create in Access that makes it easier for users to enter data.

____ 8. Record

h. The section of the Access window where you work on the current object (table, form, query, etc.).

____ 9. Relational database

i. A view of a table that shows the data in rows and columns.

____ 10. Table

j. A view of a table that lists the fields, field data types, and other field parameters.

Fill in the blank with the Access ribbon and group that is home to each of the following commands. Some ribbons appear only with a particular view of an object. You'll have to look for them, because we have not discussed some of them yet. Also, for a few of the blanks there may be more than one correct answer.

Command	Ribbon	Group	View
11. Refresh All			
12. Query Wizard			
13. Saved Exports			
14. Relationships			
15. Data Type			
16. New Field			

17. Primary Key	_____	_____	_____
18. Gridlines	_____	_____	_____
19. Tab Order	_____	_____	_____
20. Text Box	_____	_____	_____

21. Create the database table and form discussed in the tutorial. You should do the following to complete this exercise:

Complete the design of the database *loans* table as described in the tutorial. Note: in this and in all future creations of tables, it is essential that you spell the field names *exactly* as they are show in the tutorial. Failure to spell them correctly will result in your database not working as planned!

Complete the design of the *loans* form as described in the tutorial.

Enter the data shown in Access Table 1-3 into *loans* using the *loans* form.

Use Access Help to find the answers to the following questions:

22. How many different display formats are available for a field with the Date/Time data type?

23. What data type would you use if you wanted to store a large amount of text (more than 255 characters)?

24. What is a validation rule and how could you create one?

25. What is a split form? What would you use it for?

ACCESS TUTORIAL 1: MINI-CASE 1

Scenario: Nick, the owner of a small shop catering to the local fishermen, decided to expand his product line when the lake started to dry up after a drought. Blessed with a large parking area, he decided to add car sales, and thus his business was reborn as *Nick's Bait, Tackle, and Used Cars.* Determined to keep his used car inventory as organized as his assortment of shiners and larvae, Nick decided that he needed to build a database. He'd start small with one table and then expand it as necessary. Nick realized that it's generally better to create a design with all of the tables that would be needed first, but he figured that a one-table database would be sufficient for a while, and anyway it would be a good way to learn how to use Microsoft Access.

Your Task: Create an Access database with a table called *vehicles* to keep up with the list of cars on the lot of Nick's store.

Create your *vehicles* table to hold data listed in Access Table 1-4 for each vehicle. Set the various parameters for the field to match the description of the field provided.

Field	Description
ID Number	A 6-digit identification chosen by Nick that may use both numbers and letters.
Dealer Cost	The price that Nick paid for the car. Should be stored in the appropriate currency format.
Blue Book	The estimated used car sales price based on the industry standard "Blue Book" estimates. Should be stored in the appropriate currency format.
Type	The type of vehicle. Data values here can include *car, truck, SUV*, etc.
Sold	A Yes/No field that can be checked as *Yes* for vehicles that have been sold.

Access Table 1-4: Fields for Mini-case 1 database.

Create a form for entering data into the *vehicles* table. Use your form to enter the data listed in Access Table 1-5:

ID	Cost	Blue Book	Type	Sold
01086	$13,550	$17,888	Car	Yes
01145	$10,500	$12,599	Truck	No
01319	$8,100	$9,300	SUV	No
A0554	$11,430	$12,800	Car	Yes

Access Table 1-5: Data for Mini-case 1 database.

ACCESS TUTORIAL 1: MINI-CASE 2

Scenario: Since getting their digital cameras, the Couleur family takes a lot of pictures. As the family computer expert, Amy is usually the one who has to upload the photos to the family computer and keep them organized. She noticed that everyone seems to take and keep a lot more photos now that everything is digital. Amy would like to create an application to help her keep track of the photos that her family takes. She wants to be able to search based on date, family member, or location to find the file names of the photos on her computer. Having just studied Access at school, Amy has decided that a database might be the perfect application for storing her photo information.

Your Task: Create an Access database with a table called *photos* to keep up with the list of photos of Amy's family.

Create your *photos* table to hold the data listed in Access Table 1-6 for each digital photo. Set the various parameters for the field to match the description of the field provided.

Field	Description
photo_ID	A photo ID number that can be automatically generated.
photographer	The name of the family member who took the photo.
date	The date when the photo was taken.
location	The location where the photo was taken.
subject	A brief description of the photo's subject matter.
color	A Yes/No field that can be checked as *Yes* for color photos and *No* for black/white photos.
filename	The file name of the photo stored on Amy's hard drive.

Access Table 1-6: Fields for Mini-Case 2 database.

Create a form for entering data into the *vehicles* table. Use your form to enter data. Enter about 10 records. An example record is provided in Access Table 1-7.

Field	Data
photo_ID	1
photographer	Julie
date	8/7/2007
location	Burgundy, France
subject	The Roche de Solutre. A natural and prehistoric site in France.
color	Yes
filename	*roche001.jpg*

Access Table 1-7: Example data for Mini-Case 2 database.

Tutorial 2

QUERIES AND REPORTS IN MICROSOFT ACCESS 2007

After reading this tutorial and completing the associated exercises, you will be able to:

- Create simple queries in MS Access.
- Work with more complex queries.
- Create reports from tables and queries.

Files for Download: You must download the following files associated with this tutorial:

- The tutorial example template file: *ACC_2_Bank_Database_Example.accdb*
- The Mini-Case template file: *ACC_2_MC_Employees.accdb*

CREATING SIMPLE QUERIES

A query is the primary tool that you use in Access to get answers to your questions about the data. Queries are used to view, change, and analyze data in different ways. Queries allow you to specify what data you want to see. Usually this view is a subset of the available data that you created by selecting fields from tables or other queries. You can also use them as the source for forms, reports, and data access pages.

There are several types of queries to choose from, depending on the records that you want to retrieve from the database. In this tutorial we will limit our discussion to the most basic type of query: the **select query.** A select query will basically look through one or more tables and select and display records that match the parameters of the query. With a select query you can specify the table or tables from which you want to retrieve data, specify the fields from those tables that you want to display, and filter the records shown by some criteria. We will see that even while working only with select queries, there are several different variations to choose from and methods for creating them.

To begin your work in this tutorial, you should carry out the following operations:
- Download the database file that accompanies this lab tutorial (*ACC_2_Bank_Database_ Example.accdb*). Save it to secondary storage.
- Launch the MS Access Program.
- Choose Open an Existing file and open the *ACC_2_Bank_Database_Example.accdb* file.

A Simple Detail Query

If all we want is a simple select query—that is, one that pulls data from one or more fields and displays it without filtering—we can create one easily using the Query Wizard. Let's see how we can use the Query Wizard to create a query that will display only the Loan Type, Loan Rate, and Loan Minimum fields from our loans table.

1. After loading the database, the *loans* table in Datasheet view should be displayed. If not, you can select it in the navigation pane.

   Notice in the navigation pane that there are currently two components in the database: the *loans* table and the *loans* form.

   Select the Create ribbon.

   Now, click on the Query Wizard command in the Others group as shown in Access Figure 2-1.

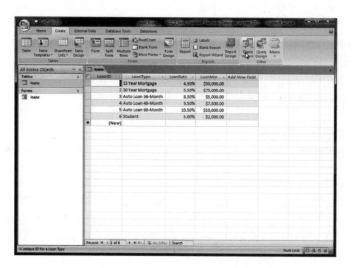

Access Figure 2-1: Starting the Query Wizard.

2. A New Query dialog will appear with a list of several types of Access queries that you can create.

   Select the first one on the list, Simple Query Wizard, and click OK as shown in Access Figure 2-2.

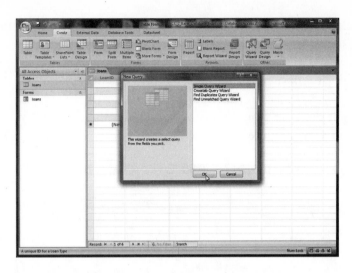

Access Figure 2-2: The New Query dialog.

The Simple Query Wizard consists of several pages. On each page you select the options that you want and then click Next to advance to the next page.

3. On the first page of the Query Wizard you select the tables and fields that you want to be a part of the database.

   We currently have only one table, but let's see how we would select a table anyway.

   Click the arrow on the list box labeled Tables/Queries, as shown in Access Figure 2-3.

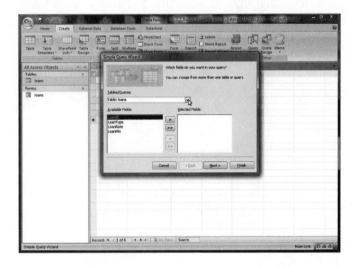

Access Figure 2-3: The Simple Query Wizard.

4. After clicking the arrow, you'll see a listing of the tables and queries that exist in the database.

Currently, we have only one table, so the list is not long.

Highlight the item from the list that includes the data that you want to select, as shown in Access Figure 2-4.

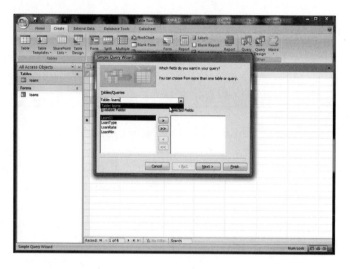

Access Figure 2-4: Choosing tables for a query.

5. After you have selected a table (or a query), a list of the Available Fields in that table will be displayed.

To choose a field, highlight it and click the arrow to add it to the Selected Fields list as shown in Access Figure 2-5.

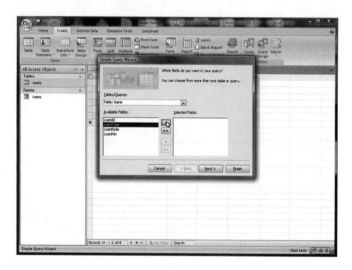

Access Figure 2-5: Selecting a field.

The right-facing arrows will add a field to the Selected Fields list, whereas the left-facing arrows will remove it. The double arrows can be used to add or remove all fields in the lists.

6. After you click the right-facing arrow, the selected field will be moved from the Available Fields list to the Selected Fields list as shown in Access Figure 2-6.

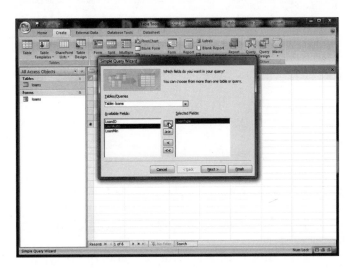

Access Figure 2-6: *LoanType* in the Selected Fields list.

7. Go ahead and select the *LoanRate* and *LoanMin* fields for the query.

Your list should resemble Access Figure 2-7.

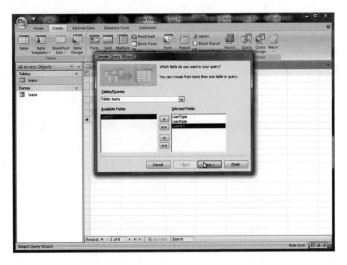

Access Figure 2-7: The selected fields.

When all of the fields that you want are displayed in the Selected Fields list, click the Next button to move to the next page of the Query Wizard.

8. On the second page of the Simple Query Wizard you can choose between two types of simple queries.

   For this one, choose Detail query, as shown in Access Figure 2-8, and click Next to go to the next page of the wizard.

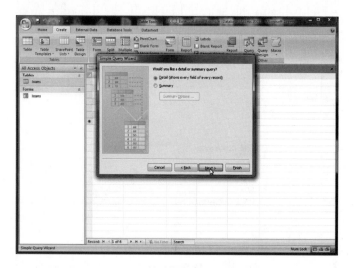

Access Figure 2-8: Selecting a Detail query type.

Note that this type of query will display all of the records from the selected fields.

We'll take a look at the Summary query type in the next section.

9. On the final page of the Wizard you can name the query and choose to either open the query or modify its design.

   Type the query title *All_Loan_Types* into the text box provided.

   Select the option that lets you open the query and click the Finish button as shown in Access Figure 2-9.

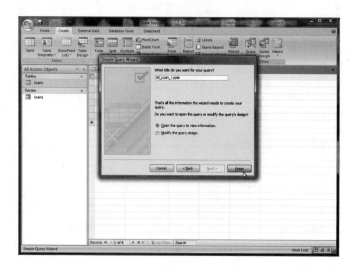

Access Figure 2-9: Naming the query.

10. You should now see the query results displayed in the Object window as shown in Access Figure 2-10.

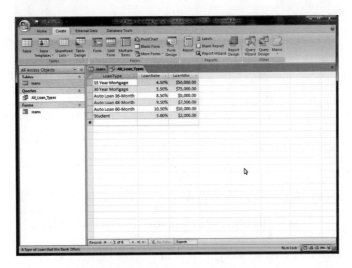

Access Figure 2-10: The query results.

Notice that this looks almost like the Datasheet view of the *loans* table. There are two major differences, however:

The *LoanID* field is not displayed. Remember that we didn't choose to add this one to the query.

We cannot add data on this view.

11. You can also see that a new section for queries and the new query have been added to the list in the Navigation Pane.

You can adjust this view somewhat.

Either right-click on the field heading or click the arrow next to the *LoanRate* field heading.

Select Sort Smallest to Largest to sort the data by increasing loan rate as shown in Access Figure 2-11.

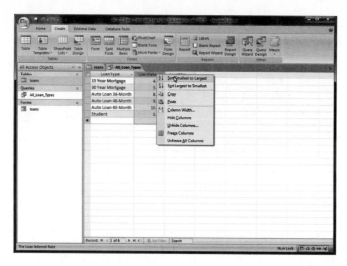

Access Figure 2-11: Sorting the query results.

12. You can see the sorted query results in Access Figure 2-12.

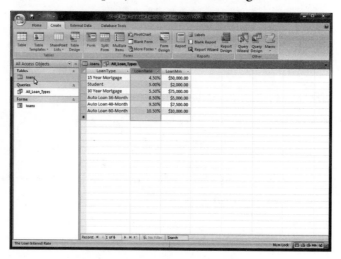

Access Figure 2-12: The sorted query results.

►Thinking Critically:

A query provides the answer to a question. Assume that the query in this first example is the answer. What is the question?

A Simple Summary Query

While making the previous query we saw that we can use the Simple Query Wizard to make two types of queries: a Detail query, which shows all of the data from the selected fields, or a Summary query. As the name implies, a summary query is used to obtain summary values such as totals and averages from the data in the database. Let's see how we can quickly create a summary query to answer the questions: What is the average loan rate? What are the minimum and maximum values in the loan minimum field? How many records are in the table?

1. As before, click the Query Wizard command on the Create ribbon to start the Query Wizard.

   Again, select Simple Query from the list as shown in Access Figure 2-13.

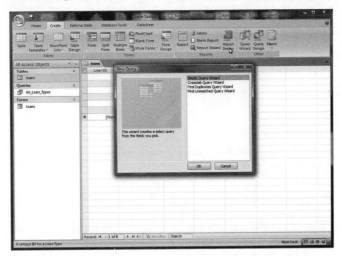

Access Figure 2-13: Starting the Query Wizard.

2. For this query, select the *LoanRate* and *LoanMin* fields as shown in Access Figure 2-14.

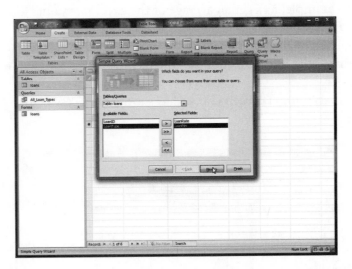

Access Figure 2-14: Selecting the *LoanRate* and *LoanMin* fields.

   Click Next.

3. This time, select the Summary query type.

   To set up a summary query, you need to select what types of summary calculations you want to see.

To do this, click the button labeled Summary Options as shown in Access Figure 2-15.

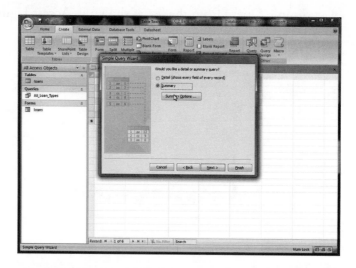

Access Figure 2-15: Selecting a summary query.

4. Notice that you have several types of summary values that you can obtain for each field.

For our example, let's get an average of the *LoanRate* values and the Min and Max of the *LoanMin* values.

Also, check the box for a counting the records in the *loans* table.

When everything has been checked as shown in Access Figure 2-16, click the OK button.

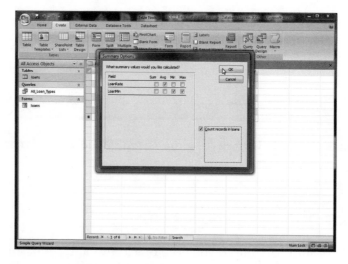

Access Figure 2-16: Choosing summary options.

5. As before, you should name your query. Use the name *Summary_loans_Query.*

   Click the Finish button to complete the query as shown in Access Figure 2-17.

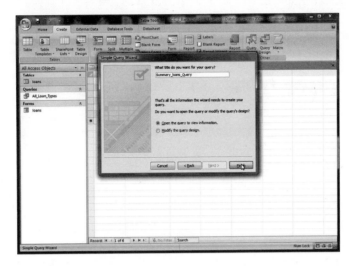

Access Figure 2-17: Naming the summary query.

6. Your query results should look like those shown in Access Figure 2-18.

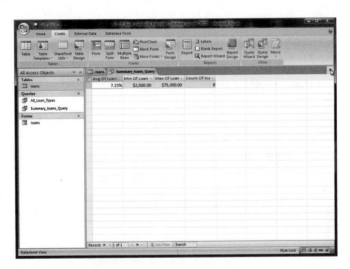

Access Figure 2-18: The summary query results.

Notice that for this query Access has summarized the values into a single set of numbers. The query field headings indicate what each summary value represents.

Using Query Design

As you might expect from the name, the Simple Query Wizard is mostly useful when we have relatively simple questions. As our questions become more complex, we need more options for creating more complex queries. Let's take a look at how we can use the Query Design tool to make more complex queries.

In this example we'll answer the question: Which loan types and rates have a minimum loan value that is greater than $10,000? To answer this question, we will want to see the *LoanType*, *LoanRate*, and *LoanMin* fields. But we will want to see only those records for which the *LoanMin* field is over 10,000.

1. This time we'll start to build the query by selecting the Query Design command on the Create ribbon as shown in Access Figure 2-19.

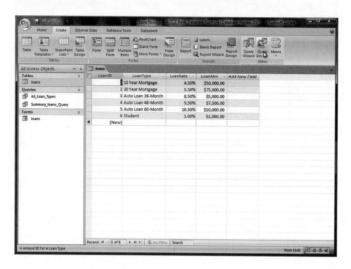

Access Figure 2-19: Selecting Query Design.

2. The Query Design view will be displayed in the Object window.

First, you'll need to select the source data for the query. This can be from tables or other queries in your database.

For now, select the *loans* table and click Add, as shown in Access Figure 2-20.

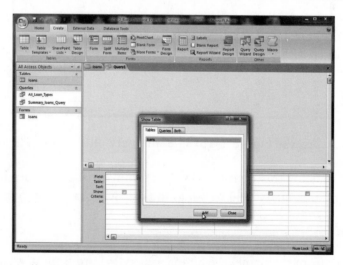

Access Figure 2-20: Selecting the query source.

Then click the Close button.

3. You should now see the Query Design view, shown in Access Figure 2-21.

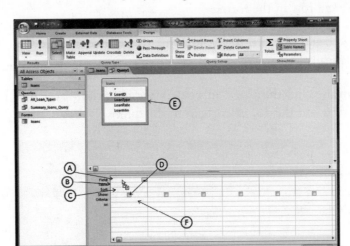

Access Figure 2-21: The Query Design view.

The Object window is divided into two parts.

In the top part you will see boxes representing the tables or queries that will be used as the source of your query. Each box is a window that you can move or resize as needed.

On the bottom is a form, which you fill out to specify what the query will show.

The query design form uses a method known as query by example (QBE). This basically means that the query is created by showing Access an example of what the query results should contain. This is in contrast to the more standard form of query, based on Structured Query Language (SQL). SQL will be covered in another unit within the Access tutorial.

The primary parts of the QBE form are shown in Access Figure 2-21. These parts are:

- Field row (A): Adds a field to the result of the active query
- Table row (B): Indicates the table in which the field is located
- Sort row (C): Used to indicate the type of sort for the field in the active query; can be ascending or descending
- Show check box (D): Determines whether or not the field is displayed in the active query
- Table(s) area (E): Displays the tables from which the fields and records of the query will be taken
- Criteria rows (F): Used to define one or more limiting conditions that are used to filter the records shown

We'll use this form to create our query. The first step is to select the fields that we need for the query. There are three ways you can do this.

4. Click and drag the *LoanType* field from the *loans* table window to the first column of the Field row in the form.

This will add the *LoanType* field to the query. Notice that the Table row is automatically set.

You can also click the arrow on a field row cell to choose the field from a list. Use this method to add the *LoanRate* field to the query, as shown in Access Figure 2-22.

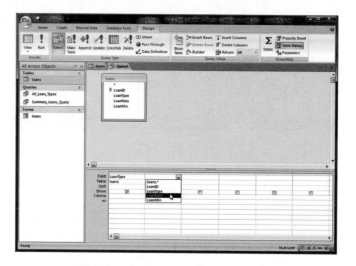

Access Figure 2-22: Adding a field to the query.

5. Select the *LoanMin* field for the third column on the form as shown in Access Figure 2-23.

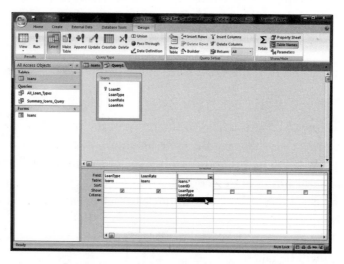

Access Figure 2-23: Adding *LoanMin* field.

Notice that the Show check box is checked by default for each of these fields.

Our next step is to adjust the settings for the fields. For this we might add filtering criteria, choose not to display some of the fields, or sort the results based on one of the fields. Let's add a filtering criterion. We'll show you an example of one now and discuss criteria in more detail later in the tutorial.

6. In the QBE form, click in the first cell of the Criterion rows for the *LoanMin* field.

   Type: >*10000* as shown in Access Figure 2-24.

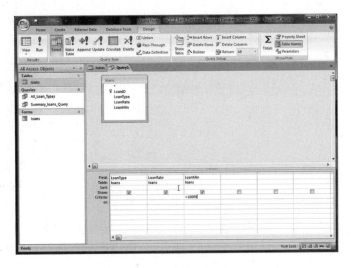

Access Figure 2-24: Add a query criterion.

With this criterion we are telling Access to show us only those records with a minimum loan amount greater than $10,000.

7. Click the Sort cell for the *LoanRate* field on the QBE form.

   When the arrow appears, click on it to see the list of sorting options.

   Select Ascending, as shown in Access Figure 2-25, to sort the records by increasing *LoanRate*.

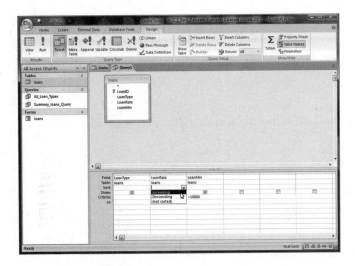

Access Figure 2-25: Sorting by *LoanRate*.

8. Your final query design should resemble Access Figure 2-26.

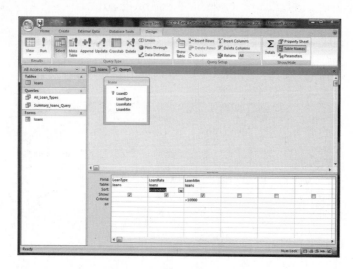

Access Figure 2-26: Final query design.

Let's save the design by clicking on the Save icon on the Quick Access Toolbar.

9. The Save As dialog will appear.

Give your query the name *Loan_Min_>10K* and click OK as shown in Access Figure 2-27.

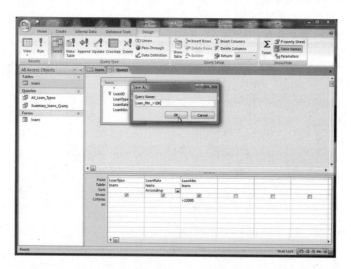

Access Figure 2-27: Saving the *Loan_Min_>10K* query.

10. As with Access tables and forms, there are several views available with queries.

Let's check the results of our query by selecting the Datasheet view.

Click the View command and select Datasheet View as shown in Access Figure 2-28.

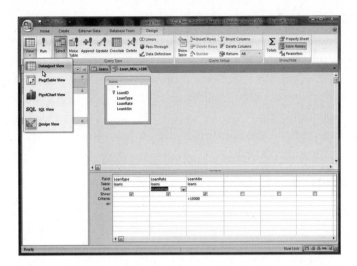

Access Figure 2-28: Switching to Datasheet view.

Your query results will appear like those shown in Access Figure 2-29.

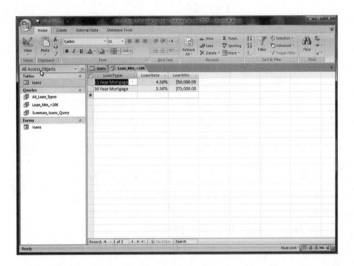

Access Figure 2-29: The *Loan_Min_>10K* query results.

▶**Thinking Critically:**
Are these query results correct? How can you check? It's important always to test your queries to see that they are formulated correctly.

Query Criteria Explained

In our most recent example we included a query criterion that was used to filter the displayed data and limit the records to only those that met the query condition. The criterion that we added to the query let us filter the results to answer the question: "What loan types have a loan minimum greater than $10,000?"

The criteria that are used to filter query records are entered into the criteria rows using conditions. These conditions are similar to those that you may encounter with IF functions in MS Excel but without the cell references. A typical query criterion will use a **relational operator** (such as =, <, >) and a value. Each record will be evaluated against the criterion, and if there is a match, then the record will be included in the query results. Access Table 2-1 lists other relational operators that may be used. Note the special characters that are used to surround text and date values in the conditions. These are known as **data type delimiters**. No delimiters are needed for numeric values.

Making an And Query

Sometimes we wish to ask questions that are a bit more complex. For example, we may wish to ask something like:

> What, if any, loans have an interest rate greater than 5% and a loan minimum less than $10,000?

Operator	Function	Examples
=	Return records that match the value exactly. Using the = sign is optional.	= 1000 "Minnesota"
>	Return records that have a field value greater than the value in the criterion. For text data, letters that are later in the alphabet are greater than earlier letters.	> 5 > "Jones"
>=	Return records that have a field value greater than or equal to the value in the criterion.	>= 5 >= "Jones"
<	Return records that have a field value less than the value in the criterion.	< 5 < "Jones"
<=	Return records that have a field value less than or equal to the value in the criterion.	<= 5 <= "Jones"
<>	Return records that have a field value that is not equal to the value in the criterion.	<> 5 <> "Jones"
Between	Return records with a field value that is between the two stated values.	Between 10 And 20 Between #01/01/03# And #03/01/03#
In	Return records that match one of several values in a list.	In(2, 4, 6, 10) In("CA", "GA", "TN", "MD")
Like	Return records that match the pattern of the entry with wildcards. * can be replaced by many characters. ? can be replaced by one character only.	Like "Mortgage*"

Access Table 2-1: Criteria operators.

These questions require more complex queries, for which we will need to set criteria on more than one field. For the first question, we would need to filter for records that have the field *LoanRate* > 0.05 and the field *LoanMin* < 10000. Note the use of the word *and* in the previous sentence. *And* is a logical operator corresponding to the intersection of two sets, shown in your math classes as the overlap of two circles in a Venn diagram. This means that when And is used to connect two criteria; both of the criteria must match before a record is shown in the query. If either one of the query criteria is not a match, then the record is filtered out and not shown in the query.

▶ **Thinking Critically:**

Draw a Venn diagram with two circles. Imagine that the circles contain the data that resulted from two Access queries. Shade in and label the area that would represent the data returned by an Or query and the area that would represent the data returned by an And query. Relative to each other, which type of query, Or or And, would generally include the broadest set of results?

To create an And question in the Query Design form, simply place each of the criteria on the same row in the criteria grid.

1. Start a query with the design shown in Access Figure 2-30. Include the *LoanType, LoanRate,* and *LoanMin* fields.

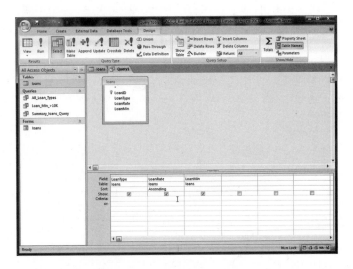

Access Figure 2-30: Start of query design.

2. For the *LoanRate* field, add the criterion: >0.05, as shown in Access Figure 2-31.

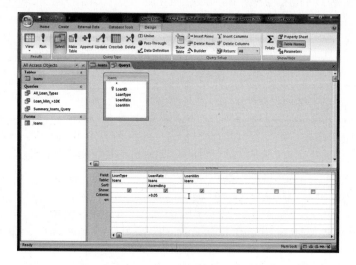

Access Figure 2-31: *LoanRate* > 5% criterion.

This criterion will filter the records to show only those with a *LoanRate* greater than 5%.

3. For the *LoanMin* field, add the criterion <10000, as shown in Access Figure 2-32.

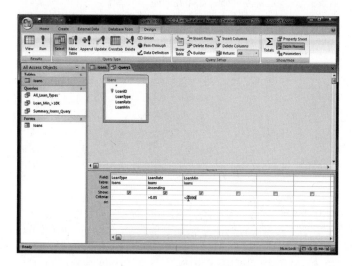

Access Figure 2-32: *LoanMin* <$10,000 criterion.

Alone, this criterion will filter the records to show only those with a *LoanMin* less than $10,000.

Together with the *LoanRate* criterion, the two criteria will filter the records to display only those records with a *LoanRate* < 5% and a *LoanMin* > $10,000.

4. To see the query results, click the Run command on the Query Tools Design ribbon as shown in Access Figure 2-33.

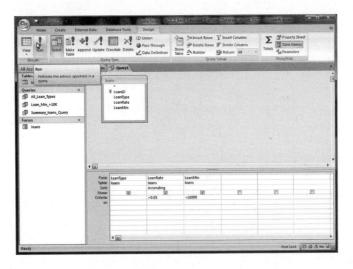

Access Figure 2-33: Using Run to get query results.

5. Your query results should be like those shown in Access Figure 2-34.

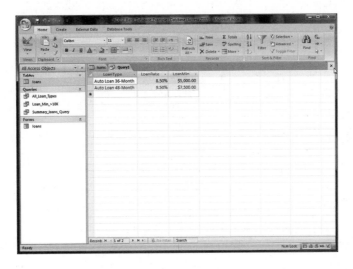

Access Figure 2-34: AND query results.

Notice that the values should correctly fit both criteria.

6. Click on the X in the upper left corner of the query Datasheet window.

Since we haven't yet saved the query, you should be prompted to save it as shown in Access Figure 2-35.

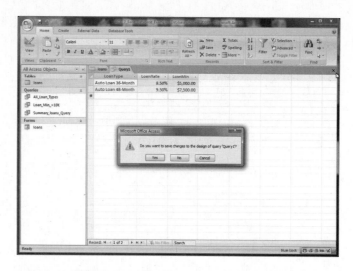

Access Figure 2-35: Prompt for saving the query.

7. Save the query with the name *Loan_Min_<10K_and_Loan_Rate_>5%* as shown in Access Figure 2-36.

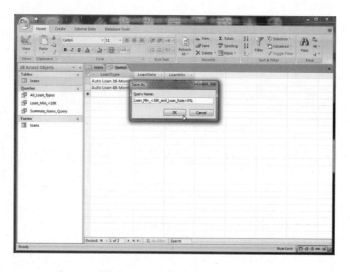

Access Figure 2-36: Naming the query.

Making an Or Query

In our last example, we looked at a query that uses an And structure for the filter criterion. That is, a record was displayed only if it satisfied both criterion 1 *and* criterion 2. Another type of question that is often asked of the data is known as an Or query. For example, we may wish to ask:

Which loans are for automobiles or have an interest rate greater than 5%?

For an Or question, a record will need to satisfy one criterion, the other, or both to be displayed. For our example, a data record will satisfy this question if it is an auto loan, if it has an interest rate more than 5%, or both. To set up an Or query, we simply place our criteria on different rows in the criteria section of the QBE form.

In this next example, we'll see how to set up an Or query. We'll also see how we can set a Like criterion on a field with the text data type.

1. Start a query with the design shown in Access Figure 2-37. Include the *LoanType, LoanRate,* and *LoanMin* fields.

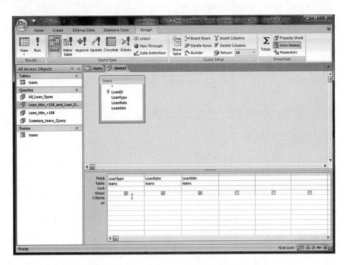

Access Figure 2-37: Starting the Or query.

2. In the first Criteria row under the *LoanType* field, type:

Like "Auto"*

You must include the quotes and the asterisk (*) as shown in Access Figure 2-38.

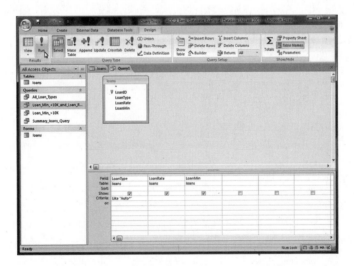

Access Figure 2-38: Settting a Like criterion on *LoanType*.

This criterion will match all records that start with the text *Auto*.

The * is known as a **wildcard**. Including it here means that any text in the field after the starting text *Auto* will be okay to match the criterion.

Click the Run command to see the results so far.

3. Notice that all of the records in the current query results shown in Access Figure 2-39 have a *LoanType* that starts with *Auto*.

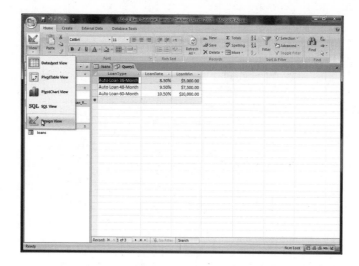

Access Figure 2-39: Results of Like query.

Let's go back to Design view to finish the query.

4. In the second criteria row below the *LoanRate* field, type:

    >5%

    We placed this criterion in a different row so that we can make an Or query.

    Notice the word "Or" to the left of the criteria grid that serves as a reminder as shown in Access Figure 2-40.

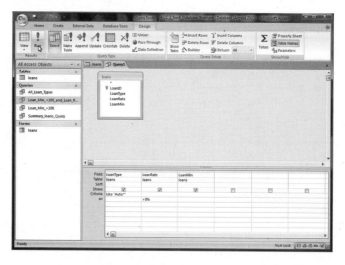

Access Figure 2-40: Adding the Or criterion.

Click the Run command to see the results so far.

5. Wait a minute! We got an error message (shown in Access Figure 2-41)!

   Whenever you get a message, be sure to read it and try to understand it before dismissing it. They generally give you a clue about what you need to fix.

   This one says, "The expression you entered contains invalid syntax."

   After reading the error and figuring out what to do, click OK to dismiss the message.

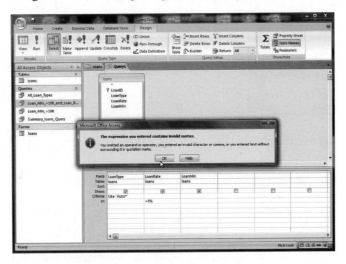

Access Figure 2-41: Invalid syntax error.

▶Thinking Critically:
Before moving on, what do you think caused this error?

---

6. Recall that the *LoanRate* field was defined with a Number data type.

   This means that we can compare the field's values only with numbers. No special characters such as % are allowed.

   No problem! Since 5% is the same as 0.05, we can fix it by changing the criterion to:

   >.05

   Make the change, as shown in Access Figure 2-42, and run the query again.

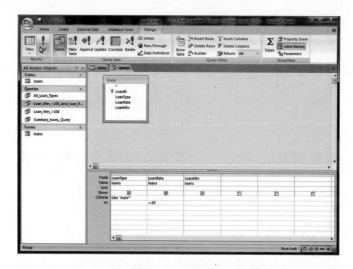

Access Figure 2-42: Correcting the *LoanRate* criterion.

7. You should see results like those shown in Access Figure 2-43.

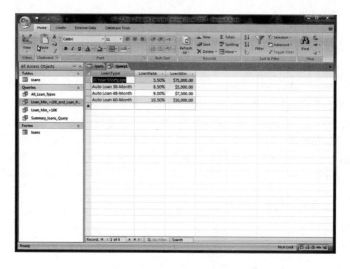

Access Figure 2-43: Or query results.

Notice that we now have four records displayed in the query results.

The first record displayed only satisfies the criterion *LoanRate* > 0.05.

The other three satisfy both the *LoanRate* criterion and the *LoanType Like "Auto*"* criterion.

Save your query as *Auto_Loan_or_Loan_Rate >5%*.

Building a Query Expression

Sometimes we want to ask questions whose answer is not explicitly stored in the database but rather is derived from the data. For example, with our database we might want to answer:

What is the average of the loan rates offered by our bank?

It wouldn't make sense to actually store the average in the database because it would be incorrect as soon as we added or deleted a new loan type or changed the rate on a loan type. It makes more sense simply to use the loan rates that are currently stored in the database to calculate the current average when we need it. We can do this in a query by building expressions into our query. Let's see how we can do this.

Keep in mind that we are building a fairly simple expression with this example. With a little imagination you should be able to see that you can follow similar steps to build more complex expressions when needed.

1. Start a query with the design shown in Access Figure 2-44. Include the only the *LoanRate* fields.

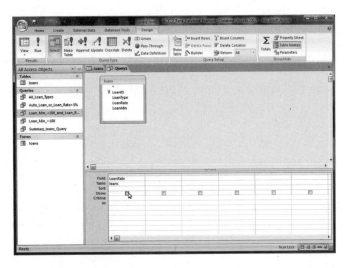

Access Figure 2-44: Starting the query design.

We don't really want to display a loan rate in the results. We just want to have the *LoanRate* field available for our expression.

Click the Show box to *uncheck* this field.

2. Click in the next field cell of the QBE form to make it active.

Don't add a field here. Instead, click the Builder command.

You'll find the Builder command in the Query Setup group on the Design ribbon under Query Tools, as shown in Access Figure 2-45.

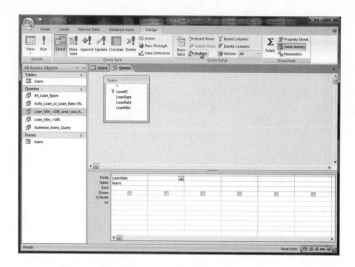

Access Figure 2-45: Starting the Expression Builder.

3. The Expression Builder dialog will appear.

You can use this dialog to create expressions that will calculate values based on the values stored in your database.

As you build the expression, it will appear in the top window of the dialog as shown in Access Figure 2-46.

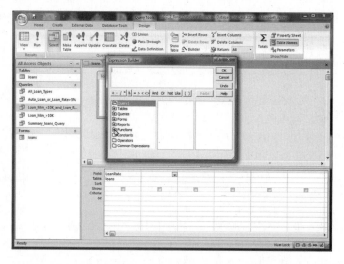

Access Figure 2-46: The Expression Builder dialog.

Of the windows on the bottom, the left window lets you navigate through folders where components for your expression may be stored.

In this window, click Functions and then the subfolder called Built-In Functions.

4. The dialog should now appear as shown in Access Figure 2-47.

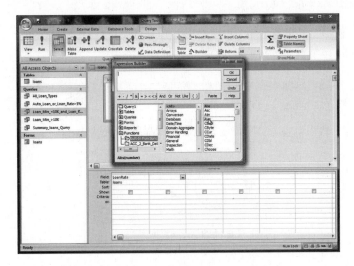

Access Figure 2-47: Built-in expression functions.

In the center window, you now see categories of built-in functions.

After you choose a category (<All> is chosen in the figure) a listing of the available functions are displayed in the rightmost window.

Double-click on the function called Avg listed in the rightmost window.

5. Now you'll see that you have started to build an expression. The text *Avg(«expr»)* is shown in the upper window of the dialog (Access Figure 2-48).

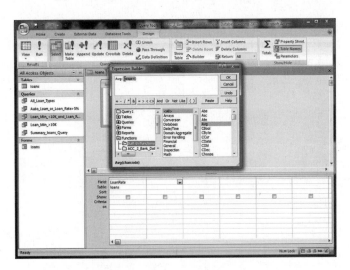

Access Figure 2-48: The Avg function.

The *«expr»* means that we need to replace this part with some type of expression that returns a set of numbers that can be averaged.

6. In the upper window of the dialog, highlight *«expr»* and replace it with the field name *LoanRate* as shown in Access Figure 2-49.

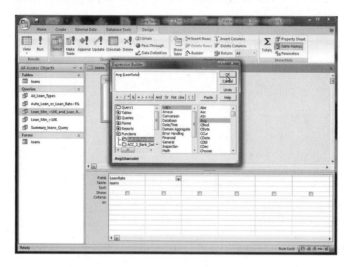

Access Figure 2-49: The Avg function applied to *LoanRate*.

In this case, the expression that we are supplying to the function is simply the name of a field in the database.

We could have also retrieved the field name by using the navigation windows in the lower portion of the dialog. Try it!

7. Click OK on the Expression Builder dialog.

You should now see the expression that you built in the field cell of the QBE form as shown in Access Figure 2-50.

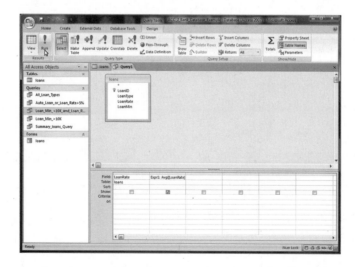

Access Figure 2-50: The expression in the QBE form.

Take a good look at how the expression looks and then run the query to see the results so far.

8. Looks pretty good!

As shown in Access Figure 2-51, we see a number that we can presume is the average of the loan rates.

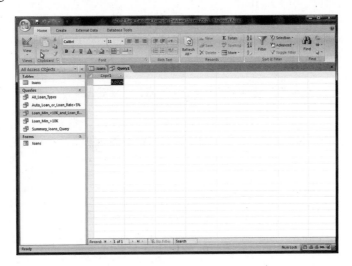

Access Figure 2-51: The expression results so far.

Notice that the average rate is shown as a decimal number and that the field heading says *Expr1*. It would be nice to make the value and the heading more meaningful.

▶**Thinking Critically:**
How could you check to see whether this query is working correctly?

---

9. Return to Design View for the query.

Right click on the field cell in the QBE form to obtain the menu shown in Access Figure 2-52.

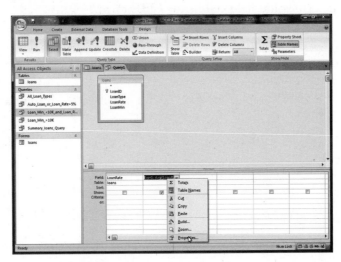

Access Figure 2-52: Adjusting the Expression field.

Select Properties.

Notice the Build option. We could have called the Expression Builder dialog here as well.

10. A dialog will appear on the right of the Design window that you can use to adjust the properties of this field.

Bring down the list for the Format property and select Percent, as shown in Access Figure 2-53.

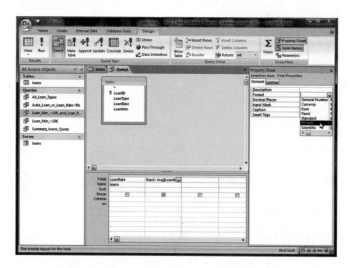

Access Figure 2-53: The Expression field properties.

Before moving along, take a moment to look at the other properties that you could adjust here.

11. The easiest way to change the displayed field heading is simply to edit it in the QBE form.

Select the expression field cell in the QBE form.

Notice that the current heading, *Expr1,* is shown before the expression itself and separated from it by a colon.

Adjust the text by replacing *Expr1* with *Loan_Rate_Average* as shown in Access Figure 2-54.

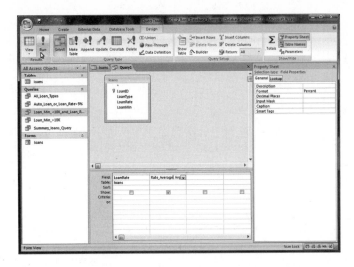

Access Figure 2-54: Editing the field heading.

12. After running the query, you'll see the results shown in Access Figure 2-55.

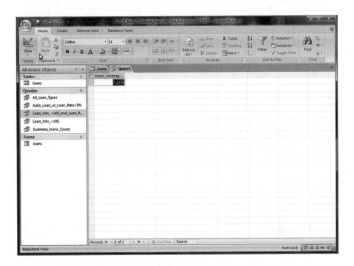

Access Figure 2-55: The final query results.

The value is the same, but what you are looking at makes a little more sense with the new heading and the % symbol as clues.

Save your query as:

Loan_Rate_Average.

COMMUNICATING RESULTS USING ACCESS REPORTS

Reports are snapshots of selected parts of your data. The contents of a report are based on the criteria you specify; for example, base the report on a table or a query. When you create an Access report, you are basically defining the fields and records in the database that will be a part of the report, and you are defining formatting options that will determine how your report will look. Reports display the data in only those fields that you included when you built the report. If you left out a field in a table or a query, it will be present elsewhere in your database but it will not appear on your report.

You can use reports to organize and view your data, and you can share these views with others. Reports and queries are two ways to create information from your data. In this section we'll look at how we can create a report based on our *loans* table. The same process can be used to create a report from a query.

1. To begin, open the *loans* table.

   Before starting a report it's best to have open the component that you want to base the report on.

   Now, click the Reports command in the Reports group on the Create ribbon as shown in Access Figure 2-56.

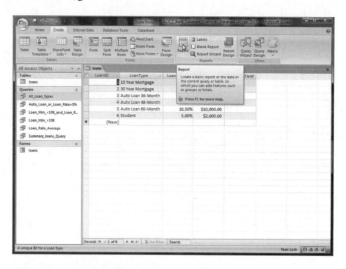

Access Figure 2-56: Starting to create a report.

2. A report is generated and is shown in the report Layout view as in Access Figure 2-57.

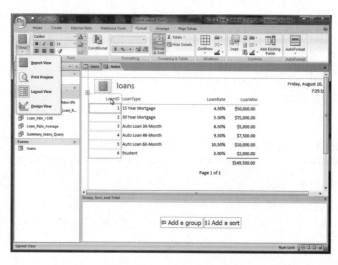

Access Figure 2-57: The initially created *loans* report.

Notice that the report is showing the data that is currently in the table.

It's pretty good already, but we can do a few things to make it better.

Since the Loan ID is automatically generated by Access, it doesn't mean much for our report, so let's delete it from the report.

3. Right-click on the column heading for the *LoanID* on the report.

Select Delete from the context-sensitive menu as shown in Access Figure 2-58.

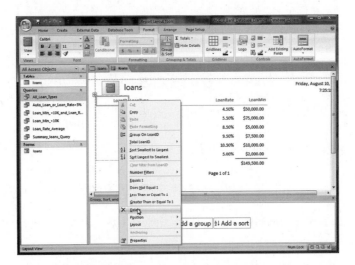

Access Figure 2-58: Deleting *LoanID* from the report.

The *LoanID* column will disappear from the report and the other fields will adjust to the left.

Note that this does not delete the field from the table, only from the report.

4. Let's make the report more attractive.

Bring up the AutoFormat layouts available on the Format ribbon under Report Layout Tools, as shown in Access Figure 2-59.

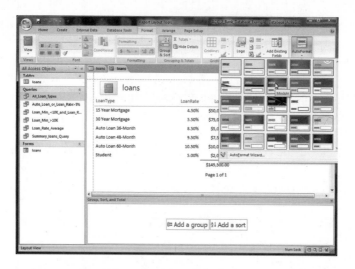

Access Figure 2-59: Selecting an AutoFormat.

Choose a look that you think is attractive.

We chose the one called Module.

5. Let's also sort the records on the report in increasing order of *LoanRate*.

    Click the box at the bottom of the window labeled Add a Sort as shown in Access Figure 2-60.

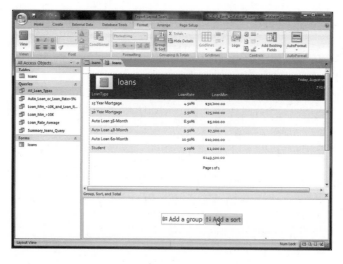

Access Figure 2-60: The AutoFormatted report.

6. A list of the fields that are available in the report is displayed.

    Select the *LoanRate* field from the list as shown in Access Figure 2-61.

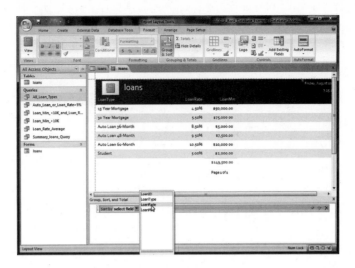

Access Figure 2-61: Sorting the report records by *LoanRate*.

If you wanted, you could add second and third levels of sorting to the report. We'll stop with one.

7. We should also make the report title a bit more descriptive.

    Double-click on the report title.

    A text box will open, and you can edit the text within it.

    Edit the title to read *Bank Loan Types* as shown in Access Figure 2-62.

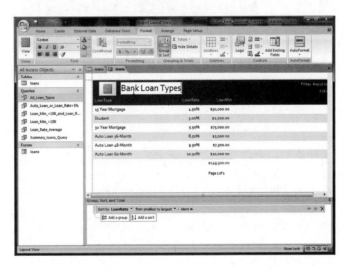

Access Figure 2-62: Editing the Report Title.

8. You can edit the column headings in the report in the same way.

    Edit the column headings to make sense like those shown in Access Figure 2-63.

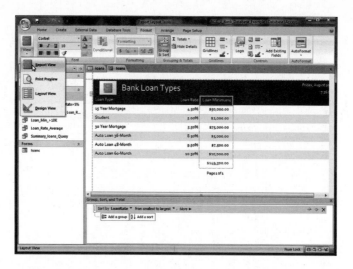

Access Figure 2-63: Final report in Layout view.

Let's have a look at the final report.

Select the Report view.

9. The Report view is shown in Access Figure 2-64.

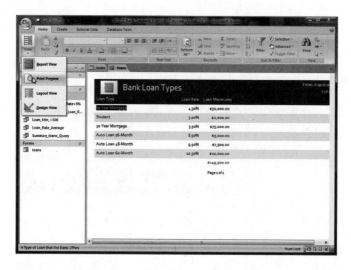

Access Figure 2-64: The final report in Report view.

This is how the report will appear if displayed on the screen.

Now, select the Print view.

10. The Print view shows the report as it will look when printed.

Notice that the ribbon has changed to provide you with various print options (Access Figure 2-65).

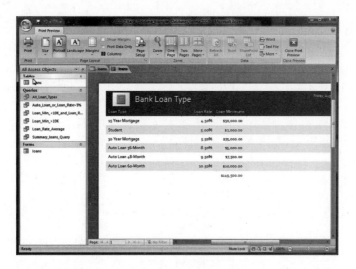

Access Figure 2-65: The final report in Report view.

> ► **Thinking Critically:**
> What more could you do to the report to make it better? Give some of your ideas a try.

EXERCISES TO BUILD YOUR KNOWLEDGE OF MS ACCESS

Match each of the Access terms with its description.

____ 1. AND query

____ 2. Detail query

____ 3. Expression Builder

____ 4. OR query

____ 5. Query

____ 6. Query by example (QBE)

a. A tool for selecting data from a database that can help you answer a specific question.

b. A tool for presenting the data in a database by preparing a nice-looking template.

c. An Access dialog that helps you build query fields that are calculated or derived from data stored in the database.

d. A query that shows all data that satisfies the query design and criteria.

e. A query in which the data that satisfies the query design and criteria is aggregated into values such as totals, averages, minimum values, and maximum values.

f. The use of a form to create the design for a query rather than a text description.

_____ 7. Report

g. A standard, textual language that can be used to create query designs.

_____ 8. Structured query language (SQL)

h. A query that uses two or more filter criteria. A record will satisfy the criteria only if it simultaneously satisfies all of the criteria.

_____ 9. Summary query

i. A query that uses two or more filter criteria. A record will satisfy the criteria if it satisfies just one of the criteria.

_____ 10. Wildcard

j. A special character such as **?** or ***** that can be included in a query filter and used to represent any character or string of characters.

Follow the directions in this Access tutorial to create and execute queries to the *loans* table discussed in the tutorial using QBE. In addition, you should create and run queries using QBE to answer these questions:

11. Which loans have an interest rate less than 6%?

12. Which loans have a *LoanType* of "Student Loan"?

13. Which loans have a loan minimum between $5,000 and $10,000?

14. Which loans are either a Mortgage loan or an Auto loan?

15. Which loans have an interest rate less than 5% and a loan minimum greater than $10,000?

16. Copy the *ACC_2_Bank_Database_Example.accdb* file to a new folder and complete the following exercises (do *not* modify the original version of the file because you will need it for future tutorials).

    You should add the following new loan types to *loans* table:

LoanType	LoanRate	LoanMin
Personal	12%	$1,000
Credit Card	18%	$10

Once you do this, open your customer report (*rptLoan*). Has it been updated?

17. Now go back to the loans table and add a *LoanTerm* field between *LoanType* and *LoanMin*. Once you've done this, give all loans in the database the appropriate term length in months (for the student loan, make it 120 months; for the personal loan, make it 60 months; and

for the credit card loan, make it 12 months. All other loan terms should be evident to you.) Close the table and open the loans report. Is it updated? Hmmmm. Why not? See if you can use the Report Design or Layout view to add the new field to the report.

Assume that you have a table called *stocks* with the following fields:

Field Name	Data Type	Description
stockSymbol	Text	A text symbol up to 5 characters long.
stockName	Text	The full name of the stock.
purchaseDate	Date/Time	The date when the block of stock was purchased.
purchasePrice	Currency	The price per share at which the block of stock was purchased.
numberOfShares	Number (Integer)	The number of shares in the block of stock.

Access Table 2-2: *stocks* table fields.

Answer the following questions (keep in mind that you could create an example database in Access to help you obtain the answers):

18. What field(s) and criterion(criteria) would you use in a query designed to answer the questions: "Which stocks were bought before August 2007?"

_____

_____

_____

_____

19. What field(s) and criterion(criteria) would you use in a query designed to answer the questions: "Which stocks were bought before August 2007 that has a stock purchase price less than $100 per share?"

_____

_____

_____

_____

20. What field(s) and criterion(criteria) would you use in a query designed to answer the questions: "Which stocks were bought before August 2007 or after December 2007?"

_____

_____

_____

21. Suppose you wanted a query that included a derived field showing how much a block of stock was worth when purchased. Describe how you would set up this query:

_____

_____

_____

22. Suppose that over the last year you have made several separate purchases of a stock with the symbol *IBM*. Describe how you would design a query that showed you the average purchase price per share, the total number of shares owned, and the number of different purchase transactions for this stock.

_____

_____

_____

Use Access Help to find the answers to the following questions:

23. If applied to a Text field in a query, what would the criterion *Is Not Null And <>* show us?

24. When is it possible and when is it not possible to edit data with a query?

25. What is report grouping used for?

ACCESS TUTORIAL 2: MINI-CASE 1

Scenario: Canard and Sons, founded in 1980, was a small, family-run maker and distributor of gourmet pâtês. In 1988, the company was sold to MultiBrands, Inc. A new management team was installed, but the conglomerate retained the original name, which had become quite well known among pâté connoisseurs. Since then the enterprise has grown from a small family business to one that employs over 30 people. Toby Childers, the director of human resources, has long maintained a list of the company's employees in the form of a single-table Access database. Using the database, Mr. Childers can answer many questions that he and other managers might have about the company's associates.

File: Download and open the Access database *ACC_2_MC_Employees.accdb*.

Your Task: Use queries with the Access database *ACC_2_MC_Employees.accdb* to answer the following questions:

- What are the names, departments, and salaries of all employees? (Save this query as *EmployeeList.*)
- What are the names of all of the employees in the Accounting department? (Save this query as *AccountingList.*)
- What are the names and departments of employees who have an annual salary of at least $100,000? (Save this query as *100000.*)
- What are the names, departments, and birthdates of employees with an annual salary between $30,000 and $50,000? (Save this query as *30kto50k.*)
- Who are the employees who have worked at the company since the year 2000? (Save this as *after2000.*)
- Who are the employees who have worked at the company since the year 2000 and have an annual salary at least $35,000? (Save this as *after2000and35k.*)
- List the employees that are in both the Finance (FIN) and Operations (OPS) departments. (Save your query as *FINorOPS.*)
- Which employees will have been with the company for more than 10 years at the start of 2007? (Save your query as *10Years.*)
- Which employees will have been with the company for more than 10 years or will be over 30 years of age as of the start of 2007? (Save your query as *10Yearsor30.*)

Make a report based on *salary30kto50k*. Group the data by the birth date and sort the data within groups by salary.

ACCESS TUTORIAL 2: MINI-CASE 2

Scenario: Pepé L'Arrange is organizationally challenged. He's very talented and when he gets around to doing anything he generally does it very well. The problem is that he just can't keep up with what it is he needs to do next. He's decided that he needs to take the database skills that he learned in class and build himself a tool that he can use to organize his life. Unfortunately, Pepé has forgotten to get it built, so he needs your help. What's needed is a database table that Pepé can use to keep up with the tasks that he needs to do and when they need to get done. In a moment of organizational inspiration, he did manage to make a list of the fields that are needed in this table. These are shown in Access Table 2-3.

Field Name	Data Type	Description
taskDesc	Text	A description of the task that needs to be done.
taskPriority	Number (Integer)	How important the task is relative to others in the database. Stored as a number from 1 to 5 with 1 being the most important.
taskDueDate	Date/Time	The date when the task needs to be completed. For some items there may be no due date.
taskCompleted	Yes/No	Whether or not the task has been completed.
taskCategory	Text	The number of shares in the block of stock.

Access Table 2-3: *Tasks* table fields.

File: There is no file to download for this case.

Your Task: Build a database with the table described in the Scenario. Create a form that Pepé can use to enter tasks. Add queries to the database that will help Pepé by answering the following questions.

- What items are due within the next week? (Save this query as *weeklyTasks.*)
- What tasks are stored for the "school" category? (Save this query as *schoolTasks.*)
- Are there any tasks with a priority of 1 that are due today? (Save this query as *highToday.*)
- How many tasks for the "Work" category have been completed? (Save this query as *workDone.*)
- How many tasks from last week were completed? (Save this as *lastCompleted.*)
- Which tasks are stored that have no due date or a priority of 5? (Save this as *lowTasks.*)

Also, create a report based on one of the queries that will show the tasks for the next week in order of due date and priority. You should make up data and enter it into your table to test the components that you create.

Tutorial 3

WORKING WITH TABLES IN MICROSOFT ACCESS 2007

After reading this tutorial and completing the associated exercises, you will be able to:

- Work with related tables in Access using primary and foreign keys.
- Set input masks and LookUp fields.
- Implement referential integrity between tables.
- Create QBE queries for related tables.

Files for Download: Files associated with this tutorial for you to download include:

- The tutorial example template file, *ACC_3_Bank_Database_Example.accdb*

MICROSOFT ACCESS: A RELATIONAL DATABASE APPLICATION

Since Microsoft Access is a relational database application, it can work with more than one table. The relational model enables Access to store data in tables and then link tables via common fields. For example, assume we have the same banking application as covered in the first two Access tutorials. In that case, in addition to the *loans* table discussed earlier, we might have two other tables—say, a table of customer information, named *customers,* and a table of information on which customers have which loans, named *customerLoans.* In this case, the primary key (*LoanID*) field in the *loans* table and a copy of the *LoanID* field (a foreign key) in the *customerLoans* table are used to link these two tables. Similarly, the primary key in the *customers* table (*CustomerID*) and a copy of it in the *customerLoans* table (a foreign key) are used to link these two tables. In the process, the *loans* and *customers* tables are also linked.

Note that a customer's information is stored only once, in the *customers* table. This reduces data redundancy and improves updating and other database functions. The decision as to exactly which tables to create is discussed in more detail in the Appendix on Data Modeling that is part of the Access Tutorial.

As with other tutorials, most of this tutorial will be spent *learning by building.* First you will expand the *BankDatabaseExample* database by adding the *customers* and *customerLoans* tables. You will then learn how to link the tables by creating relationships. Once the tables are linked, you will learn how to query a multi-table database and to create reports from it.

BUILDING MULTIPLE TABLES

To work with multiple tables, you first need to start MS Access and open the *ACC_3_Bank_Database_Example.accdb* file. From the database window, click the Table command on the Create ribbon to begin creating a new table named *customers* in the Design view. The required field names and data types for the *customers* table are shown in Access Table 3-1, and the description for the *customerLoans* table is provided in Access Table 3-2. You should use this information to create the two new tables in the database. Be sure to define a primary key for each table.

Field Name	Data Type	Comments
custID	Text	9-digit social security number (primary key)
custLastName	Text	Last name
custFirstName	Text	First name
custBirthDate	Date/Time	Used for promotional purposes
custEMail	Text	Point of contact for customer

Access Table 3-1: *customers* table fields.

Repeat the table creation process to create the fields for the *customerLoans* table shown in Access Table 3-2.

Field Name	Data Type	Comments
custLoanID	AutoNumber	(primary key)
custLoanStartDate	Date/Time	Date when the loan began
custLoanAmount	Currency	Amount of loan
custLoanStatus	Text	Status of loan (Current, Late, Paid-in-full, etc.)
FKcustID	Text	Foreign key from the *customer* table
FKloanID	Number	Foreign key from the *loan* table

Access Table 3-2: *customerLoans* table fields.

Notice in Access Table 3-2 that we have two fields in this table with the prefix FK. These two fields are foreign keys that correspond to the primary keys in the *customers* and *loans* tables, respectively. One rule of relational databases is that when there is a one-to-many relationship between two entities in the data model, the primary key of the entity on the "one" side of the relationship will be used as a foreign key in the table on the "many" side of the relationship. These foreign keys should already be listed in the logical data model that you are using for your blueprint. The important thing to watch out for here is that you need to make sure the data type used for a foreign key field is compatible to that used when the attribute is used as a primary key. After adding the two tables just described, your database will have three tables as shown in the navigation pane displayed in Access Figure 3-1.

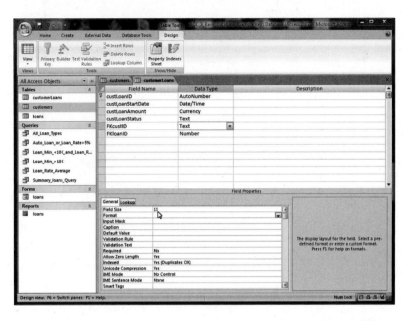

Access Figure 3-1: Tables in *BankDatabaseExample* database.

Input Masks

In regard to formatting fields, an input mask is a useful tool. An input mask prevents users from such errors as entering improper characters, too many characters, or forgetting a character. In other words, input masks help the users enter the correct data, thereby improving the accuracy and integrity of the data in our database. Before we enter data into the tables, let's make a few changes to the basic table design by adding input masks to some fields. For example, we will show you how to create a social security number input mask for the *custID* field and a short date input mask in the *customers* table.

1. Start by going to the Design view of the *customers* table.

   The first field that we want to set an input mask for is the *custID* field. So select it by clicking on the *custID* field name.

   In the field properties form, click in the Input Mask field. A button with an ellipsis (...) will appear as shown in Access Figure 3-2. Whenever you see this type of button, a dialog will appear when you click it.

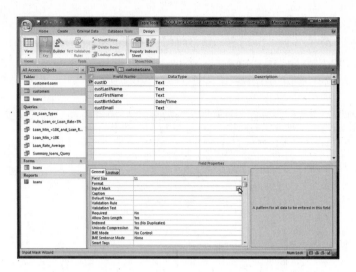

Access Figure 3-2: The *customer* table in Design view.

2. In this case, the Input Mask Wizard dialog appears as shown in Access Figure 3-3.

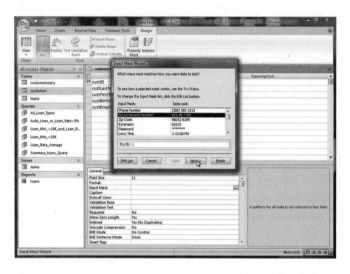

Access Figure 3-3: The Input Mask Wizard dialog.

An input mask basically defines a pattern that the data must fit.

On the first page of the Wizard you'll find a list of patterns that represent the most commonly used input masks for the data type.

Select the Social Security Number pattern and click Next.

3. The pages in the Wizard may appear differently for different types of patterns.

Here, we are presented with a text box in which we can make adjustments to the pattern. This is currently beyond our knowledge, so we'll rely on the built-in pattern.

We can also select a placeholder character that the user will see when entering data into the field.

Since the user will be entering numbers, let's select the # symbol for the place holder, as shown in Access Figure 3-4, and click Next.

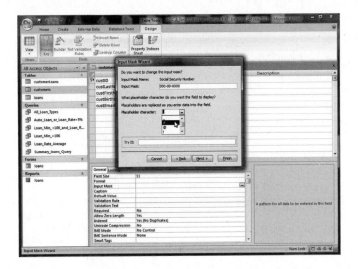

Access Figure 3-4: Setting a placeholder.

4. On the next page of the Wizard we are presented with choices for how the data will be stored.

   We'll choose to store the data with the symbols so the social security number will have hyphens wherever it appears.

   Select the option that reflects this choice, as shown in Access Figure 3-5, and click Next.

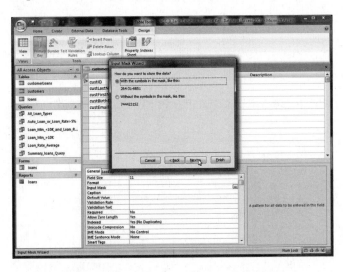

Access Figure 3-5: Selecting storage format.

▶ **Thinking Critically:**
Assume that one day your bank will be as big as the Bank of America. The Input Mask Wizard asks you whether you want to store the "-" symbols or just the numbers. What are you going to choose? Why?

5. The final page just indicates that you are finished.

So, unless you want to go back and adjust something, click Finish as shown in Access Figure 3-6.

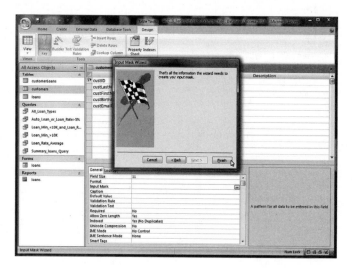

Access Figure 3-6: Last page of Input Mask Wizard.

6. Another likely candidate for an input mask is the *custBirthDate* field.

Select this field and pull up the Input Mask Wizard.

Notice that the patterns available for the Date/Time data type are different from those for the Text data type.

Select the Short Date pattern and click the Finish button as shown in Access Figure 3-7.

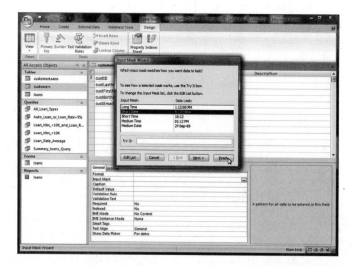

Access Figure 3-7: Selecting Date/Time input mask.

Important! When working with multiple tables, it's a "best practice" to wait until the relationships between the tables have been defined (see a later section in this tutorial) before entering data. However, we want to show you the results of the input masks that you just created, so we are going to violate that practice just this once. Usually, it's not a good idea to do this, and we (the authors) will follow the "best practices" when creating our own databases. For now though, please bear with us.

7. With the input masks set, go to the Datasheet view of the *customers* table as shown in Access Figure 3-8.

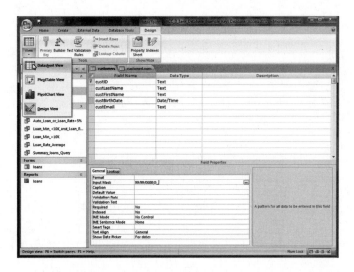

Access Figure 3-8: Switching to Datasheet view.

8. Notice that when we make changes to the table design, these need to be saved before we can switch views.

   Click Yes when asked to save the table, as shown in Access Figure 3-9.

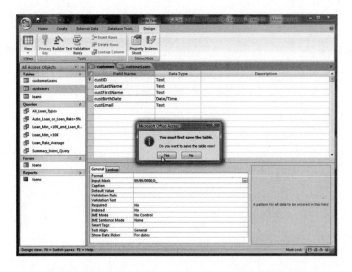

Access Figure 3-9: Saving the *customers* table.

9. Click in the *custID* field and start typing a social security number. (Make one up; don't use your real one!)

   Notice that a pattern appears showing you where to type the digits, as shown in Access Figure 3-10.

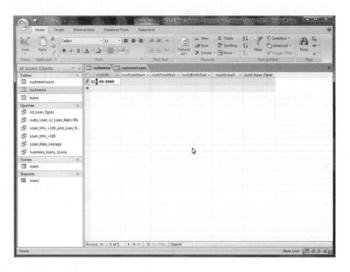

Access Figure 3-10: Typing data into a field with an input mask.

   Remember that you selected the # sign to designate where to type when you set up the input mask.

10. Type a last name (we used *Trump*) and a first name (ours is *Daffy*).

    Now enter in a birth date.

    Notice again that an input mask guides how you can enter the date data, as shown in Access Figure 3-11.

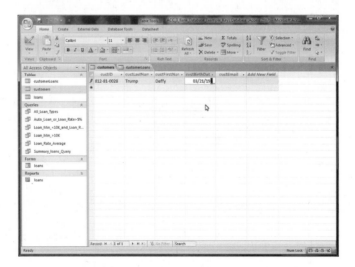

Access Figure 3-11: Entering data into a date input mask.

11. Go ahead and add a couple more records, as shown in Access Figure 3-12, to get used to how the input masks work.

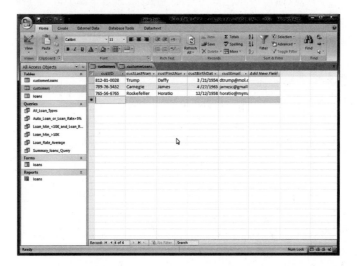

Access Figure 3-12: Entering a few more records.

Can you see how input masks can be helpful in making sure that users enter valid data?

Lookup Fields

Let's adjust a couple of fields in the *customerLoans* table to make data entry a little more user friendly. Specifically, we will change the data type of the foreign key fields so that the user entering data can easily look up a record in a related table that they want to reference. Recall that a foreign key is primarily a reference to a record in another table. Since the primary key of the record in the other table is a unique value, whenever that value is used in a foreign key, it serves as a reference to that single record.

A value that we want to enter into a foreign key field must already exist as a primary key value in the related table. One difficulty in entering foreign key values is that it can be difficult to remember the possible values available to enter. This is especially true if the primary key has the AutoNumber data type (automatically generated by Access).

One way to overcome this difficulty is to allow the user to actually look up values from a list when entering the foreign key. Access provides the Lookup Wizard data type just for this. Let's see how we can use this to improve data entry from the *customerLoans* table.

1. Pull up the *customerLoans* table in the Design view.

Click on the Data Type field on the QBE form for the *FKCustID* field.

On the Data Type list select Lookup Wizard as shown in Access Figure 3-13.

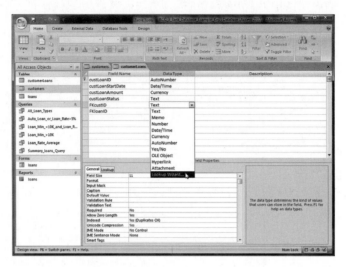

Access Figure 3-13: Selecting the Lookup Wizard data type.

2. You have the option of looking up values that exist in another table or typing in values that you want the user to see.

   For our use, we need to look up existing primary key values from a related table.

   Select this option and click Next, as shown in Access Figure 3-14.

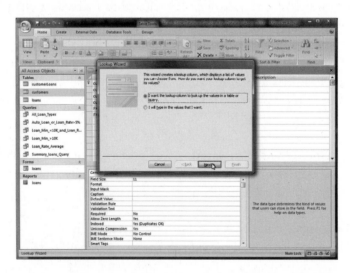

Access Figure 3-14: First page of the Lookup Wizard.

3. On the next page of the Wizard you'll see a list of the tables in the database.

   If you wanted, you could also base your lookup on a query.

   Select the *customers* table and click Next, as shown in Access Figure 3-15.

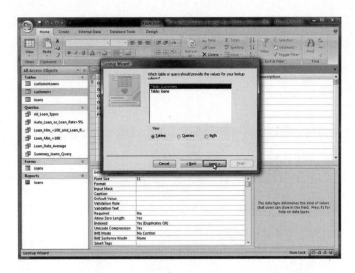

Access Figure 3-15: Selecting the lookup table.

4. You'll now see the fields that are available in the selected table.

Recall that we are trying to set up the lookup in order to enter data into the *FKcustID* field.

So, it makes sense that we select the *custID* field.

Also, select the *custLastName* field, as shown in Access Figure 3-16.

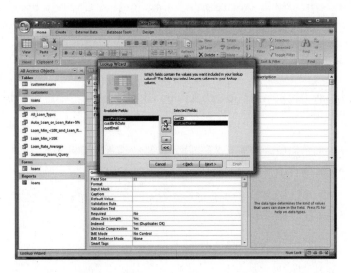

Access Figure 3-16: Selecting the lookup fields.

We'll see why in a moment.

5. On the next page you can choose to sort the lookup list based on one of the fields.

To do this, select the field and then the type of sort (ascending or descending) that you want to do.

We'll skip this and go to the next page by clicking Next, as shown in Access Figure 3-17.

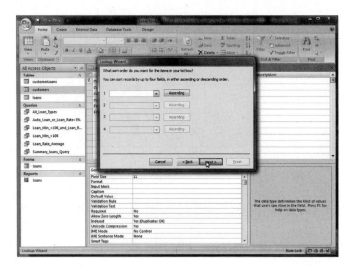

Access Figure 3-17: Sorting the lookup list.

6. Next you're asked how you want the lookup to look.

When entering the data, the user will be presented with a list of options.

The data that we want stored will be the primary key value, but this value will probably have no meaning to the user.

Instead, let's check the box that says the key value will be hidden, as shown in Access Figure 3-18.

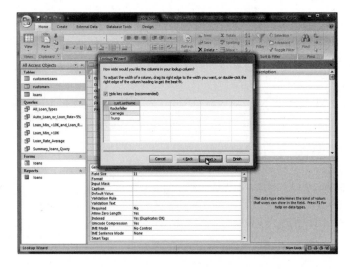

Access Figure 3-18: Adjusting the lookup look.

The remaining list that you see is what the user will see when entering data.

Click Next.

7. The final page of the Lookup Wizard will ask two questions.

    First is what the label for the lookup field should be. For now let's leave it with the original field name, *FKcustID*.

    Second, we can choose to store all of the values.

    Since we really want to store only the reference to the primary key, leave this unchecked.

    Click Finish, as shown in Access Figure 3-19.

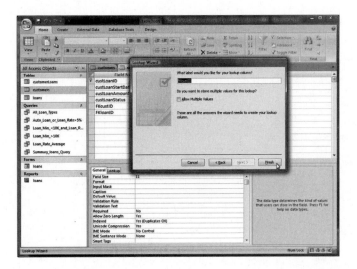

Access Figure 3-19: Final page of Lookup Wizard.

8. Switch over to the Datasheet view of the *customerLoans* table, saving the table when asked.

    Enter some data into the table.

    Click on the arrow that appears in the *FKcustID* field to see a list of values as shown in Access Figure 3-20.

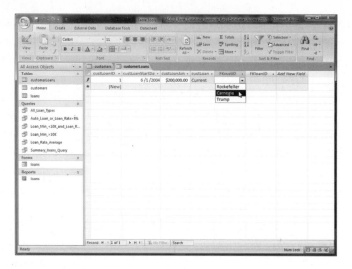

Access Figure 3-20: Entering data using a lookup.

Select the customer last name from the list.

9. Notice that we have a date field in the *customerLoans* table, as shown in Access Figure 3-21. We also have another foreign key field: *FKloanID*.

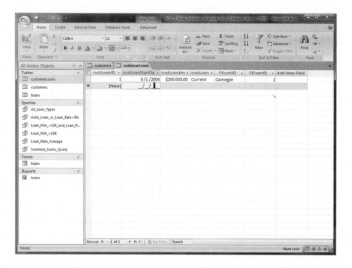

Access Figure 3-21: The *customerLoans* Datasheet view.

Test your skills by adding input masks and/or lookups to these fields as appropriate.

TABLE RELATIONSHIPS

Relationships are a very important part of a relational database. In fact, you might say that they are what make the database, well, relational. Relationships define how the tables in your database are related. As you may have read or will read in our data modeling tutorial, a relational database may contain relationships that are either one-to-one or one-to-many. Recall that a one-to-one relationship means that a record in one table may be related to one and only one record in the related table. One-to-many means that a record in one table may be related to one or more records in the related table.

The foreign keys in the database exist solely for making these relationships. A foreign key provides a reference in one table to a record that is stored in another table. Determining what relationships should be in the logical model and which tables need foreign keys is part of database design, which you can read about in our data modeling tutorial. For now, we need to see how we can specify our intended relationships while we are creating the database in Access.

For our example, we have two relationships. The first is a one-to-many relationship between the *loans* table and the *customerLoans* table. A record in the *loans* table can be related to one or more records in the *customerLoans* table. That is, there can be many customer loans for a single loan type. The second is a one-to-many relationship between the *customers* table and the *customerLoans* table. In other words, a single customer may have one or more loans.

Creating Relationships with Referential Integrity

In Access, you create relationships by specifying a connection between a primary key in one table and a foreign key in another. Let's see how that is done for our example.

1. Open the database and navigate to the Database Tools ribbon.

    You'll find the Relationships command in the Show/Hide group, as shown in Access Figure 3-22.

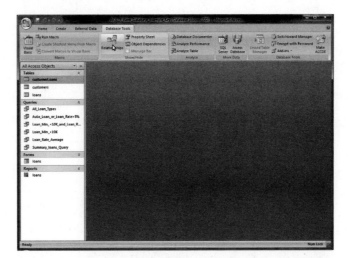

Access Figure 3-22: The Relationships command.

Click it!

2. A blank workspace will appear with a tab labeled "Relationships," as shown in Access Figure 3-23.

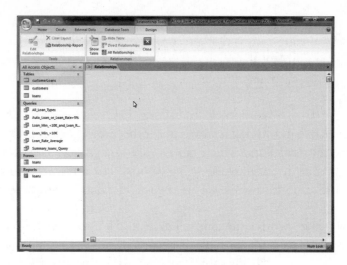

Access Figure 3-23: The Relationships workspace.

Our first step will be to add the tables that we want to connect with relationships.

To do this, click Show Tables on the Design ribbon under Relationship Tools.

3. The Show Table dialog will appear with a list of the tables that are available in the database.

To use this dialog, select each table that you want to see in the workspace and click the Add button.

Click on the *customerLoans* table and click Add, as shown in Access Figure 3-24.

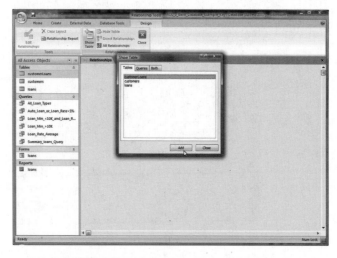

Access Figure 3-24: The Show Table dialog.

4. After selecting a table, a box representing the table will appear in the Relationships workspace.

The box will include a list of the fields in the table.

Now select and add the other two tables, as shown in Access Figure 3-25.

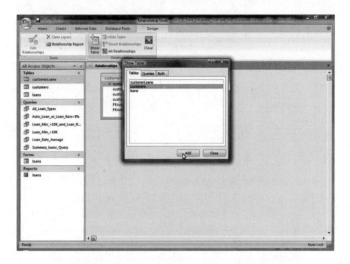

Access Figure 3-25: Showing the tables.

5. You should see the table boxes displayed in the workspace in the order in which you chose them.

We want to connect *customers* to *customerLoans* and *loans* to *customerLoans*.

It would be easier if the *customerLoans* were in between the others.

Fortunately, we can move these boxes around.

Click and hold the top of the *customers* box as shown in Access Figure 3-26.

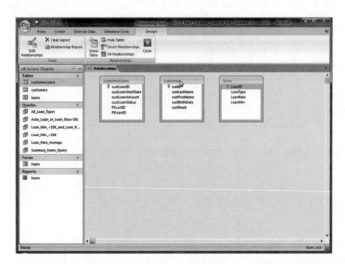

Access Figure 3-26: Tables on the relationships workspace.

6. Now drag that box out of the way so we that you can move *customerLoans* to the center as shown in Access Figure 3-27.

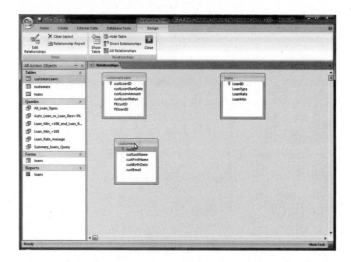

Access Figure 3-27: Moving the table boxes.

Using the same method, drag the *customerLoans* table to the center and arrange the *customers* table on the left.

Arrange the boxes to look something like the arrangement in Access Figure 3-28.

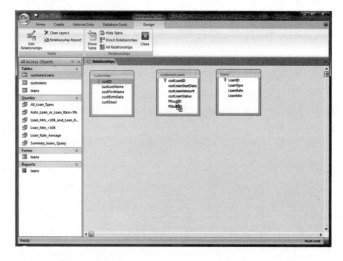

Access Figure 3-28: The relationships table arrangement.

7. It doesn't matter that the boxes line up perfectly. We are moving them for convenience only.

To connect the tables in a relationship, you need to indicate which primary key corresponds to which foreign key.

You can do this by clicking and dragging the name of a primary key field from one table over the foreign key of another.

8. Drag the *custID* field from the *customers* table over the *FKcustID* field in the *customerLoans* table.

   The Edit Relationships dialog will appear.

   The related fields will be shown in the dialog. Check that these are correct.

   Also, check the box labeled Enforce Referential Integrity (more about this later) and click Create as shown in Access Figure 3-29.

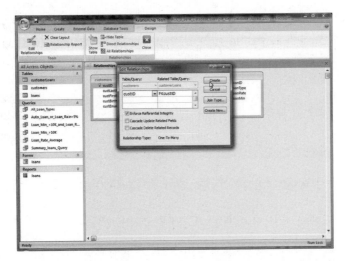

Access Figure 3-29: Edit Relationships dialog.

9. A line connecting the two, now-related tables will appear as shown in Access Figure 3-30.

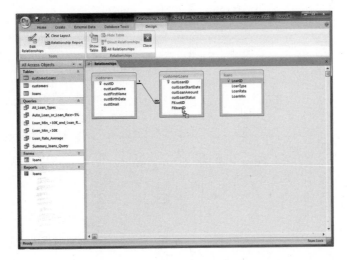

Access Figure 3-30: The newly added relationship.

Since we enforced referential integrity, you should also see that the line is labeled with a 1 and ∞, signifying a one-to-many relationship.

10. Go ahead and create a relationship between the *customerLoans* table and the *loans* table.

The Edit Relationship dialog for this relationship is shown in Access Figure 3-31.

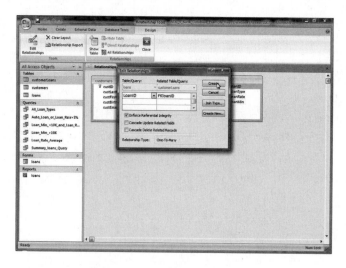

Access Figure 3-31: Edit Relationships dialog.

The completed relationships for our example are shown in Access Figure 3-32.

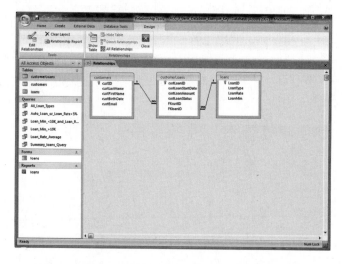

Access Figure 3-32: Completed relationships.

Why Enforce Referential Integrity?

You should think of the values stored in a foreign key as a reference to a record in another table. For example, a value of 10 in the *FKcustID* field of the *customerLoans* table is a reference to the unique record with *custID* = 10 in the *customers* table. Enforcing referential integrity helps us to make sure that there are no references in our database to nonexistent records. If we try to add a record to *customerLoans* that tries to reference a *custID* that does not exist in *customers*, Access will display a message to warn us about it and will not add the erroneous record. Conversely, if we try to remove a customer record from *customers* and that customer has outstanding loans listed in *customerLoans,* we would also get a warning message and would not be permitted to delete the customer. This feature helps to maintain the overall integrity of our database.

Entering Data

You are now ready to enter data into the *customers* and *customerLoans* tables. Sample data for you to use is shown in Access Tables 3-3 and 3-4. You can add data directly using the Datasheet view, or better yet, create a couple of form objects and use them.

custID	*custLastName*	*custFirstName*	*custBirthDate*	*custEMail*
765-56-6765	Rockefeller	Horatio	12/12/1958	horatio@mymail.com
789-76-5432	Carnegie	James	4/27/1963	jamesc@gmail.com
812-81-0028	Trump	Daffy	3/21/1954	dtrump@mol.com
999-11-1111	Patrick	Chris	04/27/1973	cpatrick@abac.not
999-22-2222	Mullins	Jesse	07/24/1985	jmullins@vstate.not
999-33-3333	Crider	Russ	08/22/1974	rcrider@uga.not
999-44-4444	Goodly	Alice	01/31/1962	agoodly@negia.not
999-55-5555	Roberts	John	03/15/1977	jroberts@fsu.not
999-66-6666	Carrall	Ann	11/15/1978	acarrall@aow.not
999-77-7777	Arons	Suzy	09/07/1944	sarons@uf.not
999-88-8888	Allman	Keegan	06/08/1972	rrand@fgcu.not
999-99-9999	Hyatt	Ashley	08/22/1969	ahyatt@uncch.not

Access Table 3-3: *customers* data.

custLoanStart Date	custLoan Amount	custLoan Status	Customer (FKcustID)	Loan (FKloanID)
06/01/2004	$200,000.00	Current	Carnegie	15 Year Mortgage
01/09/2005	$150,000.00	Current	Patrick	15 Year Mortgage
01/15/2005	$14,000.00	Paid in Full	Crider	Auto Loan 48-Month
02/20/2005	$280,000.00	Current	Mullins	30 Year Mortgage
05/22/2005	$28,000.00	Current	Hyatt	Auto Loan 60-Month
10/10/2005	$3,500	Current	Roberts	Student
03/13/2006	$125,000	Current	Goodly	30 Year Mortgage
05/15/2006	$11,500	Current	Carrall	Auto Loan 48-Month
08/31/2006	$3,500	Delinquent 30 Days	Crider	Student
09/30/2006	$15,500	Delinquent 90 Days	Roberts	Auto Loan 60-Month
11/22/2006	$19,500	Current	Crider	Auto Loan 60-Month

Access Table 3-4: *customerLoans* data.

QUERYING A RELATIONAL DATABASE

Now that you've created a relational database composed of three related tables, you are ready to query that database. Creating queries involving multiple tables with the MS Access Query by Example (QBE) facility works just like it does for one table—you add all of the tables needed for the query to the QBE window, select the fields from one or more tables that you wish to see in the query, and then add criteria.

For example, let's create a query that shows us the names of customers who have a loan with an amount that is greater than $30,000. The data with this information is found in two tables: the names in the *customers* table and the loan amount in the *customerLoans* table. We can create this query as follows.

1. Open the database and click the Query Wizard command on the Create ribbon as shown in Access Figure 3-33.

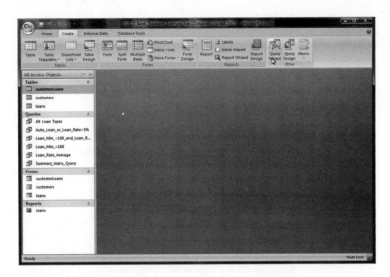

Access Figure 3-33: Starting the Query Wizard.

2. The New Query dialog will appear.

    Select Simple Query Wizard from the list and click OK as shown in Access Figure 3-34.

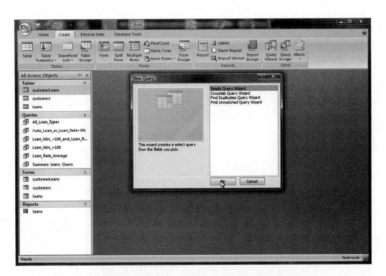

Access Figure 3-34: The New Query dialog.

3. On the next page of the New Query Wizard, you can select the fields that we want to be part of the query.

Select the *customers* table from the Tables/Queries list as shown in Access Figure 3-35.

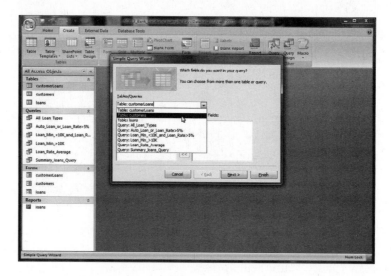

Access Figure 3-35: Selecting the *customers* table.

4. A list of the *customer* table fields will be displayed in the Available Fields list.

   Highlight the *custLastName* field and click the right arrow to add it to the Selected Fields list as shown in Access Figure 3-36.

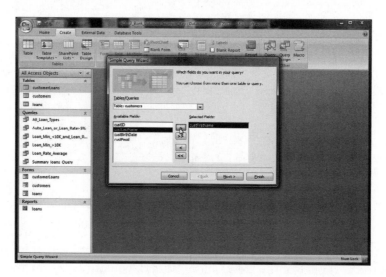

Access Figure 3-36: Selecting *custLastName* field.

5. Use the same technique to add the *custFirstName* field from the *customers* table and then the *custLoanAmount* from the *customerLoans* table.

   Click Next to go to the next page of the Wizard as shown in Access Figure 3-37.

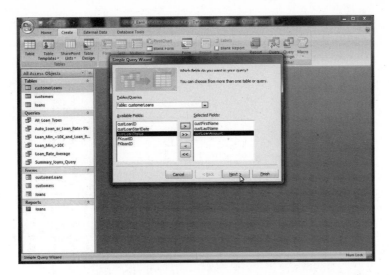

Access Figure 3-37: Adding the remaining query fields.

6. Select Detail Query and click Next as shown in Access Figure 3-38.

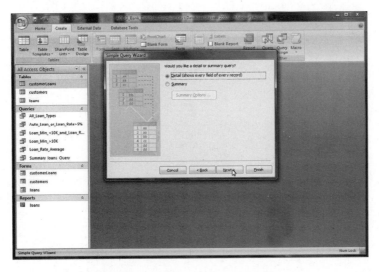

Access Figure 3-38: Selecting detail query.

7. On the final page, name the query *loans*>30K.

We're not really through designing the query, but that is all we can do with the Query Wizard.

Select "Modify the query design" before clicking Finish as shown in Access Figure 3-39.

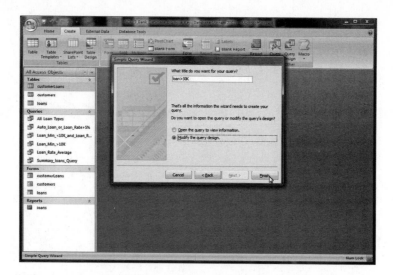

Access Figure 3-39: Naming the query.

8. You'll then see the QBE query design as shown in Access Figure 3-40.

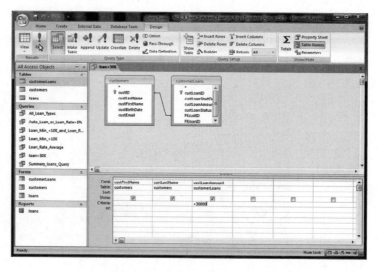

Access Figure 3-40: The Query Design

To complete the query, we need to add the criterion

> 30000

to the *custLoanAmount* field.

Do that and then click the Run command on the Design ribbon under Query Tools, as shown in Access Figure 3-40.

9. You should now see the query results as shown in Access Figure 3-41.

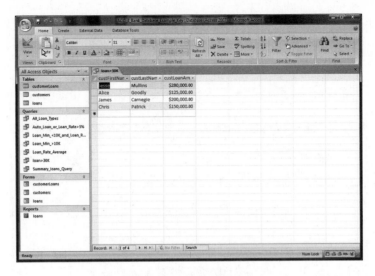

Access Figure 3-41: The query results.

Notice that all loan amounts are above $30,000.

Remember that this query drew results from two different but related tables.

Queries that draw data from two or more tables are known as **join queries**.

Let's adjust the design to add some data from the *loans* table as well.

10. In Design view, right-click anywhere in the workspace to get the context-sensitive menu shown in Access Figure 3-42.

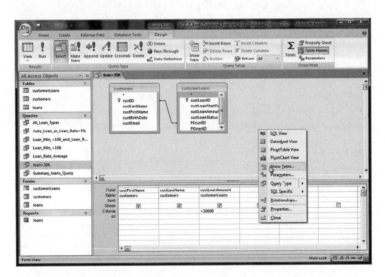

Access Figure 3-42: QBE context-sensitive menu.

Have a look at the options available.

For now, select Show Table.

11. You'll see the Show Table dialog again with the list of tables.

This time, select the *loans* table and click Show.

After it appears as shown in Access Figure 3-43, close the dialog.

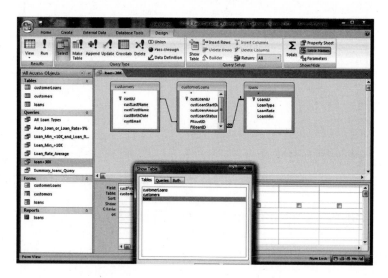

Access Figure 3-43: Adding the *loans* table to the query.

12. Now add the *loanType* and *loanRate* fields to the query.

Finally, click the Run command as shown in Access Figure 3-44.

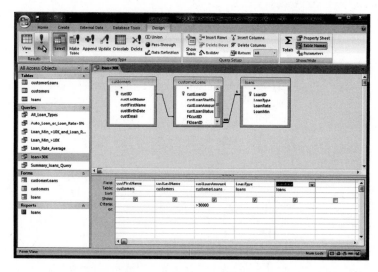

Access Figure 3-44: Adding fields from the *loans* table.

13. Your results should appear like those shown in Access Figure 3-45.

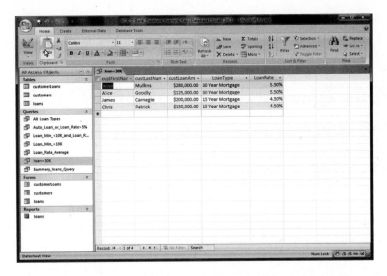

Access Figure 3-45: The three-table query results.

Now we have a query that draws from three different but related tables.

Using these techniques you can create the more complex queries like those discussed in Access Tutorial 2.

EXERCISES TO BUILD YOUR KNOWLEDGE OF MS ACCESS

Match each of the Access terms with its description.

____ 1. Input mask

a. A query that draws data from two or more related tables.

____ 2. Join query

b. A pattern you can set on a field to make sure that the user enters data in a valid format.

____ 3. Lookup field

c. Setting a data type so that the user can select the value to enter in a field from a list of available values.

____ 4. Referential integrity

d. A connection between two tables that is created by linking the primary key of one table to a corresponding foreign key in another table.

____ 5. Relationship

e. A feature that ensures that the foreign key values entered into a database are valid references.

6. Follow the directions in this Access tutorial to add the *customers* and *customerLoans* tables to the *ACC_3_Bank_Database_Example.accdb* database file. Be sure to include creating the relationships between the tables and then adding the data shown in Access Tables 3-3 and 3-4.

7. Follow the directions in this Access tutorial to use QBE to create and execute *all* of the queries to the tables in the *ACC_3_Bank_Database_Example.accdb* database discussed in the tutorial.

In addition, you should create and run queries to display the following information:

8. List all customers with a loan having an interest rate greater than 6%.

9. List the e-mail address and birth date of all customers with a loan amount greater than $50,000.

10. List the SSNs and first and last names of all customers who are delinquent on their loans. Also include the loan amount and loan type.

Use Access Help to find the answers to the following questions:

11. An input mask can contain three sections. What are they?

12. What are a bound value and a display value in a lookup column?

13. What is an inner join? Do the queries discussed in the tutorial use inner joins?

14. When you choose to enforce referential integrity, what does Access do to make sure that references are correct?

15. On the Database Tools ribbon next to the Relationships command in the Show/Hide group there is a command called Object Dependencies. What is an object dependency and what is shown when you click this command?

ACCESS TUTORIAL 3: MINI-CASE 1

Scenario: Breanna had always been a voracious reader. She read just about anything she could get her hands on: mysteries, romance, biographies, science fiction. You name a book and there's a high probability that Breanna has read it. She also owns many of the books that she's read. Breanna is about to go off to college in another city, and her vast book collection has become a bit of a problem. She can't take them with her—too much to transport and too many to fit in her dorm room. In addition, her entrepreneurial parents are eager to rent out her room. The solution? Store the books in the attic. But, before she does, Breanna wants to take an inventory and store her book lists in a database rather than keep paper-based lists.

Your Task: Help Breanna by creating the Access database tables shown in the Access data model in Access Figure 3-46. Use appropriate data types for each field. Fields that are bold in the figure represent the primary keys for each table. (Note: both fields in the *authorISBNs* are bold. This is known as a **compound primary key**. It means that the *combination* of the two field values should be unique for each record.) Use the Access Relationship window to add the relationships between tables. Remember to enforce referential integrity.

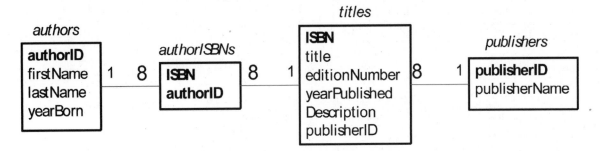

Access Figure 3-46: Book inventory database.

Create data entry forms for your database. Make one form for each table.

Enter appropriate data into your database using the forms that you created. You may make up the data, or you can find inspiration using your personal library.

Create Access queries that will answer the following questions:

- What authors (first and last name) wrote what books (title, year published, and description) by what publisher (publisher name)? (Save your query as *bookList*.)
- Choose one of the authors in your database. What publishers published books by this author)? (Save your query as *authorPub*.)
- What books if any have more than one edition (title, author, publisher, edition, year published)? (Save your query as *edition*.)
- What authors wrote a book that was published before 1990? (Save your query as *1990Entries*.)

Create a report based on the query *bookList*. Group by authors' last names. Subgroup by publisher name.

ACCESS TUTORIAL 3: MINI-CASE 2

Scenario: Melita Voiture is the proud owner of a car service in the big city. Her cars are hired out on a daily basis to her customers. In addition to Melita's fleet of cars, she owns a garage with several mechanics on staff to maintain the fleet. Melita's customers prefer their cars in perfect working order. While Melita covers the costs of preventive maintenance, other repairs are paid for by the customer. Melita needs to keep track of when the cars are hired out and to whom. In addition, she wants to keep careful track of how often cars have been maintained, who worked on them, and the details of the work performed. In order to keep up with this data, she's commissioned you to create a database based on the model shown in Access Figure 3-47.

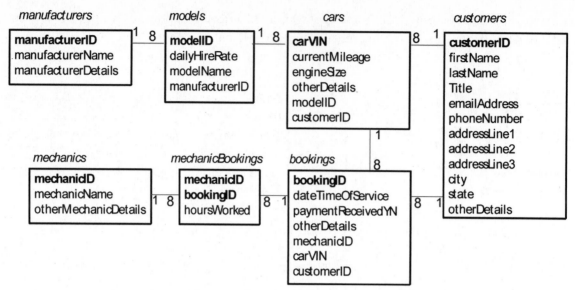

Access Figure 3-47: Car maintenance database.

Your Task: Create a database based on Melita's data model. Your database should include the tables, fields, and relationships shown. Choose appropriate data types and set input masks and lookup fields as appropriate. In addition, create queries to answer the following questions:

- Which customers use which cars and at what daily rate?
- What is the total daily rate for all cars?
- Which mechanics worked on a car for more than 5 hours?
- Which cars have been worked on in the last 3 months?
- Which customers still owe for repair work? (Create a query and a report based on the query.)

Tutorial 4

MICROSOFT ACCESS 2007 AND SQL

After reading this tutorial and completing the associated exercises, you will be able to:

- Discuss the use of SQL to query a relational database.
- Find matching records using a SELECT query.
- Carry out computations using aggregate functions.
- Insert, delete, or change records into a table.
- Use SQL with multiple tables.

Files for Download: Files associated with this tutorial for you to download include:

- The tutorial example template file, *ACC_4_Bank_Database_Example.accdb*
- The mini-case template file, *ACC_4_MC_Students. accdb*

LEARNING ABOUT SQL

For a relational database, the instructions for finding records are written in the form of queries in **Structured Query Language (SQL)**, which is a computer language for manipulating data in a relational database. SQL queries also enable database users to add new records or change or delete records in a database that meets some stated criterion. The **Query By Example (QBE)** system that you have been using to query databases takes the design you give it and converts it into SQL when it actually queries the database.

The general form of an SQL query to search for matching records is:

SELECT *fields* FROM *tables* WHERE *fields match query condition*

In the SQL statement, the **SELECT** keyword designates which fields will be displayed as a result of the query, the **FROM** keyword designates which tables are to be searched, and the **WHERE** keyword specifies the search criteria or query condition to be used in finding records. In our use of SQL, we will put keywords in uppercase to make them stand out. In practice, you don't necessarily type them in uppercase.

In addition to the SELECT keyword, there are keywords that can be used to **CREATE** a table, **INSERT** new records in a table, **DELETE** records from a table, and to **UPDATE** one or more records in a table. We can also search for records that are *like* a specific condition as well as computing sums, averages, and so on, for all records that match some criteria.

SQL WITH ONE TABLE

In our discussion of SQL, we will use the same example as shown earlier—the *ACC_4_Bank_Database_Example.accdb* file. We start by creating a query and then switching to the SQL view as follows.

1. Start by clicking the Query Design command on the Create ribbon.

    Close the Add Tables dialog.

    Your Access Window should now look like that shown in Access Figure 4-1.

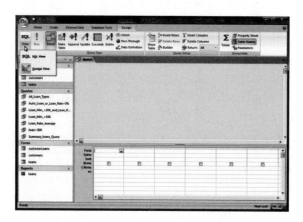

Access Figure 4-1: Selecting SQL view.

On the Design ribbon under Query Tools, click SQL View.

2. The workspace will change to look as shown in Access Figure 4-2.

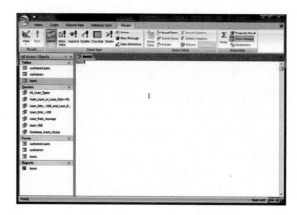

Access Figure 4-2: The SQL view.

This workspace is basically a simple text editor that allows you to type an SQL command.

As you'll see, most SQL queries begin with the SELECT keyword, so that is provided for you.

To use SQL to display the *loanType, loanRate,* and *loanMin* fields from the *loans* table, as we did using QBE in Access Tutorial 2, the SQL command is:

SELECT *loanType, loanRate, loanMin* FROM *loans*

and the resulting output would display information on all of the loan types. To sort these in order of *loanRate,* you simply add the clause ORDER BY *loanRate* to the end of the SQL statement.

3. Type the query as shown in Access Figure 4-3.

Access Figure 4-3: SQL query to display *loanType, loanRate,* and *loanMin* in order of *loanRate.*

Click the Run command on the Design ribbon.

4. The results of your SQL query will look like those shown in Access Figure 4-4.

loanType	loanRate	loanMin
15 Year Mortgage	4.50%	$50,000.00
Student	5.00%	$2,000.00
30 Year Mortgage	5.50%	$75,000.00
Auto Loan 36-Month	8.50%	$5,000.00
Auto Loan 48-Month	9.50%	$7,500.00
Auto Loan 60-Month	10.50%	$10,000.00
*		

Access Figure 4-4: Results of SQL *loans* query.

Follow this same procedure for each of the SQL queries described in this tutorial.

Fact: You can replace the list of fields with the asterisk if you want to display all of the fields in a table. For example, to display all of the fields in the *loans* table, the SQL statement is:

SELECT * FROM *loans*

In many cases, we will want to display only selected fields for records that match some condition. To do this we need to use the WHERE keyword followed by a comparison condition involving one of six comparison operators: equals (=), greater than (>), less than (<), greater than or equal to (>=), less than or equal to (<=), or not equal to (<>), plus a fieldname and a value (see Acess Table 2-1 in Access Tutorial 2). The general form is:

> SELECT *FieldName1,FieldName2,* ... FROM *TableName* WHERE
> *Query Condition*

To find all loan types that have a loan minimum greater than or equal to $10,000, the SQL statement is:

> SELECT *loanType, loanRate, loanMin* FROM *loans* WHERE
> *loanMin* >=10000

5. Create and run this SQL query.

The results should appear as shown in Access Figure 4-5.

loanType	loanRate	loanMin
15 Year Mortgage	4.50%	$50,000.00
30 Year Mortgage	5.50%	$75,000.00
Auto Loan 60-Month	10.50%	$10,000.00

Access Figure 4-5: Results for *loanMin* >=10000.

Whenever you use the equals sign in a SELECT query, you are looking for an exact match. When working with character data, there is a very good way to look for something other than an exact match: using the LIKE operator. The LIKE operator uses the **wildcard** character as a replacement for unknown or nonexisting characters in attempting to find matches to a group of characters (commonly referred to as a character **string**). The wildcard character is either the asterisk (*) in MS Access or the percent sign (%) in other database management systems. The general form of this type of query is:

> SELECT *FieldName1, Fieldname2,*... FROM *TableName* WHERE
> *FieldName* LIKE "**value***"

For example, the query to find the same fields as the previous example for automobile loans would be:

> SELECT *loanType, loanRate, loanMin* FROM *loans* WHERE
> *loanType* LIKE "Auto*"

6. Create and run this SQL query.

The results should appear as shown in Access Figure 4-6.

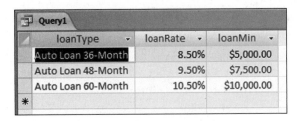

Access Figure 4-6: Results for LIKE SQL query.

USING AGGREGATE FUNCTIONS IN SQL

One operation that is easier to use with SQL than with QBE is to compute certain values about the records in the table using five different aggregate functions—COUNT, AVG, SUM, MIN, and MAX, where their purpose is indicated by their name. In each case, you must use a dummy name for the result of the computation. The form of the calculations is similar among AVG, SUM, MIN, and MAX, whereas that for the COUNT function is somewhat different. The form for the AVG function would be:

SELECT AVG(*fieldname*) AS *DummyName* FROM *TableName*
WHERE *Query condition*

In this SQL statement, the average value is stored in the *DummyName* variable, which is displayed when the query is run. For example, to find the average interest rate for all items in the *tblLoan* table, the query would be (the WHERE portion is not needed since all records are averaged):

SELECT AVG(*loanRate*) AS *AvgRate* FROM *loans*

7. Create and run this SQL query.

The results should appear as shown in Access Figure 4-7.

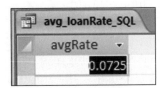

Access Figure 4-7: Result of average interest rate calculation.

Using the SUM, MAX, and MIN functions would have the same form as the AVG function. On the other hand, to use the COUNT function, the form is different, as follows:

SELECT COUNT(*) AS *DummyName* FROM *TableName* WHERE
Query condition

For example, to count the number of items in the table with an interest rate of more than 8 percent, the SQL statement would be:

SELECT COUNT(*) AS *Over8Percent* FROM *loans* WHERE
loanRate >.08

8. Create and run this SQL query.

The results should appear as shown in Access Figure 4-8.

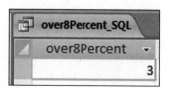

Access Figure 4-8: Counting items with
interest rates more than 8 percent.

INSERTING OR DELETING RECORDS

As we have discussed earlier, you can use MS Access or another database management package to add records to or delete records from a database table. It is also possible to carry out both of these operations using SQL. To insert a record into a table, you would use a statement of the form:

INSERT INTO *TableName(field1, field2, . . .*) VALUES (*value1, value2, . . .*)

where the values must be entered in the *exact order* as the fields in the record separated by commas. Not all fields must be included, but there must a value for any field name that is included.

Fact: If a record with an AutoNumber field is being inserted, the field name for the AutoNumber field must *not* be included in the list of fields, and no value should be included for it in the Values list.

For example, to insert a new record for a loan with a loan type of "Auto Loan 72 Months," an interest rate of 11.5 percent, and a minimum loan amount of $20,000 into the *loans* table, the SQL statement would be:

INSERT INTO *loans* (*loanType, loanRate, loanMin*) VALUES ('Auto Loan 72 Months', 0.115, 20000)

Note that the *loanID* field is not mentioned in the *loans* list because it is an AutoNumber field.

On the other hand, to delete an existing record from a database table, you would use an SQL statement of the form:

DELETE FROM *TableName* WHERE *FieldName = value*

We could also use the LIKE operator if the value is a text string to avoid problems with finding exact matches of case or spacing. In either case, this will delete *all* records that match the criteria. For example, assume that the bank no longer wishes to offer the 36-month automobile loan and needs to remove it from its database. To do this, the SQL command would be:

DELETE FROM *loans* WHERE *loanType* LIKE "*36 month*"

1. Let's add and delete records to the *loans* table using SQL.

The current *loans* table records are shown in Access Figure 4-9.

	LoanID	LoanType	LoanRate	LoanMin	Add New Field
⊞	1	15 Year Mortgage	4.50%	$50,000.00	
⊞	2	30 Year Mortgage	5.50%	$75,000.00	
⊞	3	Auto Loan 36-Month	8.50%	$5,000.00	
⊞	4	Auto Loan 48-Month	9.50%	$7,500.00	
⊞	5	Auto Loan 60-Month	10.50%	$10,000.00	
⊞	6	Student	5.00%	$2,000.00	
*	(New)				

Access Figure 4-9: *loans* table before adding and deleting records.

2. Create an SQL query to insert the new 72-month auto loan record as described previously.

Then click Run to insert the record as shown in Access Figure 4-10.

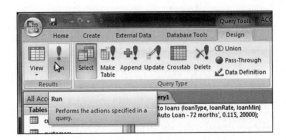

Access Figure 4-10: Running the INSERT query.

3. Since we are making a change to the database, Access will check to verify that we want to make the change.

A message like that in Access Figure 4-11 will be displayed.

Access Figure 4-11: Access verification message for the INSERT query.

Click Yes to actually insert the new record.

4. Create an SQL query to delete the old 36-month auto loan record as described previously.

Then click Run to insert the record.

You'll see a message like that in Access Figure 4-12 to verify that you want to delete the record.

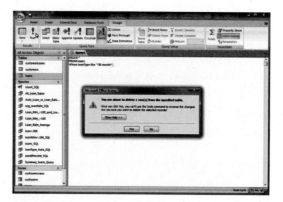

Access Figure 4-12: Access verification message for the DELETE query.

After reviewing the message, click Yes to actually delete the record from the table.

5. The *loans* table should contain the records shown in Access Figure 4-13 after you have successfully inserted and deleted the two records.

Access Figure 4-13: *loans* table after insertion and deletion.

To change values in a row of a database, you can use the UPDATE and SET keywords in the form:

UPDATE *TableName* SET *FieldName1* = *value* WHERE *FieldName2* = *value*

For example, assume the interest rate for the student loan has increased by 0.5%. To account for this increase in the database table, the SQL statement would be:

UPDATE *loans* SET *loanRate* = *loanRate* + 0.005 WHERE *loanType* = "Student Loan"

Executing this SQL statement would result in the interest rate for all student loans to increase by 0.5%. The student loan in the current table would increase from 5% to 5.5%.

USING SQL WITH MULTIPLE TABLES

So far in our discussion of relational databases, we have used a single table to demonstrate the use of SQL. However, the power of a relational database comes from the use of multiple tables that are related by a common field and in which different types of data are stored. We can use SQL to query multiple tables to determine information of interest in a manner similar to querying a single-table database.

The Join Operation

The most common operation on a two-table database is the **join** operation, in which we create a single table from two (or more) tables. Once you understand the join operation, you can then use it to perform calculations and carry out grouping of products. The simplest join operation is creating one table from two. For our example, the SQL instruction to join the *loans* and *customerLoans* tables showing all fields in both tables is:

SELECT * FROM *loans, customerLoans* WHERE *loans.loanID* = *customerLoans.FKloanID*

In looking at this query, you can see that even though the field name for the *loanID* foreign key in *customerLoans* (*FKloanID*) is already different from the primary key field name in *loans* (*loanID*), we further distinguish between them by combining the table name and the field name using a period, that is, *loans.loanID* and *customerLoans.FKloanID*. While this is more for the human users of Access than for the database management system, it is still good form. If this query is run on the database, the result is as shown in Access Figure 4-14. In this example, the two tables, loans and customerloans, are joined by virtue of the fact that all records from each table that share the same loan ID are displayed in the resulting view.

LoanID	LoanType	LoanRate	LoanMin	custLoanID	custLoanStartDa	custLoanAm	custL
1	15 Year Mortgage	4.50%	$50,000.00	1	6/1/2004	$200,000.00	Curr
1	15 Year Mortgage	4.50%	$50,000.00	2	1/9/2005	$150,000.00	Curr
2	30 Year Mortgage	5.50%	$75,000.00	4	2/20/2005	$280,000.00	Curr
2	30 Year Mortgage	5.50%	$75,000.00	7	3/13/2006	$125,000.00	Curr
4	Auto Loan 48-Month	9.50%	$7,500.00	3	1/15/2005	$14,000.00	Paid
4	Auto Loan 48-Month	9.50%	$7,500.00	8	5/15/2006	$11,500.00	Curr
5	Auto Loan 60-Month	10.50%	$10,000.00	5	5/22/2005	$28,000.00	Curr
5	Auto Loan 60-Month	10.50%	$10,000.00	10	9/30/2006	$15,500.00	Delir
5	Auto Loan 60-Month	10.50%	$10,000.00	11	11/22/2006	$19,500.00	Curr
6	Student	5.00%	$2,000.00	6	10/10/2005	$3,500.00	Curr
6	Student	5.00%	$2,000.00	9	8/31/2006	$3,500.00	Delir

Access Figure 4-14: Result of two-table join operation.

As another example of the join operation, consider again the query we ran in Tutorial 3; that is, to display the first and last names of customers from the *customers* table and the amount outstanding field from the *customerLoans* table (*custLoanAmount*) for loans of more than $30,000. In SQL the query would be:

SELECT *custLastName, custFirstName, custLoanAmount* FROM *customers, customerLoans* WHERE *customers.custID* = *customerLoans.FKcustID* AND *customerLoans.custLoanAmount* > 30000

Note that we have used the AND operator to combine the join and comparison operations in this query.

The result of running this query is shown in Access Figure 4-15.

custLastNam	custFirstNan	custLoanAm
Carnegie	James	$200,000.00
Patrick	Chris	$150,000.00
Mullins	Jesse	$280,000.00
Goodly	Alice	$125,000.00

Access Figure 4-15: Two-table join with condition.

As we did in Tutorial 3 with QBE, it is possible with SQL to create a three-table join. To display the loan type and interest rate on the loans over $30,000, the SQL statement is an extension of the one shown above:

SELECT *custLastName, custFirstName, custLoanAmount, loanType, loanRate* FROM *customers, customerLoans, loans* WHERE *customers.custID = customerLoans.FKcustID* AND *customerLoans.FKloanID = loans.loanID* AND *customerLoans.custLoanAmount* > 30000

As before, running this query will result in the same output as shown in Tutorial 3, shown here as Access Figure 4-16.

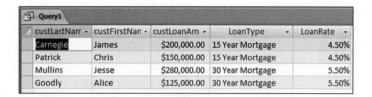

Access Figure 4-16: Three-table join.

CARRYING OUT CALCULATIONS WITH SQL

It is also possible to carry out calculations and display them as the result of a join query. For example, we can modify the query associated with Access Figure 4-16 to calculate the amount of simple interest due on each loan this year by multiplying the interest rate times the loan amount. The previous SQL query can be modified as follows to output the first and last names of the customer, loan amount, loan type, interest rate, and interest due:

SELECT *custLastName, custFirstName, custLoanAmount, loanType, loanRate, loanRate* * *custLoanAmount* AS *InterestDue* FROM *customers, customerLoans, loans* WHERE *customers.custID = customerLoans.FKcustID* AND *customerLoans. FKloanID = loans.loanID* AND *customerLoans.custLoanAmount* > 30000

If we run this query, the result is as shown in Access Figure 4-17. Note in this figure that the result is the same as was shown in Access Figure 3-17 in Tutorial 3 with the addition of a new field, *InterestDue,* that has been created as the product of the interest rate and the loan amount. For example, Jesse Mullins owes $15,400 on his loan amount of $280,000 at 5.5 percent interest.

custLastNam	custFirstNan	custLoanAm	LoanType	LoanRate	InterestDue
Carnegie	James	$200,000.00	15 Year Mortgage	4.50%	9000
Patrick	Chris	$150,000.00	15 Year Mortgage	4.50%	6750
Mullins	Jesse	$280,000.00	30 Year Mortgage	5.50%	15400
Goodly	Alice	$125,000.00	30 Year Mortgage	5.50%	6875

Access Figure 4-17: Inclusion of calculated field.

EXERCISES TO BUILD YOUR KNOWLEDGE OF MS ACCESS

Match each of the Access terms with its description.

___ 1. COUNT   a. An SQL keyword that is used to retrieve records from a relational database.

___ 2. DELETE   b. An SQL keyword that is used to set a condition on the records to retrieve or modify from a relational database.

___ 3. FROM   c. An SQL keyword that is used to add records to a table in a relational database.

___ 4. INSERT   d. An SQL keyword that is used to change values in a relational database.

___ 5. JOIN   e. An SQL keyword that is used to remove records from a relational database.

___ 6. ORDER BY   f. An SQL keyword that is used to sort the retrieved records from a relational database.

___ 7. SELECT   g. An SQL keyword that is used to combine records from multiple tables from a relational database.

___ 8. SQL   h. An SQL keyword that is used to specify the tables from which records will be retrieved.

___ 9. UPDATE   i. A standard language that can be used to work with the data in a relational database.

___ 10. WHERE   j. A function that can be used in an SQL query to obtain the number of records that satisfy a query.

Follow the directions in this Access tutorial to use SQL to write and execute all of the queries to the *loans* table in the bank database example database discussed in the tutorial. In addition, you should create and run queries to display the following information:

11. List all the loans.

12. How many automobile loan types are there?

13. What loan type has the lowest minimum loan amount?

14. Which loans have a loan minimum between $5,000 and $10,000?

15. Which loans have an interest rate less than 5% and a loan minimum greater than $10,000?

Follow the directions in this Access tutorial to use SQL to write and execute all of the queries to multiple tables in the bank database example database discussed in the tutorial. In addition, you should create and run queries to display the following information:

16. List all customers with a loan having an interest rate greater than 6%.

17. List the e-mail address and birth date of all customers with a loan amount greater than $50,000.

ACCESS TUTORIAL 4: MINI-CASE 1

Scenario: MyFace.com, a social networking Web site popular with the cool kids, just bought a database of student names from the local community college for use in marketing the features of their site. They hope to mine the data to identify trends that they can use to improve their services and attract more eyeballs. For example, if they were to find out that there is a significant number of students majoring in fifteenth-century Asian art, they could add provocative photos of Ming vases to their Spring Break pages. The folks at MyFace.com are willing to provide an extra 10Mbytes of Web storage and status as a gold platinum user to anyone who can help them query the database to answer the following questions.

File: Download and open the Access database *ACC_4_MC_Students.accdb.*

Your Task: Use SQL to query the Access database *students.accdb* to answer the following questions:

- Who are the students listed in the database? (Show all fields in student table; save this query as *studentList.*)
- What is the major of Alexis Allen? (Save this query as *alexis.*)
- Which students are over 30? (Show name and age; save this query as *over30.*)
- What are the names, ages, and majors for those students who enrolled in March 2007? (Save this query as *march2007.*)
- Which students are journalism majors who enrolled in March 2000? (Save this query as *marchJour.*)
- How many students were born on a Monday? (Save your query as *monday.*)
- What is the average age of students who are majoring in computer science? (Save your query as *avgCSCI.*)

ACCESS TUTORIAL 4: MINI-CASE 2

Scenario: Jacquey Sparrow works for a small Web2.0 startup. A new feature that she wants to add to the Web site is an online "link-saver" application. This application will let people store bookmarks online so that a user may log in to access links to his or her favorite Web sites from any computer connected to the Internet. As a first step, she has created a database that can be used to store the links. She wants to test the data model before writing instructions for the Web developers. To do this, Jacquey needs to run SQL queries against the data model that might be implemented in the Web application.

The initial design for the Web application includes (1) the *links* database, (2) a main page that shows a brief introduction to the purpose of the link-saver Web page and links users to other pages; (3) a new-user function that allows a new user to create an account; (4) a login function for an existing user to log in; (5) a logout function for a logged-in user to log out; (6) a page where users may view their personally stored bookmarks, a new bookmark can be added, and a bookmark may be deleted.

File: Download and open the Access database *ACC_4_MC_LinkSaver.accdb.*

Your Task: Use SQL to query the Access database *linkSavers.accdb* to test the following tasks or answer the following questions:

- List the usernames and passwords. (Show all fields in *user* table; save this query as *userList.*)
- What are the e-mails of all users who have entered a link? (Save this query as *activeUsers.*)
- What are the URLs for all links that are in the Search category? (Do not show duplicates. Save this query as *searchURLs.*)
- What links are available for .com sites? (Include title, link, and category. Save this query as *dotComs.*)
- Write the SQL command to add a new link to the *links* table. (Save this query as *addLink.*)
- Write the SQL command to add a new user to the *user* table. (Save your query as *newUser.*)
- Write the SQL command to delete all records in the *userLinks* table related to user 1. (Save your query as *linkDelete.*)

Appendix

INTRODUCTION TO DATA MODELING

After reading this appendix to data modeling and completing the associated exercises, you will be able to:

- Discuss the use of logical modeling for database design.
- Describe an ERD and create one.
- Understand data models and create one.

THE IMPORTANCE OF RELATIONAL DATABASES

As a relational database application, MS Access can work with more than one database table. As discussed in the Access Tutorials, the relational model enables Access to store data in tables and then link tables via common fields. You may ask why it is necessary to do this. Why not just use one table with all of the information in it? To help you understand the reasons for using multiple tables, consider a revised version of the *customer* table from the Access Tutorials, shown here in Appendix Figure 1. Note that we have included all of the information about each customer plus information about the customer's loans.

CustomerID	CustomerLNam	CustomerFnam	CustomerBDate	CustomerEmail	CLOriginationDa	CLAmount	CLStatus
999-11-1111	Patrick	Chris	4 /27/1973	cpatrick@uga.n	1 /9 /2005	$150,000.00	Current
999-33-3333	Crider	Randy	8 /21/1975	rcrider@uga.not	1 /15/2005	$14,000.00	Paid in full
999-22-2222	Mullins	Jesse	7 /24/1985	jmullins@vstate	2 /20/2005	$280,000.00	Current
999-99-9999	Hyatt	Ashley	8 /22/1969	ahyatt@uncch.r	5 /22/2005	$28,000.00	Current
999-55-5555	Roberts	John	3 /15/1977	jroberts@fsu.no	10/10/2005	$3,500.00	Current
999-44-4444	Goodly	Alice	1 /31/1962	agoodly@negia	3 /13/2006	$125,000.00	Current
999-66-6666	Carrall	Ann	11/15/1968	acarrall@aow.r	5 /15/2006	$11,500.00	Current
999-33-3333	Crider	Randy	8 /21/1975	rcrider@uga.not	8 /31/2006	$3,500.00	Delinquent 30 Days
999-44-4444	Goodly	Alice	1 /31/1962	agoodly@negia	9 /30/2006	$15,500.00	Delinquent 90 Days
999-55-5555	Roberts	John	3 /15/1977	jroberts@fsu.no	11/22/2006	$19,500.00	Current

Appendix Figure 1: Single table with all data.

In looking closely at Appendix Figure 1, you can probably see a big reason for not using a single table: **redundancy**. Note that the Customer table now lists each customer's ID, first and last names, birth date, e-mail address, loan origination date, and loan amount, status, type, and interest rate. For customers with multiple loans, we have repeated all of the information about them for each loan.

Note that this redundancy not only can result in the database table taking up unneeded storage space (especially for a realistic-sized database table involving millions of records) but also causes problems when trying to insert new records, delete existing records, or update records. These problems, typically referred to as **anomalies**, can harm the integrity of the database records.

Therefore, to solve the problems associated with storing all the data in one table, relational databases are used. Relational databases store data in multiple tables in which records in one table can be related to records of another table. To create the appropriate tables, most knowledge workers rely on logical modeling. **Logical modeling** provides tools to help analyze and understand what data items are important and the relationships between the data.

> ▶**Thinking Critically:**
> Relational database proponents often highlight the reduction in data redundancy inherent in relational databases. What redundancy does the relational model add? Think about why a relational database can store data in discrete but related tables. How could data redundancy increase lack of data integrity?

LOGICAL MODELING: ENTITY-RELATIONSHIP DIAGRAMS (ERDs) AND DATA MODELS

Businesses generate important data as a result of their day-to-day operations. In order to store and use this data, databases are created and updated as necessary. Prior to creating a database it is important to understand what data your business needs. Logical modeling provides tools to help businesses analyze and understand what data items are important and the relationships between the data. Logical modeling creates a picture of this world of data and relationships. An accurate logical model provides a business with a solid foundation upon which to build its database(s).

In logical modeling terms, **entities** are important things, such as customers, products, or students, about which a business or an organization wants to capture and store data. Entities have **attributes**, or characteristics, which are also important and serve to organize the data stored about an entity. For example, most databases have customer ID numbers or social security numbers (SSNs) that identify customers.

> ▶**Thinking Critically:**
> Would your phone number be a good unique identifier (primary key) for you? How about your birthday? Can you think of a good primary key (unique identifier) other than SSN?

Let's try an example that involves reading a business scenario, picking out the entities and attributes, and creating the **entity-relationship diagram (ERD)** and the **data model**. Some people use only one or the other of these models, but they work well together, too. The ERD is uncluttered by attributes, so you can focus on the entities and the relationships. The data model adds the attributes and helps to organize them before you actually create the database. Primary and foreign keys are identified as well.

The data model is built after the ERD by adjusting some symbols and adding more detail. It becomes your blueprint for building your database using software such as Access. Using both an ERD and a data model allows knowledge workers to focus first on what's important in the real-world scenario—entities and relationships—and then, by transforming the ERD into a data model, to organize the data to conform to the rules of relational databases.

Scenario 1: Kraig's Kayak Shoppe (note the spelling of "shoppe"; these are fancy kayaks!) sells kayaks and related products. He has a *very* limited inventory, so he limits his customers to one kayak/related product per customer. (OK, I'm reaching on this one, but bear with me.) He wants to keep track of each customer and the product the customer bought.

Determine each "important thing" about which Kraig needs to capture and store data. Recall what the database term for an "important thing" is: *entity*.

Customer is a good start, and so is Product. Notice how these entities are all nouns. Noun-hunting is a good way to spot entities, but you may bag a few attributes, too, so you have to be careful.

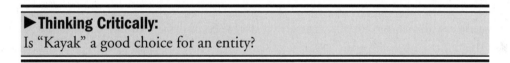

▶**Thinking Critically:**
Is "Kayak" a good choice for an entity?

Using standard symbols, draw the entities and the relationships between the entities. The standard symbols for an ERD are shown in Appendix Figure 2. In the figure, we see that entities are represented by box shapes in the ERD and the relationships are represented by lines with a diamond shape in the middle. Relationship symbols are labeled to indicate the **cardinality/ordinality** of the relationship. In other words, labels indicate the number of records that can be related between tables. The relationship symbols shown here represent the three possible relationships between data: one-to-one, one-to-many, and many-to-many, respectively.

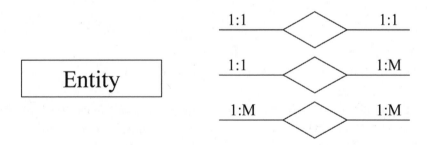

Relationships

Appendix Figure 2: Standard ERD symbols.

Once an ERD is drawn, you can actually "read" the ERD to understand the relationships between entities. For example, in the ERD snippet of Appendix Figure 3, reading from left to right, "a customer buys one-to-many products." Note that the 1:M is next to the Product entity. Note also that we have added the verb in the sentence, "Buys," as an additional label to the diagram.

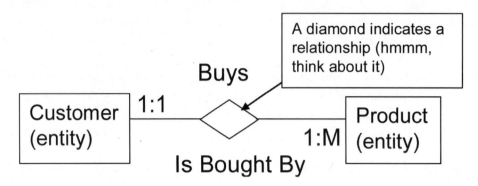

Appendix Figure 3: One-to-many relationship.

Reading from right to left, "a product is bought by 'one instance of a customer' or 'one and only one customer.'" Note that the 1:1 is next to the Customer entity and that we have once again labeled the diagram so this relationship is easy to read.

Now consider this more realistic, revised scenario 2: Kraig's Kayak Shop (note the spelling of "shop"; the fancy kayaks are gone!) sells kayaks and related products. His inventory is extensive, so customers can buy as many of each product as they need or want. Kraig wants to keep track of each customer and the products that the customer purchases.

Reading from left to right in Appendix Figure 4, "a customer buys one-to-many products." Note that the 1:M is next to the Product entity.

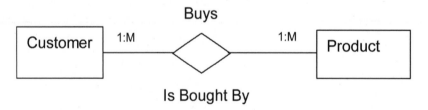

Appendix Figure 4: Many-to-many relationship.

Reading from right to left, "a Product is bought by one-to-many customers." Note that this time the 1:M is next to the Customer entity. (So, each time you make a sentence to describe the relationship from one entity to another, it is standard convention to place the label next to the second entity in the sentence.)

The revised ERD includes what is known as a **many-to-many relationship** between the Customer and Product entities, because many customers buy many products and many products are bought by many customers. You must resolve (change) these relationships, because many-to-many relationships violate the rules upon which your relational database will be built.

Typically, a many-to-many relationship is drawn as a new **relational entity** (note the dashed box around the diamond in Appendix Figure 5) that lies between the original two entities. From the standpoint of the original entities, the relational entity is connected to each original entity by a one-to-many relationship. You can say that the many-to-many relationship (Appendix Figure 5) has been transformed into two one-to-many relationships and a relational entity (Appendix Figure 6).

THIS ...

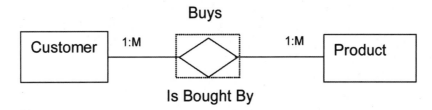

Appendix Figure 5: Many-to-many relationship (before transformation).

... BECOMES THIS

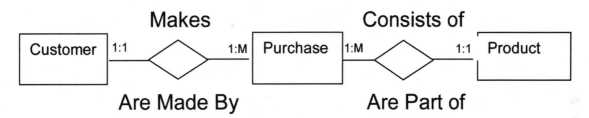

Appendix Figure 6: Two one-to-many relationships with relational entity (after transformation).

▶**Thinking Critically:**
How would you read these relationships, from left to right and from right to left? What does this tell us?

Now we'll show you the Data Model for the ERD shown in the first scenario (Appendix Figure 7).

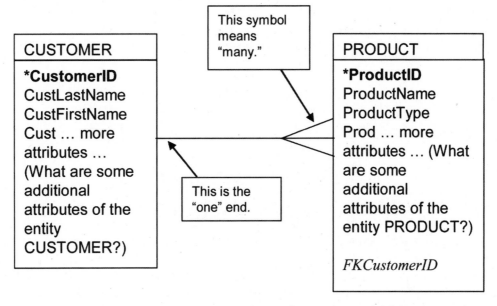

Appendix Figure 7: One-to-many relationship in data model (Scenario 1).

Reading from left to right, "a customer buys one to many products," and reading from right to left, "a product is bought by 'one instance of a customer' or 'one and only one customer.'" Notice how the symbols changed when the ERD was converted to a data model. The relationship symbol has changed from a "labeled diamond" to a "line with crow's foot." The **crow's foot** is placed on the "many side" of the relationship. We have also added more detail to the entities. This additional detail includes a listing of the attributes (fields) for the entities and indicators for the primary and foreign keys.

So why are there asterisks in front of *CustomerID* and in front of *ProductID?* This indicates that these attributes are the unique identifiers for their respective entity. *CustomerID* uniquely identifies each instance of a customer, and *ProductID* uniquely identifies each instance of a product. A more common term for unique identifier that you have already seen is *primary key*. We will use the two terms interchangeably to remind us that, ultimately, we will create a physical database from this logical model. Primary keys are fields in the tables in a relational database. The physical database uses primary keys to identify each row in each table uniquely.

If an asterisk indicates a primary key, then what is *FKCustomerID* and why is it in the PRODUCT entity? FK stands for *foreign key*, and it designates the attribute from the "one" end of the relationship that is duplicated and placed with the attributes of the entity that serves as the "many" end of the relationship. In the physical database, using the primary key from the table at the "one" end as a foreign key in the table at the "many" end will enable us to link the two entities and establish a relationship when we create our database.

CREATING A DATA MODEL FOR THE BANK EXAMPLE

Let's think about the bank example that is used in our Access tutorials. In that example, we have a Loan entity that contains information on the various types of loans available from the bank. We also have a Customer entity that contains information about the customers of the bank. Many customers can take out many different types of loans. In terms of an ERD, we have the situation shown in Appendix Figure 8, with a many-to-many relationship between the Customer entity and the Loan entity.

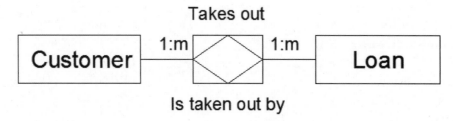

Appendix Figure 8: Many-to-many relationship between Customer and Loan entities.

We now convert this ERD from an m:m relationship into two 1:m relationships as was done earlier, only this time using the *CustomerLoan* entity, we now have the ERD shown in Appendix Figure 9.

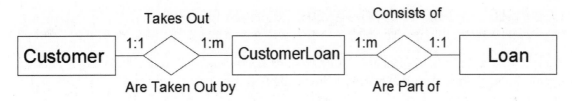

Appendix Figure 9: Conversion of ERD to two 1:m relationships.

The next step is to convert this into a data model using the three entities: Customer, CustomerLoan, and Loan. If this is done, the result is shown in Appendix Figure 10.

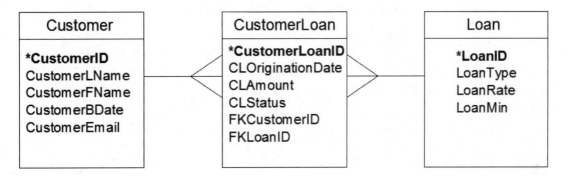

Appendix Figure 10: Data model for bank example.

This is the same data model we used in Access, only there it is shown in a different fashion. Compare Appendix Figure 10 with the copy of the relationships from Access shown here in Appendix Figure 11. Note that instead of the crow's foot symbol used to show the "many" side of the relationship in the data model, Access uses a key symbol to identify the primary key of each table and the infinity symbol to indicate "many" relationships. Other than that, they are very similar.

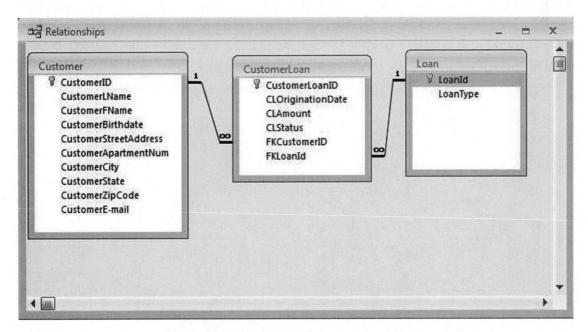

Appendix Figure 11: Relationships in Access.

EXERCISES TO BUILD YOUR KNOWLEDGE OF DATA MODELING

Assume that a certain state in the United States has two state parks: Heart State Park and Diamond State Park. Appendix Table 1 shows the two state parks and any hiking trails that are in them or go through them along with the trail length in that park. (Trails may go outside the state parks as well.) The state division of natural resources wants to create a database for the hiking trails that go through its state parks that will include such information as park name, county, address, and so on as well as trail name and trail length.

Heart State Park	Diamond State Park
Star (5 miles)	Arrow (8 miles)
Arrow (10 miles)	Boomerang (4 miles)
Boomerang (3 miles)	

Appendix Table 1: State parks and hiking trails.

Your assignment is to create an ERD for this situation. Then using the ERD you have created, create a data model. If you are feeling ambitious, create a database that is based on your data model.

DATA MODELING TUTORIAL MINI-CASE

Scenario: NP Watersports, Inc., sells and services personal watercraft at Lake Vickery, Georgia. Nicolas P., the owner of NP Watersports, wants to create a database that will help him run his business. Eventually, he wants to track sales and service, but first he wants you to model a database that will let him know which of his customers own which watercraft. Customers can have more than one personal watercraft, and personal watercraft can be associated with more than one customer. He needs to track customers' first and last names, address, type of watercraft purchased or serviced, and other information. If you can model this part of the database, Nicolas will award you the contract.

Your Task: Create the ERD and the data model for the scenario.

MICROSOFT ACCESS PROJECT 1: THE WILDOUTFITTERS "HOW-TO" COURSES DATABASE

By reading the business case sections and completing the three parts of this project (Parts A, B, and C) you will:

- Extend your knowledge of Microsoft (MS) Access tables, forms, queries, and reports.
- Understand the relationship between the logical model of a database and the physical implementation of that database.
- Understand how to implement referential integrity and discover its purpose.
- Learn how to apply Access to solve business problems.

Files for Download: Files associated with this project for you to download are the following:

- The Mini-Case data model file, *ACC_Project_WildOutfitters_Data_Model_1.pptx*

PROJECT INTRODUCTION

Data and databases are at the heart of many business information systems. If you think about the daily interactions you have with organizations, you will discover that many of these interactions generate data that organizations use to create value for you and for them. For example, when you shop at a retail grocery store, data is gathered about your purchases and your method of payment. If you choose to pay with a debit or credit card, then additional data may be gathered about you and your purchase. Many stores offer a discount if you use some type of "customer" card. This enables the store to gather data about your specific purchases and to provide value to you through coupons and other sales promotions. It also enables store management to make better decisions about product selection, pricing, promotions, and so forth. This project will focus on how a retail firm might achieve its goals of generating new business and increasing customer satisfaction by providing a knowledge-oriented service to its customers. You will create the database that will allow this company to accomplish these goals.

GENERAL BUSINESS CASE

Wild Outfitters, Inc. is a well established national outdoor-sports retail products chain with a local store in your area. It carries a complete line of name brand and locally produced equipment and supplies for outdoor enthusiasts. Through customer surveys, Wild Outfitters discovered that many of its customers are beginners and buy equipment but do not know how to use it properly. Rather than view this as a problem, Wild Outfitters sees this as an opportunity to provide better service to its customers and to gain a business advantage over its competitors. Wild Outfitters is going to offer "how to" courses for its customers. During these courses, customers will learn how to use the equipment they purchased, but they will also learn about other equipment they need and might want to purchase. Wild Outfitters will use this free (to the customers) service to increase sales and customer satisfaction. Isaac Timberlake, a student at your business school, is an intern at Wild Outfitters, and Sara Johns, the store manager, asks Isaac to create a Course Management System that she can use to track the courses customers take and the employees who teach the courses. Isaac understands the business requirements, but he needs your help in designing the database that will be at the heart of the Course Management System. The end result of your collaboration with Isaac will be the relational database and associated features specified in the MS Access Project instructions that follow.

Project Data Model Instructions

You will need to download the PowerPoint file *ACC_Project_WildOutfitters_Data_Model.ppt*. Your instructor will tell you how to do this. This file contains the data model you will reference in order to create your database. There are several slides in the presentation. The first slide is the data model, and the remaining slides are examples of how your tables might look. Remember, you will have to use MS Access to create the actual tables, and you will have to add additional data to meet project requirements.

PART A: CREATING THE TABLES

Part A Problem Definition

Isaac Timberlake welcomed the challenge of creating an information system that will help create business value for Wild Outfitters, Inc. This project focuses on the database component of that IS, and accomplishing this project will enable you to help Isaac by applying and refining the IS skills you've learned. Before you can build the database, you will have to understand the data that must be captured by the system and sketch out how this data will be stored. You should try this on your own and then compare your model to the one found in the *ACC_Project_WildOutfitters_Data_Model.pptx* file.

Part A Problem Requirements

Remember, tables are the objects that MS Access uses to store data. Your first task in this part of the project is to help Isaac by using Microsoft Access to create the required tables (see the *ACC_Project_WildOutfitters_Data_Model.pptx* file). You should use input masks for fields where appropriate (e.g., zip code). If you do not know what an input mask is, use MS Access's Help function to find out. Next, you will need to populate the tables with data. You should make up the data yourself, following the examples in the *ACC_Project_WildOutfitters_Data_Model.pptx* file. You should create at least 10 records (rows) in the customer table and five records each in the employee, class, and course tables. Your instructor may require that you add more data. You may want to accomplish Part B of the project before you enter all of your data. Lastly, you will need to create the appropriate relationships between the tables. When creating relationships, you should ensure that referential integrity is enforced.

Part A Interpretive Questions

Based on your work in Part A, answer the following questions:

1. What is the relationship between an instance of a primary key and a record (row) in a table?

2. What is referential integrity and why is it important for Isaac (and you) to enforce referential integrity in the database you create?

PART B: INPUTTING DATA INTO THE DATABASE AND CREATING FORMS

Part B Problem Definition

Isaac discovered that, rather than entering data directly into the tables, he could use the MS Access database objects known as forms to enter data into the database. He used the forms that you created to make data entry more efficient and less error-prone.

Part B Problem Requirements

Use the Form Wizard to create a form that will allow you to input data into each of the tables. Although the forms that you create are useful tools for entering data, when a customer makes a purchase, it would be useful to have the option to sign the customer up for a class.

Part B Interpretive Questions

Based on your work in Part B, answer the following questions:

1. In Part A of the project, you may have entered data directly into the tables. Although this is convenient, why are forms a better way to do this? Why might it be a good idea to avoid entering data directly into the tables?

2. Forms work well, but given additional hardware and software resources, how could you improve the data entry process to reduce errors?

PART C: CREATING DIFFERENT VIEWS OF DATA FOR DECISIONS; CREATING DATABASE QUERIES

Part C Problem Definition

Ms. Johns asked Isaac to find out which employees are leading which courses and classes and when they are leading them. She also wants to know which customers are taking classes and when. Lastly, she wants to be able to view the data for each instructor and for each month. Although the data stored in your database is organized into tables, looking at all of the tables to answer her questions or to help her make decisions is inefficient. Fortunately, MS Access provides an object—the query—and a query tool—query by example (QBE)—which makes it easy for you to view selected subsets of your data. In other words, Access makes it easy for you to ask and answer questions about your data and then use this information to make business decisions.

For the purposes of this project, you can think of a query as a question you ask of your database. In addition to QBE, the visually oriented tool you will use here, Access also provides another tool to create queries, although this tool is actually a computer language. Structured Query Language (SQL) is a standardized language for querying databases. With it you can create complex queries of almost any database; however, using SQL is beyond the scope of your project requirements (see Part C Interpretive Question 2).

Part C Problem Requirements

Using the Design view and QBE, create the following queries. You may need to add more data to your database so that you can test your query results.

Query 1: What customers have signed up to take classes from which instructors? (This query should return the data in your database for all courses, classes, customers taking classes, and employees leading classes.)

Query 2: Who is taking and leading a course in September? (This query should return the courses, classes, customers taking classes, and employees leading classes for September only.)

Query 3: What classes is Sara Johns teaching in September? (This query should return the courses and classes that Sara Johns is leading in September only.)

Query 4: What classes are being lead by either Sara Johns or Isaac Timberlake in September? (This query should return the all of the courses and classes that Sara Johns and Isaac Timberlake are leading in September only.)

Part C Interpretive Questions

Based on your work in Part C, answer the following questions:

1. When querying a database using QBE, what are criteria used for?

2. When using QBE, what is the difference between asking, "What are all the classes that Employee A and Employee B are teaching?" and "What are all the classes that both Employee A and Employee B are teaching together?"

3. Although we mentioned that SQL was beyond the scope of this project, you can look at the SQL view for any of your queries. It is one of the choices on the same View menu that you used to select the design view after running your queries.

Look at the SQL for Query 2 above. Can you make sense of the SQL query? Look for things like table and field names. You can even change the September query to an August query by changing only one character—try it!

PART D: OUTPUTTING DATA TO DECISION MAKERS AND OTHER KNOWLEDGE WORKERS; CREATING REPORTS

Part D Problem Definition

Queries are useful tools for asking questions of your data and for transforming data into information that is useful to decision makers. However, the standard query table view is not as useful or as easily readable as most users need or want. Ms. Johns asked Isaac to organize the views of Wild Outfitters data and present it in a well-organized form.

Part D Problem Requirements

To organize the views of Wild Outfitters data and present it in a well-organized form, Isaac will use the MS Access Report object. A report can be based on a table or a query or a combination of tables and queries; however, for Part D of this project you need only to create a report based on Query 2 from Part C above. You can use the Report Wizard to create your report. The report should show all of the data contained in Query 2. When responding to the Report Wizard's prompts, you should select to view your data by class, add "class date" as grouping level, and sort the detailed records by customer last name in ascending order. The layout and style choices are up to you. Finish the report and name it *septemberQuery.*

Review your report and note the "database speak" used for the title and headings. Since the purpose of a well-crafted report is to convey useful information effectively and efficiently, you will need to edit your report. Here are the minimum requirements for Part D of the project.

1. Change the orientation of the report from portrait to landscape.

2. Change the title of the report to "Wild Outfitters September 2008 Classes."

3. Move the customer first name label and data so that they are next to each other, last name then first name.

4. Transform all field names into easily readable headings; for example, *CourseName* should become *Course Name*, *CourseType* should become *Course Type*, and so forth.

Your instructor may add additional requirements or you may want to explore just how professional you can make the report appear.

Part D Interpretive Questions

Based on your work in Part D, answer the following questions:

1. What other reports would you suggest that Isaac should create for Ms. Johns to help her understand and manage the courses and classes that Wild Outfitters provides to its customers?

2. We have mentioned several Access objects throughout this project. Did you notice any additional objects when you were working in the Design view? What were some of these objects, and how did you know that you were looking at an object?

MICROSOFT ACCESS PROJECT 2: THE WILDOUTFITTERS EMPLOYEE SERVICE DATABASE

By reading the business case sections and completing the three parts of this project (Parts A, B, and C) you will:

- Extend your knowledge of Microsoft (MS) Access tables, forms, queries, and reports.
- Understand the relationship between the logical model of a database and the physical implementation of that database.
- Understand how to implement referential integrity and discover its purpose.
- Learn how to apply MS Access to solve business problems.

Files for Download: Files associated with this project for you to download are the following:

- The data model file, *WildOutfittersDataModel_2.pptx*

PROJECT INTRODUCTION

Data and databases are at the heart of many business information systems. The daily interactions you have with businesses and other organizations generate data, which enables management to make more efficient decisions about product selection, pricing, and promotions.

Businesses' own internal activities also generate data that the businesses use to manage programs and projects, and databases are used to track such data as well. Recently, many businesses have been emphasizing the good works that their employees perform for their local communities and beyond. This project will focus on how a retail firm might track the community service activities of its employees. The company will use this data to publicize its achievements and to enhance its standing in the local community. The goodwill and publicity created by community service can result in the generation of new business and increased name recognition in the community.

GENERAL BUSINESS CASE

Wild Outfitters, Inc., is a well-established national outdoor-sports retail products chain with a local store in your area. Seeing an opportunity to gain publicity through the community service performed by its employees, Wild Outfitters wants to track all of the community service activities performed by its employees nationwide. Wild Outfitters plans to establish annual awards for outstanding service by an employee and by a store.

Jennifer Franklin, a student at your business school, is an intern at Wild Outfitters, and Nicolas Isaacson, the store manager, asked Jennifer to create an Employee Community Service Management System (ECSMS) that he can use to track the community service performed by his employees. Jennifer understands the business requirements, but she needs your help in designing the database that will be at the heart of the ECSMS. The end result of your collaboration with Jennifer will be the relational database and associated features specified in the MS Access Project instructions that follow.

Project Data Model Instructions

You will need to download the PowerPoint file *WildOutfittersDataModel.ppt*. Your instructor will tell you how to do this. This file contains the data model you will reference in order to create your database. There are several slides in the presentation. The first slide is the data model, and the remaining slides are examples of how some of your tables might look. Remember, you will have to use MS Access to create the tables, and you will have to add additional data and at least one entity to meet project requirements.

PART A: CREATING THE TABLES

Part A Problem Definition

Jennifer Franklin welcomed the challenge of creating an information system that will help create business value for Wild Outfitters, Inc. This project focuses on the database component of that IS, and accomplishing this project will enable you to help Jennifer by applying and refining the IS skills you've learned. Before you can build the database, you will have to understand the data that must be captured by the system and sketch out how this data will be stored. You should try this on your own and then compare your model to the one found in the *WildOutfittersDataModel.pptx* file.

Part A Problem Requirements

Remember, tables are the objects that MS Access uses to store data. Your first task in this part of the project is to help Jennifer by using Microsoft Access to create the required tables (see the *WildOutfittersDataModel.pptx* file). You should use input masks for fields where appropriate (e.g., zip code). If you do not know what an input mask is, use MS Access's Help function to find out. Next, you will need to populate the tables with data. You should make up the data yourself following the examples in the *WildOutfittersDataModel.pptx* file. You should create at least ten records (rows) in the employee table, and five records each in the other tables. Your instructor may require that you add more data. You may want to accomplish Part B of the project before you enter all of your data. Lastly, you will need to create the appropriate relationships between the tables. When creating relationships, you should ensure that referential integrity is enforced.

Part A Interpretive Questions

Based on your work in Part A, answer the following questions:

1. What is the relationship between an instance of a primary key and a record (row) in a table?

2. What is referential integrity and why is it important for Jennifer (and you) to enforce referential integrity in the database you create?

PART B: INPUTTING DATA INTO THE DATABASE AND CREATING FORMS

Part B Problem Definition

Jennifer discovered that rather than entering data directly into the tables, she could use the MS Access database objects known as forms to enter data into the database. She used the forms that you created to make data entry more efficient and less error-prone.

Part B Problem Requirements

Use the Form Wizard to create a form that will allow you to input data into each of the tables.

Part B Interpretive Questions:

Based on your work in Part B, answer the following questions:

1. In Part A of the project, you may have entered data directly into the tables. Although this is convenient, why are forms a better way to do this? Why might it be a good idea to avoid entering data directly into the tables?

2. PC-based forms work well but given additional hardware and software resources, how could you improve the data entry process to allow employees to enter their activities regardless of location?

PART C: CREATING DIFFERENT VIEWS OF DATA FOR DECISIONS, CREATING DATABASE QUERIES

Part C Problem Definition

Mr. Isaacson asked Jennifer to find out which employees are performing which activities and at which events they performed these activities. He also wants to know how many hours of community service are performed each month by each employee and the total number of community service hours performed by each store. Although the data stored in your database is organized into tables, looking at all of the tables to answer his questions or to help him make decisions is inefficient. Fortunately, MS Access provides an object—the query—and a query tool—query by example (QBE)—which makes it easy for you to view selected subsets of your data. In other words, Access makes it easy for you to ask and answer questions about your data and then use this information to make business decisions.

For the purposes of this project, you can think of a query as a question you ask of your database. In addition to QBE, the visually oriented tool you will use here, Access provides another tool to create queries, although this tool is actually a computer language. Structured Query Language (SQL) is a standardized language for querying databases. With it you can create complex queries of almost any database; however, using SQL is beyond the scope of your project requirements.

Part C Problem Requirements

Using the Design View and QBE, create the following queries. You may need to add more data to your database so that you can test you query results.

Query 1: Create a query that returns the first names, last names, and one other item of data (your choice) for each employee in your database. If you input the 10 employees as required, then your query should return 10 rows of data.

Query 2: What employees performed which activities on which dates? (This query should return the data in your database for all activities for all employees.)

Query 3: Using just two fields, one from each table, create a query that will tell you what store an employee works in and the employee's last name. You can use *storeID* or *storeName* to indicate which store.

Query 4: What employees performed which activities in a given month? You pick the month. (This query should return the data in your database for all activities for all employees for the month you picked.)

Query 5: List the first names of all of the employees who performed one specific type of activity (your choice) for any event. For example, suppose the following people had the following community service opportunities: Mark picked up trash at the Relay for Life, Craig picked up trash at the Dance Marathon, and Jay picked up trash at the Botanical Gardens 5K. Then the query would use *picked up trash* as the activity regardless of event.

Query 6: Chose one other employee besides Jennifer. In which events did Jennifer and the other employee participate together, and what activities did they each perform? (This query should return all of the events that Jennifer and the other employee participated in together.)

Query 7: Jennifer Franklin performed community service while she was an intern. In which events did she participate, and what activities did she perform?

Part C Interpretive Questions

Based on your work in Part C, answer the following questions:

1. When querying a database using QBE, what are criteria used for?

2. When using QBE, what is the difference between asking, "What are all the events that Employee A and Employee B participated in individually?" and "What are all the events that *both* Employee A and Employee B participated in together?"

3. Although we mentioned that SQL was beyond the scope of this project, you can look at the SQL view for any of your queries. It is one of the choices on the same View Menu that you used to select the Design view after running your queries. Look at the SQL for Query 4 above. Can you make sense of the SQL query? Look for things like table and field names. Try changing the month by changing only one character.

PART D: OUTPUTTING DATA TO DECISION MAKERS AND OTHER KNOWLEDGE WORKERS, CREATING REPORTS

Part D Problem Definition

Queries are useful tools for asking questions of your data and for transforming data into information that is useful to decision makers. However, the standard query table view is not as useful or as easily readable as most users need or want. Mr. Isaacson asked Jennifer to organize the views of Wild Outfitters data and present them in a well-organized form.

Part D Problem Requirements

To organize the views of Wild Outfitters data and present it in a well-organized form, Jennifer will use the MS Access Report object. A Report can be based on a table or a query or a combination of tables and queries. However, for Part D of this project you need only to create a report based on Query 4 from Part C above. You can use the Report Wizard to create your report. The report should show all of the data contained in Query 4. When responding to the Report Wizard's prompts, you should select to view your data by community service event, add a grouping level that makes sense to you, and sort the detailed records by customer last name in ascending order. The layout and style choices are up to you. Finish the report and name it *monthlyEventQuery*.

Review your report and note the "database speak" used for the title and headings. Since the purpose of a well-crafted report is to convey useful information effectively and efficiently, you will need to edit your report. Here are the minimum requirements for Part D of the project.

1. Change the orientation of the report from portrait to landscape.

2. Change the title of the report to "Wild Outfitters *name-and-year-of-month-you-chose* Community Service Events."

3. Move the employee first name label and data so that they are next to each other: last name, then first name.

4. Transform all field names into easily readable headings; for example, *CommServEvent* should become *Community Service Event*, and so on.

Your instructor may add additional requirements or you may want to explore just how professional you can make the report appear.

Part D Interpretative Questions

Based on your work in Part D, answer the following questions:

1. What other reports would you suggest that Jennifer Franklin should create for Mr. Isaacson to help him understand and manage the community service activities and events that Wild Outfitters supports?

2. We have mentioned several Access objects throughout this project. Did you notice any additional objects when you were working in the design view? What were some of these objects, and how did you know that you were looking at an object?

Tutorial 1

INTRODUCTION TO MICROSOFT EXCEL 2007

After reading this tutorial and completing the associated exercises, you will be able to:

- Know what type of software application MS Excel is.
- Understand the meaning and function of MS Excel objects, such as workbooks, worksheets, columns, rows, and cells.
- Enter data into cells and manipulate and format the data contained in cells.
- Create and use absolute and relative cell references.
- Save your Excel workbook and use Excel Help.

MICROSOFT EXCEL: A SPREADSHEET APPLICATION AND MORE

Microsoft Excel is a versatile software application that is part of the Microsoft Office Suite of applications. MS Excel is commonly referred to as a **spreadsheet** application. MS Excel allows you to enter, organize, and use data to solve business problems, especially problems involving mathematical calculations and financial decision making.

First, you need to know a few terms that will help you understand how Excel works. Next, you will create an Excel worksheet that helps you calculate how much currency you have (in U.S. dollars—USD), and then helps you convert your USD to euros (EUR). Lastly, you will practice what you have learned by adding to this worksheet (see the Build section below).

TOUR OF THE EXCEL INTERFACE

The Excel user interface is shown in Excel Figure 1-1. You can see that the majority of the interface is represented by a grid of **cells**. Each cell is created by the intersection of a **row** and a **column**. It is within this area that you will enter the text, data, formulas, and functions that you need to perform your calculations and analyses. The remaining components shown in Excel Figure 1-1 represent the various features that are available in Excel. To perform your work efficiently, you will need to learn and become comfortable with using these features. A brief description of each of these components is provided in Excel Table 1-1.

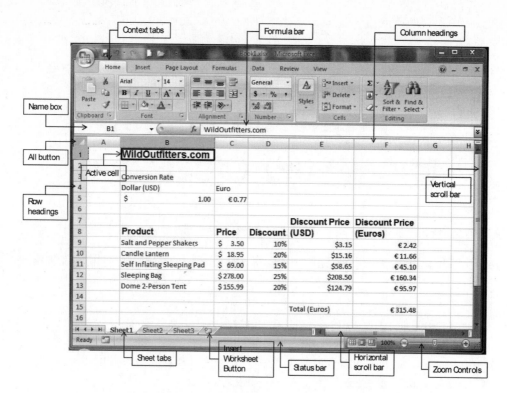

Excel Figure 1-1: The Excel user interface.

Because cells are containers for important data, whenever possible, cells are referred to by their names. For example, in Excel Figure 1-1, the cell with the dark, thick border is currently selected. Notice that the column header, column B, is highlighted and that the row header, row 1, is also highlighted. The cell is at the intersection of this row and column. Hence, the current name of this cell is B1. The name of the current selection is also indicated in the **name box**.

The actual contents of the cell are visible in the **formula bar**. Note that in this case, we see that the cell holds a formula, which is a combination of cell names and mathematical operators. Excel calculates the final **value** of the formula by substituting the values that are located in the cells that are named in the formula. The final value then appears in the cell itself.

Further, if the value located in a cell named in the formula changes, Excel automatically recalculates the values of this formula and of every other formula that depends on the altered cell. This is one of the primary features that make Excel a powerful tool for quantitative analysis. You will learn how to create simple formulas later in this tutorial and how to make more advanced formulas in tutorials to come.

Component	Description
Context tab	As with other Office 2007 applications, Excel commands are provided on visual components known as ribbons. The context of each ribbon is listed on a tab on which you can click to access the ribbon.
Formula bar	The actual contents of the selected cell will be displayed here. If a formula or function is in the cell, you'll see it here, while the final calculated value will be displayed in the cell.
Column headings	These provide identifiers for each column in the worksheet grid. The heading(s) of the selected column(s) will be highlighted.
Row headings	These provide identifiers for each row in the worksheet grid. The heading(s) of the selected row(s) will be highlighted.
Name box	The name of the selected cell or range of cells will be displayed here. By default, names are based on the column and row headings, but you can actually give cells a different name if you want.
All button	The button provides a shortcut for selecting the entire active worksheet. You can also use the hot key combination Ctrl-A.
Sheet tabs	Think of each Excel file that you create as a workbook that can have one or more **worksheets** included in it. You can click on the tab for each sheet when you want to work with it. It turns out that you can reference cells from one worksheet in a formula located in another.
Insert Worksheet button	This provides as shortcut for adding a new worksheet to your workbook.
Status bar	Provides information on the status of Excel such as the sum, count, and average of selected cells.
Horizontal scrollbar	Sometimes you will want to use more of the worksheet than can be displayed on the screen. The horizontal scrollbar lets you slide the worksheet leftward or rightward to view more of the worksheet.
Vertical scrollbar	The vertical scrollbar lets you slide the worksheet up or down to view more of the worksheet.
Zoom Control	Allows you to adjust the display size of the worksheet quickly.

Excel Table 1-1: Components of the Excel user interface.

Excel Ribbons

As you can see in Excel Figure 1-1, Excel typically has seven different ribbon contexts that make it easy to find the commands that you need. (You can actually customize Excel and add one or two more if needed.) The next several figures will provide a quick overview of the primary Excel ribbons. You will get very familiar with these as you work through these tutorials, so there is no need to memorize them now. Just take a quick look now and then refer back to these pages as needed.

Notice that each ribbon has some things in common. Commands are arranged in a series of groups. Each group includes a set of commands that let you do related tasks. Some controls are accompanied by downward-pointing arrows. When these are clicked, a menu or palette with more related options is displayed. You should also notice that each group has a small arrow in the lower right corner. By clicking this arrow you can open a dialog box for the group that provides even more options that you can use to complete your work.

Excel Figure 1-2: The Home ribbon.

The Home ribbon, shown in Excel Figure 1-2, contains the most commonly used Excel commands. Commands such as Copy, Cut, and Paste are located here in the Clipboard group. Cell formatting commands are provided in the Font, Alignment, Number, and Styles groups. The Cells group provides commands for adding, deleting, and formatting cells in the worksheet. Finally, the Editing group provides some more commonly used commands.

Excel Figure 1-3: The Insert ribbon.

You'll find a myriad of different objects that you can add to your worksheet on the Insert ribbon, shown in Excel Figure 1-3. The types of objects that you can use are included the groups Tables, Illustrations, Charts, Links, and Text.

Excel Figure 1-4: The Page Layout ribbon.

The Page Layout ribbon, shown in Excel Figure 1-4, provides commands that you can use when you want to control how the overall worksheet will be printed. The commands on this ribbon are organized into the groups Themes, Page Setup, Scale to Fit, Sheet Options, and Arrange.

Excel Figure 1-5: The Formulas ribbon.

Commands for working with formulas and functions are provided on the Formulas ribbon, shown in Excel Figure 1-5. You can search through a vast array of prebuilt formulas, called **functions**, using the Function Library group. You can name **ranges** of cells and work with named ranges using commands in the Defined Names group. The Formula Auditing group provides commands that allow you to check and debug the formulas and functions in your worksheet. You can also adjust how Excel calculates formulas by using options in the Calculations group.

Excel Figure 1-6: The Data ribbon.

The Data ribbon, shown in Excel Figure 1-6, provides tools for working with data. Groups included here are Get External Data, Connections, Sort & Filter, Data Tools, and Outline.

Excel Figure 1-7: The Review ribbon.

Options available on the Review ribbon, shown in Excel Figure 1-7, are typically used when you are working with other people on the workbook. These commands allow you to check the spelling and grammar of the worksheet (Proofing group), add comments to cells for you or others to read (Comments group), and track the changes made to the worksheet by you or others over time (Changes group).

Excel Figure 1-8: The View ribbon.

The View ribbon, shown in Excel Figure 1-8, provides commands that you can use when you want to control how the overall worksheet will be displayed on the screen. The commands on this ribbon are organized into the groups Workbook Views, Show/Hide, Zoom, Window, and Macros. A **macro** is a saved set of Excel or programming commands that you can create to automate various actions and/or functions in your workbook.

BUILDING YOUR FIRST SPREADSHEET SOLUTION: THE CASH AND CURRENCY CALCULATOR WORKBOOK

Now that you are at least a little familiar with what you are looking at in Excel, let's create your first Excel workbook.

Opening a New Excel Workbook

Before you can start, you need to open a new Workbook. Opening, closing, and saving files is done by using the Microsoft Office button.

1. Click on the Microsoft Office button to open the dialog box shown in Excel Figure 1-9.

Excel Figure 1-9: Starting a new workbook.

Notice that this dialog provides several options (some are grayed out because they are not currently available):

- Open an existing file.
- Select a recent document and open it.
- Save Excel files.
- Print a worksheet.
- Set some Excel options.
- Exit Excel.

2. Click on New.

   You should now see the dialog shown in Excel Figure 1-10.

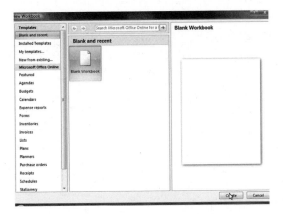

Excel Figure 1-10: Blank worksheet.

3. For now, make sure that Blank Worksheet is selected and click the Create button.

   Notice that you could also start with a **template**.
   A template is a prebuilt workbook that you can alter for your own use.
   Excel comes with a library of templates for many common applications.

At this point you should see a new workbook. By default, you will see the first of three blank worksheets ready for you to begin entering your text and data.

Using Excel to Solve Business Problems

You can use Excel to help you perform business calculations. For a simple example, let's assume that the outdoor supply store WildOutfitters.com needs to ship a number of products to a new client in France. Nick, who took the order, needs to provide a quote to the client in euros. For each item, the client was quoted a different percentage discount. Let's see how Nick can use Excel to provide a breakdown of prices for the products ordered with the price for each item after a discount converted to euros.

First, when creating a spreadsheet solution, you should think about what problem you are trying to solve. It is often a good idea to think about the types of data that you will need and how you will organize and manipulate the data. If you have values that you will use more than once, or values that you wish to change and see "what-if" effects, you should put these values in an easily viewed area of the spreadsheet and refer to the cells, not the values in those cells. You may want to sketch a possible layout for the spreadsheet.

For Nick's mini-project we will need the following data shown in Excel Table 1-2.

WildOutfitters.com				
Conversion Rate				
Dollar (USD)	Euro			
1	0.8321			
			Discount Price	Discount Price
Product	Price	Discount	(USD)	(Euro)
Salt and Pepper Shakers	3.5	0.1		
Candle Lantern	18.95	0.2		
Self-Inflating Sleeping Pad	69	0.15		
Sleeping Bag	278	0.25		
Dome 2-Person Tent	155.99	0.2		
			Total (Euros)	

Excel Table 1-2: Data for example worksheet.

From the data, you see that we can calculate the discounted price for each product. Then we can convert each price to euros. Finally, we can calculate a total value for the order in euros. When complete, our spreadsheet solution will appear, as shown previously in Excel Figure 1-1. To get the most of the next few sections, you should read and then do the Excel skills that we demonstrate to build this example.

Entering Text Labels

Entering text into a cell is probably the easiest thing that you can do while working with Excel. Primarily you just select the cell in the worksheet into which you want to enter the text, and then type the text. To begin entering the text labels for our example, follow these steps:

1. Click on the cell into which you want to enter text.

   For now, select cell B3.

   Note from Excel Figure 1-11 how the selection is highlighted in three ways:

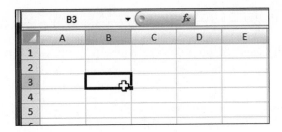

Excel Figure 1-11: Selecting cell B3.

- The selected cells are highlighted with bold rectangles.
- The range of selected cells is listed in the Name Box.
- The column headings and row numbers are highlighted along the edge of the worksheet.

2. Type in the Cell.

With the cell selected, begin typing the text data that you want to be stored in the cell.

Type *Conversion Rate* into the selected cell B3 as shown in Excel Figure 1-12.

Excel Figure 1-12: Entering text in cell B3.

As you type, your text will appear in the cell and will also be shown in the formula bar.

3. Adjust column width (if necessary): Sometimes the text that you type will be wider than the cell into which you are typing.

Notice that this is the case for our example. It's possible to adjust the column width, if desired.

First, place your cursor on the line separating columns B and C so that the cursor looks like that shown in Excel Figure 1-13. When you click and hold, the column width will be displayed as shown in the figure.

Excel Figure 1-13: Adjusting column B width.

Now you can drag the column to the width that you want it to be.

You can do this with rows as well. See whether you can figure out how to adjust the height of row 2. When would you want to do this?

It's also possible to have Excel automatically adjust the column width based on the largest number of characters in a cell. To do this, double-click on the column separator.

Now that you know how to enter text into cells, practice by entering the rest of the text labels that are shown in Excel Table 1-2. Don't worry about formatting cells (for example, making the text bold). We will look at how to do that in just a few pages.

Entering Numbers

Entering numbers into a cell is just about as easy as entering text. The main thing we need to remember is that the cell is a container. If we want the contents of the cell to be used in a calculation, then it is usually best to type a numerical value in the cell only (or an expression that will result in a numerical value.) We usually do not want to type any character data into the cell such as dollar signs, percent signs, or others.

1. As with text data, simply select the cell into which you want to type the number and then type.

   Excel Figure 1-14 shows us typing the value 3.5 into cell C9.

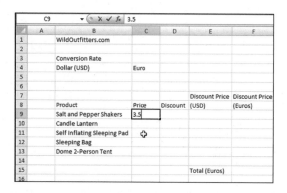

Excel Figure 1-14: Entering a number into cell C9.

   On your own, finish adding the rest of the numbers to the worksheet as shown in Excel Figure 1-15.

Excel Figure 1-15: Numbers entered into the worksheet.

2. As you type, your number will appear in the cell and will also be shown in the formula bar.

   Remember not to type in characters other than digits or the decimal point, such as $ or %. We will add those in a little while using formatting.

   A cell is a container. When a cell contains only a numerical value, it is easy to use in calculations.

Entering Formulas

In this tutorial, we will briefly discuss how to enter a formula. A more in-depth coverage of entering formulas is available in Excel Tutorial 2. As with all data that is entered into a worksheet, we begin by selecting the cell into which we want to type a formula. For our example, we need formulas to calculate the discounted price in dollars for each product, the discounted price in euros for each product, and the total price in euros.

To calculate a discounted price in dollars, we can use the formula in words as: price * (1 − percent discount). For the first product, Salt and Pepper Shakers, the price is in cell C9, and the discount is in cell D9. We can translate our word formula into one that will work in Excel using the cell addresses. This corresponding Excel formula will be: *=C9*(1-D9)*. Let's see how we can "build" this formula in a cell.

1. Select the cell into which you want to build the formula.

   For this example, select cell E9.

   Building an Excel formula is typically a mix of typing and clicking on cells to select them.

   Excel formulas should always begin with an = sign. Type that now as shown in Excel Figure 1-16.

Excel Figure 1-16: Starting a formula with =.

2. When you need to refer to a value stored in another cell in your formula, simply click on that cell to select it.

   Click on cell C9 to add it to the formula that we are building.

   Notice how the cell that you have selected is now highlighted, as shown in Excel Figure 1-17.

Excel Figure 1-17: Clicking on a cell to add to a formula.

3. The next few characters in the formula are not cell references, so we need to type them.

   Continue building the cell by typing *(1- as shown in Excel Figure 1-18.

Excel Figure 1-18: Adding values and operators to a formula.

Notice how the formula is displayed both in the cell and in the formula bar.

4. Next, click on cell D9 to add it to the formula as shown in Excel Figure 1-19.

Excel Figure 1-19: Adding another cell reference.

5. Next, complete the formula by typing the closing parenthesis as shown in Excel Figure 1-20.

Excel Figure 1-20: Completing the formula.

Notice how each cell reference in the formula is color-coded. The color will correspond to the highlights around each of the referenced cells. This provides a visual way for you to check that you've selected the correct cells.

6. Finally, press the Enter key to store the completed formula in the cell.

Notice that the cell now displays the value that is the result of the formula instead of the formula itself, as shown in Excel Figure 1-21.

	E10	▾	*fx*		
	A	B	C	D	E	F
1		WildOutfitters.com				
2						
3		Conversion Rate				
4		Dollar (USD)	Euro			
5			1	0.769		
6						
7					Discount Price	Discount Price
8		Product	Price	Discount	(USD)	(Euros)
9		Salt and Pepper Shakers	3.5	✛ 0.1	3.15	
10		Candle Lantern	18.95	0.2		
11		Self Inflating Sleeping Pad	69	0.15		
12		Sleeping Bag	278	0.25		
13		Dome 2-Person Tent	155.99	0.2		
14						
15					Total (Euros)	

Excel Figure 1-21: The resulting value.

What would happen to this value if you were to change a value in one of the referenced cells, C9 or D9? Try it and see.

Let's leave the rest of the Discount Price (USD) formulas for later and move on to converting this value into euros in cell F9. Keep in mind the following things to remember:

- Cell formulas are always started by selecting a cell and then entering an = sign in that cell.

- The formula is shown in the formula bar as it is entered or when the cell is selected. When completed, the formula can still be seen in the formula bar, but the resulting value is displayed in the cell.

To calculate a discounted price in euros, we can use the formula (price in dollars * exchange rate). For the first product, Salt and Pepper Shakers, the discount price is in cell E9 (calculated from our first formula). The exchange rate is in cell C5 for all of the products. Since the exchange rate is the same for all conversions, we have chosen to enter it in one cell only. We can translate our word formula into one that will work in Excel using the cell addresses.

7. First, type = in cell F9 and then click on cell E9.

Then, type the multiplication symbol *.

Finally, click on the cell with the exchange rate, C5, as shown in Excel Figure 1-22.

	MAX	▾	X ✓ *fx*	=E9*C5	
	A	B	C	D	E	F
1		WildOutfitters.com				
2						
3		Conversion Rate				
4		Dollar (USD)	Euro			
5			1	0.769		
6						
7					Discount Price	Discount Price
8		Product	Price	Discount	(USD)	(Euros)
9		Salt and Pepper Shakers	3.5	0.1	3.15	=E9*C5
10		Candle Lantern	18.95	0.2		
11		Self Inflating Sleeping Pad	69	0.15		
12		Sleeping Bag	278	0.25		
13		Dome 2-Person Tent	155.99	0.2		
14						
15					Total (Euros)	

Excel Figure 1-22: Entering the Discount Price (Euros) formula.

Store the final formula by pressing the Enter key.

8. The result of the formula in F9 is shown in Excel Figure 1-23.

	A	B	C	D	E	F
						F10
1		WildOutfitters.com				
2						
3		Conversion Rate				
4		Dollar (USD)	Euro			
5			1	0.769		
6						
7					Discount Price	Discount Price
8		Product	Price	Discount	(USD)	(Euros)
9		Salt and Pepper Shakers	3.5	0.1	3.15	2.42235
10		Candle Lantern	18.95	0.2		
11		Self Inflating Sleeping Pad	69	0.15		
12		Sleeping Bag	278	0.25		
13		Dome 2-Person Tent	155.99	0.2		
14						
15					Total (Euros)	

Excel Figure 1-23: Discount Price (Euros) formula result.

As before, let's leave the rest of the Discount Price (Euros) and move on to calculating converting the total in cell F15. To calculate the total price in euros we could simply add all of the cells from F9 to F13 together. One way to do this is shown in Excel Figure 1-24. We'll learn a better way in the next tutorial.

9. Enter the formula as shown in Excel Figure 1-24.

MAX — =F9+F10+F11+F12+F13

	A	B	C	D	E	F	G
1		WildOutfitters.com					
2							
3		Conversion Rate					
4		Dollar (USD)	Euro				
5			1	0.769			
6							
7					Discount Price	Discount Price	
8		Product	Price	Discount	(USD)	(Euros)	
9		Salt and Pepper Shakers	3.5	0.1	3.15	2.42235	
10		Candle Lantern	18.95	0.2			
11		Self Inflating Sleeping Pad	69	0.15			
12		Sleeping Bag	278	0.25			
13		Dome 2-Person Tent	155.99	0.2			
14							
15					Total (Euros)	=F9+F10+F11+F12+F13	

Excel Figure 1-24: Entering the Total (Euros) formula.

Try to click on cell references rather than type them in.

10. Your result should look like Excel Figure 1-25.

	A	B	C	D	E	F
						F16
1		WildOutfitters.com				
2						
3		Conversion Rate				
4		Dollar (USD)	Euro			
5			1	0.769		
6						
7					Discount Price	Discount Price
8		Product	Price	Discount	(USD)	(Euros)
9		Salt and Pepper Shakers	3.5	0.1	3.15	2.42235
10		Candle Lantern	18.95	0.2		
11		Self Inflating Sleeping Pad	69	0.15		
12		Sleeping Bag	278	0.25		
13		Dome 2-Person Tent	155.99	0.2		
14						
15					Total (Euros)	2.42235

Excel Figure 1-25: Result for Total (Euros) formula.

What would happen if you needed to add another product to the list? How do you think that would affect this formula?

Copying the Contents of a Cell

Recall that we haven't completed adding our formulas. We still have to add the rest of the formulas for discounted price in dollars and the discounted price in euros. To be honest, we wanted you to wait so that we could use those cells to show you how to copy formulas. Let's first look at copying the formula for discounted price in dollars.

Think about it for a moment. We could simply go to each cell for discounted price and type in the formula. This wouldn't be too hard for a small set of formulas like this, as there are only five in all. But, what if instead of five products, we had 10, or 50, or 100, or even 1000? That starts to become a lot of typing.

Fortunately, Excel provides a way to copy formulas into other cells in such a way that the cell references in the new cells will automatically be correct (at least most of the time, as we will see). Let's look at a couple of ways to do this.

Most software made for Windows includes Copy, Cut, and Paste options. Excel includes these on the Home ribbon. You can use these to copy formulas.

1. Select the cell with the formula to copy (in this case, cell E9).

    Select Copy from the Clipboard section of the Home ribbon as shown in Excel Figure 1-26.

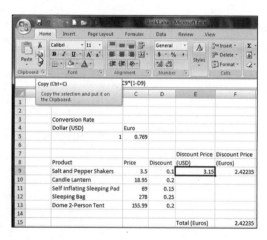

Excel Figure 1-26: Copying Cell formula in cell E9.

This will copy the contents of the cell—in this case, the formula—to the Windows Clipboard.

Notice that the keyboard shortcut for Copy is Ctrl-C.

2. Select the cell or cells into which you want to copy the formula.

   In this case, that's the range of cells from E10 down to E13, referred to as E10:E13 for short.

   Select Paste from the Paste drop-down menu in the Clipboard group of the Home ribbon, as shown in Excel Figure 1-27.

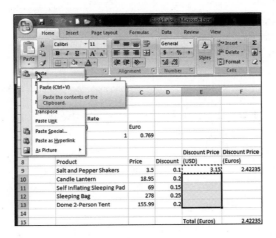

Excel Figure 1-27: Pasting cell formula in cells E10:E13.

   Notice that the keyboard shortcut for Paste is Ctrl-V.

   You can also copy cell formulas a little quicker by *dragging*. Let's try this method on the same Discount Price (USD) formula in cell E9.

3. Select the cell E9 with the formula to copy.

   Place the cursor on the lower right corner of the cell until it resembles a small cross, as shown in Excel Figure 1-28.

	A	B	C	D	E	F
	E9			*fx*	=C9*(1-D9)	
1		WildOutfitters.com				
2						
3		Conversion Rate				
4		Dollar (USD)	Euro			
5			1	0.769		
6						
7					Discount Price	Discount Price
8		Product	Price	Discount	(USD)	(Euros)
9		Salt and Pepper Shakers	3.5	0.1	3.15	2.42235
10		Candle Lantern	18.95	0.2		
11		Self Inflating Sleeping Pad	69	0.15		
12		Sleeping Bag	278	0.25		
13		Dome 2-Person Tent	155.99	0.2		
14						
15					Total (Euros)	2.42235

Excel Figure 1-28: Copying Cell Formula by Dragging

4. Click and drag until the entire range of cells into which you want to copy the formula is covered.

In this case, drag until the box covers the entire range of cells from E9 to E13 as shown in Excel Figure 1-29.

Excel Figure 1-29: Dragging the cursor.

5. Release the mouse button.

    The values that result from the new formulas will be shown in the cells as shown in Excel Figure 1-30.

Excel Figure 1-30: The results of copying the formula.

After you have copied the discount price formula, the formulas in the cells E9 to E13 should be as shown in Excel Figure 1-31.

Discount Price (USD)
=C9*(1-D9)
=C10*(1-D10)
=C11*(1-D11)
=C12*(1-D12)
=C13*(1-D13)

Excel Figure 1-31: Results of copying the discount price formula.

Notice what has happened to the formula. C9, which refers to the cell two spaces to the left from the original formula, has automatically changed to C10, C11, and so forth. In each of the new cell formulas, the reference also refers to the cell two spaces to the left. Similarly, cell D9 (one cell to the left) has automatically changed to D10, D11, D12, and D13.

As you can see, by simply copying the cell contents we have let Excel automatically adjust the formula so that it works for the new cells.

Relative versus Absolute Cell Addressing

Let's see if copying will work the same for the Discount Price (Euros) formula. Try the next few steps to see what happens.

1. To start, use one of the methods above to copy the Discount Price (Euros) formula in cell F9 to cells F10 through F13.

   Your results should be similar to those in Excel Figure 1-32.

F9		fx	=E9*C5		
	A	B	C	D	E	F	G
1		WildOutfitters.com					
2							
3		Conversion Rate					
4		Dollar (USD)	Euro				
5			1	0.769			
6							
7					Discount Price	Discount Price	
8		Product	Price	Discount	(USD)	(Euros)	
9		Salt and Pepper Shakers	3.5	0.1	3.15	2.42235	
10		Candle Lantern	18.95	0.2	15.16	0	
11		Self Inflating Sleeping Pad	69	0.15	58.65	0	
12		Sleeping Bag	278	0.25	208.5	#VALUE!	
13		Dome 2-Person Tent	155.99	0.2	124.792	436.772	
14							
15					Total (Euros)	#VALUE!	

Excel Figure 1-32: Results of copying the Discount Price (Euros) formula.

What happened? Do the values look correct to you? What does the "#VALUE!" mean in that one cell? Why did this mess up the totals formula value? As it turns out, there is a slight hitch when you simply copy this cell formula. The problem is that the exchange rate is in a single cell that applies to all the copied formulas, not in a different cell for each occurrence of the formula as the discounted price in dollars is.

As you can see, when the cells were copied, the cell reference E9 was supposed to change to reference cells E10 to E13, and it did. The cell reference C5 also changed in the same way, to C6 through C9. The exchange rate, however, is in only one cell, so the reference needs to stay C5 in all the destination cells (Excel Figure 1-33).

Discount Price
(Euros)
=E9*C5
=E10*C6
=E11*C7
=E12*C8
=E13*C9

Excel Figure 1-33: Resulting formulas.

Fear not: Excel provides a way to alter the formula so that we can simply copy it and get the right values.

When we use a cell reference in a formula, we usually just enter the cell reference in a format like C5. This format is known as a **relative cell reference** (or **relative cell address**). When copied, a relative reference in a formula will automatically change to reference the cell the same relative distance away.

Think about where C5 is located relative to the cell we are copying, F9. You should notice that C5 is three cells to the left and four cells above cell F9. When we copied cell F9 to cell F10, what reference was used to replace C5? Cell reference C5 changed to cell reference C6. Where is cell C6 in relative to the new formula cell F10? Again, C6 is three cells to the left and 4 cells above cell F10. When you copy relative cell references in Excel, they automatically change to reference a different cell that is the same relative distance in rows and columns away.

In this case, however, we want C5 to remain C5 in all cells and not change when we copy it. In order to do this, we need to adjust how we reference the cell. Instead of using a relative cell reference format we will use what is known as an **absolute cell reference**.

An absolute cell reference contains a $ (dollar sign) in front of each part of the cell reference that you want to remain absolute when the formula is copied. For example, using a cell reference of C5 will ensure that neither the column nor the row will change when the reference is copied. Let's see how this works with our example.

2. Select cell F9 and re-enter the formula using an absolute cell reference for the exchange rate.

   One way to do this is to simply type the cell reference with the dollar ($) signs.

   There is also a way to edit the formula more quickly. In the formula bar, click on the reference that you want to change, as shown in Excel Figure 1-34. Then press the F4 key. Each press of the F4 key will change the reference from one combination of relative and absolute references to the next.

	A	B	C	D	E	F
						=E9*C5
1		WildOutfitters.com				
2						
3		Conversion Rate				
4		Dollar (USD)	Euro			
5		1	0.769			
6						
7						
8		Product	Price	Discount	Discount Price (USD)	Discount Price (Euros)
9		Salt and Pepper Shakers	3.5	0.1	3.15	=E9*C5
10		Candle Lantern	18.95	0.2	15.16	0
11		Self Inflating Sleeping Pad	69	0.15	58.65	0
12		Sleeping Bag	278	0.25	208.5	#VALUE!
13		Dome 2-Person Tent	155.99	0.2	124.792	436.772
14						
15					Total (Euros)	#VALUE!

Excel Figure 1-34: Entering Discount Price (Euros)
formula with absolute reference.

There are four different combinations of relative-absolute referencing that you can use as needed: C5, $C5, C$5, and C5. In this way, you can choose to make all or part of the cell reference absolute. You can use the F4 key to toggle (switch) between each possible absolute cell reference combination.

In Excel Figures 1-35 and 1-36 you can see the results of copying your formula with the absolute cell address.

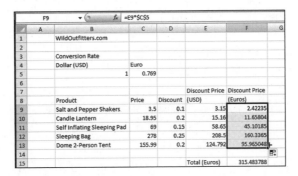

Excel Figure 1-35: Results of copying the Discount Price (Euros) formula with absolute reference.

Discount Price (Euros)
=E9*C5
=E10*C5
=E11*C5
=E12*C5
=E13*C5

Excel Figure 1-36: Formulas resulting from copying the Discount Price (Euros) formula with absolute reference.

Note that the cell reference to E9, which is still relative, automatically changed as the formula was copied while the reference to C5 remained the same.

▶**Thinking Critically:**

An important use of Excel is called **what-if analysis**. The idea is that since Excel formulas change automatically in response to changes to the spreadsheet values, you can ask "What if . . . ?" questions about the data in the spreadsheet and immediately see an answer. What are some of the what-if questions that you could ask about this spreadsheet? How would you use the spreadsheet to answer them? Why is what-if analysis a powerful use of Excel?

Formatting Cells

Recall that you can think of worksheet cells as containers. So far we've seen how to put things into the cells (text, numbers, and formulas). Let's see how we can adjust how the cell contents are displayed. To do this we use the cell formatting features. Here we'll look at just a few things you can do with cell formatting.

Generally, you can format a cell by first highlighting the cell (or cells) that you want to format and then selecting the options from the Home ribbon. Let's use these options to change the formats of some of the text labels and how the numbers are displayed on our worksheet.

1. Let's start by changing the table headings to use the Arial font, adjust the font size to 12, and make these labels bold.

   Notice that options for changing these items are included in the Font group on the Home ribbon, shown in Excel Figure 1-37.

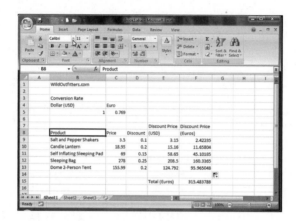

Excel Figure 1-37: The Excel Font group.

   To start, select the cell or cells that you want to change. In this case select B8.

2. Click on the arrow next to the name of the current font. A drop-down list is displayed with a huge list of available fonts.

   Scroll down the list and select the Arial font as shown in Excel Figure 1-38.

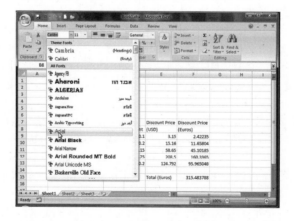

Excel Figure 1-38: Selecting a font.

3. Similarly, use the drop-down list for the font size to adjust the size of the font to 12 points, as shown in Excel Figure 1-39. (Recall from the Word tutorials that 1 inch equals 72 points.)

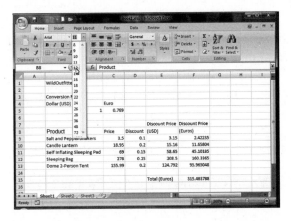

Excel Figure 1-39: Adjusting font size.

4. Now click on the bold **B** icon in the Font group, as shown in Excel Figure 1-40, to display the text in bold font.

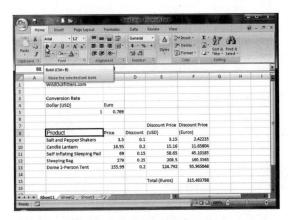

Excel Figure 1-40: Making the text bold.

Notice that you could also use the keyboard shortcut Ctrl-B to make text bold.

Go ahead and change the other column headings in the table to match the new format.

Take a moment to look at the other options in the Font group. You can change the text to italic or underlined, adjust the font size larger or smaller, change the color of the text, add borders, and fill the cell with color. Even more options are available in the Format Cells dialog (available by clicking the small arrow in the bottom right corner of the Font, Alignment, or Number group). Additional options here include adjusting the cell alignment and the ability to protect or lock the cell so that it can't be changed. You can also change how numbers are displayed in the cell.

With numbers, we often need to display the number with a certain common symbol or a certain number of decimal places. When we do this, we will be adjusting only the format of how the number is displayed, not the value or formula that is contained in the cell.

5. Let's select the cells with the product prices so that we can display them in a currency format in U.S. dollars.

   Notice that there are several options for changing the number format in the Number group on the Home ribbon.

   Click on the $ symbol as shown in Excel Figure 1-41.

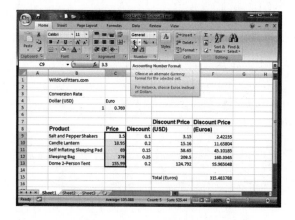

Excel Figure 1-41: The Number group.

6. Now select the range with the Discount values, D9 to D13.

   We can click on the % icon in the Number group, as shown in Excel Figure 1-42, to format these as Percent style.

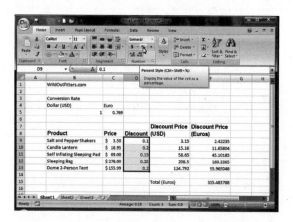

Excel Figure 1-42: Setting Percent format.

7. Let's now have a look at another way we can set the number format by setting the Discount Price (USD) to currency format.

Select the range E9 to E13.

Now, click on the small arrow in the bottom right of the Number group as shown in Excel Figure 1-43.

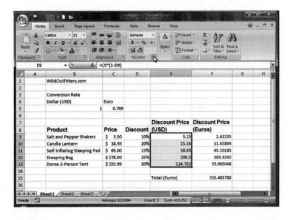

Excel Figure 1-43: Selecting the Number page to set the format for Discount Price (USD).

8. You should now see the Number page of the Format Cells dialog.

Select Currency under the Category list as shown in Excel Figure 1-44.

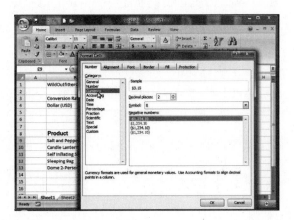

Excel Figure 1-44: Formatting currency in U.S. dollars.

You should take a moment to look at the other types of number formats in that list before moving on.

Check that the decimal places, currency symbol, and way of showing negative numbers are as desired; then click on OK.

9. You can also use this method to format the Discount Price (Euros) to currency with a euro symbol.

   Select the range and format as before.

   This time, click the arrow next to the Symbol drop-down box.

   Scroll through the list of currencies to select the symbol for Euros (€123), as shown in Excel Figure 1-45.

Excel Figure 1-45: Formatting currency in euros.

10. Another way to format cells is to right-click on a cell that you want to format.

    You should now see a Quick Format toolbar and a context-sensitive pop-up menu.

    Options for formatting the cell appear on the toolbar.

    The Format Cells option on the pop-up menu (Excel Figure 1-46) will display the Format Cells dialog that we have already seen.

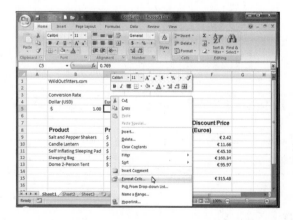

Excel Figure 1-46: Quick Format toolbar and context-sensitive menu.

11. Now, you try your hand at formatting the worksheet so that it appears like that shown in Excel Figure 1-47.

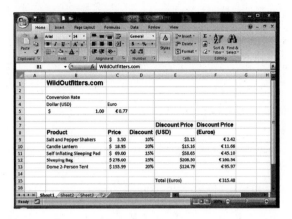

Excel Figure 1-47: Worksheet with final formats.

Saving Your Excel Workbook

Now that you have completed your worksheet, you need to save your file. Actually, it's best to save and name your file when you start and then save it periodically as you work by clicking the Save icon ( ), but this is the best place to discuss the topic in our tutorial.

1. Click on the Microsoft Office button to open the dialog box shown in Excel Figure 1-48.

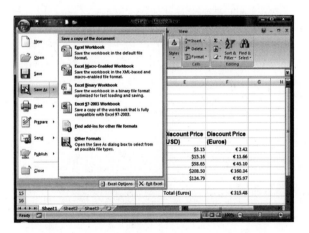

Excel Figure 1-48: Saving an Excel file.

This time, select the Save As option.

You should notice that there are several ways (formats) that you can use to save your file.

2. Select Excel Workbook, and you will see the Save As dialog shown in Excel Figure 1-49.

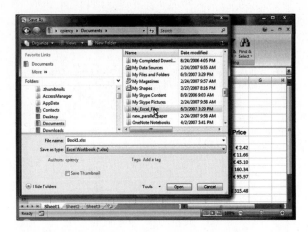

Excel Figure 1-49: Selecting a folder to save your file.

Scroll through the folders in the right and left panes to select the storage location where you want your file to be saved.

Notice that the left pane will display the current folder that you are viewing, while the right pane will show the contents of that folder.

As you click on a folder in the right pane, the left pane will expand to display your selected folder, and the right pane will display the contents of the newly selected folder.

3. In the File name: text box, type the name of your file as shown in Excel Figure 1-50.

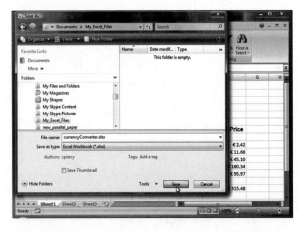

Excel Figure 1-50: Naming your Excel file.

In this case, we are using the file name *currencyConverter.*

Notice that the file extension for an Excel 2007 Workbook is *xlsx.*

If you want to save your file as a different type, you can click the arrow for the Save as Type list for other options.

Once you have set the location and file name, simply click on Save to save your file to storage. Now, you can retrieve it at a future date to work with or edit the workbook.

USING THE EXCEL HELP FEATURE

At times you may find yourself wanting to do something to a workbook that you don't know how to do. Fear not! Like all Microsoft Office software, Excel comes with an extensive Help feature that can answer just about all of your questions about using Excel. Help topics are loaded onto your local computer for most questions, and even more is available online if you are connected. Getting to know how to use, and becoming comfortable with, Excel Help are important parts of mastering the software. Let's take a quick look at using Excel Help.

1. The Help button (a circle icon with a question mark inside) is located near the top right corner of the Excel window. Click on this when you need help, as shown in Excel Figure 1-51.

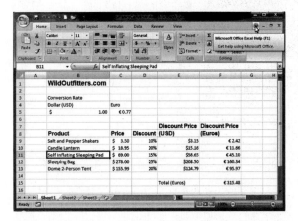

Excel Figure 1-51: Getting Help from Excel.

Notice that while using Excel, you can also simply press the F1 key on your keyboard to get help.

2. The Excel Help browser will be displayed as shown in Excel Figure 1-52. There are two main ways to search Excel Help:

Excel Figure 1-52: Excel Help browser.

- You can browse the Table of Contents by clicking on the hyperlinks.
- You can enter keywords into the text box and click on the Search link.

Type *insert a row* into the text box and click Search.

3. If you are connected to Office Online, this will be indicated at lower right on the Help browser.

A message will be displayed, as shown in Excel Figure 1-53, while the Help system searches your computer and the on-line resources for pages that may contain the answer to your question.

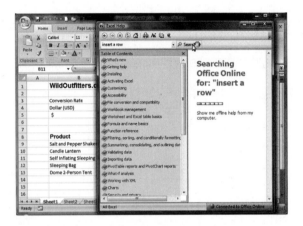

Excel Figure 1-53: Searching Office Online.

If not connected, you can still search for Help pages stored on your computer.

4. Results will be displayed as a list of hyperlinks in the right pane of the browser.

Scroll the list and click the link that seems most likely to lead to the answer you are seeking, as shown in Excel Figure 1-54.

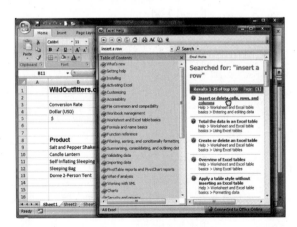

Excel Figure 1-54: Selecting a Help topic.

You may need to go through two or three of these before you find the answer.

The browser has buttons to help you browse back and forward to different topics.

5. Results of your searching and browsing will be displayed in the right pane of the browser.

    Results will include descriptions of Excel features and step-by-step instructions for doing something.

    Note that you can adjust the browser and browser panes sizes for easier reading.

    See if you can find the page displayed in Excel Figure 1-55.

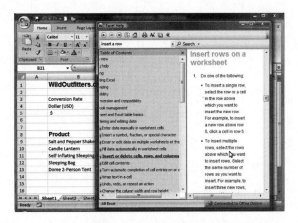

Excel Figure 1-55: Excel Help Text

At the risk of sounding repetitive, the Help feature of any Microsoft Office application is one of the most important tools available to you. Anything that you want to know about the software is presented somewhere within this vast knowledge base. It is especially important to you when you move beyond the forgiving environment of your courses and out into the big cruel world. Learn Help! Use Help!

EXERCISES TO INCREASE YOUR KNOWLEDGE OF MS EXCEL

Match each of the Excel terms with its description.

_____ 1. Absolute reference   a. The primary space for entering your data, formed by the intersection of a row and a column.

_____ 2. Cell   b. A cell reference that does not change when a cell formula is copied.

___ 3. Cell format

   c. A cell reference that changes to refer to a cell the same relative distance away (in rows and columns) when a cell formula is copied.

___ 4. Formula bar

   d. A sheet within your Excel file that is made up of a grid of cells formed by rows and columns.

___ 5. Name box

   e. Your complete Excel file, which typically includes multiple worksheets and other objects.

___ 6. Relative reference

   f. Settings used to adjust the appearance of a cell and its contents without changing the actual value stored in the cell.

___ 7. Ribbon

   g. A portion of the workbook that displays the name of the cell or cells that are currently selected.

___ 8. Workbook

   h. The default file extension for Excel 2007 files.

___ 9. Worksheet

   i. A portion of the Excel interface that displays the contents of the currently selected cell without formatting applied.

___10. xlsx

   j. One of several groups of Excel commands that are organized according to context.

Fill in the blank with the Excel ribbon and group that is home to each of the following commands. You'll have to look for them because we have not discussed some of them yet.

Command	Ribbon	Group
11. Align		
12. Conditional Formatting		
13. Copy		
14. Freeze Panes		
15. Insert Function		
16. Picture		
17. Print Area		
18. Sort		
19. Track Changes		
20. WordArt		

21. Complete the worksheet described in this tutorial. Remember to save it often during the process of completing the spreadsheet and when you finish it.

Expand your worksheet to let you convert from U.S. dollars to British pounds (check out the latest exchange rate on the Web).

Answer the following questions in an empty location on your worksheet.

Q1: Why should values that are used many times but that are subject to change be placed in a separate but easily referenced area of the spreadsheet?

Q2: What does this have to do with "what-iffing" a business decision? *Hint:* Imagine the euro rises or falls (is worth more or less) against the U.S. dollar.

Use Excel Help to find the answers to the following questions:

22. Can you add commands to the Quick Access Toolbar?

23. What should you do if you want to share a Workbook file with a colleague who has an older version of Excel?

24. What can you do to make a long text item fit within a cell without changing the column width?

25. What letter, number, or symbol is represented by the decimal value 60 in ASCII?

EXCEL TUTORIAL 1: MINI-CASE 1

Scenario: Dexter Lampe is excited. His new boss in the accounting department, Mr. Chaise, has asked him to spruce up a spreadsheet that he wants to present to the board of directors in the next board meeting. The spreadsheet contains financial information about the company's current balance sheet. In addition, it contains a section for forecasting sales for the next 3 years and analyzing how the forecast changes impact the balance sheet. It's the first opportunity that Dexter has had to show what he can do. He's sure that this will be the first of many successful assignments that will allow him to move up the corporate ladder at UltraCorp, Inc. Mr. Chaise attached the spreadsheet to an e-mail along with his instructions to Dexter. When Dexter opened it, he smiled and thought to himself, "Piece of cake!" All he would need to do is add a few formulas and do some formatting to make the spreadsheet presentable. The hard part would be in holding back and not getting too wild with the colors. He decided to get right to work.

Your Task: Download the Excel file *EXC_1_MC_Balance_Sheet.xlsx* from the student section of http://www.wiley.com/college/piercy. Use this spreadsheet to help Dexter by completing the missing formulas in the spreadsheet and adjusting cell formats and font styles to make the balance sheet presentable for your boss. At a minimum, you should do the following:

- Complete the missing formulas. Comments are provided on each cell (indicated by little red triangles in the cell) that describe the formula that you should enter. Simply place the cursor on the cell to read the comment.
- Adjust all numeric values to display as currency format.
- Use font styles (bold, italics, etc.) to highlight the various headings in the balance sheet.
- Center the heading information at the top of the spreadsheet above the balance sheet and adjust the font and font style.

- Use cell borders to separate the various sections of the balance sheet.
- Fill the blank cells between the balance sheet columns with color to separate the columns visually.
- Don't forget to save the file when you complete your work.

If you are not sure how to do some of these tasks, be sure to use Excel Help to find out how.

EXCEL TUTORIAL 1: MINI-CASE 2

Scenario: Pepé Valise scored a lucrative consulting job right out of college. While his job was challenging and paid well, it did require a lot of traveling to meet with clients. His responsibilities include keeping track of his spending so that he can submit a report to be reimbursed for his expenses. Pepé is allowed $2000 per trip. He needs to be able to compare his actual trip expenses to this target value. Having learned Microsoft Office software in college, Pepé thinks that Excel will be a good tool to keep track of his travel expense.

Your Task: Create an Excel worksheet from scratch that Pepé can use to keep track of his expenses and compare the total expense to his budget. Make sure that your worksheet has the following features:

- Include a cell label for Target Trip Budget and a cell for entering the target value.
- Create a table on your worksheet for Pepé to record his expenses. The table should include columns for the expense item, the unit cost of each expense item, the number of units for each item, and the subtotal for each item (the unit cost times the number of units). For example, one entry might be Hotel at $75 per night for 3 nights for a total of $225.
- Include a cell and label for the total of all expenses.
- Include a cell and label for the difference between the overall total and the budget target. Format the value to display as currency with negative values in parentheses.
- Adjust numeric values to display as the appropriate number format (Currency, etc.).
- Use font styles (bold, italics, etc.) to highlight the various headings in the table.
- Use cell borders to separate the various sections of the expense table.
- Don't forget to save the file when you complete your work.

If you are not sure how to do some of these tasks, be sure to use Excel Help to find out how.

Tutorial 2

FORMULAS AND FUNCTIONS
IN MICROSOFT EXCEL 2007

After reading this tutorial and completing the associated exercises, you will be able to:

- Understand formulas and functions.
- Insert functions using the Formulas ribbon and Insert Function dialog.
- Use the following functions: SUM, AVERAGE, PMT, IF (and nested-IFs), and VLOOKUP.
- Use conditional functions.

MICROSOFT EXCEL FORMULAS AND FUNCTIONS

Recall that cells are the building blocks of worksheets. Cells can contain data, or they can contain a formula or a function that transforms data. Within a formula or function you can refer to individual cells (e.g., B2), or to a range of cells (e.g., D2:D5). The use of **formulas** and **functions**, which can reference other cells and then automatically change when a referenced cell value changes, is one of the most important and powerful features of Excel.

Often when using formulas and functions, it is appropriate and more convenient to refer to a range of cells. When you refer to a range of cells, you are including all the data in the cells beginning with the first cell in the range and ending with the last cell in the range. You can think of a cell range as a rectangle on the worksheet (in fact, this is what a cell range looks like when you select it). The *first* cell is the cell that is in the upper left corner of the rectangle, while the *last* cell is in the lower right corner of the rectangle.

So, if you used the cell range D2:D5 from Excel Figure 2-1, you would be referencing the following values: {88, 52, 56, and 60}. If you used the cell range B2:C5, you would be referencing the following values: {145, 207, 125, 195, 66, 70, 64, and 75}.

Formulas and functions are related but slightly different concepts. According to Microsoft Excel Help, formulas are "equations that perform calculations on values in your worksheet," and functions are "predefined formulas that perform calculations by using specific values, called arguments, in a particular order, or structure." The following example will help you understand how formulas and functions are used and the difference between them. To see what else Microsoft says about formulas and functions, you can go to Microsoft Excel Help, type *formula* in the search box, and press Enter.

Example 1: Formulas and functions. In Excel Figure 2-1, data for four clients, A–D, are shown. In cells B7, C7, and D7, formulas are used to sum the data, and in cells B9, C9, and D9, formulas are used to average the data. Contrast this with cells B8, C8, and D8 and with cells B10, C10, and D10, respectively. In these cells, functions are used to SUM or AVERAGE the data. Excel Figure 2-2 shows the spreadsheet as you would normally see it; the values that result from the formulas and functions are displayed in the appropriate cells.

	A	B	C	D
1	Fitness Client	Weight (in pounds)	Height (in inches)	Age
2	A	145	66	88
3	B	207	70	52
4	C	125	64	56
5	D	195	75	60
6				
7	Sum using Formula	=B2+B3+B4+B5	=C2+C3+C4+C5	=D2+D3+D4+D5
8	Sum using Function	=SUM(B2:B5)	=SUM(C2:C5)	=SUM(D2:D5)
9	Average using Formula	=(B2+B3+B4+B5)/4	=(C2+C3+C4+C5)/4	=(D2+D3+D4+D5)/4
10	Average using Function	=AVERAGE(B2:B5)	=AVERAGE(C2:C5)	=AVERAGE(D2:D5)

Excel Figure 2-1: Formula and function example (showing formulas and functions in each cell).

	A	B	C	D
1	Fitness Client	Weight (in pounds)	Height (in inches)	Age
2	A	145	65	88
3	B	207	70	52
4	C	125	64	56
5	D	195	75	60
6				
7	Sum using Formula	672	275	256
8	Sum using Function	672	275	256
9	Average using Formula	168	68.75	64
10	Average using Function	168	68.75	64

Excel Figure 2-2: Formula and function example (showing result values in each cell).

▶Thinking Critically:
Given the data, is the "middle" age of the members 64 as reported, or is it closer to another number? What function would provide a more accurate representation of the "middle" age of the members?

Look at the values in the range of cells B7:D8. Why would the owners be concerned with total weight, total height, or total age of their clients? Just correctly applying a formula or a function to your data does not necessarily create useful information.

HOW TO CREATE AND USE FORMULAS

Now that you have seen what a formula is and what a function is, let's look at how to describe them using Excel terms. In Excel Figure 2-3, cell B4 contains a typical formula that returns the average of the values in cells B2 (value = 88) and B3 (value = 52).

As in the figure, we begin all cell formulas and functions with the equal sign. After that, formulas can be made up of cell references (in this case. B2 and B3), literal values (in this case, 2), and mathematical operators (in this case, =, +, /, and ( )).

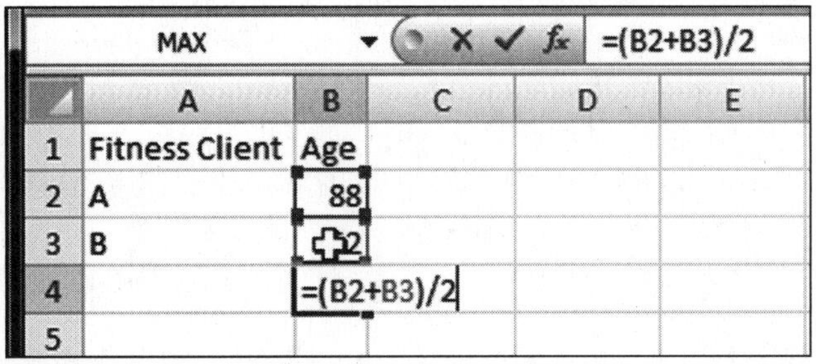

Excel Figure 2-3: Formulas and functions, construction example.

▶Thinking Critically:
Why do you think that there are parentheses () around B2+B3? Excel executes various mathematical operators in order of a predetermined precedence. Try typing the formula in B4 like this: =B2+B3/2. Do you get the same answer?

Mathematical Operators and Precedence for Formulas

From Excel Help (keyword: *calculation operators*), the operators you can use in Excel and the order in which Excel performs the operations when used in a formula are presented in Excel Table 2-1. If two operations have equal precedence, they are performed in a left to right order relative to their appearance in the formula.

Operator	Description	Examples
: (colon) (single space) , (comma)	Used as reference operators	A1:D10 refers to the cell range from A1 to D10
=	Negation	−B10: If the value in B10 is 10, then −B10 = −10
%	Percent	=20% will result in a value of .2 in the cell
^	Exponentiation	= 10^2 = 100
* and /	Multiplication and division	If A1 = 5, B1 = 4, and C1 = 2, then =A1*B1/C1 = 10
+ and −	Addition and subtraction	If A1 = 5, B1 = 4, and C1 = 2, then =A1+B1−C1 = 7
&	Concatenation (connects two strings of text together)	If A1 = Cold; B1 = play, then if we put the formula =A1&B1 into C1 = Coldplay
= (equals) <> (not equals) > (greater than) => (greater than or equal to) < (less than) <= (less than or equal to)	Comparison (generally used in expressions that will end up being true or false depending on the outcome of the comparison)	Assume A1 = 5, B1 = 4, and C1 =2: (A1 = B1) this expression is false (A1 <> B1) this expression is true (A1 * C1 > B1) this expression is true (A1 * C1 >= B1) this expression is true (A1 * C1 < B1) this expression is false (A1 * C1 <= B1) this expression is false

Excel Table 2-1: Operators and precedence.

Here are two examples to help you understand how formulas work. Based on the data in Excel Figure 2-4, can you evaluate each formula and find the answer?

Formula A: =A1^B2*C3/D3

Formula B: =A1*B2^C3/D3

	A	B	C	D
1	21	1	87	67
2	34	2	68	35
3	45	3	98	86

Excel Figure 2-4: Data for Formulas A and B.

Given the data shown in Excel Figure 2-4, which formula produces the largest value? *Hints:* (1) the cell references represent the values in the cells, and (2) You might read . . .

Formula A as "A1 is raised to the power of B2, then this result is multiplied by C3, then this result is divided by D3," and . . .

Formula B as "B2 is raised to the power of C3, then this result is multiplied by A1, then this result is divided by D3."

In Excel Tutorial 1, you read about how to enter a simple formula into an Excel cell. Try that now with these formulas to check your answer to the question.

▶**Thinking Critically:**
The best practice is to build your formulas in the following manner. When you need to enter an "=": a mathematical operator, or a number, you should type it. When you need to enter a cell reference, you should click on the cell to be referenced. It will then appear as part of the formula. Why would this be better than typing the cell reference? For large applications, knowledge workers may store values on multiple worksheets and even in multiple workbooks. It turns out that you can just click on the cell reference to add it to a formula. What happens when you are building a formula on one worksheet in a workbook, and click on a cell in another worksheet of the same workbook? How is the cell reference different? What if you are building a formula and click on a cell located in a totally different workbook?

HOW TO USE FUNCTIONS

Now that you have learned how formulas are put together, let's look at functions. Remember that functions are formula components that Excel has built for you. For example, you can use the SUM function in a formula to add together all the values in a range of cells rather than listing each cell and using the addition operator between the cells. Formulas can be created using combinations of cell addresses, mathematical operators and built-in functions. Here's an example (assuming the cells contain some numeric data):

The formula =SUM(A2:D3) using the SUM function provides the same answer as the formula =A2+A3+B2+B3+C2+C3+D2+D3 and is easier to type. You can also type the =*SUM* (and then drag and highlight the correct range, add the closing parenthesis, press Enter, and you're done. For large ranges of data, this can save time and prevent errors.

The IF Function

Functions can also help you make decisions. Many decisions you make are similar in nature to **IF functions**: If X happens, then I'll do A, but if X doesn't happen, I'll do B. Let's look at an IF function and learn the standard way in which we'll talk about functions.

The IF function checks to see whether a condition is true or false and then returns one value if true and another value if false. The IF function looks like this:

IF(logical test, value_if_true, value_if_false)

Let's take the function apart. The name of the function is followed by an open parenthesis and the **logical test**. What is a logical test? It is a test you set up using cell references or values or text and certain operators such as =, <, and >, as listed in Excel Table 2-1. The logical test is followed by a comma, the value that is returned if the logical test is true, another comma, and then the value that is returned if the logical test is false.

Whew! What did he say? Here's an example in English:

You are leaving for class and you are not sure whether or not to take an umbrella. So you check to see if it is raining. If it is true that it is raining, grab an umbrella. If it is not true that it is raining (in other words, if it's not raining), then don't take an umbrella.

Let's write this out again to see how the parameters of the IF function match up with the words we use in the form of an IF-THEN-ELSE rule:

IF

It is raining   ← logical test

THEN

Grab the umbrella   ← value if true

ELSE

Don't take the umbrella   ← value if false

For this example you could set this up in Excel (you wouldn't, but humor us here) as follows:

1. As with any formula, start by typing =.

   Now start typing *if* by typing the *i*.

Notice what happens—a list of possible built-in functions pops up that begin with the letter *i*.

Highlight IF (the function we want to use). As you highlight a function in the list, a brief description pops up to help you decide which function to use, as shown in Excel Figure 2-5.

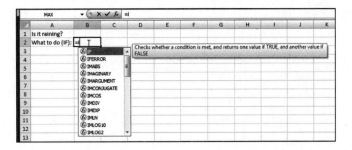

Excel Figure 2-5: Entering the IF function.

2. Double-click on the IF. Your cell entry will now appear as in Excel Figure 2-6.

Excel Figure 2-6: Components of the IF function.

Note that the arguments that you need to enter as part of your IF function are displayed.

Let's take a moment to look at the look of an Excel function. Functions start with a **function name** that reflects what the function does. For example, the SUM function can add up a range of values, the IF function can be used to choose options based on a logical test, the NPV function can calculate the net present value for an investment, and so on.

The function name is typically followed by a list of one or more **arguments** (also known as **parameters**) enclosed in parentheses. The arguments represent the input values that are needed for the function to perform its calculation. Each argument in the list is separated by a comma. Arguments may be required or optional. What you enter for an argument will depend on what the function requires, but it can be a value, a formula, or even another function—anything that ultimately returns an appropriate value for the function to use.

Most functions have at least one argument that is required (a few can be used with no arguments). Excel Figure 2-6 shows that the IF function has one required argument ("logical_test") and two optional arguments ("value_if_true" and "value_if_false"). Optional arguments are indicated by the square brackets. When using a function, you must enter something for a required argument, but it's up to you whether or not you need to enter a value for an optional argument.

Let's complete the IF function by entering appropriate arguments.

3. For the logical_test enter: *B1="Yes"* as shown in Excel Figure 2-7.

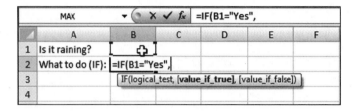

Excel Figure 2-7: Entering the logical test.

A logical test will return a value of True if the test statement is true and False if the test statement is false.

So, if the value in cell B1 is *Yes,* our test will return a value of true. Otherwise, it will return a value of false. Now we need to enter something for the other arguments.

4. Let's enter *"grab the umbrella"* for the value_if_true argument as shown in Excel Figure 2-8.

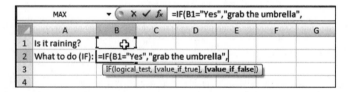

Excel Figure 2-8: Entering the value_if_true.

5. Let's enter *"don't take the umbrella"* for the value_if_false argument as shown in Excel Figure 2-9. Type a closing parenthesis and press Enter.

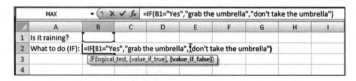

Excel Figure 2-9: Entering the value_if_false.

Note that when you want a value to be a literal string of characters, you need to put quote marks around the value. If the value to be displayed by a function is a number or the result of a formula nested within the function, quotes are not needed.

6. Just because we've finished entering the function, we haven't finished yet. We need to test our function.

Excel Figures 2-10 and 2-11 show the results of the function when the values of *Yes* and *No*, respectively, are entered in B1.

B2					=IF(B1="Yes","grab the umbrella","don't take the umbrella")				
	A	B	C	D	E	F	G	H	I
1	Is it raining?	yes							
2	What to do (IF):	grab the umbrella			✚				
3									

Excel Figure 2-10: Testing the function with a true condition.

B2					=IF(B1="Yes","grab the umbrella","don't take the umbrella")				
	A	B	C	D	E	F	G	H	I
1	Is it raining?	no							
2	What to do (IF):	don't take the umbrella			✚				
3									
4									

Excel Figure 2-11: Testing the function with a false condition.

In Excel Figures 2-10 and 2-11, you can see that when *Yes* is typed into cell B1, the IF function stored in B2 will display *grab the umbrella*. When *No* is typed into cell B1, the message *don't take the umbrella* is displayed.

So far we have tested our IF function using a data value that we expect to be entered into cell B1. In computer development parlance, this is known as **positive testing**. So far our function is working well and has passed positive testing. Let's see what happens, however, when we perform **negative testing** by typing something unexpected, but possible, into cell B1.

In Excel Figure 2-12, you can see that when the phrase *anything but yes* is typed into cell B1, the IF function stored in B2 will display *don't take the umbrella* just as if *No* had been entered.

B2					=IF(B1="Yes","grab the umbrella","don't take the umbrella")				
	A	B	C	D	E	F	G	H	I
1	Is it raining?	anything but yes							
2	What to do (IF):	don't take the umbrella			✚				
3									
4									

Excel Figure 2-12: Negative testing the function.

What if we wanted to ensure that only the values of *Yes* or *No* would return a value? Or, what about a third option, *Maybe*? Maybe if it does rain, we would want to keep the umbrella handy without actually having to carry it around. Maybe we would want to take it and leave it in the car. Our current function fails to take this or any other option into account and thus fails our negative test. What can we do to change it to take into account this new option?

The answer lies in the ability to **nest** functions within other functions. This means that we can type one or more functions as arguments of another function. The "outer" function will use the values determined by the "inner" function to determine its own results. With IF functions, nesting can be used when we have a more complex rule. Consider the following:

IF

it is raining   ← **logical test**

THEN

Grab the umbrella   ← **value if true**

ELSE   ↓ value if false (the whole thing!)

IF

it's not raining   ← **logical test**

THEN

Don't take the umbrella   ← **value if true**

ELSE

Put umbrella in car for later. ← **value if false**

In this structure, the second (inner) IF-THEN-ELSE rule is inside, or nested within, the value-if-false part for the first (outer) IF-THEN-ELSE rule. In Excel Figure 2-13 we can see how we can enter this into the spreadsheet as one IF function nested within another IF function.

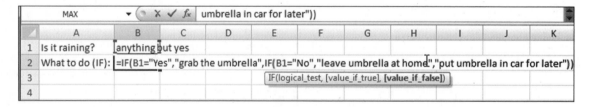

Excel Figure 2-13: Entering a nested IF function.

In Excel Figure 2-14 you can see that now the function works when we enter *Maybe* into cell B1.

Excel Figure 2-14: Results of nested IF with *Maybe* value in cell B1.

What do you think? We have made a pretty big change to our function. Has this function been fully tested? In general, you need to perform both positive and negative testing on your functions any time you create or alter them to ensure they will always be correct.

▶**Thinking Critically:**

Can you think of other possible values that could be entered into cell B1? What would the function display if those values were entered? What could you do to correct the function if needed?

INSERTING THE VLOOKUP FUNCTION USING THE FUNCTIONS RIBBON

For this section pretend that you are the professor. You feel like you have about a million students this academic term, and you need to assign each of them a letter grade based on the percentage of points they have earned for your course. The data for this example is shown in Excel Table 2-2. It may also be downloaded from the student section of http://www.wiley.com/college/piercy as the file *EXC_2_Student_Example_Data.xlsx.*

Student ID	Percent Score	Letter Grade	Student ID	Percent Score	Letter Grade
723800	90%		322163	73%	
640071	78%		724799	58%	
168435	76%		479850	60%	
588368	87%		693746	80%	
660214	93%		535107	76%	
286923	80%		298502	83%	
213264	64%		875125	71%	
227477	91%		324865	91%	
690209	78%		736643	82%	
178328	82%		214971	58%	
232434	76%		880789	69%	
769560	67%		109401	88%	
600369	80%				

Cutoff Values	Letter Grade
0%	F
60%	D
70%	C
80%	B
90%	A

Excel Table 2-2: Student grade data.

The students' IDs and percentage grades are already in the spreadsheet shown in Excel Table 2-2. But the part that you dread is manually moving down through the list in the spreadsheet, determining the letter grade, and typing the letter grade into the appropriate cell. While trying to avoid getting started, you try to estimate how long this will take you. Let's see: 1 second per student times 1 million students = 1,000,000 seconds = 16,666.7 minutes = 277.8 hours = 11 days straight. Uh oh! Either you need to ask for some time off to get this done, or you need to find something in Excel than can save you some time.

Vaguely, you recall a colleague telling you about an Excel function that can look up values in a table. That's all you know, so how are you going to find the function?

1. Select the Formulas tab as shown in Excel Figure 2-15.

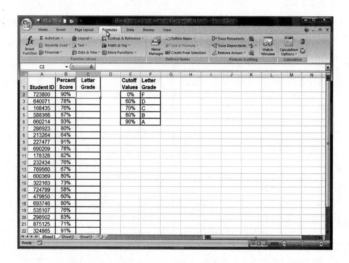

Excel Figure 2-15: Student grades spreadsheet.

Notice the group called Function Library. As the name implies, this group provides a browsable library of built-in functions.

We'll find the function we want in the library and then build it using a Function Wizard.

2. The Function Library is organized by category.

Let's think about what we want: a function that will refer to values in another table to "look up" related values.

A likely category for this type of function is "Lookup and Reference."

Click on this category, as shown in Excel Figure 2-16, to get a list of related functions.

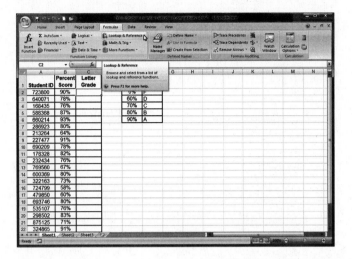

Excel Figure 2-16: Selecting the Lookup and Reference function category.

3. As you hover over an item in the list, you can read a description of what the function will do.

   Check out the VLOOKUP function and read its description, as shown in Excel Figure 2-17.

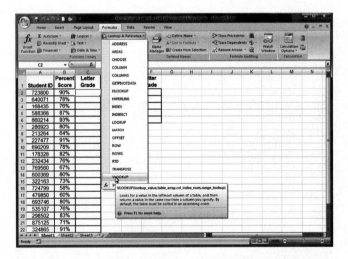

Excel Figure 2-17: Selecting the VLOOKUP function.

This function sounds made to order!

4. In Excel Figure 2-18 we have the dialog box for entering the parameters of VLOOKUP.

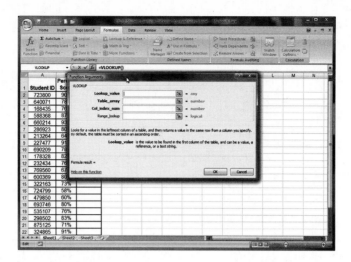

Excel Figure 2-18: The VLOOKUP dialog.

Note that when you select a text box, the description of that parameter is shown.

You should also notice that Excel has started entering the function in the selected cell (C2).

Let's start entering parameters.

5. Select the Lookup_value parameter and read its description.

   For cell C2, the value that we need to look up a letter grade for is in cell B2.

   Click on cell B2 to set it as the Lookup_value, as shown in Excel Figure 2-19. Notice that the function in cell C2 has been updated with this parameter value.

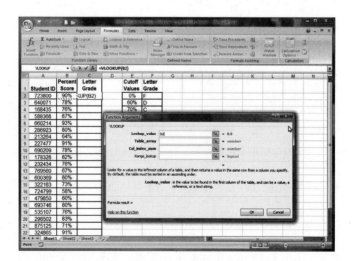

Excel Figure 2-19: Setting the lookup parameter.

Now click on Table_array.

6. The range of cells with the table from which we can look up the appropriate letter grade is E2:F6.

   Use the mouse to select this range. Wait before moving to the next parameter!

   Remember, we will be copying this function. What should you do to the table array range? Excel Figure 2-20 should give you a clue.

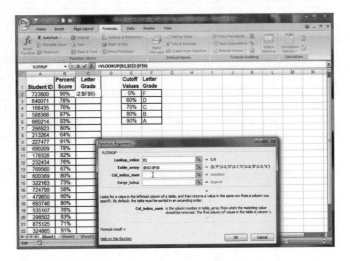

Excel Figure 2-20: Setting the Table_array parameter.

7. The Col_index_num is the column number from the lookup table that holds the value we want to look up.

   Columns are numbered starting with far left column as 1, the next as 2, and so on.

   For our example, we need to enter a 2 in this parameter, as shown in Excel Figure 2-21, because the letter grades are in the second column.

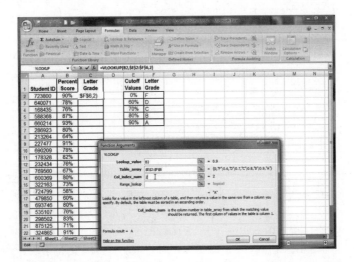

Excel Figure 2-21: Setting the Col_index_num parameter.

What about the optional Range_lookup parameter? Based on the description, if you don't enter a parameter here, the VLOOKUP function will assume True by default.

Parameters with default values are considered optional. Required parameters are shown in bold print, while optional parameters are not in bold.

▶**Thinking Critically:**

If a parameter is optional for an Excel function, does this mean that it is optional for what you want to accomplish with the function? Based on the description of Range_lookup, what should we enter (or not) here?

---

8. Excel Figure 2-22 shows the results after copying our finished VLOOKUP function into the remaining cells of the table.

Note that we elected to leave the Range_lookup parameter empty or True by default.

Why does this work?

It must come as a relief to finish that so quickly. With this function you estimate that you have saved approximately 10 days, 23 hours, and 50 minutes of typing in letter grades.

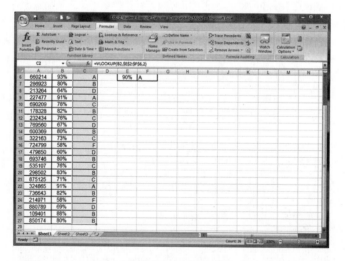

Excel Figure 2-22: VLOOKUP function results.

▶**Thinking Critically:**

Your students beg and plead for you to adjust your cutoff values for the letter grades. Bowing to the pressure, you agree to award an A for 88% or higher and allow 78% for a B, 68% for a C, and 58% for a D. How should you adjust your spreadsheet?

USING THE INSERT FUNCTION DIALOG

While the ability to browse through the Function Library is a very nice feature, it might be nice to search for a function using keywords. Fortunately, this feature is also available through the Insert Function option on the Formula Ribbon. We'll look at an example to see how this works.

1. Create a brief worksheet like that shown in Excel Figure 2-23.

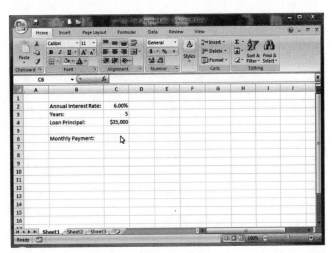

Excel Figure 2-23: Loan Payment worksheet.

Here, we want to calculate a Monthly Payment on a 5 Year, $35,000 Loan Principal with a 6% Annual Interest Rate.

You might find this formula in your finance or accounting text, but it can be difficult to remember and enter. Let's see whether a function is already available in Excel.

2. Click the Formulas ribbon tab.

On the far left of the ribbon you should find the f_x (Insert Function) button as shown in Excel Figure 2-24.

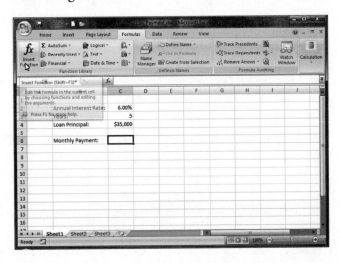

Excel Figure 2-24: The f_x (Insert Function) button.

Note: Insert Function is also available by clicking the f_x icon next to the formula text box.

3. Click the f_x button to get the Insert Function dialog.

    This dialog gives you the ability to browse the Function Library or to search it using a question or keyword list.

    Notice in Excel Figure 2-25 that when a function has been highlighted, a description of the function is provided.

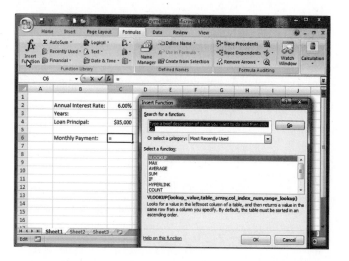

Excel Figure 2-25: The Insert Function dialog.

4. Type "Calculate a monthly payment" into the Search for a Function text box and click the Go button.

    The result will be a list like that shown in the Select a Function list box of Excel Figure 2-26. This list consists of those functions that Excel thinks might be a match for your search query.

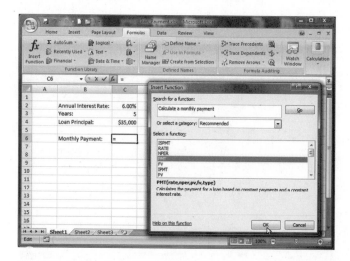

Excel Figure 2-26: Searching for a function using search query.

Highlight the PMT function and read its description.

5. With PMT highlighted, click OK. You could also double-click what you want in the list.

The result will be the dialog for the selected function, such as the PMT dialog shown in Excel Figure 2-27.

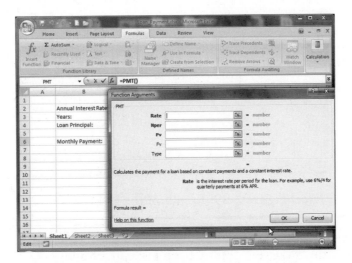

Excel Figure 2-27: The PMT dialog.

You should recognize that you are now at the same stage of building your function as you would be had you browsed using the Formulas ribbon.

6. Enter the values in the PMT dialog that are shown in Excel Figure 2-28.

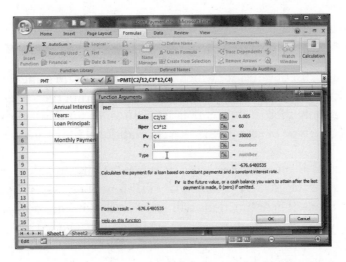

Excel Figure 2-28: Parameters for the PMT function.

Click the OK button when you are finished entering the values.

Notice that it's possible to enter formulas as parameters for a function.

7. The complete function should appear as shown in Excel Figure 2-29.

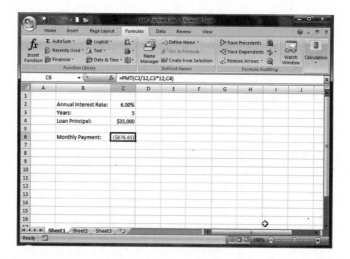

Excel Figure 2-29: Results of the PMT function.

▶**Thinking Critically:**

Think about the PMT function that you just entered and the parameters used in the example. Do you understand why the particular parameter values in the example were used? Why did we divide the given interest rate by 12? Why did we multiply the given years by 12? Should we have used the FV or Type parameters? Why or why not? Finally, how would you check to see that the value returned by the function is correct and reasonable?

CONDITIONAL FUNCTIONS

Imagine that you have a list of values for which you want to perform some calculations. Imagine further that the calculations need to be performed on only part of the values. For example, you may want to average only those numbers that are positive or sum only those number that are above 1000. This is the type of activity that Excel conditional functions were designed for.

A conditional function is one that performs its function only on values that match a given criterion. Examples are the SUMIF and COUNTIF functions, which have been around in Excel for several versions. These functions will respectively sum or count the values within a range that meet a given criteria. With Excel 2007, Microsoft has added several new conditional functions as a direct response to user requests. We've listed the Excel conditional functions along with a brief description in Excel Table 2-3.

Function	Description
AVERAGEIF	Calculates the average value of cells in a range for cells that meet a single criterion.
AVERAGEIFS	Calculates the average value of cells in a range for cells that meet multiple criteria.
SUMIF	Calculates the sum of cell values in a range for cells that meet a single criterion.
SUMIFS	Calculates the sum of cell values in a range for cells that meet multiple criteria.
COUNTIF	Calculates the number of cell values in a range for cells that meet a single criterion.
COUNTIFS	Calculates the number of cell values in a range for cells that meet multiple criteria.
IFERROR	An extension of the IF function that lets you tell Excel what to do in case a cell's formula generates an error.

Excel Table 2-3: Conditional functions.

Let's take a quick look at how you might use a conditional function.

1. Consider the worksheet shown in Excel Figure 2-30, which includes a set of positive and negative values in the range B3:E21.

Excel Figure 2-30: A set of values.

The sum of all of these values is shown in cell G6.

Let's see how we can use a conditional function to obtain the sum of only the positive values.

2. You can find the SUMIF function in the Math & Trig Library or by using the Insert Function feature.

Enter the parameters that are shown in Excel Figure 2-31.

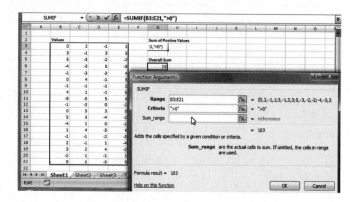

Excel Figure 2-31: SUMIF parameters.

The Criterion is entered just like the logical test for the IF function. You don't have to type the quotes; these will appear automatically when you tab to the next parameter.

3. We can view the results of the SUMIF function in Excel Figure 2-32.

	A	B	C	D	E	F	G	H	I
1									
2		Values					Sum of Postive Values		
3		0	2	-1	1		103		
4		3	-1	3	3				
5		5	-3	-2	-2		Overall Sum		
6		-4	-3	5	-3		23		
7		-1	-3	-3	4				
8		0	4	-1	3				
9		-1	-1	-1	1				
10		4	1	-1	5				
11		-5	-5	5	4				
12		-1	-3	0	-1				
13		0	5	3	0				
14		5	3	-4	-2				
15		-4	1	0	-1				
16		1	4	-3	4				
17		-1	-1	-2	-3				
18		2	-1	1	-4				
19		3	2	4	-2				
20		-2	1	-1	1				
21		5	2	-3	3				

Formula bar: G3 = SUMIF(B3:E21,">0")

Excel Figure 2-32: Results of using SUMIF on the values.

Notice how the sum of only the positive values is much greater than the sum that includes all the values in the range.

▶**Thinking Critically:**
If these conditional functions did not exist, could you still get the desired result in another way? If so, how would you do it?

EXERCISES TO INCREASE YOUR KNOWLEDGE OF MS EXCEL

Match each of the Excel terms with its description. You may have to browse the features of Excel or use Excel Help to find the answers.

____ 1. Argument

    a. A combination of the equal sign, values, and mathematical operators that you can enter into a cell to perform a calculation.

____ 2. AutoSum

    b. A built-in formula that you can use by entering the function name and a set of parameters.

____ 3. Conditional function

    c. A function that will perform its calculation on only those values that match a given criterion.

____ 4. Financial

    d. Displays the sum of selected cells directly after the selected cells.

____ 5. Formula

    e. The section of the Function Library that includes functions that perform financial calculations.

____ 6. Function

    f. The section of the Function Library that includes functions that performs tests and returns the values of true or false.

____ 7. Logical

    g. The section of the Function Library that includes functions that are used to look up values from other areas of a worksheet.

____ 8. Logical test

    h. A parameter or input value that is used with a function.

____ 9. Lookup and Reference

    i. A test that can return the value of true or false, typically used with the IF or conditional functions.

____10. Mathematical operator

    j. The symbols such as +, −, =, or * that are used within formulas or functions to signal the arithmetic operations that are needed to perform the calculation.

For each of the following, write a formula in Excel form:

11. The area of a circle can be calculated by multiplying pi by the square of the radius. Assume that the radius of a circle is stored in cell A1 and that the value of pi is approximately 3.1416. Write a formula in cell B1 to calculate the area of the circle.

12. Assume that there are three values stored in cells A1 to A3. Write a formula (not a function!) to calculate the average of these values in cell B1. Recall that an average can be found by

summing a set of numbers and then dividing by the number of values there are (in this case 3).

13. Given that the temperature in Fahrenheit is stored in cell A2, write a formula in cell B2 that will calculate the corresponding temperature in Celsius. In words, the formula is degrees Celsius = (degrees Fahrenheit − 32) times 5/9.

14. An appropriate sample size for a statistical test can be determined using the formula: sample size n = (reliability coefficient $\times$ standard deviation / tolerance level)^2. Assume that the reliability coefficient, standard deviation, and tolerance level are stored in cells B2, C2, and D2, respectively. Place a formula to calculate an appropriate sample size in cell E2.

15. Assume that a set of 5 cash flow values are stored in cells B1:B5. In the range A1:A5 are the numbers 1 through 5 corresponding to the period of each cash flow. Also, the interest rate is stored in cell C1. Write a formula (not a function!) to calculate the net present value (NPV) for these values. If n is the number of cash flows in the list of values, the formula for NPV is:

$$NPV = \sum_{i-1}^{n} \frac{values^i}{(1+rate)^i}$$

Browse or search the Excel Function Library to find functions that match the following descriptions:

16. A function that returns TRUE if number is even, or FALSE if number is odd.

17. A function that returns the future value of an investment based on periodic, constant payments and a constant interest rate.

18. A function that returns the average of the absolute deviations of data points from their mean.

19. A function that will join two or more text strings into one text string.

20. A function that will return the kth smallest value in a data set.

Use Excel Help to find the answers to the following questions:

21. How are date values stored in Excel, and what date is used as the basis (first) date?

22. What has happened when you see a cell with ##### as a value? What should you do?

23. What does it mean when you see the value #REF! in a cell?

24. What are some common errors when entering formulas, and how can you correct them?

25. What can you use a Watch Window for?

EXCEL TUTORIAL 2: MINI-CASE 1

Scenario: Tom Voiture's dad needs some help. Mr. Voiture is interested in getting a new car. He says that he is tired of driving a mini-van, which is no longer needed because Tom is the last of the kids to move out of the house, and is looking for something "a little more sporty." Mr. Voiture wants Tom to utilize that "high-priced education" of his to help him compare car loan scenarios. Tom decides that they can start by building an Excel worksheet that they can use to try different "what-if" cases. Help Tom by building the worksheet described below.

Your Task: Your job is to help Tom by creating a worksheet solution like that shown in Excel Figure 2-33 by doing the following:

Look up Section:

Model:	Camry
Manufacturer:	Toyota
MSRP	$27,000.00
MPG:	48

Car List Section:

Model	Manufacturer	MSRP	MPG
300	Chrysler	$32,000.00	22
360 MF1	Ferrari	$141,525.00	21
911 Turbo	Porsche	$116,000.00	25
Camry	Toyota	$27,000.00	48
Caprice	Chevrolet	$24,000.00	22
Caravan	Dodge	$25,000.00	18
Civic	Honda	$23,000.00	55
Esteem	Suzuki	$13,999.00	24
Explorer	Ford	$28,000.00	16
XKR	Jaguar	$85,155.00	19

Payment Section:

Interest Rate:	5.0%
Down Payment:	$3,000.00
Loan Term (years):	3
Months/Year:	12
Payment:	($719.30)

Excel Figure 2-33: An example of Tom's worksheet.

- Create a worksheet with a table of four columns listing car models, manufacturer, MSRP, and gas mileage rating. Add at least ten cars to your list. After the table is created, add a section of labels and functions that can help Tom's dad look up values in the table. He should be able to enter the car model into a cell and then see the corresponding manufacturer in a second cell, the MSRP in a third, and the gas mileage rating in a fourth.
- Create a section on your page to help Tom's dad determine the amount of monthly payment he would need to pay for his chosen car. Assume that despite the hefty tuition at your college, Tom's dad has managed to save $3000 for a down payment. Also assume that he can get financing for the rest for a three-year loan at an annual rate of 5%. To do this, you will need to look up and use a financial function from the Excel Function Library.

EXCEL TUTORIAL 2: MINI-CASE 2

Scenario: Justine Temps received a large sum of money last year for graduation from her grandmother. Rather than spend it on a new car, Justine decided to try her hand at investing in stocks. After spending some time researching how the stock market works and how to evaluate the value of a company's stock, she decided to jump in with both feet and purchased shares of twenty stocks. Justine also decided to use her Excel skills to create a workbook that she can use to track the performance of her portfolio. Her workbook consists of two spreadsheets. One (the portfolio sheet) lists all of her stocks. The other (the summary sheet) provides a summary of the portfolio and includes a section that will let her see a summary of an individual stock from the portfolio based on entering the stock market symbol.

Your Task: Your job is to complete the stock portfolio workbook for Justine. To do this, you will need to download the Excel file *EXC_2_MC_Stock Portfolio.xlsx* from the student section of http://www.wiley.com/college/piercy. Open it in Excel and carry out the following operations. (Comments are provided within the worksheets to remind you what to do.)

Portfolio sheet: Look up each of the stocks that are listed in your local paper or on the Web and enter the current price. (Remember, the purpose of this exercise is to practice Excel, so it may be permissible to enter fake data.)

Portfolio sheet: Enter a formula for calculating the purchase commission. The purchase commission is equal to the value of the stock when purchased (quantity times purchase price) times the purchase commission rate that is provided at the top of the spreadsheet. Copy this formula to the rest of the column.

Portfolio sheet: Enter a formula for calculating the commission if sold. The commission if sold is equal to the value of the stock when sold (quantity times current price) times the sales commission rate that is provided at the top of the spreadsheet. Copy this formula to the rest of the column.

Portfolio sheet: Enter a formula for calculating the return value of the stock if it were to be sold at the current price. The return value is equal to the value of the stock when sold (quantity times current price) minus the value of the stock when purchased (quantity times purchase price) less the purchase and sales commissions. Copy this formula to the rest of the column.

Summary sheet: Complete the Portfolio Summary section by entering the appropriate formulas/functions for each item in this section.

Summary sheet: The Lookup section should allow Justine to type a stock symbol into the appropriate cell. When this is done, the other cells should display the appropriate values that correspond to the entered stock symbol. Enter the appropriate formulas/functions into each of these cells.

Both Sheets: Format all numeric values appropriately.

Both sheets: Be sure to test all your formulas and functions thoroughly.

Tutorial 3

DISPLAYING INFORMATION USING CHARTS IN MICROSOFT EXCEL 2007

After reading this tutorial and completing the associated exercises, you will be able to:

- Understand how charts can be used in Excel to display information.
- Create a chart with Excel.
- Work with and edit an Excel chart after it has been created.

UNDERSTANDING YOUR DATA USING CHARTS

So far you have seen how you can use MS Excel to organize and analyze data with formulas and functions. Excel also provides the ability to create a visual depiction of your data in a chart. Charts make it easier for users to spot trends and patterns in data or to make comparisons between groups. In addition, charts can help to spice up an analysis with the addition of color and graphics. Chart graphics are linked to the data in the worksheet. If the data in a worksheet changes, then an Excel chart will change automatically.

The chart capabilities of Excel are a form of business graphics. When creating business graphics, the user can choose one of a variety of chart types that can efficiently illustrate important relationships within the data. A list of some business graphics charts that can be created with Excel is provided in Excel Table 3-1.

Chart Type	Example	Description
Column		A column chart shows data changes over a period of time or illustrates comparisons among items.
Bar		A bar chart illustrates comparisons among individual items.
Line		A line chart shows trends in data at equal intervals.
Pie		A pie chart shows the size of items that make up a data series proportional to the sum of the items.

XY Scatter		An XY scatter chart shows the relationships between two numeric values at each data point by plotting the point with the numbers as its (x, y) coordinates.
Area		An area chart emphasizes the magnitude of change over time.
Doughnut		A doughnut chart shows the relationship of parts to a whole for one or more data series.
Surface		A surface chart is useful when you want to find optimum combinations between two sets of data.
Radar		A radar chart compares the aggregate values of a number of data series.
Stock		This type of chart (also known as a box-and-whisker plot) is most often used for stock price data, but it can also be used for scientific data.
Bubble		The bubble chart compares a set of three values for each data point.
Cylinder		A cylinder chart is just like a column or bar chart but uses a cylinder instead of a bar.
Cone		A cone chart is just like a column or bar chart but uses a cone instead of a bar.
Pyramid		A pyramid chart is just like a column or bar chart but uses a pyramid instead of a bar.

Excel Table 3-1: Excel chart types.

▶ **Thinking Critically:**

As the creator of your Excel spreadsheets you will be the one who will need to select the appropriate chart type to display your data. What would be the best type of Excel chart to select for each of the following scenarios?

- Your company has been collecting data about the sales of several products for the last several years. You'd like to make a chart that shows, and allows you to compare, how the relative number of sales of each product has changed in that time.
- The cars sold by your company have been malfunctioning in strange ways in southern and western areas of the country. You have been able to collect data about the number of malfunctions and the mean ambient temperature for each region. You'd like to be able to see visually whether or not there is a relationship between these two variables.

LEARN AND USE: MAKING A CHART

To create a chart, you first need data in a spreadsheet. For the next several examples, we will use a spreadsheet with the data in Excel Table 3-2.

Client	Gender	Age	Weight (lb.)	Height (in.)	3-Mile Time	Adjusted Time	Fitness Level
Kara Vunderbar	F	40	120	62	50	50	1
Nicolas Alexander	M	22	164	71	42	40	3
Jill Princess	F	33	110	62	43	43	3
Carol Christie	F	21	131	69	47	47	2
Bobby Jones	M	26	172	64	30	28	5
Bonnie Asinatti	F	53	115	61	47	47	2
Bill Bailey	M	51	159	70	49	47	2
Chiara Davis	F	47	105	58	32	32	5
David Hastings	M	52	146	65	42	40	3
George Hudson	M	28	210	65	51	49	1
Paula Gambino	F	55	147	62	48	48	1
Charlyne Palmero	F	25	138	72	48	48	1
Keith Partridge	M	50	195	64	35	33	5
Earl Sandwich	M	53	160	65	30	28	5
Rick Springfield	M	46	152	68	32	30	5
Thomas Engine	M	21	187	67	32	30	5
Mabel Skarloey	F	38	123	67	43	43	4

Excel Table 3-2: Sample performance data.

Once you have entered your data into a spreadsheet, you can then begin to create charts that may help in understanding the data. Working with Excel charts typically involves six main activities. With Excel, we can quickly generate an initial chart and then make adjustments to the generated settings. The main steps in creating an Excel chart are:

- Selecting the data series
- Generating an initial chart
- Selecting or modifying the "look" of the chart (chart type, layout, and design)
- Adjusting individual chart components (legend, data points, etc.)
- Checking and adjusting the data series
- Selecting a Location for your chart

Selecting the Data Series

1. Our preferred method of creating an Excel chart is to start by selecting the range of cells that include the data that you want to chart.

   For our example, we will create a chart that plots the clients' weights against their names.

   Let's start by selecting the Client Name data—cells B2:B20, as shown in Excel Figure 3-1.

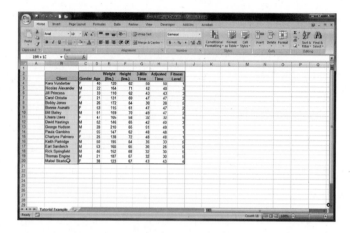

Excel Figure 3-1: Selecting the client name data.

2. We also need to select the corresponding Weight data.

   To select a disconnected range of cells, click and drag to select the initial cell range; then press and hold down Ctrl; and then click and drag to select the next cell range.

   So, while the names are still selected, hold the Ctrl key down and select the Weight data, as shown in Excel Figure 3-2.

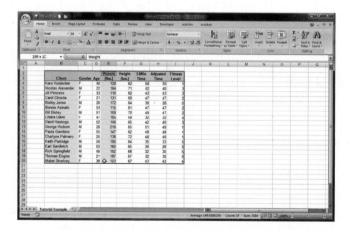

Excel Figure 3-2: Selecting the client weight data.

When selecting the range that you want, be sure to select the cells that contain the appropriate labels for the data along with the cells that hold the data. In this case, we have included the cells that hold the labels *Client* and *Weight (lbs)*. We will see the usefulness of this in a little while.

Generating an Initial Chart

Once you have selected the desired data ranges, you can start to create a chart.

1. Click on the tab for the Input ribbon.

   In the center of this ribbon you'll notice the Charts group, which includes buttons for selecting from different chart types.

   We'll use a Column chart for this example, so click the arrow that goes with this option, as shown in Excel Figure 3-3.

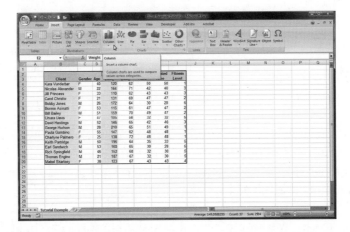

Excel Figure 3-3: Selecting a chart type from the Input ribbon.

2. When the chart type has been selected, you will see a set of chart subtype options from which to choose, as shown in Excel Figure 3-4.

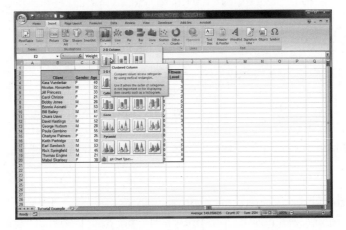

Excel Figure 3-4: Selecting a chart subtype.

We will select the first one in the list, called Clustered Columns.

3. After you select the chart subtype, your chart will appear above the worksheet as shown in Excel Figure 3-5. It's that simple!

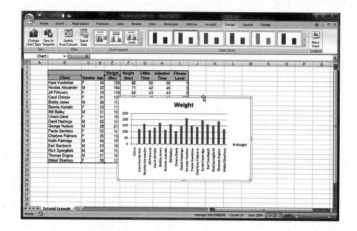

Excel Figure 3-5: The generated chart.

The chart is a graphic object that you can move around. Place the cursor on the edge of the chart object, then click and drag to move it.

Take a moment to look at your current Excel worksheet or the one shown in Excel Figure 3-5. Do you notice anything different about the ribbons? You should see that three new tabs are included, all under Chart Tools. These ribbons (Design, Layout, and Format) include options that we can use to modify a selected chart.

Try clicking a cell in the worksheet away from the chart. What happened? Now, click somewhere on the chart itself to select the chart object. The Chart Tools ribbons automatically appear when you select a chart object and then disappear when you are not working with a chart object.

Note that another way to make a quick chart is to select your data and then press the F11 key. This will quickly create a chart of the data using the default type (usually Column, but you can change that), default layout, and default format.

Selecting or Modifying the "Look" of the Chart

There are several ways that we can change the overall look of the chart once it's created. The main categories of changing the overall look of the chart are covered by the groups on the Design ribbon. Let's take a look how we can adjust the layout, style, and type of the chart.

1. With the chart selected, click on the arrows of the Chart Layout group on the Chart Tools Design ribbon to browse the possible layouts for this type of chart.

The layout options will change along with the type of chart selected.

One layout option is shown in Excel Figure 3-6.

Excel Figure 3-6: The Design ribbon.

2. After trying several layouts, you can see the layout we selected in Excel Figure 3-7.

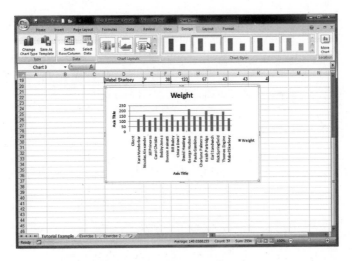

Excel Figure 3-7: Selecting a chart layout.

As you could see as you browsed the layouts, each layout may include different components, and these components can be arranged in different ways.

3. The colors and shapes of the major components can be adjusted using the commands in the Chart Styles group, as shown in Excel Figure 3-8.

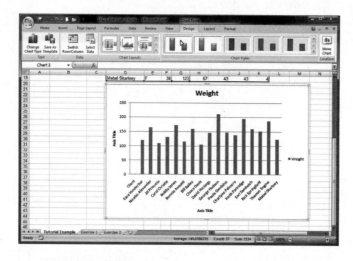

Excel Figure 3-8: Adjusting the chart style.

With this group you can also use the arrows on the right to browse through the predefined styles that are available.

4. After we have selected style 31, our chart looks like that shown in Excel Figure 3-9.

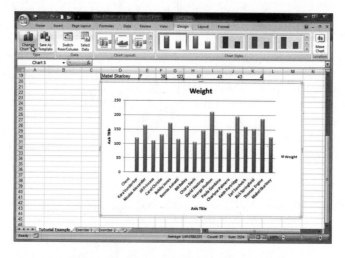

Excel Figure 3-9: The selected chart style.

Note that if you want to see all of the available predefined styles at once, you can click on the double arrow.

5. We might decide later that a different type of chart will suit our purposes better.

If so, we can click the Change Chart Type button in the Type group as shown in Excel Figure 3-10.

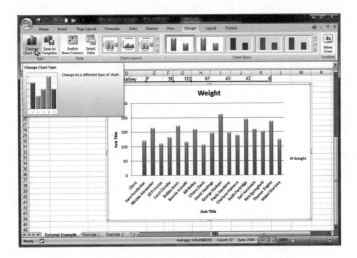

Excel Figure 3-10: Changing the chart type.

6. A dialog with all the different chart types will appear.

Let's change our column chart to a bar chart.

Choose the major type, Bar, from the list on the left.

Then select the chart subtype from the options in the dialog window on the right, as shown in Excel Figure 3-11.

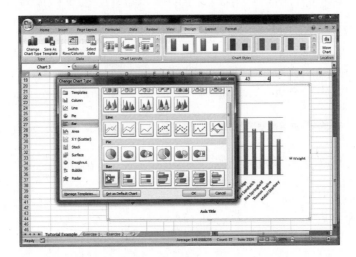

Excel Figure 3-11: Chart type options.

Finally, click OK.

7. The chart will now appear as shown in Excel Figure 3-12.

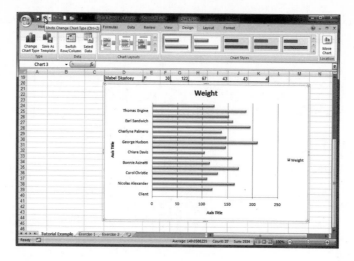

Excel Figure 3-12: New chart type.

Notice that the general layout and style are still the same. Only the type of chart has changed.

Now that you've seen how to change the chart type, go ahead and change it back to the clustered column type.

Adjusting Individual Chart Components

You can think of your chart as a single object. However, it's better to think of the chart as a container of multiple objects that make up the chart. The chart is made up of objects including the chart title, a legend, the data series, the plot area, and the horizontal axis, to name just a few. In addition to selecting the overall look and feel of your chart, you can adjust these objects individually. Let's take a few moments to see how we can adjust the format or design of some chart component objects.

You can select an individual chart component by clicking on it. In Excel Figure 3-13, we have clicked on the chart legend. Most of the time, you can tell that an item has been selected because you will see an outline around the object. Once the component is selected, you can make adjustments to it.

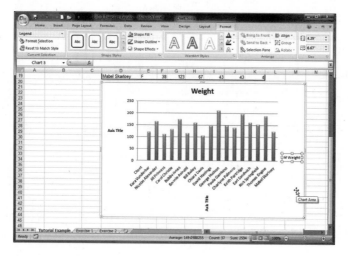

Excel Figure 3-13: Selecting a chart component.

1. Possibly, the simplest adjustment is to delete the object. Do that now with the legend.

   Click on the legend to select it.

   Press the Delete key on your keyboard.

   Why delete the legend? When multiple data series are included on a chart, a legend can help readers in understanding which charted series are which. A legend lists the data series of a chart by showing a symbol and the series name for each. For our chart with only one data series, a legend is not needed.

   Let's get a little more advanced and make some changes to the horizontal axis text.

2. With the chart selected, move the mouse over the horizontal axis labels. Hover for a moment; a label should appear indicating where you are on the chart.

   Click to select this axis.

   Your selection is indicated in two places. First, the component is outlined. Second, you should see it in the list box of the Current Selection group of the Layout and Format ribbons.

   Now, click Format Selection in the Current Selection group of the Format ribbon under Chart Tools, as shown in Excel Figure 3-14.

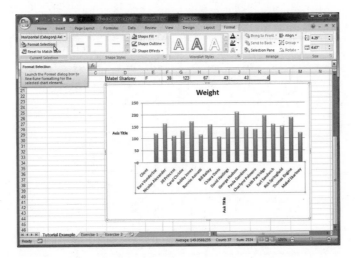

Excel Figure 3-14: Selecting the horizontal axis.

3. The Format Axis dialog appears, as shown in Excel Figure 3-15.

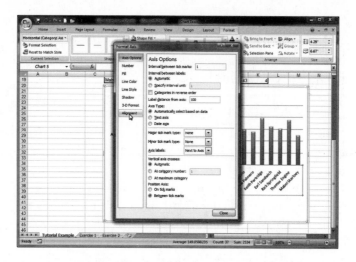

Excel Figure 3-15: The Format Axis dialog.

Browse and try the various options that you have to change the axis. Remember, you can use Undo (Ctrl-Z) to remove an unwanted change.

For our example, we'll leave the axis as is.

4. Now select the horizontal axis title.

Then, click on Format Selection in the Current Selection group of the Format ribbon, as shown in Excel Figure 3-16.

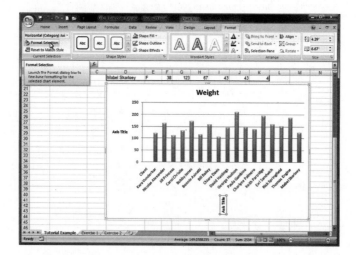

Excel Figure 3-16: Selecting the horizontal axis title.

5. We'd like to change the alignment of the axis title from vertical to horizontal.

To do this, select Alignment in the left pane of the dialog, as shown in Excel Figure 3-17.

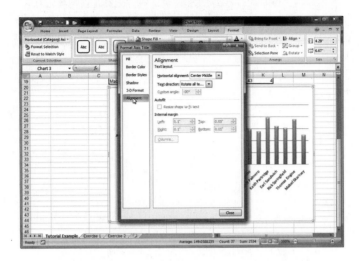

Excel Figure 3-17: The Alignment dialog.

6. Click the arrow for Text Direction to view the options.

You'll see the list along with samples of how the text will look.

Select the Horizontal option for the text as shown in Excel Figure 3-18.

Excel Figure 3-18: Choosing the horizontal text direction.

7. Our current chart with the latest changes is shown in Excel Figure 3-19.

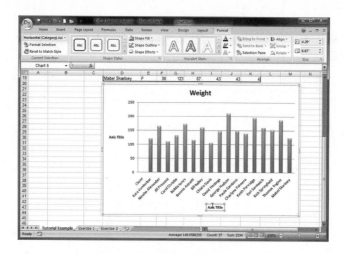

Excel Figure 3-19: The current chart.

Every once in a while, take a moment to review what you have and figure out what you need to change. One thing we need to change on our current chart is the text for the axis titles. Let's try changing those now.

8. Select the horizontal axis title.

Once the title is selected, click and drag the cursor over the text that you want to change to highlight it, as shown in Excel Figure 3-20.

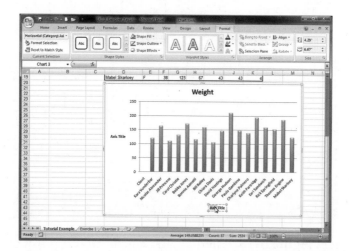

Excel Figure 3-20: Highlighting text in the axis title.

9. Now simply type what you want to replace the current text.

In Excel Figure 3-21 you can see that we changed the horizontal axis title to read *Client Name.*

Excel Figure 3-21: Changing axis title text.

10. Now, edit the vertical axis title to read *Weight* as shown in Excel Figure 3-22.

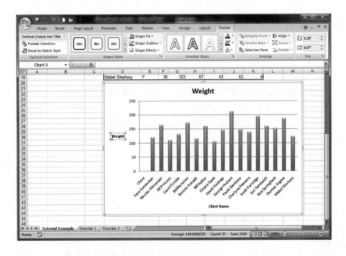

Excel Figure 3-22: Adjustments to vertical axis title.

Let's focus on the vertical axis. When first generated, Excel chose a range of values for this axis that seemed to make sense based on the data. It's possible, though, that we would prefer a different range, and Excel provides the capability to make changes to the values used for the axis.

11. First, select the axis that you want to change (in this case the vertical axis).

Again, you'll see a border highlighting this component, as shown in Excel Figure 3-23, and the Current Selection changes to reflect your selection.

Excel Figure 3-23: Selecting the vertical axis.

12. Let's learn another way to get to the formatting options.

Right click on your selection.

You'll now see a context-sensitive menu like that shown in Excel Figure 3-24.

Excel Figure 3-24: Context-sensitive menu for chart axis.

Select the Format Axis option to get to the Format Axis dialog.

13. The first item on the list in the Format Axis dialog is Axis Options. Take a moment to look at the options provided here, as shown in Excel Figure 3-25.

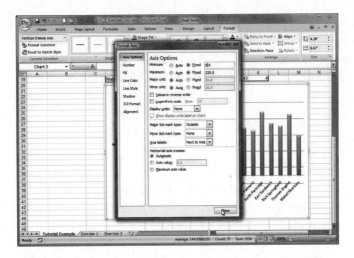

Excel Figure 3-25: Adjusting axis value range.

We would like to change only the range (low and high values) on the axis.

For Minimum, choose the Fixed option and type the value *0.0* in the text box.

For Maximum, choose the Fixed option and type the value *225.0* in the text box.

14. The chart will now appear as shown in Excel Figure 3-26.

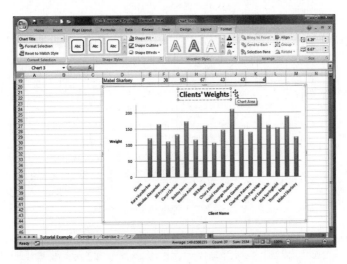

Excel Figure 3-26: Result of changing vertical axis values.

Notice that the vertical axis starts at zero and ends at 200, but the chart extends a little way above 200.

Why do you think that is? What could you do to change the actual values shown on the axis? Try it and see.

Also, change the chart title as shown in the figure.

By now you should have noticed that there are lots of things you can do to change how the components look and behave on a chart. It should be apparent that you can actually change any item in just about any way that you want. To do so, you select the object and then use the options on the dialog that appears after you select Format Selection, use options that appear directly on a ribbon, or right-click the object and use options on a context-sensitive menu.

For good measure, let's do a couple more things to alter the look and feel of our chart. Namely, we'll add data labels and some more gridlines. Data labels can be located within the chart itself to indicate the values of the data symbols (bars, in this case.) You might recall that we could have chosen a layout that includes these already when we first generated the chart. Now, we'll see how we can add them at a later time.

15. On the Layout ribbon, click the Data Labels icon.

    There are five main locations for the data labels including None. You can read a description of each before making a selection.

    We'll choose Outside End as shown in Excel Figure 3-27.

    Note that you can also adjust data label formats by clicking on More Data Label Options.

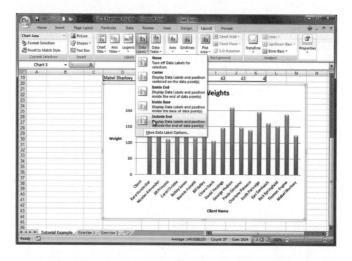

Excel Figure 3-27: Adding data labels.

16. Excel Figure 3-28 shows you how the chart looks with the added data labels.

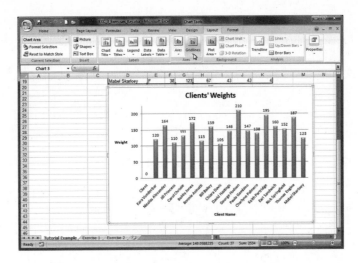

Excel Figure 3-28: Chart with data labels.

17. Now we'll add some vertical gridlines so that we can more easily see a separation between categories.

    Click Gridlines, found in the Axes group of the Layout ribbon.

    We'll choose Primary Vertical Gridlines and then select Major Gridlines from the list as shown in Excel Figure 3-29.

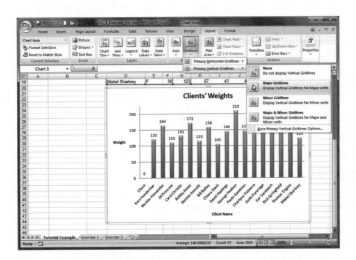

Excel Figure 3-29: Adding gridlines.

18. We can see how our chart currently looks with the new data labels and gridlines in Excel Figure 3-30.

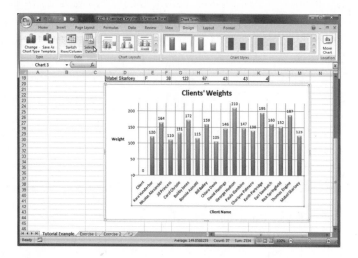

Excel Figure 3-30: Chart with data labels and new gridlines.

So far in our discussion, we've dwelt on the steps to follow to adjust your chart design. You should also be thinking about what the appropriate changes should be. For this, you need to think about the value of each element to the chart and how you might improve it.

In general, it's better to minimize the number of elements on your chart. For example, a data label provides additional information about a data marker, which represents a single data point or value that originates from a worksheet cell. If it would be valuable to have this additional information, then use data labels. If not, you should remove them.

You should also think about the value of gridlines. Gridlines come in two types: major and minor gridlines. Gridlines are tied to an axis, and they emanate perpendicular to that axis. For example, the gridlines for the horizontal axis are drawn vertically starting on the horizontal axis line. Gridlines can make a chart easier to read, but be careful of overuse, which can make the chart too busy.

Checking and Adjusting the Data Series

For some sharp-eyed readers there is one flaw in our chart that has been there from the start. Why is the first category labeled "client" with no bar indicated? The answer is that the original data series was selected in a way that made Excel think that the first value to be charted was labeled this way. Basically, Excel thought that cell B3, which stores the text *Client*, represented a category rather than a label for the category list.

It's now time to set Excel straight! We'll do this by adjusting the range of cells that are used as the source data for the chart. (Note that we could have done it right from the beginning, which is what you should usually do, but then we wouldn't be able to show you how to do it like this.)

1. On the Design ribbon click Select Data.

   The Select Data Source dialog will appear over a portion of the data in the worksheet as shown in Excel Figure 3-31. Also, notice that the currently selected data is highlighted and bounded by a flashing, dashed border.

   The currently selected data range is shown in the text box labeled Chart Data Range on the dialog.

In Excel, chart data is usually composed of two parts: the range of cells that represent the values of one axis (category labels, independent variable values, X axis values, etc.) and the range of cells that represent the values of the other axis (category amounts, dependent values, Y axis values, etc.). Look close and you'll see that both of these are listed in the Chart Data Range text box. The ranges are separated by a comma, with the X axis (usually horizontal) data range listed first.

You can also enter more than one series or set of data to chart against the X axis. If you do, then each additional series data range will also be listed in the Chart Data Range text box. You can also see a list of the series in the Select Data Source dialog in the Legend Entries (Series) list. We currently have only one series for client weights, as shown in Excel Figure 3-31.

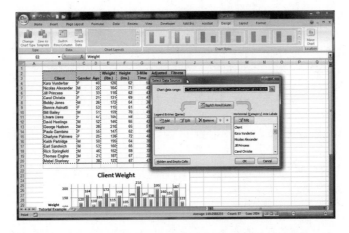

Excel Figure 3-31: The Select Data Source dialog.

Another component of the Select Data Source dialog is Horizontal (Category) Axis Labels list. In this list you can view the values that are to be displayed for the horizontal axis. Since you may have many series charted against this horizontal axis, a separate list for vertical axis values is not provided. Notice that the first label in the list in Excel Figure 3-31 is *Client.*

Finally, notice the buttons on the dialog that let us add, edit, or remove series and edit category labels. We'll use these in the rest of the example to fix our category label range and add a new series.

▶**Thinking Critically:**

When we refer to the *X* axis for many charts, such as the column chart, this is the horizontal axis. However, if we were to use the bar chart instead, as in Excel Figure 3-12, then it's as if we just turned the chart 90 degrees to where the *X* axis is now vertical. How would you describe the *X* axis and *Y* axis for a pie chart?

2. Click on *Series1* (yours may already say *Weight*) to select it in the Legend Entries (Series) list.

    The click on the Edit button for this list as shown in Excel Figure 3-32.

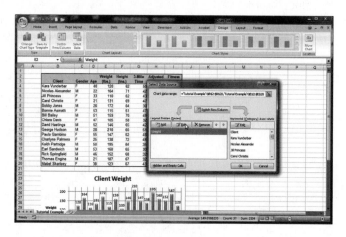

Excel Figure 3-32: Selecting a series to edit.

3. You should now see the Edit Series dialog shown in Excel Figure 3-33.

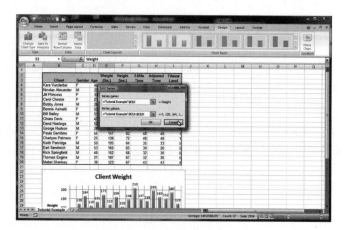

Excel Figure 3-33: Editing a data series.

To fix our chart, we will be adjusting the entries here.

We can indicate the cell that holds the name of the series in the Series Name box and the range with the corresponding values in the Series Values box.

Click on the icon on the right of the Series Values box.

4. With the dialog minimized, highlight the correct range of data values for the series on the worksheet.

    In this case, highlight the client weights in the range E4:E20, as shown in Excel Figure 3-34.

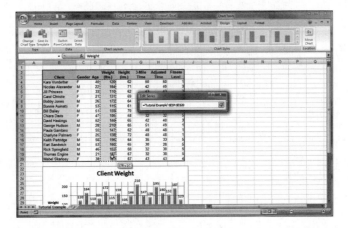

Excel Figure 3-34: Selecting the data series values.

5. After selecting the Series Values range, select the cells E2:E3, with the words *Weight* and *(lbs)*, respectively, for the Series Name box.

    Your Edit Series dialog should now appear like that shown in Excel Figure 3-35.

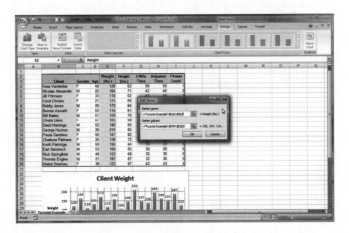

Excel Figure 3-35: Edit Series dialog with correct ranges.

Click OK when you are done with this dialog.

6. You should now see that the item in the Legend Entries (Series) list has changed from *Series1* to *Weight (lbs)* (for some of you it was already *Weight* because you selected this to begin with).

   Now, click the Edit button for the Horizontal (Category) Axis List as shown in Excel Figure 3-36.

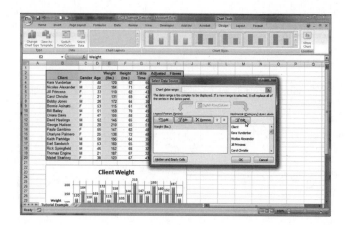

Excel Figure 3-36: Editing the horizontal axis label range.

We need to make sure that this range includes only the client names.

7. Now select the correct range for the axis labels as before.

   This should be the range B4:B20 with the clients' names, as shown in Excel Figure 3-37.

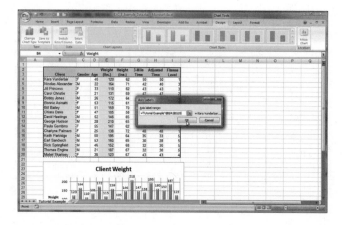

Excel Figure 3-37: Selecting the correct axis labels range.

8. The Select Data Source dialog should now look like that shown in Excel Figure 3-38.

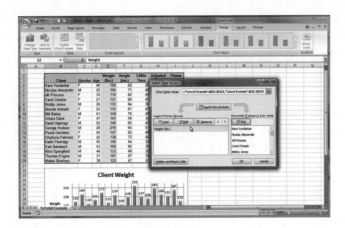

Excel Figure 3-38: Select Data Source dialog with correct ranges.

Notice that the label *Client* no longer appears in the Horizontal Axis Labels list.

The corresponding column has also been removed from the chart.

While we're working with the chart data, let's go ahead and add the clients' heights to the chart. We do this by adding a new range of values to the Legend Entries (Series) list.

9. Click the Add button for the Legend Entries (Series) list.

    The Edit Series dialog will appear as shown in Excel Figure 3-39, just as if we were editing an existing series.

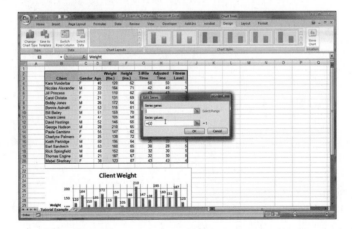

Excel Figure 3-39: The Edit Series dialog for the new (height) data series.

We just need to enter the appropriate cell ranges.

10. Select cell range F2:F3 as the range for the new series name.

    Select the cell range F4:F20 for the new series values.

Click OK as shown in Excel Figure 3-40.

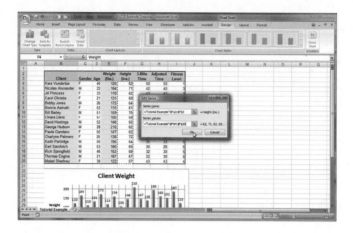

Excel Figure 3-40: Edit Series with ranges for new series.

11. The final chart should appear as shown in Excel Figure 3-41.

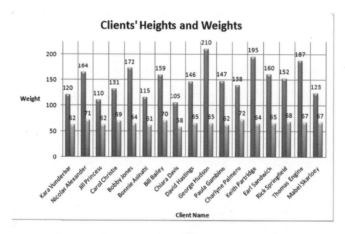

Excel Figure 3-41: The final chart design.

Go ahead and change the chart title to be like the figure and reflect the additional series.

Selecting a Location for Your Chart

So far, we have been working with our chart located on the same worksheet as the data. It's possible to place it on another worksheet (in which case it is known as an embedded chart) or on a sheet with a tab of its own. Let's take a brief look at how we could choose a different chart location.

1. Click on the Move Chart icon in the Location group on the Design ribbon, as shown in Excel Figure 3-42.

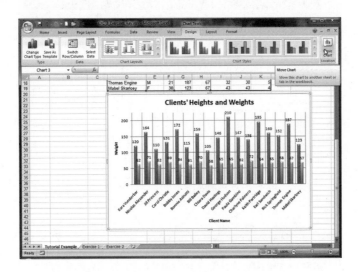

Excel Figure 3-42: The Move Chart command.

2. The Move Chart dialog will appear as shown in Excel Figure 3-43.

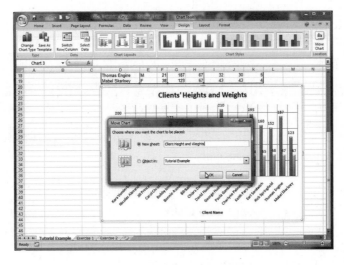

Excel Figure 3-43: The Move Chart dialog.

You have two main options. You can place the chart on an existing worksheet chosen from a list, or you can place it by itself on a new sheet.

Select New Sheet and type the words *Clients' Heights and Weights* in the text box, as shown in the figure.

3. Your chart will now appear as shown in Excel Figure 3-44.

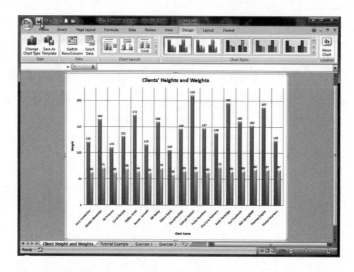

Excel Figure 3-44: The chart on its own sheet.

Notice that the tab for the new sheet has the same text that you typed in the previous step.

A chart on its own sheet can often be easier to work with and print than one that remains on a worksheet.

EXERCISES TO INCREASE YOUR KNOWLEDGE OF MS EXCEL CHARTS

Match each of the Excel terms with its description. You may have to browse the features of Excel or use Excel Help to find the answers.

____ 1. Axis

a. A collection of commands that are available for modifying the design of a chart.

____ 2. Chart Styles group

b. A collection of commands that are available for modifying the format of a chart.

____ 3. Data labels

c. A collection of commands that are available for modifying the layout of a chart.

____ 4. Data series

d. A set of values from a worksheet that are represented on a chart.

____ 5. Design ribbon

e. A set of predefined styles that you can choose from for your charts.

____ 6. Format ribbon

f. A box that identifies the patterns or colors that are assigned to the data series or categories in a chart.

___ 7. Gridlines

g. A line bordering the chart plot area used as a frame of reference for measurement.

___ 8. Layout ribbon

h. Labels that provide additional information about each data marker, which represents a single data point or value that originates from a datasheet cell.

___ 9. Legend

i. Lines you can add to a chart that make it easier to view and evaluate data. Gridlines extend from the tick marks on an axis across the plot area.

___10. Plot area

j. In a 2-D chart, the area bounded by the axes, including all data series. In a 3-D chart, the area bounded by the axes, including the data series, category names, tick-mark labels, and axis titles.

What would be the best type of Excel chart to select for each of the following scenarios? (While a scenario may have multiple blanks, each blank represents the same scenario.)

11. Data that is arranged in columns or rows on a worksheet can be plotted in an _____. A(n) _____ emphasizes the magnitude of change over time and can be used to draw attention to the total value across a trend. For example, data that represents profit over time can be plotted in a(n) _____ to emphasize the total profit.

12. Data that is arranged in columns or rows in a specific order on a worksheet can be plotted in a(n) _____. As its name implies, a(n) _____ is most often used to illustrate the fluctuation of stock prices. However, this chart may also be used for scientific data. For example, you could use a _____ to indicate the fluctuation of daily or annual temperatures.

13. Data that is arranged in columns or rows on a worksheet can be plotted in a(n) _____. A(n) _____ is useful when you want to find optimum combinations between two sets of data. As in a topographic map, colors and patterns indicate areas that are in the same range of values.

14. Data that is arranged in columns or rows on a worksheet can be plotted in a(n) _____. _____ are useful for showing data changes over a period of time or for illustrating comparisons among items. In _____, categories are typically organized along the horizontal axis and values along the vertical axis.

15. Data that is arranged in columns or rows on a worksheet can be plotted in a(n) _____. _____ can display continuous data over time, set against a common scale, and are therefore ideal for showing trends in data at equal intervals. In this kind of chart, category data is distributed evenly along the horizontal axis, and all value data is distributed evenly along the vertical axis.

16. Data that is arranged in one column or row only on a worksheet can be plotted in a(n) _____. A(n) _____ shows the size of items in one data series proportional to the sum of the items. The data points in a(n) _____ are displayed as a percentage of the total.

17. Data that is arranged in columns or rows only on a worksheet can be plotted in a(n) _____. Like a pie chart, a(n) _____ shows the relationship of parts to a whole, but it can contain more than one data series.

After completing the example in the tutorial, you should be able to make and modify your own charts. Use the example data in the tutorial to make and print the charts described in the following exercises.

18. The objective of this first chart exercise is to see whether the data indicates a relationship between the heights and weights of the clients.

Which of the chart types available in Excel is designed to illustrate the relationship between two sets of values? _____

Create a chart to help us determine visually whether or not there is some relationship between the heights and weights of the clients. Create your chart to meet the following specifications:

- Plot the heights on the X axis and the weights on the Y axis of your chart.
- Include appropriate titles on your chart.
- Choose a pleasing symbol and color for the data points.
- Adjust the axis scales on your chart to the following: Y axis minimum = 50; Y axis maximum = 230; X axis minimum = 50; X axis maximum = 75.
- Add a "best-fit" straight line to your chart. *Hint:* Open the drawing toolbar and use the straight-line tool.

Based on your chart, does this data show a relationship between height and weight?

    YES   NO

19. The objective of the second chart exercise is to be able to compare visually how many of the clients are at each fitness level.

Which of the chart types available in Excel is designed to show the proportion of data items in a category relative to the total? _____

20. Create a chart that lets us see the proportion of clients in each fitness level category. You will need to add some values representing the count of clients in each fitness level to the worksheet. (Check out the COUNTIF() function!) Create your chart to meet the following specifications:

- Include appropriate titles on your chart.
- Choose pleasing colors and patterns for the sections of your chart.
- Separate the portion of the chart that represents the largest category so that it stands out.

Use Excel Help to find the answers to the following questions:

21. How would you go about adding a trend line to an Excel chart?

22. Which types of charts are available in 3-D formats?

23. What types of chart components can you change using a custom shape effect?

24. What are error bars and how would you use them in a chart?

25. What is the difference in a chart wall and a chart floor?

26. What are drop lines and high-low lines? When would you use them?

EXCEL TUTORIAL 3: MINI-CASE 1

Scenario: Portalis, Inc. is a Web incubator. That is, the company creates and maintains new Web sites until each site is well enough along that Portalis can spin the site off as a new start-up company. The firm currently has five promising Web sites. Kelly Fenetre has been put in charge of monitoring the number of unique visitors to the sites. The end of the fiscal year has just passed, and Kelly has been invited to the managers' retreat to present the performance of each Web site over the past year. Kelly has been told to focus on two things: (1) the relative trends in numbers of unique site visits, and (2) the proportion of total visits on each site. Kelly has been keeping track of the site visits in an Excel workbook and would like to generate a couple of charts to tell the story behind the numbers.

Your Task: Your job is to complete the Site Visits Excel file for Kelly by creating the following charts using the data found *EXC_3_MC_Site_Visits.xlsx*, which you can download from the student section of http://www.wiley.com/college/piercy.

Relative Visit Trends Chart: Select the appropriate chart type to show how the number of unique visits to each site has changed over time. Your chart should allow for the trends of all five sites to be seen at once. Complete your chart with the following:

- Add the following titles: Main title: *Unique Site Visits by Month (FY: 06)*; *X* axis: *Months*; *Y* axis: *Unique Visits.*
- Place the legend underneath the chart.
- Include horizontal and vertical main gridlines.

Save your chart as a separate sheet in the workbook

Site Proportions Chart: Select the appropriate chart type to show how the proportion of total visits that each site received during the month of May. Complete your chart with the following:

- Choose a three-dimensional chart type for greater effect.
- Add the following titles: Main title: *Unique Site May-06.*

- Do not include a legend.
- Label each portion with the site and the percentage of the overall visits to the site.
- Highlight the site with the largest number of unique visits in May 06 by separating it from the rest of the chart.
- Save your chart as a separate sheet in the workbook.

EXCEL TUTORIAL 3: MINI-CASE 2

Scenario: Michelle Encre works for an office supply retail chain. She has been asked to evaluate and compare several computer printers for her company's Web site and catalog. Typically, information about six different criteria is presented for each printer. These criteria are metrics of how well a printer works to print photos and text. For each format, there are measures of quality and cost, as shown in the column headings of Excel Table 3-3. Using these measures, Michelle has ranked four printers based on these measures. She has used a ranking from 0 to 5, with higher values representing better values of the metric. In addition to presenting a table in the catalog, Michelle would like to display this information in a graphical format so that readers can more quickly compare the printers and choose the one that best meets their needs. She needs your help to create a chart using Excel.

Printer	Cost (Photo)	Resolution (Photo)	Depth of Color (Photo)	Speed (Photo)	Cost (Text)	Quality (Text)	Speed (Text)
MaxiPrint 500	3.5	3.5	2.5	4.5	3.5	3.5	4
Photosharp 10×4	3	3.5	3	4.5	3.5	3	4
Printique 2500	3.5	3	4.5	3.5	4.5	2.5	3.5
Nikus Printall A10	3.5	5	4.5	3.5	4	4	2

Excel Table 3-3: Printer rankings.

Your Task: Your job is to enter the printer ranking values shown in Excel Table 3-3 into a worksheet and create a chart that can be used to compare the four printers. Your chart should be created based on the following guidelines:

- Choose the Radar type for your chart, with all four printers on the same chart.
- Locate your chart on a new sheet.
- Include the chart title: *Printer Comparison.*
- Include a legend on your chart.
- Expand the plot area to fill as much of the chart area as possible.

Tutorial 4

UNDERSTANDING DATA USING TABLES AND PIVOT TABLES IN MICROSOFT EXCEL 2007

After reading this tutorial and completing the associated exercises, you will be able to:

- Understand how to format your data in tables.
- Understand how PivotTables can be used in Excel to create different views of data useful to decision makers.
- Create a PivotTable using Excel.
- Work with and edit a PivotTable after it has been created.
- Create a PivotChart.

WORKING WITH DATA IN TABLES

Based on the way that an Excel worksheet is laid out (i.e., a grid of columns and rows), it's natural to arrange much of your data in a table format. That is, data is often entered into a worksheet where each column contains a specific data element and each row contains data for a specific entry (as in the columns and rows in Access tables). Excel provides several features that can help us easily work with data that is arranged in a table.

With an Excel table you can easily enter and summarize your data. Table features let you add data to the table, add totals to the bottom of the table, and format the table with many predefined styles. Let's take a look at how we can use these feature to work with data tables. You can find a workbook called *EXC_4_Data_Table_Example.xlsx* that you can download from the student section of http://www.wiley.com/college/piercy.

Creating a Data Table

1. To use an Excel data table, your data should be arranged like the sales data shown in Excel Figure 4-1.

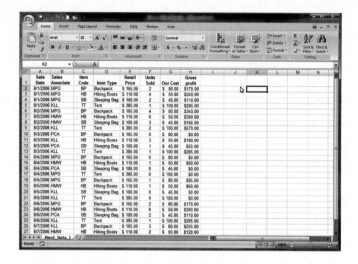

Excel Figure 4-1: Data arranged in a table.

Each column stores specific data such as Sales Data or Item Type.

Each row stores the data for a specific entry, such as the entry for the sale of a tent on 8/1/2006.

2. To format this as a data table, first select any cell within the range of the data that you want to format, as shown in Excel Figure 4-2.

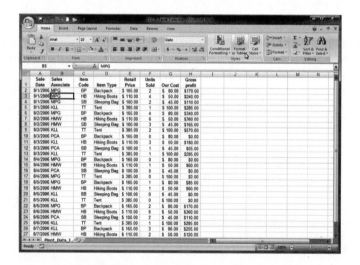

Excel Figure 4-2: Selecting a table cell.

3. Now, click the Format as Table icon, which you will find on the Home ribbon.

You'll see a number of predefined table styles from which to choose, as shown in Excel Figure 4-3. Select one that looks good to you.

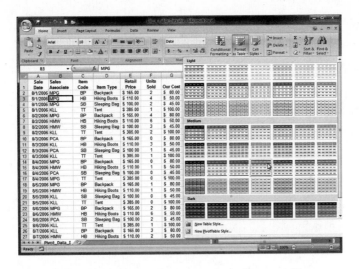

Excel Figure 4-3: Choosing a table style

We chose Table Style Medium 18.

Notice the options at the bottom that will let you create your own styles if needed.

4. Excel will detect the range of cells with the table data.

   The dialog shown in Excel Figure 4-4 will appear. You should verify that the correct range was chosen. Adjust the range as needed.

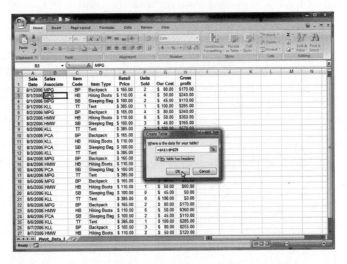

Excel Figure 4-4: Checking data range and heading option.

If your data has a row of headings, as our example does, then make sure that the "My data has headings" option is checked.

5. You should now see your data formatted using your predefined style selection.

   Our example table is shown in Excel Figure 4-5.

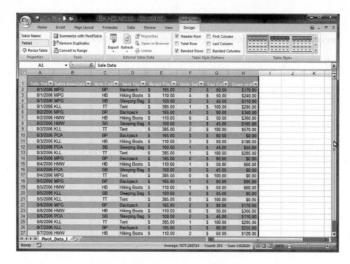

Excel Figure 4-5: Formatted data table.

Wasn't that pretty quick and easy?

Working with a Data Table

In addition to a quick way for you to make your data tables look good, Excel data tables have several features that can help you work more productively with your data. Many of these are accessible on the Table Tools Design ribbon, which appears any time a portion of the table is selected. Let's take a look at the things that you'll want to do most often with a data table.

6. There are two ways to enter new data into the table.

    One way is to click the cell in the bottom right corner of the table and press Tab.

    Another is to type data into the cell below the bottom left corner of table and then move to the next cell in the row.

    With either method, a row will be added for data entry with the proper table format as shown in Excel Figure 4-6.

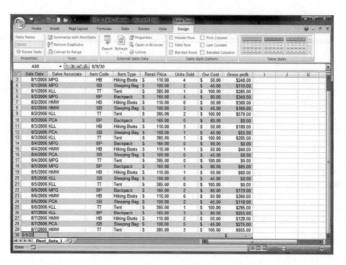

Excel Figure 4-6: Adding a new data row.

7. You can provide a name for your table. This can make it easier to refer to a table using functions or formulas.

    To give the table a name, find the text box labeled Table Name on the Table Design ribbon.

    Type in a name for the data. In Excel Figure 4-7, you can see that the example table has been named *Sales*.

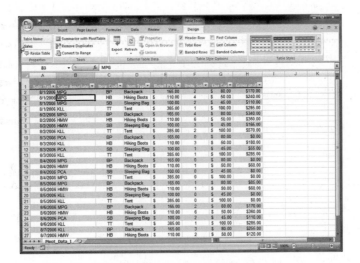

Excel Figure 4-7: Naming the data table.

8. What if you have another column of data to add?

    Simply place the cursor on the bottom right corner edge of the table and drag to add columns (Excel Figure 4-8).

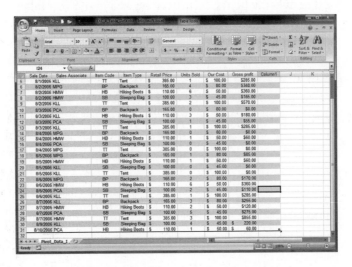

Excel Figure 4-8: Adding table columns.

Give it a try, but we'll end up with the original number of columns for the rest of the example.

9. Possibly the most useful thing about data tables is how easy it is to sort or filter the data in the table.

Filtering means setting the table to display only data that matches certain criteria.

To start, click on the arrow in the column heading that you want to use to sort or filter.

Excel Figure 4-9 shows the *Item Code* column selected.

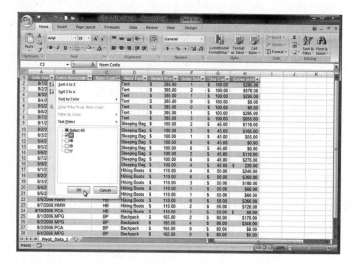

Excel Figure 4-9: Filtering by item code.

10. Make sure that only the Item Code *BP* is checked in the Text Filters. Then the data table will display only those rows with an Item Code for backpacks (Excel Figure 4-10).

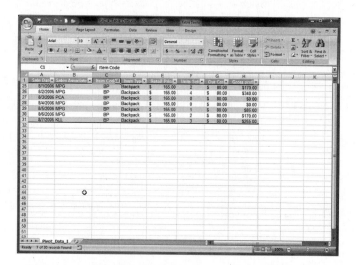

Excel Figure 4-10: Data filtered for backpacks.

What happened to the rest of the data?

Don't worry! It hasn't been erased. It's just been hidden from view so we can focus on a single item.

11. Once again, click on the arrow in the column heading for the *Item Code.*

   Now, check the Select All box for the Text Filters, as shown in Excel Figure 4-11.

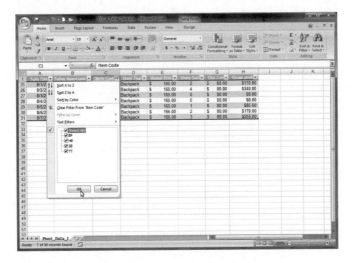

Excel Figure 4-11: Choosing Select All.

To see how sorting works, click on Sort Z to A.

12. Excel Figure 4-12 shows that the rest of the data is back, and the rows have been sorted based on *Item Code.* The sort has arranged the items with the code further along in the alphabet listed first.

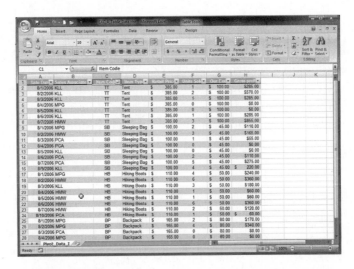

Excel Figure 4-12: All data sorted by item code.

13. Excel adjusts the Text Filtering options based on the data in a column.

Have a look at the options for the Sales Date column.

As you can see in Excel Figure 4-13, the filtering options for date data are provided.

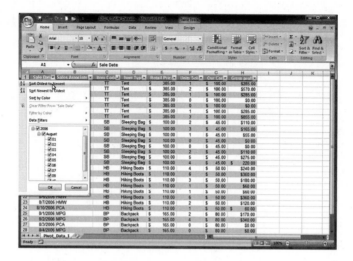

Excel Figure 4-13: Date filter options.

INCREASING YOUR UNDERSTANDING OF DATA USING PIVOT TABLES

So far you have seen how you can use MS Excel to organize and analyze the data in basic data tables. PivotTables provide a more powerful tool that enables users to go beyond organizing and analyzing data. PivotTables can help you understand the relationships that are in your data, and they can do this for very large data sets.

For example, retail businesses gather large amounts of data about sales, salespeople, customers, products, and so on. They combine this data in many ways. Sometimes they look at just two combinations or two dimensions, such as sales per month (unit of time). Using a simple Excel worksheet and formulas might provide enough understanding of the relationship between sales and time. However, if we add more dimensions, things become more complex. If we want to answer questions such as which customers are sold which products by which salespeople at what cost and when, then we need to analyze multi-dimensional data, and PivotTables are a great tool to use.

We begin our study of PivotTables with the same small data set as before, which shows the daily sales for a hypothetical backpacking store, WildOutfitters.com. With a small data set like our example you can easily determine the answers to questions such as "Which item generates the most weekly profit?" "What item was our sales leader?" or "Which sales associate had the highest total sales?" You might wonder why PivotTables are necessary. Later in the tutorial, we will use a larger data set and the answers will be much less obvious, unless you use a PivotTable!

Creating a PivotTable

For our PivotTable examples, we will use the sample in the Excel file *EXC_4_Pivot_Table_Data. xlsx* that you can download from the student section of http://www.wiley.com/college/piercy. Although PivotTables can handle data from external (non-Excel) sources, we will use data that is found on the two Excel worksheets contained in the file. For the next several examples, we will use the data on the worksheet labeled *Pivot_Data*.

When working with the data for a PivotTable, it's important that the data is organized properly. As in the data table we created earlier, data should be organized in rows and columns. The columns contain data items that you want to keep about specific objects (these are called fields when working with a database, as described in the Access tutorials), and the rows each represent all of the data for a specific object. You can also run into problems if there are blank rows of data and rows that summarize data but are not themselves data. It's best to make sure that the data is organized correctly before creating the PivotTable.

1. We will use the data labeled "Sample Daily Sales at WildOutfitters.com" on the *Pivot_Data* worksheet.

   To begin, select (click on) a cell in the data set (for example B4), as shown in Excel Figure 4-14.

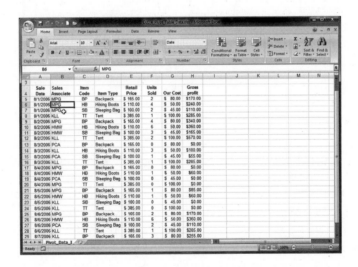

Excel Figure 4-14: Selecting a cell in the data set.

2. Now, select PivotTable from the Tables group on the Insert ribbon as shown in Excel Figure 4-15.

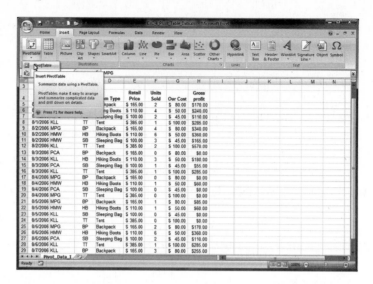

Excel Figure 4-15: Inserting a PivotTable.

3. The Create PivotTable dialog will appear, as shown in Excel Figure 4-16.

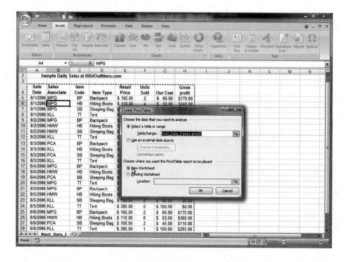

Excel Figure 4-16: The Create PivotTable dialog.

Notice that Excel has selected the table range as the source of the data. This is highlighted on the worksheet with a dotted line.

Notice that you can also choose to get your data from an external source (e.g., another Excel file or an Access database).

You can also select where you want to place the PivotTable, either on an existing worksheet or in a new worksheet.

Go ahead and check that the data range is correct, and select the New Worksheet option. Then, click OK.

4. A new sheet with the template for a PivotTable will appear as shown in Excel Figure 4-17.

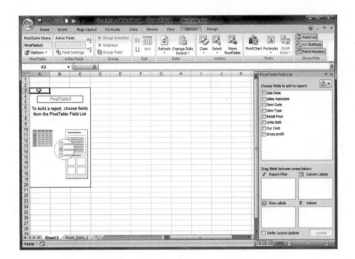

Excel Figure 4-17: PivotTable template.

Notice that when a cell within the PivotTable range is selected, the PivotTable Field List dialog will be displayed at the right of the worksheet.

Also, two PivotTable Tools ribbons will appear, labeled Options and Design.

Before moving along, let's take a moment to understand how Excel relates the data in the worksheet (or external source) with a PivotTable. The relationships among the data source, the Field List dialog, and the PivotTable are illustrated in Excel Figure 4-18. As discussed, the data source (1) can be an Excel worksheet or another external data source. The data should be organized as one or more fields (the columns). These fields will be displayed in the Field List. To include fields in our PivotTable, we need to check the box next to each field name that we want to use.

To build the PivotTable, we will drag field names into the four areas (number 2 to 4) at the bottom of the dialog. Excel Figure 4-18 shows how each area corresponds with a section of the PivotTable. The components shown in the figure are related as follows:

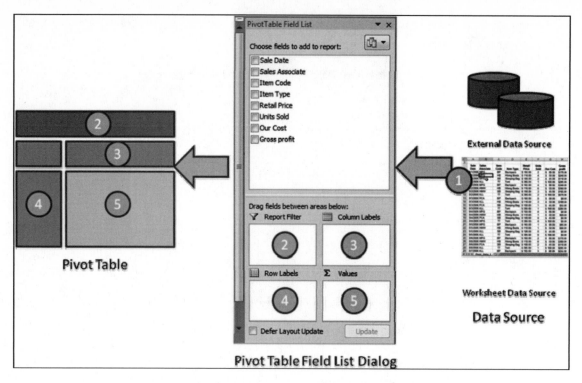

Pivot Table Field List Dialog

Excel Figure 4-18: PivotTable source, Field List, and template relationships.

1. Data Source: Fields in the data source correspond to fields in the Field List.

2. Report Filter: Moving a field to the report filter area in the Field List will simultaneously move the field to the Report Filter area in the PivotTable report. The report filter is used to focus on a subset of data in the report, such as a product or a time span.

3. Column Label: Moving a field to the Column Label area in the Field List will simultaneously move the field to the Column Label area in the PivotTable report. As the name indicates, fields here will be used as the column headings in the PivotTable report.

4. Row Label: Moving a field to the Row Label area in the Field List will simultaneously move the field to the Row Label area in the PivotTable report. Fields here will be used as the row headings in the PivotTable report.

5. Values: Moving a field to the Values area in the Field List will simultaneously move the field to the Values area in the PivotTable report. The fields included here will be summarized to make up the main area of the PivotTable.

Don't worry if you don't fully understand how this works yet. It should become clearer as we proceed with the example. Let's do that now and fill our PivotTable with fields.

Creating a Simple PivotTable

Imagine that you are the manager of WildOutfitters.com. You may want to analyze the weekly sales data for several reasons. One reason may be to understand how well your sales associates are performing. Based on this assumption, you'll need to see the results broken down by sales associate. This corresponds to the row area of your PivotTable.

1. To make this happen, select the *Sales Associate* field from the Field List by clicking on it.

    Next, click and drag the field (or just drag if you held on) and drop it in the Row Labels area of the Field List dialog, as shown in Excel Figure 4-19.

Excel Figure 4-19: Adding *Sales Associate* field to Row Labels.

You now see the data that corresponds to the *Sales Associate* field (all four of your associates) listed in the Row Labels area.

2. Next we need to know what data is important to us. What do we want to know related to each sales associate?

    In this case we want to see how each employee is contributing to our gross profit. The way to do this is to drag and drop the appropriate field, *Gross profit*, into the Values area as shown in Excel Figure 4-20.

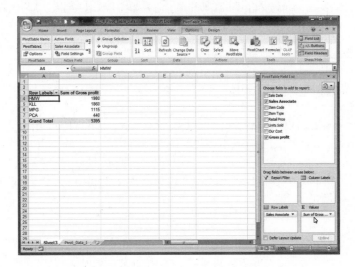

Excel Figure 4-20: Adding *Gross Profit* to Values.

Well, it seems for this week the summary is fairly clear. We can see how each sales associate performed relative to the others. Notice that the data is already sorted based on the row labels (currently alphabetically ordered). It's just a coincidence, in this case, that the gross profit is sorted from highest to lowest. In addition, the Grand Total Gross Profit has been calculated and included in the table. Do we stop now, or can we learn more? Let's try for more detail.

3. Drag the *Item Type* from the Field List to the cell with the Column Labels area, as seen in Excel Figure 4-21.

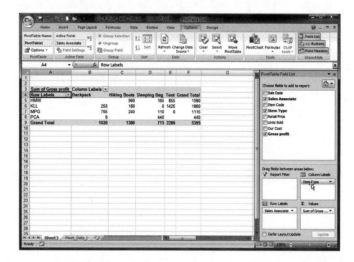

Excel Figure 4-21: Adding *Item Type* to Column Labels.

By adding *Item Type*, we now see the Gross Profit by Sales Associate for each of the four items that we sell.

> ▶**Thinking Critically:**
> So far, we have created a pretty simple PivotTable, but, as you can see, we can answer some questions that might have been difficult to answer by just looking at the raw data. See whether you can answer these questions: In terms of gross profits, which sales associate has been the most productive? Which product item has contributed the most to gross profits? What other questions could you ask and answer with the current PivotTable?

Working with a Simple PivotTable

While our current PivotTable is not so complex, there are still a few things we can do with it to drill deeper into the data. Let's start with the row labels.

1. Click on the arrow next to the Row Labels heading to see the menu shown in Excel Figure 4-22.

Excel Figure 4-22: Filtering by row label.

Notice that we can sort the table based on Row Labels, either A to Z or Z to A.

We can also filter the view to show just a few of the row label values.

Change the filter to check only the sales associate MPG.

2. The results are shown in Excel Figure 4-23.

Excel Figure 4-23: PivotTable filtered by row label.

See how the table has been compressed to show only the data related to the sales associate MPG.

Go ahead and adjust the filter to show the data for all of the sales associates again.

3. Now, click on the arrow next to the label Column Labels.

You'll see a menu as before with sorting and filtering options.

For practice, adjust the view to show only data for hiking boots (Excel Figure 4-24).

Excel Figure 4-24: PivotTable column label options.

4. You can now see that the data in the PivotTable allows you to focus only on hiking boot sales, as shown in Excel Figure 4-25.

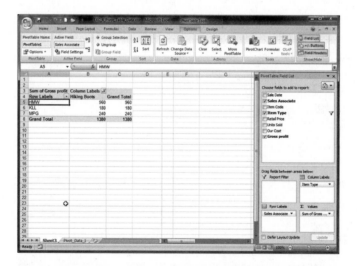

Excel Figure 4-25: PivotTable filtered by column label.

Adding Data to the PivotTable

Continuing to analyze the data, we may want to add in the dates of the sales, and we can do this by simply dragging the *Sales Date* field from the Field List to the Row Label area.

1. Click and drag the *Sales Date* after the *Sales Associate* label in the Row Label area.

Your table should now look like that shown in Excel Figure 4-26.

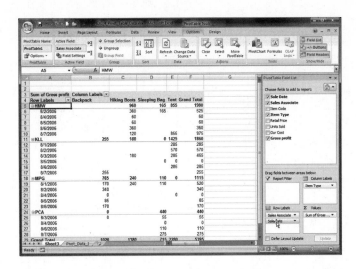

Excel Figure 4-26: PivotTable with sales date added.

The Row Labels are now shown in a hierarchy. The *Sales Associate* data is now broken out by *Sales Date*.

> ▶**Thinking Critically:**
> Look closely at the current PivotTable. Why is the Sales Associate field at the top of this hierarchy? What do the values listed in the row at the top of each group represent? What questions could you answer with this data?

2. In the Row Label area of the Field List, click the arrow next to the *Sales Date* field.

    You should see a menu like that shown in Excel Figure 4-27 with options that let you make adjustments to this label.

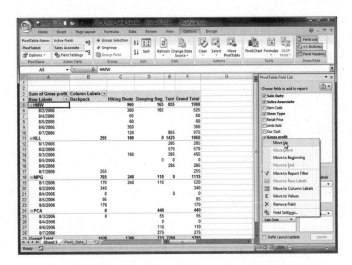

Excel Figure 4-27: Row Label item menu.

Let's choose Move Up to put the *Sales Date* at the top of the hierarchy.

3. Excel Figure 4-28 shows the PivotTable with the new row label order.

Excel Figure 4-28: PivotTable with new row label order.

Now the sales for each day are summarized, and then the data is broken out by sales associate.

From a managerial perspective, the use of additional fields of data has given us more to think about. For the Sales Associate *PCA*, what do you notice about the sales and gross profits? It seems that PCA must have a deep understanding of sleeping bags and customers' needs related to sleeping bags, because PCA's sales are responsible for over 60% of the week's gross profits for sleeping bags. Perhaps this associate should be training others to increase overall sales of sleeping bags.

> ▶ **Thinking Critically:**
> If you study the data, do you see any other sales associates who might be able to share their knowledge or expertise? Perhaps this expertise could be used to guide customers through the store from one expert to another to fill all of their equipment needs? Are there products that outsell others? Would this influence your layout of the store (if you had more than a week's data)?

Using the Report Filter Area

Imagine that you are the manager of the WildOutfitters.com store. You want to call in each sales associate to discuss his or her weekly performance, but you don't want to share all the data with each associate. Perhaps you noticed that we did not use one of the areas of the PivotTable Field List. We did not yet use the Report Filter. Let's see how we can use this area to modify our report.

1. Move the *Sales Associate* field from the Row Labels area to the Report Filter area, as shown in Excel Figure 4-29. You can do this in either of two ways:

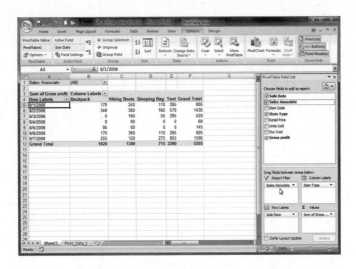

Excel Figure 4-29: Using the Report Filter.

- Click on and drag the field from one area to the other.

- Click on the arrow next to the field and select the appropriate option.

2. Click the arrow to the right of the field name in the Report Filter area of the PivotTable itself (not the Field List).

   You will see all of the associates as individuals and a choice to display all of the associates' data.

   Select the *Sales Associate* with the initials *MPG* (Excel Figure 4-30).

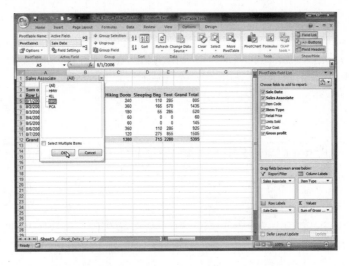

Excel Figure 4-30: Selecting filter options.

3. Now, your PivotTable should look like the one shown in Excel Figure 4-31.

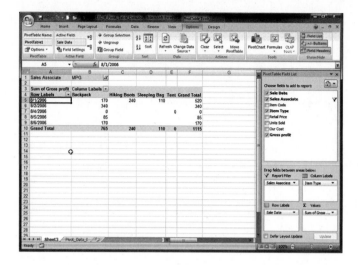

Excel Figure 4-31: PivotTable filtered by sales associate.

Notice that all four areas of the PivotTable are now being used.

You can easily get back to earlier version of your PivotTable by moving the fields among the various areas on the Field List dialog.

▶**Thinking Critically:**

Examine the results in your PivotTable. Did you lose any detail in your data? What conclusions can you draw from the filtered report?

Formatting a Pivot Report

Our current pivot table works pretty well and provides us with the ability to focus on aspects of the data that will help us answer our business questions. However, it could use some work in making it presentable. Let's use a couple of formatting options to make our PivotTable a little more pleasing to the eye.

1. With a cell in the table selected, click on Format as Table on the Home ribbon.

   Note that you could also select PivotTable Styles on the Design ribbon.

   In either case, you will be presented the predefined table formats shown in Excel Figure 4-32.

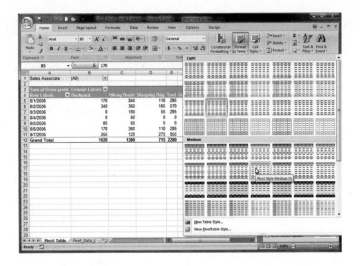

Excel Figure 4-32: Formatting the PivotTable.

Select one that you like.

2. Next, let's change the number format of the Value cells to Currency.

    While this may sound easier than formatting the entire table, it actually takes a few more steps.

    Start by clicking the arrow for the values field to get the menu shown in Excel Figure 4-33.

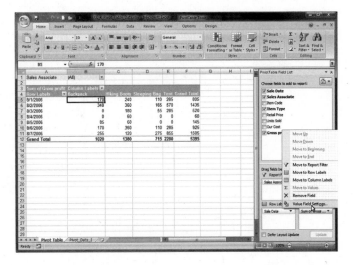

Excel Figure 4-33: Value Field Settings.

Select Value Field Settings.

3. The Value Field Settings dialog will be presented as in Excel Figure 4-34.

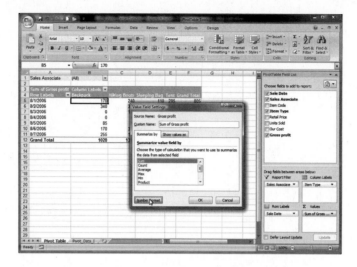

Excel Figure 4-34: Value Field Settings dialog.

Have a look at the options available here.

Then, click the Number Format button.

4. The familiar Format Cells dialog appears with just the Number tab available.

Select the Currency settings as shown in Excel Figure 4-35.

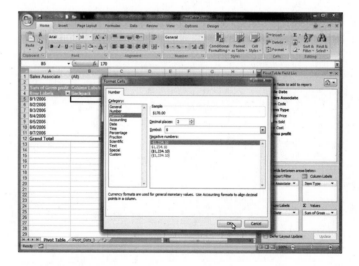

Excel Figure 4-35: Formatting cells to Currency.

5. Your final, formatted PivotTable should look similar to that shown in Excel Figure 4-36.

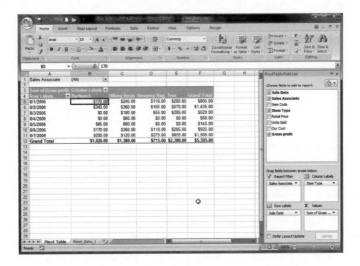

Excel Figure 4-36: The formatted PivotTable.

CREATING A QUICK PIVOT CHART

Like the charts discussed in Tutorial 3, a PivotChart can provide a graphical representation of the data displayed in a PivotTable. A PivotChart will always have an associated PivotTable, and their layouts will correspond. Both the PivotTable and the PivotChart will have fields that correspond to each other. When you make adjustments to a field in the PivotTable, the related field in the PivotChart will be adjusted accordingly, and vice versa.

You can create a PivotChart from scratch by following just about the same steps we took to create a PivotTable. The only difference is at the beginning, when we would choose PivotChart rather than PivotTable from the menu. Since we've already done the hard work to create a PivotTable, let's see how we can use it to create a corresponding PivotChart quickly.

1. To start, make sure that a cell within the PivotTable is currently selected.

   Then, choose a Chart Type for insertion from the Insert ribbon.

   We've selected a Stacked Cylinder chart type in Excel Figure 4-37.

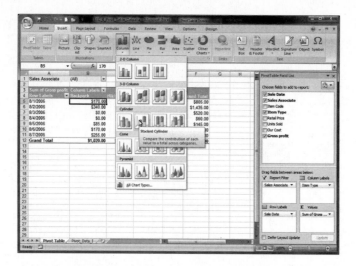

Excel Figure 4-37: Selecting a PivotChart type.

2. The PivotChart will be displayed like that shown in Excel Figure 4-38.

Excel Figure 4-38: PivotChart displayed.

You'll also see a dialog called the PivotChart Filter Pane.

Take a moment to look over the chart and the Filter Pane. Can you see how the chart is related to the PivotTable?

When you create a PivotChart report from a PivotTable report, the positions of the fields on the PivotChart report are determined initially by the layout of the PivotTable report. Notice that the category labels (horizontal axis labels) of the PivotChart correspond to the row labels of the PivotTable. In this case that's the *Sales Date* field.

Have a look at the legend of the PivotChart. This shows us that there are four series on the chart corresponding to the column labels. For this example we have a series (cylinder) for each of the *Item Type*s in the PivotTable.

The PivotTable values are represented on the vertical axis (y-axis) of the PivotChart. Thus, we can compare overall sales for each sales date and see a visual breakdown of each item type's contribution to sales for each date.

What about the Report Filter? As with the PivotTable, the filter simply determines which values are used to make the PivotChart and which are left out. So far, all of the PivotTable values are displayed in the chart. Let's see how we can look at only a subset of the data by filtering on the *Sales Associate* field.

3. Click the arrow next to the *Sales Associate* field displayed under Report Filter in the PivotChart Filter Pane.

   Select *MPG*, as shown in Excel Figure 4-39, to see a PivotChart based on only the sales for the Sales Associate with initials MPG.

Excel Figure 4-39: Report Filter in PivotChart Filter Pane.

4. Our chart now appears as shown in Excel Figure 4-40.

Excel Figure 4-40: Filtered PivotChart.

We can now easily see sales associate MPG's data. What conclusions can you draw from this chart?

Notice that the Pivot Table has also been filtered to show only the data for MPG. Since the PivotChart and the PivotTable are related, you can filter either one and the other will automatically adjust to match.

5. Let's drill down a little further into the data.

    Click the arrow next to the *Item Type* field displayed under Legend Fields in the PivotChart Filter Pane.

    Let's adjust the check boxes so that we see only the data for backpacks, as shown in Excel Figure 4-41.

Excel Figure 4-41: Filtering by legend field.

6. The PivotChart and PivotTable showing only the backpack sales for MPG are shown in Excel Figure 4-42.

Excel Figure 4-42: Backpack PivotTable and PivotChart.

You should take a little time to play around with the various ways that you can adjust the filters and fields of the PivotChart and PivotTable.

▶Thinking Critically:

As the manager of WildOutfitters, assume that you'd like to promote your most profitable item. Which item is it? Which sales associate has been the most successful in selling this item? Work with the PivotTable and PivotChart to answer these questions.

EXERCISES TO INCREASE YOUR KNOWLEDGE OF MS EXCEL PIVOTTABLES

Match each of the Excel terms with its description. You may have to browse the features of Excel or use Excel Help to find the answers.

____ 1. Axis Field

a. A range of cells that are arranged in columns and rows. Each column contains a specific data element, and each row contains data for a specific entry.

____ 2. Column Labels

b. A set of ribbons with options available for working with PivotTables and PivotCharts.

____ 3. Data table

c. An interactive way to summarize large amounts of data quickly in a graphical form.

____ 4. Legend Fields

d. An interactive way to summarize large amounts of data quickly in a tabular form.

____ 5. PivotChart

e. The area of a PivotChart that is used to display fields as an axis in the chart.

____ 6. PivotTable

f. The area of a PivotChart that is used to display fields in the legend of the chart.

____ 7. PivotTable Tools

g. The area of a PivotTable that is used to display fields as columns at the top of the report.

____ 8. Report Filter

h. The area of a PivotTable or PivotChart that is used to display summary numeric data.

____ 9. Row Labels

i. The area of a PivotTable or PivotChart that is used to filter the entire report based on a selected item.

____10. Values

j. The area of a PivotTable that is used to display fields as rows on the side of the report.

After completing the example in the tutorial, you understand enough about PivotTables to use Excel's Help function to guide you as you accomplish new tasks with PivotTables. Try your hand with the following exercises.

Modify the PivotTable created for the last part of the tutorial to carry out the following operations:

11. Create a calculated field (formula) that calculates a 10% commission. Write the name of your new field here _____ and write the formula you used here _____.

12. Now that you've done this, the CEO wants to know the impact of the commission on gross profit. You can do this with another calculated field that you should name "Net Profit." Write the formula you used to calculate Net Profit here _____.

13. Now it's time to create a PivotChart. If the PivotChart shows that commissions reduce gross profit, why should WildOutfitters.com pay commissions to its sales associates? _____

The power and advantages of PivotTables and PivotCharts become more evident when you are working with large data sets. Download the file *EXC_4_Large_Data_Set.xlsx* from the Wiley Web site. Use a PivotTable and a PivotChart to answer the following questions:

14. What time period might be a more appropriate time period for displaying the data than daily? _____. Adjust your PivotTable accordingly.

15. Which sales associate had the highest overall sales? _____

16. Which item type had the highest overall sales? _____

17. During which month were the highest sales obtained? _____

18. Who was the most successful sales associate in terms of gross profit during the highest sales month? _____

19. Which sales associate was most successful during the lowest sales month? _____

20. Which sales associate sold the most of the highest-selling product? _____

Use Excel Help to find the answers to the following questions:

21. What are banded rows and columns?

22. What wildcards can you use with a text data filter?

23. By default, the values in a PivotTable are summed to get the grand total and sometimes subtotals. How would you add other types of calculations (for instance, averages) to your PivotTable?

24. How would the fields from a data source with multiple dimensions (such as an OLAP data source) be displayed?

25. What are the primary differences between basic Excel charts and PivotCharts?

EXCEL TUTORIAL 4: MINI-CASE 1

Scenario: Imagine that your spending has gotten out of control. No matter how hard you try, you can't seem to make ends meet. Where does all the money go? Your parents have been stressing lately about your college expenses and have warned you to get your act together or else. They recommend that you first get a handle on what you've been spending your money on and then look for places where you can cut back. Fortunately, you've recently discovered PivotTables and PivotCharts in your IS class. You decide to list your spending data for a month, create a PivotTable from the data, and then analyze the data to improve your fiscal control.

File: There is no file to download for this mini-case. You'll need to enter your own data in the proper format.

Your Task: Keep records of your daily spending for one month. Enter this data in a spreadsheet for each item for each day. Create a PivotTable and PivotChart based on the following:

- Categorize each amount spent by category. You should come up with categories such as food, gas, electric, auto insurance, and rent. Remember that each item should have a category—don't summarize or leave blank cells/rows, or the PivotTable Wizard will use an incorrect _____ (fill in what will be incorrect).
- After you've collected your data, create a PivotTable that lets you analyze your total spending for each category.
- Change your report to show weekly totals and not the data for each day.
- Create a PivotChart that shows your weekly spending by category. Your final report calls for analyzing such information as percentages spent by category, so what type of chart is good for showing parts of a whole?
- Write a brief analysis of your spending using MS Word. You should cut and paste your PivotChart into your analysis. You may want to answer questions such as "What category is my biggest expense?" or "How much cash do I spend on nonessential items?"

EXCEL TUTORIAL 4: MINI-CASE 2

Scenario: Amelie, the excursions manager for the outdoor recreation retailer WildOutfitters, has started to offer guided raft trips to rivers in the southeastern United States. Groups of clients can select and reserve trips to one of seven rivers: the Chattooga, Ocoee, Pigeon, Nantahala, Nolichucky, French Broad, or Cheoah. The store offers one trip a day, and each trip is led by a certified raft guide. Amelie has collected data about each of the river trips taken during the 2006 season. She would like to use this data to make decisions about how to reward her guides. The main problem is that the data is listed in order of occurrence. Amelie would like to look at the data in various ways to see what it tells her.

File: Download and open the Excel spreadsheet *EXC_4_MC_WO_River_Trips.xlsx*

Your Task: Your job is to create a PivotTable and PivotChart that will help Amelie evaluate the number of clients supported by each WildOutfitters guide. Create your PivotTable so that you can answer the following questions:

- Which guide served the most clients in the 2006 season?
- Which guide served the least number of clients during the 2006 season?
- Which guide guided the most clients down the Cheoah River?
- Which guide guided the most "long" trips (4.5 hrs)?
- How many trips did Luz guide on the Pigeon River? (*Hint:* Use the Show Detail feature of the PivotTable).

MICROSOFT EXCEL PROJECT 1: GLOBAL RIVER CONSERVANCY SURVEY ANALYSIS

By reading the business case sections and completing the three parts of this project (Parts A, B, and C) you will:

- Extend your knowledge of MS Excel.
- Learn how to apply MS Excel to solve business problems.
- Understand how to find and use built-in MS Excel functions.

PROJECT INTRODUCTION

The Global River Conservancy (GRC) is a nonprofit environmental group whose primary purpose is the protection of free-flowing rivers. Lisa Rios, a business school graduate, has recently become a brand manager for a major corporation. In her spare time she works as a volunteer for the GRC.

The GRC is interested in starting a major fund-raising drive. The funds will then be used to lobby Congress in an effort to designate the Broad River as a Wild and Scenic River. GRC has asked Lisa to use her marketing skills to develop effective advertising for the drive. Lisa will first need to determine the target market, which you will help her do in Part A of the Excel project. She will then conduct a phone survey to determine the best form of advertising to promote the fund-raising effort. In Part B you will help Lisa analyze the budget for the survey, and in Part C you will help her analyze the results of the survey. When Lisa and you have finished all the parts of the project, the GRC should have some valuable information with which it can begin its fund-raising effort.

Project Spreadsheet Instructions

You will need to download the Excel file *globalRiverConservancy.xls* from the Web site for this text. This workbook contains three worksheets: one worksheet for each part of this project.

PART A

Part A Business Case

Lisa is excited about this opportunity. Not only will she be working for a cause that she believes in, but the project will also enable her to apply and refine the marketing skills she learned in school. Lisa knows that the marketing concept can be applied to any organization, and her knowledge of it will be beneficial.

One hurdle that Lisa must cross is the limited budget that she has to work with. She will have to plan carefully to achieve the maximum benefit from the available funds and also be able to justify her expenses to the GRC board of directors. Lisa decides that she needs to be armed with the proper information to best prepare and justify the plan.

The board has indicated that it wants Lisa to develop an advertising campaign for the fund-raising effort. The goal, as with any advertising campaign, is to reach the target market effectively and efficiently. Lisa concludes that she first needs to determine who the target market is and then find out the best way to reach them. To do so, she chooses first to study demographic information, with the hope that it will indicate the best market segments to target. Then she will conduct a survey of the target market to discover which media would most effectively reach them.

Lisa has learned that there is much demographic data available. However, she has also learned that data is useless without an effective way to analyze and interpret the information. Fortunately, Lisa had a lot of practice using electronic spreadsheet software, such as Excel, to analyze data while she was an undergraduate. She thinks she sees a way to use a spreadsheet to help her determine her target market.

Part A Problem Definition

Your job in this first project is to help Lisa by using MS Excel to analyze the required demographic data. Lisa has determined that a good way to select target markets is to examine household information based on income level. She reasons that such an analysis will point to the groups that are most likely to contribute to environmental causes.

She has already found information gathered by other groups that shows the percentage of households in each income level that have contributed to environmental causes in the past. In addition, the data includes the average annual amount of total environmental contributions by households that have made donations. She has also been able to obtain household figures from census reports and other marketing sources (this information is included in the project spreadsheet file). With this information she will be able to calculate the expected environmental contribution per household to all environmental causes. She can then estimate the total contribution for each group. By looking at the percentage figures for each group, she eventually wants to target advertising toward the group or groups that give the most contributions. She is also interested in seeing whether there are any recognizable trends in the data that might help her make future decisions.

Part A Spreadsheet Instructions

To complete the analysis, you need to perform the following calculations *using the spreadsheet.*

- Contributions per household for all households in an income level are calculated by multiplying the percentage of households contributing for each income level by the average contributions for the income level. For example, 7.00% of $55 = $3.85/household.
- Lisa wants to forecast the numbers of households by income level for the years 2005 and 2010. She will do this using the following growth/decline rates, which she calculated earlier using estimates of relevant households. The numbers represent the growth rates between 1990 and 2000. Without evidence to the contrary, these growth rates are assumed to remain the same through the year 2010. Format these as percentages with 1 decimal place.

$0-$20K	$20-$40K	$40-$70K	$70-$100K	Over $100K
−11%	22.5%	66%	77%	70%

- Enter the values into the column marked Growth Rates under the basic assumptions section of the spreadsheet. For example, the Over $100K group was expected to grow at a rate of 70% over the five-year period from 2000 to 2005. Assume this growth rate will also apply from 2005 to 2010.
- Calculate the forecast number of households for this income level in 2005 using the equation:

$$2005 \text{ households} = 2000 \text{ households}*(1 + \text{growth rate})$$

- Similarly, calculate the forecast number of households for each income level in 2010. Use the same growth rates and the 2005 forecasts to calculate forecasts for 2010. (Format these values to 0 decimal places, since households are counted in whole numbers.)
- Use an appropriate function to obtain a total estimate of households for each of the years in the table.
- Next, we need to calculate the total estimated environmental dollar contributions by income level for each of the years in the table.
- Therefore, calculate these dollar figures by multiplying the number of actual or estimated households in an income level by the previously computed contributions per household. This latter number, we remember, takes into account both the households who gave and the others who did not. Compute the total dollar figures for 1990, 1995, 2000, 2005, and 2010. Format these as currency with 0 decimal places. (*Hint:* By carefully using absolute cell references and copying, you can save yourself some time here. See whether you can type the formula only once into cell B31 and then copy the formula to the rest of the table.)
- Compute the total contributions for all income levels for each year by using the appropriate spreadsheet function.
- To calculate the percentage of environmental contributions by income level, simply divide the estimated contribution for each level and year by the total contributions

for that year. Format as a percent with two decimal places. (*Hint:* Keep absolute cell referencing in mind here.)

- Lisa is also interested in obtaining a good graph that indicates the target market to use in a presentation for the GRC board, so you will need to create one. She decides she needs a histogram (column chart) of the percentage of environmental contributions by income level for the year 2005. The graph should be created as a column chart with the income levels as the labels for the columns and the percentages for 2005 as the heights of the columns. Since the graph will be used in a presentation, it should also have titles and legends where appropriate.

Part A Interpretative Questions

Based on your analysis of your results, answer the following questions.

1. Which is the best single-income level for Lisa to target for her advertising campaign? Why?

2. Briefly explain any trends you detect from the data in the spreadsheet, especially in terms of the number of households per income level. How might this affect future GRC fund raising?

PART B

Part B Introduction

After studying the demographic analysis (which you did for Lisa in project A), Lisa has decided that the demographic group $40–$70K is the target market for her survey. The next step is to determine the details of the survey: sample size, timing, and budget. She can use this information to prepare a report to the GRC board and request the necessary funds.

Part B Business Case

The GRC board has promised Lisa a total budget of $18,000 for the survey but will allow her a little extra if it is justified. She now needs to analyze her expected costs to see whether it is feasible to do the survey within budget. She has already decided that she will conduct a phone survey, so there will be several sources of expenses. These are wages, employee training, the costs of making phone calls, telephone rental, office rental, and miscellaneous supplies. The company Lisa works for has done extensive marketing research, and it has donated the use of a computerized phone number list for the survey. The list has the names and numbers of the heads of households divided into income groups.

Lisa tried to get volunteers to man the phones, but given the short notice and the fact that most of the GRC's members work or go to school during the day, she was unsuccessful. One of the members gave her the name of a good temporary employment agency where she could get employees to work the phones. She would pay the agency $17.50 per hour for the workers, who would each work 8 hours per day. The agency has several workers who have experience conducting phone surveys, so training costs will be minimal. Lisa expects that training costs will be about $23 per person. This assumes that once an employee is trained, that employee will work every day until the project is completed.

Lisa has scheduled the survey for one week in the near future. This allows 5 days for the survey to be conducted. She will need to take this into account in her analysis in determining how many temporary workers and phones she will need. Through some other contacts, Lisa found office space she could rent for $220 a day and telephones she can rent for $30 each per day.

Based on previous surveys conducted by the GRC, Lisa figures that each call will average 9 minutes in length. This average is for all calls, including both those that reach a cooperative respondent and those that do not. The average excludes training time, which precedes actual phone calls. Unsuccessful calls include those calls in which no one answers and those in which someone answers but refuses to participate in the survey. Some time for paperwork and caller breaks is also built into this average.

A major consideration when designing a survey (and many other types of marketing research) is that of selecting an appropriate sample. A sample is a small portion of the population. Data from the sample is then used to deduce information about the entire population. Sampling is necessary in cases where it would be difficult or too expensive to collect information about the entire population. Three questions to answer when selecting a sample are (1) who is to be sampled, (2) how big the sample should be, and (3) how the sample should be selected. Lisa has already determined the answer to the first question using the demographic analysis you completed in Project A. The target population for the survey was chosen to be households with income between $40,000 and $70,000.

The sample size should be large enough to provide statistical validity to the survey. One method of determining the sample size for a random sample is based on statistical precision. This method uses a **confidence interval** for each important criteria measured in the survey. A confidence interval gives a range into which the true population value of the characteristic being measured will fall, assuming a given level of certainty. The smaller this range, the more precise our conclusions about the true population value of the characteristic are. A confidence interval is calculated using:

$$C.I. = \bar{x} \pm Z_{\alpha/2} \frac{s}{\sqrt{n}}$$

Where

$C.I.$ = the range in which the true value lies

$\bar{x}$ = the estimated value of the characteristic

$Z_{\alpha/2}$ the reliability coefficient

s = standard deviation of the estimated value

n = the sample size

By making estimates of our characteristic and our desired precision, we can calculate the necessary sample size. The last term of the preceding equation, which includes the reliability coefficient, standard deviation, and sample size, determines the tolerance level we can accept. By selecting an acceptable tolerance level, which represents the allowable difference permitted between the estimate and its known true value, we can manipulate this part of the equation and solve for the sample size.

For our survey Lisa has decided that the most critical question involves how much respondents are likely to donate to the GRC. She wants to have a large enough sample size to estimate the average donation to within a tolerance level of plus or minus $3.25.

Next, we will choose the reliability coefficient. Reliability coefficients can be found on statistical tables based on how much confidence one wants to have in the estimate. Lisa would like to have 99% confidence in the result. For this confidence level we need $Z_{1-\alpha} = 2.33$.

We also need an estimate of the standard deviation. This can be estimated using a small test sample or through the use of past data. Lisa has analyzed the past contributions to GRC fund raising and she found that these averaged $96 with a standard deviation of $38.

With these values we can use the following formula to calculate the sample size:

$$n = (Z_{1-\alpha})^2(s)^2/h^2$$

where

n = sample size

$Z_{1-\alpha}$ = the reliability coefficient

s = standard deviation of the estimated value

h = tolerance level

Lisa must also decide how the sample will be selected. Since the list includes addresses, it is easy to divide the list into different geographic regions. Then, samples can be selected at random and analyzed from each of the regions. This method is a form of sampling called **stratified sampling**.

Using stratified sampling, we will divide the total sample size among the different regions. The amount of households sampled in each region can be determined by assigning a weight to each region, which is based on the number of households in the region. The regional sample sizes can then be found by multiplying the weights by the overall sample size.

For the GRC survey, because of the demographics of her state, Lisa has divided her state into five geographic regions. Region A includes the counties within the metropolitan areas around the state capital. Regions B, C, D, and E include the counties in the northeast, northwest, southeast, and southwest, respectively. The procedure Lisa used to determine the sample size for each region is to base each regional sample size on the proportion of households in the region. For example, if 28% of the total households in our target population live in Region A, then 28% of the total sample size will be contacted from this region. The numbers of households in each region are already provided in your spreadsheet.

Because some people will either not cooperate or not be at home when called, the survey team will need to make a larger number of calls in each region in order to obtain enough valid responses to meet the sample size requirements. Lisa was able to use data from past surveys to estimate a response rate for each region. The response rate represents the percentage of total calls made that result in a valid survey response. For example, if the response rate in a region is 0.39, then 39% of the total calls made to the region will be useful for the survey. If we divide the needed regional sample size by the response rate, we can calculate the number of calls necessary to obtain the sample size in a region. The response rates for each region are already provided in your spreadsheet.

The average cost per call from Lisa's city to each region is also provided for you on the spreadsheet. These averages include the costs for all calls including those that result in invalid responses.

Now Lisa and you have enough information to complete the survey budget analysis.

Part B Problem Definition

Your job is to help Lisa with her survey budget analysis. Using Excel, you should conduct an analysis that will provide answers to the following questions:

- What is the total needed sample size for the entire survey?
- How many total calls will be needed to meet the sample size?
- How many phones and workers will Lisa need?
- What is the expected total cost of the survey?

You will answer these questions in writing in the Part B Interpretive Questions section that is found later in the project. For now, keep them in mind as you create your budget analysis.

Part B Spreadsheet Instructions

You have already downloaded the project Excel file when you downloaded the file for Part A. The spreadsheet will initially contain all labels needed and some of the values mentioned above.

To complete the spreadsheet, you need to perform the following steps:

- Enter the basic information into the appropriate cells on the spreadsheet. The numbers to be entered can be found by reading through the background section above. Remember to give them the proper format (currency, number, etc.).
- Calculate the total sample size using the formula discussed above:

$$\text{Sample Size} = Z^2 * (\text{Standard Deviation})^2 / \text{Tolerance}^2$$

- Round the answer to the nearest whole number (since we don't want to survey 1/2 of a household) using the appropriate spreadsheet function (this is *not* simply formatting the value to 0 decimal places). Be sure to use the appropriate cell addresses in all formulas.
- Complete the Call Calculations sections as follows: format all values to zero decimal places, except regional response rate, which is already formatted for you.
- Use the correct spreadsheet function to compute the total number of all households.
- Compute the Percent of Total households for each region by dividing the Number of Households in each region by the overall total Number of Households.
- Calculate the Regional Sample Sizes by multiplying the Percent of Total households in each region by the overall sample size. Use a function to round these to values with no decimal places.
- Compute the Number of Calls (to make) per region by dividing the Regional Sample Size by the Regional Response rate. Use a function to round these to values with 0 decimal places.
- Use the appropriate spreadsheet function to calculate the grand totals for Regional Sample Size and Number of Calls.

Complete the Budget Calculations section as follows:

- Compute the Regional Call Costs by multiplying the Cost per Call by the Number of Calls needed in each region. (The format for these numbers should be currency with 0 decimal places.)
- Calculate the Call Time by Region by multiplying the Number of Calls and the average time per call. Convert this to hours by dividing the result by 60. (The format for these numbers should be fixed with 0 decimal places.)
- Use the appropriate spreadsheet function to compute the grand totals for Regional Call Costs and Total Call Time.
- Compute the Total Shifts by dividing the grand total Call Time by Region by Calling Shift. A shift is equal to one 8-hour day. (The format for these numbers should be fixed with 1 decimal place.)

- Calculate the Number of Employees and Phones Required by dividing the number of Shifts Required by the number of Days for Survey. Use a function to round this value to the nearest integer.
- The following formulas are used to compute the various expenses. (The format for these numbers should be currency with 0 decimal places.)

  - Wages = (Total Call Time)*(Wage Rate)
  - Training = (Employees/Phones Required)*(Training Costs)
  - Calls = (Total Call Costs)
  - Phone Rent = (Employees/Phones Required)*(Phone Rental)*(Days for Survey)
  - Office Rent = (Office Rent per day)*(Days for Survey)
  - Miscellaneous Supplies = $1750

- Use the appropriate spreadsheet function to total the expenses.

Lisa would also like to have a horizontal bar chart she can use to compare the Number of Calls required per region. Create this chart using the data in the spreadsheet. Include appropriate titles and legends, as necessary.

Interpretive Questions

Based on your analysis results, answer the following questions.

1. Here again are the questions from the Part B Problem Definition section:

   a. What is the total needed sample size for the entire survey?
   b. How many total calls will be needed to meet the sample size?
   c. How many phones and workers will Lisa need?
   d. What is the expected total cost of the survey?

2. What effect would decreasing the average time per call from 9 minutes to 8 minutes have on Lisa's total budget? Give specific values.

PART C

Part C Introduction

Lisa and her team have completed the media survey. Thanks to the careful planning and the analyses you helped Lisa with in Project Parts A and B, there were few problems, and an adequate sample size was reached. In Part C, you will help Lisa analyze part of the results of the survey. From the analysis it will then be possible to choose the advertising medium or media that is/are expected to be most effective for the fund-raising effort.

Part C Business Case

The survey was completed as planned, in 5 days with only a few extra hours of overtime required to obtain a good sample size. The final total sample size obtained by Lisa and her team was 977 households. After carefully looking through the responses, it was determined that 43 responses were invalid. A response was designated invalid if key questions were not answered or if the answers obtained were inconsistent. Invalid responses were removed from the data set and were not used in the analysis.

The survey was designed so that each worker could first record the name, address, and telephone number of the person he or she was about to contact. This information was available on the telephone list that was donated by Lisa's company. The callers were careful not to ask for this information from the respondents, since asking for this information will often cause a respondent to choose not to respond to the survey. When a respondent was contacted, the caller would begin the conversation by reading an opening paragraph. If the respondent needed additional information about the GRC and its purpose (as was often the case), the caller would then read a second explanatory paragraph. Next, the respondent would be asked if he or she could answer some brief questions. As mentioned in Part B, many times there would be no answer to the call or respondents would refuse to participate. In these cases, the caller would simply discard the survey form and begin again with the next person on the list. The callers would also ask a first question to ascertain whether the respondent was an adult and qualified to give valid responses. If the person who answered was not an adult, the caller would then ask to speak to one.

The remaining questions were divided into three categories: Media Viewing Habits, Environmental Group Involvement, and Personal Information. The questions under Media Viewing Habits were designed to solicit information that could be used to determine the media most likely to be seen by the target market. The Environmental Group Involvement questions were designed to determine the level of potential donations from each respondent household. The purpose of the Personal Information category was to gather demographic information, which is an important part of many surveys. The demographic information could be used when designing the advertisements so that they appeal to the target market.

When giving the survey, each caller would read each question and mark the responses as instructed. At the end of each day, the completed surveys were gathered and the question responses tabulated. Those surveys judged invalid were noted and discarded. The tabulated results of the valid questionnaires are now ready for analysis.

One basic form of analysis conducted with most survey results is to examine the frequency distribution for each question. A frequency distribution breaks each question into categories and shows the number of responses that fall into each category. By dividing the number of responses in a category by the total number of responses for the question, the distribution is shown in percentage terms. Usually, a cumulative frequency is presented, which shows the percentage of responses in a category plus all previous categories. The frequency and cumulative frequency distributions can be used to calculate statistics, such as the median and the mean. For example, the frequency distribution for question 2 (television hours per day) would be:

Frequency Distribution for Television Hours:

Category	Number of Responses	Frequency	Cumulative Frequency
0 to 2 hr.	185	19.96%	19.96%
2.1 to 4 hr.	306	33.10%	52.97%
4.1 to 6 hr.	195	21.04%	74.01%
6.1 to 8 hr.	148	15.96%	89.98%
More than 8 hr.	93	10.02%	100.00%

From this frequency distribution it can be seen that the largest group of those surveyed watch television between 2.1 and 4 hours per day. In addition, over half of the respondents say they watch television 4 or less hours per day.

The frequency column was computed by simply dividing the number of responses in a category by the total responses for the question. The cumulative frequency column was calculated by adding the frequency for each category to the cumulative frequency of the previous category.

One measure of how the responses to the question are centered is the **median**. The median is the value for which there are an equal number of responses with a value greater than the median as there are responses with a value less than the median. The median can be easily calculated using the information available in the frequency distribution. First, notice in the example that 52.97% of the responses have a value less than or equal to 4 hours, and 19.96% of the responses are 2 hours or less. Therefore, the median falls somewhere between 2 and 4 hours. Using the following equation we can determine the value of the median:

$$\text{Median} = U_{n-1} + ((0.5 - \text{c.f.}_{n-1})/(\text{c.f.}_n - \text{c.f.}_{n-1}))(U_n - U_{n-1})$$

Where

n = the number of the category in which the median falls

U_{n-1} = the upper bound on the $(n-1)$th category

c.f._{n-1} = the cumulative frequency of the $(n-1)$th category c.f.$_n$ = the cumulative frequency of the nth category

U_n = the upper bound on the nth category

In the television hours example above, we can find the median by using:

$$n = 2, \qquad U_{n-1} = 2, \qquad \text{c.f.}_{n-1} = 0.1996, \qquad \text{c.f.}_n = 0.5297 \qquad \text{and} \qquad U_n = 4.$$

So the median is:

Median = 2 + ((0.5 − 0.1996)/(0.5297 − 0.1996))(4 − 2) = 3.82 hr.

This means that half of the respondents reported viewing television less than 3.82 hours per day, and half of the respondents reported viewing television more than 3.82 hours per day.

Lisa would like to analyze the frequency distribution of Question 8 of the survey, the amount of expected donation per household, to determine the expected total donation from each of several media used for advertising. To do this, she wants to complete a separate frequency distribution for each of the media categories. Using Question 6, which asks for the media a household has responded to, she can tabulate the donation responses for all survey forms with the radio answer checked, then with the cable TV answer checked and so on, until there is a separate tabulation for each of the five media. The tabulated responses are already included in the project spreadsheet file, which you downloaded earlier. A respondent may answer that she or he has responded to more than one category in the last year, so there is some overlap in the response tabulations. Surveys in which the respondent indicated the answer "don't know" were discarded as invalid surveys. After the frequency distributions are found, it will then be possible to calculate the median and the percentage of respondents who can be reached by each form of media. These values will then be used to compare the forms of media to determine which is most likely to provide the best advertising for the GRC fund-raising campaign.

The final values obtained will be in the form of expected net proceeds based on advertising from each of the forms of media. These values should be used for comparison purposes only. Many simplifying assumptions have been made for the analysis, and there are several sources of variation. Another problem frequently encountered with surveys of this nature is that the respondents' answers do not provide an entirely accurate picture of what their actions will be when the fund raising is under way. Survey respondents often say one thing and then do another. For these reasons the final net proceeds values should not be taken as accurate forecasts of the true net proceeds for each form of media.

Part C Problem Definition

In Part C, you will help Lisa determine the most effective form of advertising based on the survey results. First, open the project Excel file that you downloaded earlier. Once you have this file you can complete the analysis by following the instructions described subsequently.

Part C Spreadsheet Instructions

As you have already seen in the spreadsheet template, the responses for each form of media have been tabulated for you. The cost per 1000 for each form of media has also been entered for you. For each of the frequency distributions in the spreadsheet, complete the following calculations:

- Enter the appropriate Total Sample Size in the space provided (*Hint:* Include only the valid responses).
- Use the appropriate spreadsheet function to compute the Total Number of Households that responded to the given media for each frequency distribution. (These values should be formatted with 0 decimal places.)
- Complete the Frequency column by dividing the number of responses for each category by the total responses for the given media. For example, the frequency for the first category of radio responses can be found as follows (these values should be formatted as percent with two decimal places):

Frequency = (Number of responses in category 1)/(Total Radio Responses)

- Complete the Cumulative Frequency column by using the frequency of the first category as the first cumulative frequency and then, for each subsequent category, using the frequency of the category plus the previous cumulative frequency. (These values should be formatted as percent with two decimal places.)
- Calculate the median donation for each medium using the formula provided in the background section (format as currency with two decimal places).
- For example, the median of the contributions from the respondents who have responded to the radio advertising would be calculated as follows, assuming the median falls in the $51 to $100 category:

$$\text{Radio Median} = \$50 + \frac{(50\% - \text{c.f. of \$1 to \$50 category})(\$100 - \$50)}{(\text{c.f. of median category} - \text{c.f.of \$1 to \$50 category})}$$

- Calculate the Percent of Total responses for a medium, such as radio, by dividing the Total Responses for the individual medium by the Total Survey Sample Size. This value is an estimate of the percentage of the target population that can be reached by the individual medium (format as a percent with two decimal places).

After completing all of the Frequency Distribution sections, complete the Expected Proceeds Calculations as instructed below. The cost per 1000 people reached is already included in the spreadsheet.

- Use cell addresses to show the Median Donation values in the Median Donation column (format as currency with two decimal places).
- Compute the Households Reached for each medium by multiplying the Percent of Total Sample for each medium by the total number of Target Households provided for you in the spreadsheet (format with 0 decimal places).

- The Gross Proceeds are calculated by multiplying the Households Reached by the Median Donation for each medium (format as currency with 0 decimal places).

- Compute Expected Costs by dividing the Households Reached by 1000 and then multiplying by the Cost per 1000 (format as currency with 0 decimal places).

- Net Proceeds are simply the Gross Proceeds minus the Expected Cost (format as currency with 0 decimal places).

Interpretive Questions

Based on your analysis results, answer the following questions.

1. Which form of media appears to be most effective in soliciting donations for the GRC?

2. How can the analysis be improved so that the results are more valuable from a marketing perspective? (Provide two or three brief suggestions only.)

MICROSOFT EXCEL PROJECT 2: WILDOUTFITTERS SALES PIVOT TABLES

By reading the business case sections and completing the three parts of this project (Parts A, B, and C) you will:

- Extend your knowledge of MS Excel.
- Learn how to apply MS Excel to solve business problems.
- Understand how to find and use built-in MS Excel functions.

PROJECT INTRODUCTION

WildOutfitters is an outdoor store that sells backpacking and camping equipment. Juan Jorgé Rios, an MIS major, is interning with WildOutfitters. Last year, WildOutfitters installed a simple point-of-sale terminal system that allows them to capture sales data and then export that data to MS Excel. Over the past year, WildOutfitters has collected sales data but has not used it to help with planning or decision making. WildOutfitters' owner Michelle Kingston wants Juan to design an Excel workbook that will allow her to understand current sales quickly.

Juan knows that planning is critical to the successful design and implementation of any information system. Juan decides that what Michelle really wants is an information system to support her decision making—something with depth and details and not just a typical worksheet. Juan realizes that he will need to spend more time with Michelle to make sure he understands all of her requirements for the new Excel-based decision support system he'll build. Also, Juan remembers learning that an Excel workbook only *seems* to be a collection of two-dimensional worksheets. In reality an Excel workbook can be a "3-D collection of worksheets," and by using a very simple formula and cell references, data from one worksheet can be viewed and used on another.

After meeting with Michelle, Juan concluded that one workbook with three worksheets would meet Michelle's initial requirement with room for expansion and would enable Juan to build a working prototype fairly quickly. Juan decided that one worksheet would house the data from WildOutfitters' POS terminals, one worksheet would display the PivotTable and PivotChart data, and one worksheet would serve as Michelle's dashboard—her high-level view of the data. In Part A of the Excel project you will create the three worksheets and import the data. In Part B you will help Juan create, format, and test the PivotTables and PivotCharts, and in Part C you'll create Michelle's dashboard and answer questions about WildOutfitters' sales. By completing Parts A, B, and C of this project, you'll build a simple DSS to understand WildOutfitters' sales better and to improve your understanding of MS Excel.

Project Spreadsheet Instructions

You will need to download the file *EXC_4_Large_Data_Set.xlsx* from the Wiley Web site. Your instructor will tell you how to do this. You will need to create an additional workbook to complete Parts A, B, and C of this project.

PART A

Part A Business Case

Juan is excited about this opportunity. Not only will he be helping Michelle make better business decisions, but by completing the project he can apply and refine the information technology skills he learned in school. Also, Juan knows that the IS development and project management skills he gains during his internship will be useful to him in whatever IS career he pursues after graduation.

Part A Problem Definition

Your job in this first part of the project is to help Juan set up the Excel workbook by creating the worksheets and importing the data.

Part A Spreadsheet Instructions

You *must* first download the Excel file for this project.

To complete this part you need to perform the following tasks:

- Create a new workbook with three worksheets, save it, and name it according to your professor's instructions. For now, we'll call it *wildOutfitterDSS*.
- Name the worksheets *Michelle's Dashboard*, *PivotTblAndCharts*, and *POS Data*.
- If you haven't downloaded the file *EXC_4_Large_Data_Set.xlsx* from the Wiley Web site, do so now. Once you have downloaded the workbook, open it using Excel.

- Excel provides a useful shortcut to move worksheets between workbooks using your right mouse button. Right-click on the tab named *Large_Pivot_Data_Set* in the *EXC_4_Large_ Data_Set.xlsx* workbook. Check the box that says "Create a copy" and proceed and add a copy of the current worksheet to the wildOutfitterDSS workbook. Be sure that the new worksheet is the last worksheet in the wildOutfitterDSS workbook. You can now close the *EXC_4_Large_Data_Set.xlsx* workbook.
- Edit your current workbook so that there are only three worksheets including the one you just added. Rename the worksheet containing the data *POS Data*. Save your workbook.

Part A Interpretive Questions

Based on your analysis of your results, answer the following questions.

1. What are the advantages and disadvantages of storing the POS data in a separate worksheet? Why might you want to provide additional controls for the data in this worksheet? What is the relationship between the data in this worksheet and the decisions Michelle makes using the workbook?

2. What other techniques or tools could you have used to import the data from the *EXC_4_Large_Data_Set.xlsx* workbook? Did you have to import it, or could you use the data if you left it in the *XC_4_Large_Data_Set.xlsx* workbook?

PART B

Part B Introduction

After creating the workbook and the specified worksheets, you'll need to create the appropriate PivotTable.

Part B Business Case

Juan explained to Michelle that Excel's PivotTables and PivotCharts are an exceptionally useful way to organize, analyze, and display data. He asked her to pose a set of questions that would guide his development of the pivot table. The set of questions is found in Part B Problem Definition.

Part B Problem Definition

Your job is to help Juan set up the pivot table to answer the following questions. Use the PivotTable and a PivotChart to answer the following questions:

1. What time period might be a more appropriate time period for displaying the data than daily? _____. Adjust your PivotTable accordingly.

2. Which sales associate had the highest overall sales? _____

3. Which item type had the highest overall sales? _____

4. During which month were the highest sales obtained? _____

5. Who was the most successful sales associate in terms of gross profit during the highest sales month? _____

6. Which sales associate was most successful during the lowest sales month? _____

7. Which sales associate sold the most of the highest-selling product? _____

You will answer these questions in writing in the Part B Interpretive Questions section, which is found later in the project. For now, keep them in mind as you create your PivotTable.

Part B Spreadsheet Instructions

You already downloaded the project Excel file when you downloaded the file for Part A.

To complete the spreadsheet, you need to perform the following steps:

1. Create a PivotTable and modify it as necessary to answer the questions in the Part B Interpretive Questions section.

Part B Interpretive Questions

Based on your analysis results, answer the following questions.

1. Here again are the questions from the Part B Problem Definition section:

   a. What time period might be a more appropriate time period for displaying the data than daily? _____. Adjust your PivotTable accordingly.
   b. Which sales associate had the highest overall sales? _____
   c. Which item type had the highest overall sales? _____
   d. During which month were the highest sales obtained? _____
   e. Who was the most successful sales associate in terms of gross profit during the highest sales month? _____
   f. Which sales associated was most successful during the lowest-sales month? _____
   g. Which sales associate sold the most of the highest selling product? _____

PART C

Part C Introduction

The PivotTable that you created is working well, and now it is time to create the dashboard for Michelle.

Part C Business Case

Michelle knows that she needs to be able to understand WildOutfitters sales' and profits in order to make intelligent business decisions. She wants to be able to open the DSS and have it display some key performance indicators (KPIs). Key performance indicators are used by a business's management to understand the business's progress or lack of progress in meeting or exceeding business goals. For example, many retail businesses use a KPI that compares current monthly sales to monthly sales from one year ago, e.g., December 2007 sales vs. December 2006 sales. You will have to decide how to best display Michelle's KPIs on the worksheet labeled *Michelle's Dashboard*.

Part C Problem Definition

Michelle does not know how to use PivotTables or PivotCharts. During a recent meeting, Juan gathered an initial list of Michelle's required KPIs. You'll need to pull the data from the other two worksheets in order to display the data Michelle needs. You also may need to create one or more charts as part of the dashboard. Here are the KPIs Michelle requested:

1. Total sales

2. Gross profits

3. Monthly sales of all items for the past 12 months (see Part C Interpretive Question 2 for an extra challenge)

4. Monthly sales by item for the past 12 months (see Part C Interpretive Question 2 for an extra challenge)

5. Sales by salesperson per month

6. A KPI that you create based on what you would like to know if you were Michelle

Part C Interpretative Questions

Based on your analysis results, answer the following questions.

1. What are the advantages of creating a dashboard for Michelle?

2. For Part C, Problem Definition, Items 3 and 4, how would you change this part of the dashboard so that it recalculated and then displayed the most recent past 12 months, based on "today's" date, without asking Michelle for any input?

3. Juan's internship will eventually end. Juan has asked for your advice: How should he ensure that the DSS remains useful after he is gone?

Tutorial 2

INTEGRATING MICROSOFT OFFICE 2007 APPLICATIONS

After reading this tutorial and completing the associated exercises, you will be able to:

- Understand the powerful capabilities provided when Office applications are used together to create knowledge work.
- Use linking and embedding to add items created using one Office application into another Office application.
- Use data from an Access or Excel file as a source for a Word document.

Files for Download: Files associated with this tutorial for you to download include:

- The tutorial chart example file, *Internet_Access_By_Region.xlsx*
- The mini-case Excel file, *net_sales_by_region.xlsx*
- The mini-case Access file, *sales_managers.accdb*

INTEGRATING OFFICE APPLICATIONS

By now, you have worked with the various individual applications provided with Microsoft Office: Access, Excel, PowerPoint, Word, and possibly others. You no doubt came to appreciate the powerful tools that each of them provides to help you perform knowledge work as you learned to use these software applications. While each one of these software applications is very useful in its own right, it is not until you have started using them together that you realize the full potential of the MS Office suite of software.

Consider the following scenario: As the project leader for new product idea for your company, you and your team are responsible for developing the business plan and feasibility study for the new product. When your plan is completed, you will need to create a presentation for the board of directors and a cover letter and a snazzy brochure to be sent to over 5000 shareholders.

It could be fairly obvious how you can use the individual software provided in MS Office to complete this project. For example, you would probably use PowerPoint to create a presentation. You could use Word to prepare a document to be used as a brochure. Excel provides useful tools for performing calculations and creating charts. Data about the shareholders may be stored in an Access database.

It may be less obvious how you can use the applications together. How can you add the charts created in Excel to your PowerPoint presentation or Word document? Wouldn't it be nice to be able to create one cover letter and then automatically "personalize" it for each shareholder using the data stored in the database? These and other questions are the subject of this tutorial.

We will begin by introducing you to the many ways that the applications provided with MS Office can be used together to satisfy your knowledge work needs. You will then begin using applications together by learning two of the more fundamental yet powerful methods of combining the features of two or more office applications. First, you will learn how software objects created in one application can be incorporated into an object created with another application through the use of linking and embedding. Second, you will see how data stored using Access or Excel can be used as a source for dynamic content in a Word document.

HOW CAN MICROSOFT OFFICE APPLICATIONS WORK TOGETHER?

As we mentioned in the Office Tutorial 1, "Introduction to Microsoft Office," Microsoft Office is the most popular suite of applications available today. By a "suite" of applications, we mean a group of applications that share a similar look and feel as well as the capability to easily move data between the applications. Of primary interest here is the ability to move data easily between applications. This ability allows us to combine the features and functions of the individual applications so that Office can work as if it is one, very powerful application for working with data, information, and knowledge. Let's take a look at many of the ways that we can integrate our MS Office applications:

- *Insert data from Access into Word:* You can use a query to import data from a Microsoft Access database or other data source into Word. You can even create a link to the data source so that whenever the data is changed in the source file, it will be automatically updated in your Word document.
- *Import a Word text file into Access:* When your Word document contains one or more tables of data, you can import the data from those tables into an Access database.
- *Create a PowerPoint presentation from a Word outline:* You can use the heading styles from a Word document to create and set up the slides for a PowerPoint presentation.
- *Use Word as your e-mail editor:* Word has some useful features, such as automatic spell and grammar check and formatting options, that can help you keep your e-mail correspondence professional. The finished document can then be easily sent as e-mail using the features of Outlook.
- *Export data from an Access database to Excel and other data sources:* You can export data to a variety of formats and applications from Access. For example, you can incorporate the data into a Word document or an Excel spreadsheet or use the data as a source for an Outlook address book.
- *Move or copy information between programs:* This can be done in several ways. You can make a copy or move an object from one document to another document. For a dynamic

link to the information, you can create a linked object, a shortcut, or a hyperlink between documents.

- *Use features and commands from one application while working within another:* For example, while working within PowerPoint to create a presentation, you can insert a Word object and then proceed to create a table using the methods and techniques that you know from using Word.
- *Copy a Word table into Excel:* In Word, you can select the rows and columns of a table that you want to copy and then paste them into an Excel spreadsheet. Excel will paste the contents of each cell in the Word table to a separate Excel cell. You can then use the features of Excel to further analyze the data.
- *Create a Word mail merge with Excel data:* After placing the data in an Excel spreadsheet in a simple, standard arrangement, you can dynamically import the data into a Word file using mail merge. This works in basically the same way as importing data from a database.
- *Exchange data between Excel and Access:* While Excel offers several database features, it does not offer the full capabilities needed for a large database. On the other hand, it's usually easier to perform calculations and analysis on tabular data using the features of Excel. Fortunately, there are several ways to exchange data between these two applications. You can: copy Access records to Excel; link Excel data into an Access database; import Excel data into an Access database; convert an Excel range to an Access database; create an Access report from Excel data; or use an Access form to enter Excel data.

In addition to sharing information within Office, the Office applications can even work with some data sources created by non-Microsoft software. This is especially true of Access, which has the capability of converting multiple database formats into an Access database.

COPYING INFORMATION BETWEEN OFFICE APPLICATIONS

Two of the most basic ways to share information between documents are **embedding objects** and **linking objects**. Using these methods you can insert objects created using one Office application into another application. For example, you could create a table or chart using Excel and then include that chart within a Word document or PowerPoint presentation. In fact, you've probably already used this feature when you copied and pasted text or graphics from one application to another. Selecting text or another object, using Copy from the Clipboard group on the Home ribbon or Ctrl-C to copy it, then using Paste or Ctrl-V to paste it, is actually known as embedding the object. So, some of the actions discussed here may already be known to you. Let's learn the terminology related to linking and embedding and then we'll see how to do more.

Objects

One way to think about the things (text, images, charts, etc) that you create in your documents is to think of them as **objects**. In fact, this is how software developers think of them! To software developers, an object is something that can have characteristics (called **properties**) associated with it and also has things that you can do to or with the object (called **methods**). For example, if you think of an Excel chart as an object, its properties will include such things as the spreadsheet range that the associated data comes from, the chart title, and the colors of the chart elements. Methods for the chart let you do things like moving the chart, changing the chart title, and deleting the chart.

To work with the properties of an Office object, you first need to select it. This can be done in various ways depending on the type of object. With text, you might highlight the object. With graphical elements, you will generally select an object by clicking on it. In Office Figure 2-1, you see an Excel spreadsheet that we will use as part of our examples. This spreadsheet provides data about Internet access by language category.

A pie chart has been created based on this data. Notice the special boundary surrounding the chart area. This is an indication that the chart is currently selected. The darker areas at the corners and in the center of each edge are points on the boundary that you can used to resize the selected object. You can also move the object. When an object is selected, the cursor will change shape as you move over various parts of the chart. In Office Figure 2-1, the shape of the cursor indicates that you could click and drag the selected object.

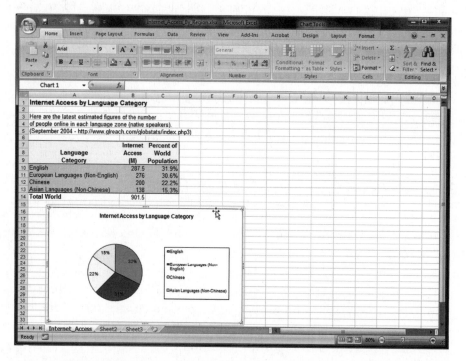

Office Figure 2-1: Example spreadsheet with selected chart.

At this point it would be a great idea for you to open Excel and create the spreadsheet shown in Office Figure 2-1. We'll be using it quite a bit in this section, and you'll learn this stuff better if you follow along and do it yourself. Be sure to use the appropriate formulas and cell formats when entering your data. It's up to you whether or not you wish to add color and cell borders in the same way that we have in the figure, but you should try to create your pie chart to look as much like ours as you can.

►**Thinking Critically:**

Click once on an empty area of the chart to select the entire chart. Now click in the legend box. What did you notice about the handles that you see? Now click on a portion of the pie. What happened to the handles now? What does this mean about objects and their relationship to other objects? What does this tell you about selecting objects?

Once an object in an Office document has been selected, there's a quick way to get to commands that are related to the object itself. Simply right-click on the selected object and a **context-sensitive menu** will appear. A context menu for the chart object is shown in Office Figure 2-2. Notice that the menu items include some general things that you can do with most objects, such as <u>C</u>opy and <u>P</u>aste (in the figure, the latter is on the menu but currently not available, as indicated by grey appearance). They also include several options that clearly make sense only in the context of working with a chart. When you select some objects, you may also have a special toolbar that pops up with contextual options that you can use to work with the object.

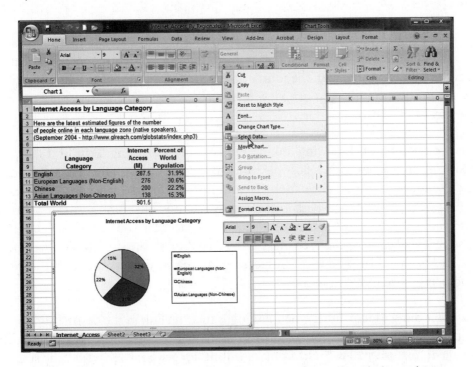

Office Figure 2-2: A context-sensitive menu for an Excel chart object.

Now that you know what we mean by an object and how to select one to work with, we can now talk about what it means to link or embed objects. As we mentioned, linking and embedding are two fundamental ways to share objects between office documents. For our purposes, we will speak of the file in which you originally create the object as the **source** file and the file into which you want to include the object as the **destination** file. The main differences between linking and embedding an object are related to where the object data is stored and how you update the object's data after you place it in the destination file.

Embedded Objects

Embedding is similar to taking a photograph of an object in the source file and then placing the photograph in the destination file. As with a photograph, while the source object might change, the photograph stays the same because it represents a snapshot of the object at a specific point in time. In this case, a representation of the original object has been copied and stored in the destination file. There are now two separate objects: one in the source file and one in the destination file. Changes made to one of the objects will not affect the other.

Embedding is different from taking a photograph in at least one respect. The destination object may actually be just a graphical snapshot of the original, or it may be an exact copy of the source object, complete with all the original data and functionality.

If you have ever copied an object in one file and then pasted into another, then you were doing embedding without even knowing it was called embedding! We'll look at the steps for embedding in a formal way soon just in case you haven't done it before.

Linked Objects

A linked object is quite different. When you place a linked object in a destination file, the only thing that is actually stored in the destination file is data indicating the location of the source object. All the data associated with the source object itself is still stored in the source file. When you view the destination file, you can view a representation of the source object as if it were actually a part of the destination file.

There are two main benefits to using linking rather than embedding. First, if it's important to keep the size of your files as small as possible, you should consider linking. Linked objects, which store only the location in the destination file and not a complete copy of the object, require less overall storage. Second, and perhaps more importantly, linked objects can be updated to match the current state of the source object. This means that you can make changes to the source object and then have those changes be reflected in all the destination files into which the object has been linked. This can be especially important if the source and the destination are maintained by two different users.

One important thing to remember when linking is that the link in the destination file specifies the location of the source object. What do you think will happen if the location of the source file is changed? You got it! The linked object will no longer be able to find the source object and may not display correctly in the destination file. Sometimes there may be no display, and sometimes the destination may display a former version of the linked object. For this reason, you will need to be careful that the source file remains in the same place relative to the destination file. Notice that we said "relative to" in the last sentence. It's possible to move the source and destination files around, as long as you move them together.

In the following examples, we'll work with the chart object of Office Figure 2-1. We'll first learn how to embed an object by embedding the chart onto a PowerPoint slide. Then we'll see how to link an object by creating a link on a separate slide.

How to Embed an Object

1. Click on an empty area of the chart object to select it.

   Make sure that the boundary indicator is around the entire chart and not an object within the chart.

   Use one of the following methods to copy the chart to the Windows clipboard:

   - Select Copy from the Clipboard group on the Home ribbon as shown in Office Figure 2-3.

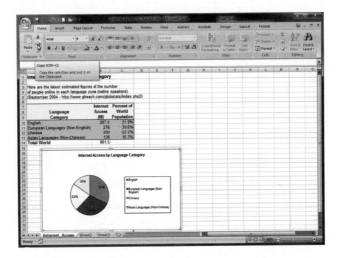

Office Figure 2-3: Copying a selected chart.

   - Press Ctrl-C.
   - Right-click on the chart and select Copy from the context-sensitive menu.

2. Open PowerPoint and set up an initial slide as shown in Office Figure 2-4.

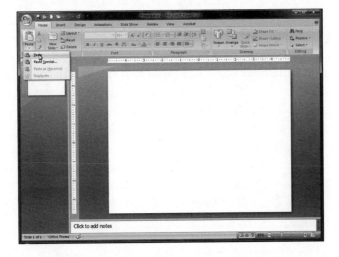

Office Figure 2-4: A blank PowerPoint slide.

   Set the slide layout as Blank.

3. Embed the chart object on the destination PowerPoint slide using one of the following:

   - Select Paste from the Clipboard group on the Home ribbon.
   - Press Ctrl-V.
   - Right-click on the slide and select Paste from the context-sensitive menu.

The chart will appear as shown in Office Figure 2-5.

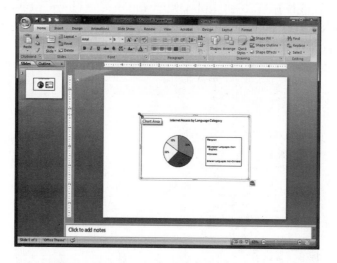

Office Figure 2-5: The embedded chart.

4. You may want to adjust the size of the chart by dragging the boundary.

   You should also add a title to the slide: *Embedded Chart.*

   The final slide with the chart embedded is shown in Office Figure 2-6

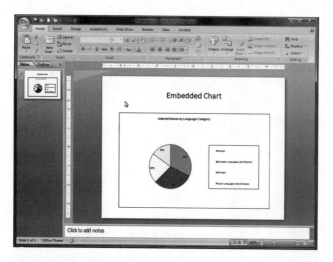

Office Figure 2-6: Final slide with embedded chart.

Editing an Embedded Chart

You can actually do quite a bit to edit embedded objects from other Office software. For example, PowerPoint will recognize the object here as a chart object and allow you to edit it appropriately.

1. To edit an embedded object, right-click on it.

    A context-sensitive menu will be displayed like that shown in Office Figure 2-7.

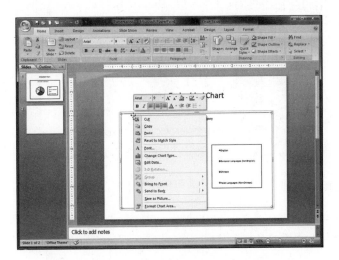

Office Figure 2-7: Editing an embedded chart.

Note: You may have limited capability to edit "non-Office" objects by converting them to drawing objects.

2. Choose the appropriate option from the context-sensitive menu, such as Edit Chart, as shown in Office Figure 2-8.

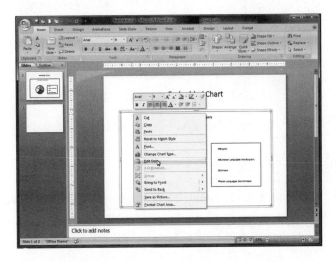

Office Figure 2-8: Edit Chart option.

3. There are also options for changing how the embedded chart looks.

For instance, select Format Chart Area from the context-sensitive menu, as shown in Office Figure 2-9.

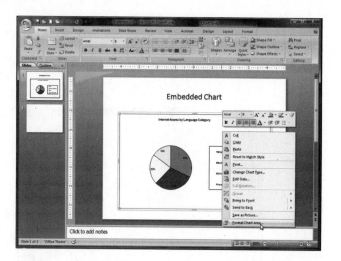

Office Figure 2-9: Format Chart Area option.

4. The Format Chart Area dialog will appear, as shown in Office Figure 2-10, with options that you can use to change how the chart looks.

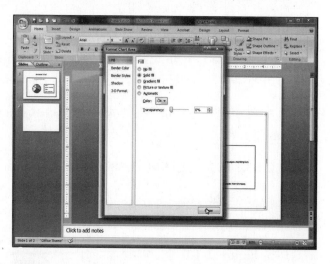

Office Figure 2-10: The Format Chart Area dialog.

How to Create a Linked Object

The task of linking an object starts much like the task of embedding an object. In fact, the first two steps are the same. First select the object and then copy it. The difference occurs when you are ready to add the object to the destination file.

1. This time click on the arrow just below the Paste command in the Clipboard group of the Home ribbon.

   Select Paste Special from the menu, as shown in Office Figure 2-11.

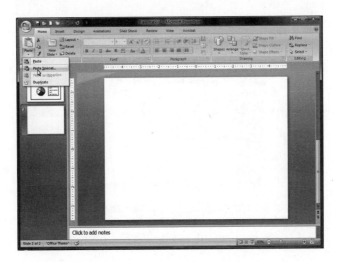

Office Figure 2-11: Selecting Paste Special.

2. The Paste Special dialog will be displayed, as shown in Office Figure 2-12.

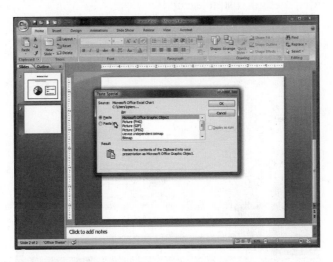

Office Figure 2-12: The Paste Special option.

With this dialog, you can choose from several options which let you paste the option in a different manner than usual.

Notice on the Paste Special dialog that there is a radio button on the left that is labeled Paste Link.

3. Select the Paste Link radio button and then click OK as shown in Office Figure 2-13.

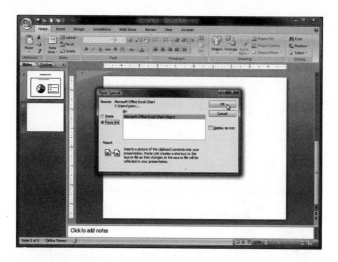

Office Figure 2-13: The Paste Link option.

4. The chart will be added to the slide.

On first glance, as shown in Office Figure 2-14, the chart looks just like the chart that we embedded on a slide earlier.

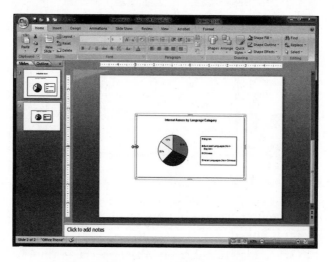

Office Figure 2-14: The linked chart.

5. Go ahead and add a title and adjust the size of the chart to match ours in Office Figure 2-15.

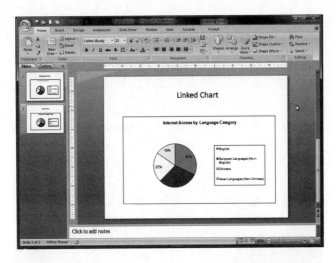

Office Figure 2-15: The final slide with the linked chart.

6. Right-click on the chart to see the context-sensitive menu as shown in Office Figure 2-16.

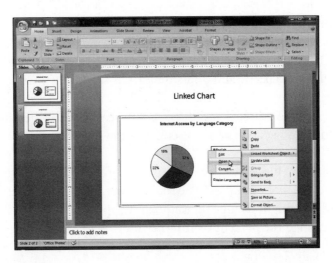

Office Figure 2-16: The linked context-sensitive menu.

You'll notice that there are now options on the Context Sensitive Menu that indicate that the object is linked.

7. When you select the Linked Worksheet Object option from the context-sensitive menu, the Excel spreadsheet will open.

You can then make adjustments to the spreadsheet.

The linked chart on the PowerPoint slide will change to reflect any adjustments made in the source spreadsheet (Office Figure 2-17).

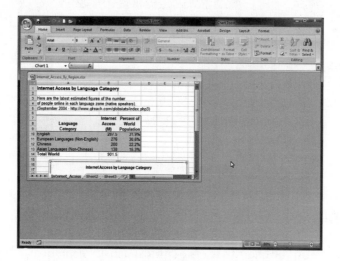

Office Figure 2-17: The source spreadsheet.

The Difference Between Linked and Embedded Objects

Have a quick look at the two PowerPoint slides that you just created. You probably don't see much difference in the two charts (and you shouldn't at this point), with the exception of the extra options on the context-sensitive menu. Keep in mind that when an object is linked, the object changes when the source is modified. So, to see the real difference between a linked object and an embedded object, we need to return to the source.

First, open the Excel source file and change one of the numbers significantly so that you can see the difference in the chart. For example, since the number of Chinese Internet users is expected to grow significantly, you might change the value in the spreadsheet from 200 (million) to 300 (million). This will change the percent of Internet users who are Chinese to 30%, which will be reflected in the chart as a larger slice of the pie.

Next, let's return to PowerPoint to see how this changes (or not) the linked and embedded charts. If you had the PowerPoint destination file open when you made the change, then you may or may not see the change in the linked chart. To update the link, right-click on the linked chart and select Update Link.

If PowerPoint is closed, then you will need to reopen the PowerPoint destination file.

When you do you will see a message like that shown in Office Figure 2-18 that tells you that there are linked objects in the file and asks whether or not you want to update the links.

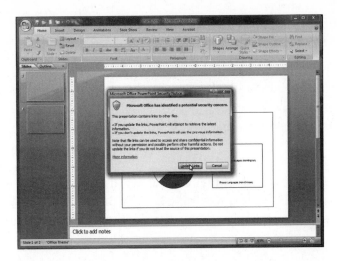

Office Figure 2-18: Opening a PowerPoint file with a linked object.

This will occur every time you open the destination file.

Once the link has been updated, you can see a difference between the embedded and linked charts. If you followed along with our example, you should see that the two charts look as shown in Office Figure 2-19. It's possible to change the link setting in any of the Office software so that links are updated automatically whenever the destination file is opened or printed.

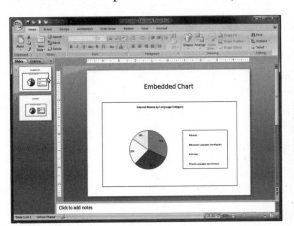 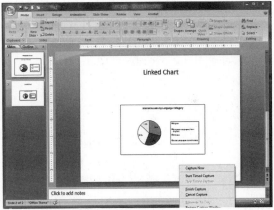

Office Figure 2-19: The two charts after updating link.
Left, embedded chart; right, linked chart.

▶**Thinking Critically:**
What do you think would happen if you moved the source file to a different place on your file system relative to the destination file? Try it! Close both files. Move the Excel source file to a different folder on your system. Now open the PowerPoint file and try to update the link. What happens? What should you think about to prevent this from occurring? If you really need to move the source file, how could you reconnect the link? (Hint: Try using Excel or PowerPoint Help to find out.)

INCLUDING ACCESS DATA IN WORD USING MAIL MERGE

As you know, Access and Excel are well suited for working with large amounts of data. Word and PowerPoint are primarily useful for communicating through the use of documents and presentations. Sometimes you may want to include data from an Access or Excel file within a Word or PowerPoint document. In other words, you will want to use a database or a spreadsheet as a **data source**.

In Word, you can easily create documents that will draw data from a data source using the Mail Merge feature. To do this, we'll rely heavily on the built-in Mail Merge Wizard. In the next few pages, we will demonstrate how you can do this using the following example scenario:

Scenario: As the human resource director for XYZ, Incorporated, you need to send a letter to prospective new hires that invites them to an interview. So far, you have been very organized, and you have kept up with job candidates in a table of an Access database (Office Figure 2-20) from a file called *candidates.accdb*. You'd like to create one letter that can be used for all of the candidates.

Office Figure 2-20: The job candidates Access database.

Starting a Word Mail Merge Document

Creating a Word document that includes data from another source is known as a **mail merge** because it was originally used for creating form letters for mailing. While mail merge is still used for that today, it can be used for any type of document regardless of whether you will actually mail it. Let's see how we can create a Word mail merge document that will use the *candidates.accdb* database as a source.

1. To begin, open Word and start a new document.

   The mail merge commands are located on the Mailings ribbon.

   Navigate to the Mailings ribbon and click on Start Mail Merge in the group of the same name, as shown in Office Figure 2-21.

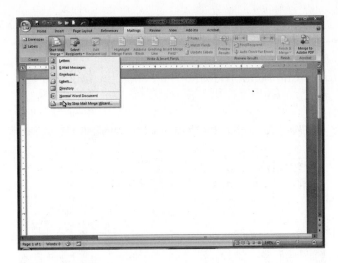

Office Figure 2-21: Starting the Mail Merge Wizard.

Notice the types of mail merge documents that are possible.

We will work within the Mail Merge Wizard, so select the option that reads Step by Step Mail Merge Wizard.

2. The Mail Merge dialog will appear to the right of the document window.

Note that this is the first of six pages in the Wizard.

Also notice that there are several types of documents that are available to choose from.

Select Letters as the document type and click the link at the bottom to move to the next page, as shown in Office Figure 2-22.

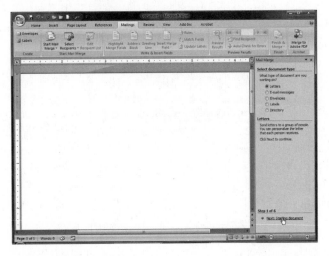

Office Figure 2-22: Selecting document type.

3. On the second page of the Mail Merge Wizard, you can select how you are going to start the document.

You may start from the blank document if you want, but we will use one of the templates supplied by Word.

Select Start from a template, and then click the link that appears that reads Select Template, as shown in Office Figure 2-23.

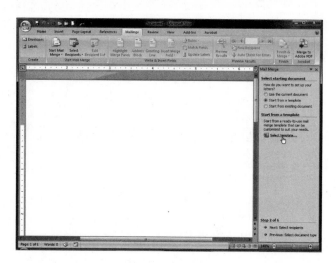

Office Figure 2-23: Selecting starting document.

4. The Select Template dialog will appear with a number of document types from which to choose.

You can select and preview a template using this dialog.

Choose one of the Letters mail merge templates and click OK.

In Office Figure 2-24, we have selected the template titled Equity Merge Letter.

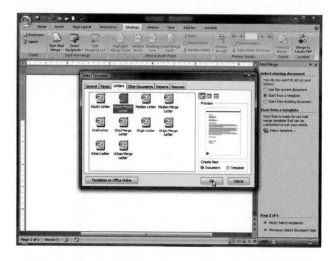

Office Figure 2-24: Selecting a document template.

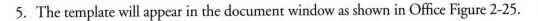

5. The template will appear in the document window as shown in Office Figure 2-25.

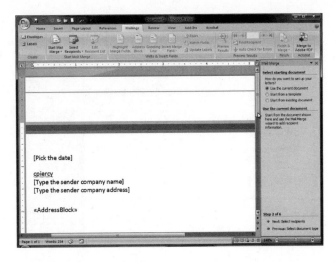

Office Figure 2-25: The Template Document.

Template documents provide fields and blocks which you can edit to include your content.

On a template, the formatting of the document is already taken care of for you to save you time.

6. You can start right away to edit the document.

For example, click on the field labeled [Pick the date].

A calendar tool will appear, from which you can choose any date.

For convenience, we'll choose the current date by clicking on the button labeled Today, as shown in Office Figure 2-26.

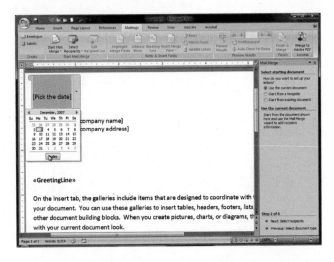

Office Figure 2-26: Picking the date value.

7. The date field will now display the data selected as shown in Office Figure 2-27.

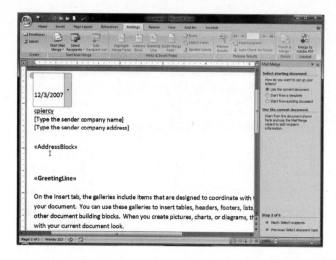

Office Figure 2-27: The date field setting.

You can also go ahead and complete other areas of the template that are not generated from the database.

8. Text that is marked with angle brackets is intended to be generated from the data source.

For example, <<AddressBlock>> should be generated from the database, since it will need to change for each letter recipient.

Click on Select Recipients, as shown in Office Figure 2-28, to go to the next wizard page.

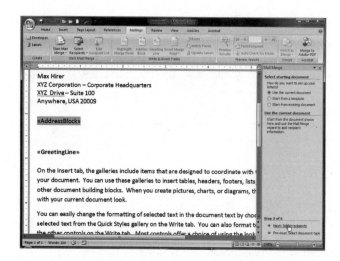

Office Figure 2-28: A block field.

9. In the next step, we need to select the data source.

    You can choose from an existing source, select from an Outlook contact list, or type a list from within Word.

    Make sure that Use an Existing List is selected then click on the Browse link, as shown in Office Figure 2-29, to search for your data source.

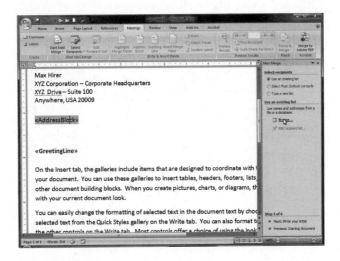

Office Figure 2-29: Source selection dialog page.

10. A Select Data Source dialog will appear.

    This dialog works just like the File Open dialog for all of the Office software.

    Find the location for your data source file, select the file (in this case *job_candidates. accdb*) and then click Open as shown in Office Figure 2-30.

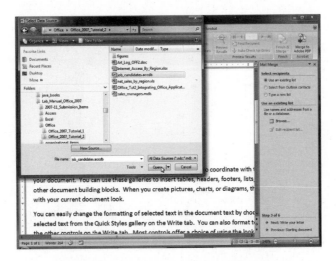

Office Figure 2-30: Selecting Source File.

11. You will now see the Mail Merge Recipients Dialog box. With this dialog box you can:

   - Review the data in the data source.
   - Select a subset of the data to be used.
   - Search for specific data records.

   Once you have selected and verified the data records to use in your mail merge, click OK, as shown in Office Figure 2-31.

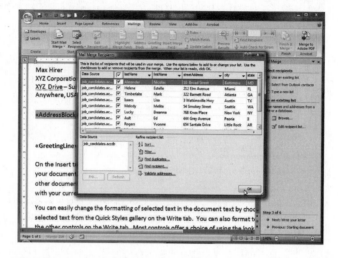

Office Figure 2-31: The Mail Merge Recipients dialog.

12. After the source has been selected, you won't see much difference in the document until you specify where in the document the data from the source should appear.

   Click the link that says Next: Write your letter, as shown in Office Figure 2-32.

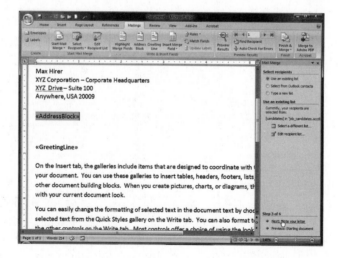

Office Figure 2-32: The current mail merge.

13. On the next page you'll notice several links that correspond to the data blocks in the template.

These will vary depending on the template that you have selected.

Click on the link labeled Address Block, as shown in Office Figure 2-33, to see how this works.

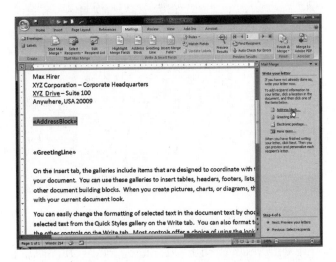

Office Figure 2-33: The Write Your Letter page of the Mail Merge wizard.

14. The Insert Address Block dialog will be displayed as shown in Office Figure 2-34.

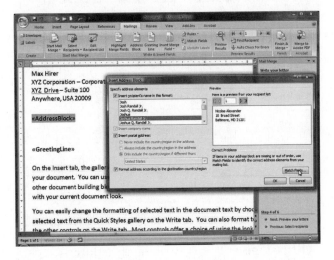

Office Figure 2-34: The Insert Address Block dialog.

The components of this dialog allow you to choose how the data will be displayed and allow you to preview it.

You may also adjust the actual data that is matched to the field in case something has been left out or you want to remove a data item.

15. To do this, click the Match Fields option.

The Match Fields dialog, shown in Office Figure 2-35, lets you match the fields needed for the Word address block to the names of the fields in your database.

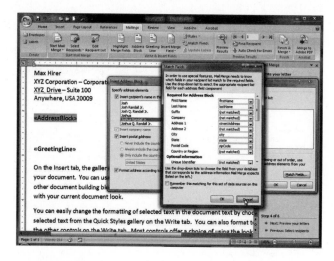

Office Figure 2-35: The Match Fields dialog.

16. After working with the Match Fields dialog, click OK or Cancel.

Then click OK on the Insert Address Block dialog, as shown in Office Figure 2-36, to continue working on the letter.

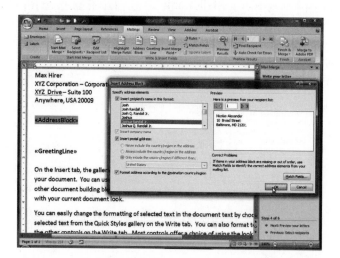

Office Figure 2-36: Finishing the address block.

17. You should see that the Address Block in the template has been replaced by an address based on data in the data source, as shown in Office Figure 2-37.

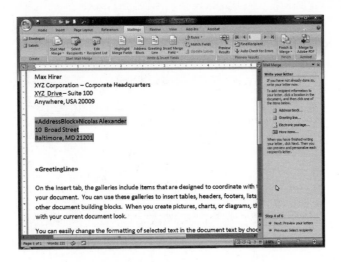

Office Figure 2-37: The address block.

If you still have the actual words <<AddressBlock>>, you can simply delete it.

18. Now, click the <<GreetingLine>> link as shown in Office Figure 2-38.

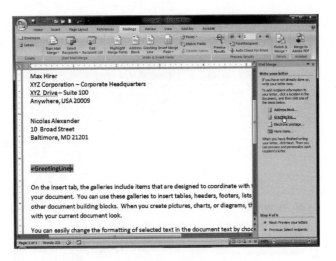

Office Figure 2-38: The greeting line.

19. The dialog that is displayed will also allow you to adjust how the Greeting Line will appear, as shown in Office Figure 2-39.

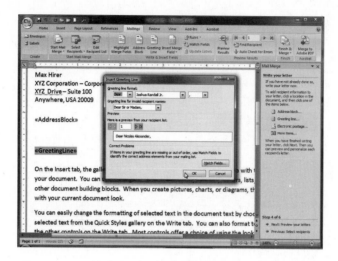

Office Figure 2-39: The Insert Greeting Line dialog.

You can change the actual greeting and see a preview.

You can also access the data source through the Match Fields button.

20. After completing the signature line, you should see the field replaced by data from the source file, as shown in Office Figure 2-40.

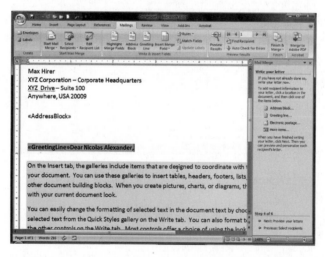

Office Figure 2-40: The Greeting Line with Data.

Again, you may need to remove the placeholder text manually.

21. In addition to the data blocks that are built into the template, you can also build the body of the letter using a combination of text and data from the source.

Highlight the filler text that was automatically added (see Office Figure 2-41) so that we can replace it with the text of the letter.

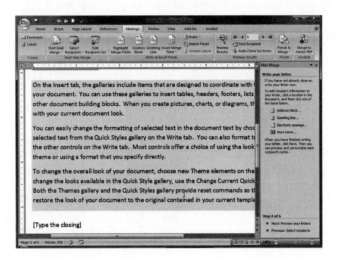

Office Figure 2-41: The filler text.

22. Type some content like that shown in Office Figure 2-42.

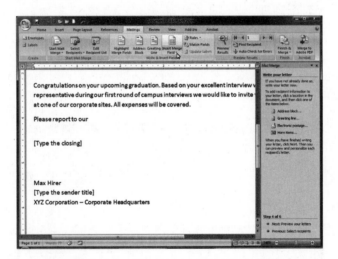

Office Figure 2-42: The body of the letter.

Some of the data in our data source includes the location, date, and time of the interview for each candidate.

Type the beginning of a sentence with the words: *Please report to our* . . . .

We'll use this sentence to see how we may include data in the text.

23. Now, on the Mailings ribbon, click on the Insert Merge Field command.

    You should see a list of the fields from the database table.

    These are available for you to insert into the body of your document.

    Select *interviewLocation* as shown in Office Figure 2-43.

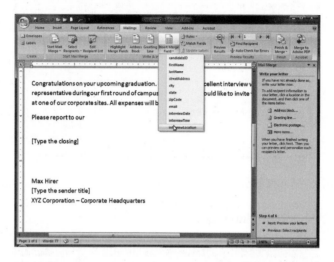

Office Figure 2-43: Inserting a Merge Field.

24. You should now see the <<interviewLocation>> placeholder inserted into the document (Office Figure 2-44).

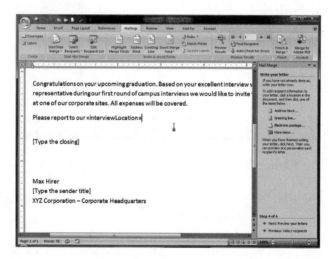

Office Figure 2-44: The <<interviewLocation>> placeholder.

When you run the merge, you will see the placeholder replaced with a location stored in the database.

25. After that, type *office on* and insert the <<interviewDate>> field as shown in Office Figure 2-45.

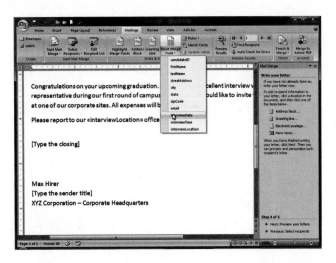

Office Figure 2-45: Inserting the <<interviewDate>> field.

26. The sentence should now appear as shown in Office Figure 2-46.

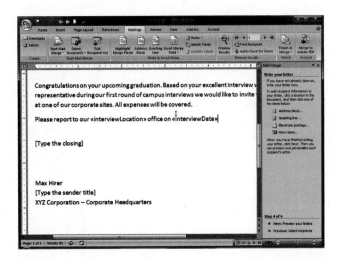

Office Figure 2-46: The inserted <<interviewDate>> field.

27. Finish the sentence by adding the word *at* and inserting the <<interviewTime>> field as shown in Office Figure 2-47.

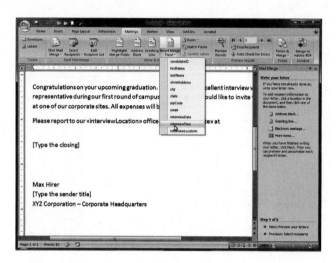

Office Figure 2-47: Inserting the <<interviewTime>> field.

28. We won't add any more fields, so go ahead and add some more text to finish the letter as shown in Office Figure 2-48.

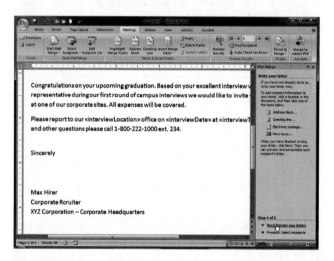

Office Figure 2-48: The completed merge document.

You can also fill in the closing and the sender title.

Click the link Next: Preview your letter.

29. When previewing the letter, you will see the document with the fields filled in from the data source (Office Figure 2-49).

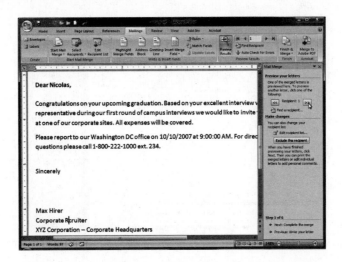

Office Figure 2-49: The Preview Letter dialog page.

You can click on the arrows to move through the records in the data source to preview.

You can also click on the button to exclude records for which you do not want to send the letter.

30. Click the arrows a few times to see the letter with different data records, as shown in Office Figure 2-50.

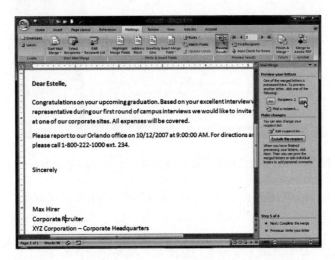

Office Figure 2-50: Preview the letter with a different record.

31. After previewing the letter, click on the link Next: Complete the merge, as shown in Office Figure 2-51.

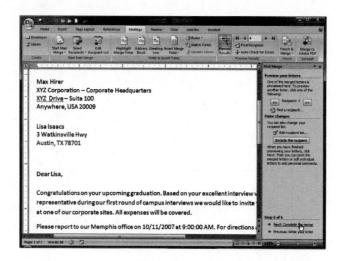

Office Figure 2-51: Complete the Merge link.

32. On the final page of the Mail Merge dialog, you can choose to print the merge, as shown in Office Figure 2-52, or edit individual letters.

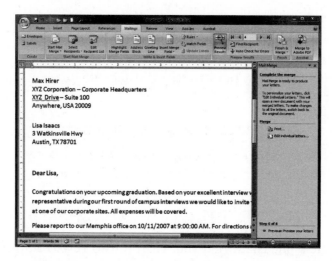

Office Figure 2-52: The final mail merge letter.

You can also return to previous dialog pages if you need to make any adjustments.

EXERCISES TO BUILD YOUR KNOWLEDGE OF MS OFFICE

Match each of the Office terms with its description.

_____ 1. Clipboard

a. An element that you have created in an Office document that can be edited, copied, and linked.

____ 2. Data source

b. A file that contains data that can be merged into a document.

____ 3. Embedding

c. A Word document that can be created to use data from another source such as a database or Outlook address book.

____ 4. Field

d. Adding a reference in a destination document that points to an object in a source document.

____ 5. Linking

e. Inserting a copy of an object from a source document into a destination document.

____ 6. Mail merge

f. A characteristic of a software object in an Office document.

____ 7. Mailings ribbon

g. A document with automatically generated text and formatting that you can use to start your own document.

____ 8. Object

h. A value in a data source or a placeholder in a mail merge document.

____ 9. Property

i. A collection of commands in Word that let you work with mail merge documents.

____ 10. Template

j. An area of memory that is used to hold document components temporarily during copying and pasting.

11. When linking an object, why are the storage locations of the destination file and the source file important?

_____

_____

_____

12. Use Excel to create a line chart. Add your chart to two PowerPoint slides. On one slide, embed the chart, and on the other link the chart. Experiment by making changes to the Excel spreadsheet. What do you notice about the two charts on the PowerPoint slides?

_____

_____

_____

OFFICE INTEGRATION: MINI-CASE 1

Scenario: Your boss, the head of the Marketing Department for XYZ, Incorporated, wants you to send a letter to the sales manager of each major sales region. The letter should summarize the sales performance for each region over the last year and compare it to sales in each region for the previous year. You have already gathered the data and created an Excel spreadsheet with the sales data. The spreadsheet includes a bar chart that displays the differences in sales between regions and between the two years. Your boss also provided you with an Access database that contains the contact information for the sales managers.

Supporting files:

- Excel spreadsheet with net sales data and chart, *net_sales_by_region.xls*
- Access database with sales manager contact information, *sales_managers.mdb*

Your Task: Create a letter using Word from your department to the sales managers. Your final letter should conform to the following requirements:

- The letter should follow a professional format (you may use a Word template, if desired).
- The chart from the spreadsheet should be linked into the body of the Word document.
- The letter should be created using the Mail Merge feature using the database file as the data source.
- The letter should be free of spelling and grammatical errors.

OFFICE INTEGRATION: MINI-CASE 2

Scenario: Marc Amusant has just been elected the Director of Fun Events for his student organization at his school, Eyeo U. He'd like to be able to write e-mails to everyone on the membership list but have them appear to be personalized for each recipient. Having used mail merge for physical letters in the past, Marc wonders whether you can do the same for e-mail. The Sadie Hawkins Formal is coming up soon, and he needs to send out an announcement to all of the club members. Marc decides that this is the perfect opportunity to try mail merge for an e-mail.

Your Task: Create an e-mail mail merge using Word. Either use your Outlook address book or create a new e-mail list to use as the data source. Your final e-mail should conform to the following requirements:

- The greeting of each e-mail should include the individual name of each club member.
- The e-mail should be free of spelling and grammatical errors. Try to use the Word AutoCorrect tool to set common e-mail abbreviations so that they will automatically replace the abbreviation to the full phrase. For example, you might add *asap* to adjust automatically to *as soon as possible.*
- What data could you add to your e-mail list to be able to send e-mail only to club officers? How about only those who have "opted-in" to the e-mail list?

Index

Microsoft Access 2007 Module

Microsoft PowerPoint 2007 Module

Microsoft Word 2007 Module

Microsoft Office 2007 Module

Microsoft Windows Vista Module